U0361938

张彭春文集

崔国良　常　健　张兰普　主编

张彭春文集·人权卷

常　健　主编　常　健　等译　常　健　校

南开大学出版社
天津

图书在版编目(CIP)数据

张彭春文集. 人权卷：汉英对照 / 崔国良，常健，
张兰普丛书主编；常健主编；常健等译. —天津：南
开大学出版社，2023.12
ISBN 978-7-310-06531-8

Ⅰ. ①张… Ⅱ. ①崔… ②常… ③张… Ⅲ. ①人权－
文集－汉、英 Ⅳ. ①C53

中国国家版本馆 CIP 数据核字(2023)第 240162 号

张彭春文集·人权卷
ZHANGPENGCHUN WENJI · RENQUAN JUAN

南开大学出版社出版发行
出版人：刘文华
地址：天津市南开区卫津路 94 号　邮政编码：300071
营销部电话：(022)23508339　营销部传真：(022)23508542
https://nkup.nankai.edu.cn

天津创先河普业印刷有限公司印刷　全国各地新华书店经销
2023 年 12 月第 1 版　2023 年 12 月第 1 次印刷
230×170 毫米　16 开本　43.5 印张　2 插页　713 千字
定价：216.00 元

如遇图书印装质量问题，请与本社营销部联系调换，电话：(022)23508339

本卷由南开大学人权研究中心资助出版

翻译

常　健　杨晗如　朱金荣　昌成程

罗　苇　丁智朗　罗泽琳　李一萌

杨茉萱　李梦瑶　陈　越　徐俊杰

校对

常　健

编译说明

　　张彭春 1892 年 4 月 22 日生于天津，又名张蓬春，字仲述。1908 年毕业于南开中学，1910 年毕业于保定高等学堂，并考取第二批庚款游美生，在美国克拉克大学就读，1913 年提前修完四年课程毕业，获得文学学士学位。后转入哥伦比亚大学，受业于教育学家杜威，1915 年获得文学和教育学硕士学位。1916 年回国后在南开中学任教，首次提出创办南开大学的建议，被南开大学校长张伯苓称为"南开大学的计划人"。1919 年担任南开大学筹备委员会主任，主持起草了《南开大学计划书》，并多次赴美为南开大学筹款和聘请教授。1919 年赴美国哥伦比亚大学攻读博士学位。1922 年回国，1923 年受聘担任南开大学教授，后被聘为清华学校教务长，提出制订清华改办大学计划。1925 年清华大学正式成立，张彭春担任校务会成员以及旧制部主任兼大学普通部主任。1926 年张彭春辞去清华大学教务长一职，回到南开大学担任教授。1928—1929 年任南开大学代理校长。

　　在南开大学任教期间，张彭春领导开展南开新剧运动，建立正规编导制度，不仅亲自编写剧本，还培养了一批成就非凡的中国剧作家，对中国现代戏剧的发展作出开创性的贡献。在赴美修读期间，他编导了《木兰》并在纽约百老汇的克尔特剧院上演，场场爆满。在梅兰芳剧团赴美国进行演出时，他担任总导演和总顾问，使西方国家了解了中国的京剧，为中西文化交流作出了重要贡献。

　　1937 年南开大学遭日军轰炸，张彭春任西南联合大学教授，并参加外交活动，赴瑞士、英国、美国宣传中国抗战，并先后担任中国驻土耳其和智利特命全权公使。

　　张彭春先生 1946 年 1 月作为四位中国正式代表之一参加了在伦敦举行的联合国创办会议，在会议期间被任命为联合国经济及社会理事会中国常任代表。1947 年 1 月，张彭春在联合国人权委员会第一届会议上当选人权委员会副主席，并于同年 6 月在人权委员会之起草委员会第一次会议上当选起草委员会副主席，与罗斯福夫人共同负责《世界人权宣言》的起草工作。在 1949 年 5 月人权委员会第五届会议和 1950 年人权委员会第六届会议上，张彭春继续当选人权委员会第一副主席，与主席罗斯福夫人和第二副主席卡森先生共同主持国际人权公约的制定工作。

根据联合国会议记录，张彭春在 1946—1950 年期间参加了联合国大会全体会议、第三委员会会议、经济及社会理事会会议、人权委员会会议、人权宣言起草委员会会议，参与了《世界人权宣言》和国际人权公约的起草工作，代表中国就人权问题作出了一系列发言。

1946 年，张彭春在联合国经济及社会理事会第二届会议上就人权问题发言。

1947 年 1 月，联合国人权委员会第一届会议举行了 22 次会议（第 1—22 次会议）。张彭春出席了除第 9、10 次会议之外的所有会议，在出席的会议中，第 2、8、15 次会议的记录中没有出现张彭春的发言。

1947 年 3 月，张彭春出席联合国经济及社会理事会第四届会议，并就人权问题作出发言。

1947 年 6 月，人权委员会之起草委员会第一届会议举行了 19 次会议。张彭春先生出席了所有会议，并在第 16、17 次会议上临时担任会议主席。

1947 年 12 月，联合国人权委员会第二届会议举行了 23 次会议（第 23—45 次会议）。张彭春因参加经社理事会会议，未能出席这届会议，由吴南如先生（Mr. Nan-Ju Wu）和吴经熊博士（Dr. C. H. Wu）代表中国参加了会议。

1948 年 2 月，张彭春出席联合国经济及社会理事会第五届会议，并就人权问题作出发言。

1948 年 5—6 月，联合国人权委员会第三届会议举行了 36 次会议（第 46—81 次会议），张彭春出席了除第 46、49、66 次会议之外的所有会议，上述三次会议由吴德耀先生（Mr. T. Y. Wu）代替他出席。在出席的会议中，第 47、79 次会议的记录中没有出现张彭春的发言。张彭春没有出席 1948 年 5 月举行的起草委员会第二届会议，由吴德耀先生代表中国出席。

1948 年 7—8 月，张彭春出席联合国经济及社会理事会第六届会议，并就人权问题多次发言。

1948 年 9—12 月，张彭春出席联合国大会第三委员会会议和全体会议，积极参与《世界人权宣言》的审议和批准工作。

1949 年 4 月 11 日，联合国人权委员会根据经济及社会理事会第 197（Ⅷ）号决议，举行了第四届特别会议（第 82 次会议），选举新闻和出版自由小组委员会的新成员。张彭春出席，并以 16 票的高票数（18 人投票）当选新闻和出版自由小组委员会成员。

1949 年 5 月 9 日，联合国人权委员会第五届会议举行了 53 次会议（第 83—135 次会议），主要工作是依据《世界人权宣言》的精神制定国际人权公约。张彭春因故缺席第 94、101、108、109、114、128、135 次会议，代他出席会议的是查修先生。在第 83、86、89、92、96、97、105、106、107、110、111、112、113、116、125、130、132 次会议的记录上没有出现张彭春的发言。张彭春在第 84、85、99、100、122、123、127 次会议上担任会议主席。

1950 年 3 月，联合国人权委员会第六届会议举行了 66 次会议（第 136—201 次会议），制定国际人权公约仍然是其最重要的工作之一。张彭春因故缺席第 141、178、179、180、181、187、188、191 次会议，代他出席会议的是曹保颐先生或查修先生。在第 144、154、156、160、162、169、172、176、177、185、190、194、200 次会议的记录上没有出现张彭春的发言。他在第 160、166、173、182、183、184 次会议上担任会议主席。

1951 年 4 月联合国人权委员会举行第七届会议，出席会议的不再是张彭春先生，而变为于焌吉先生。

为了便于对张彭春参与联合国人权文件制定工作的具体情况进行更深入的研究，我们收集并翻译了张彭春在上述会议上的发言记录，并将会议记录的英文原文附在每篇译文后面，便于读者对照。

本书涉及的联合国文件最初是由荷兰乌特勒支大学的汤姆·茨瓦特（Tom Zwart）教授提供的，此后又通过联合国网站进行了进一步的收集和补充。崔国良先生组织南开大学外国语学院的学生对 1947—1948 年间张彭春在联合国各类会议上有关人权的发言记录进行了初译，参加翻译的同学包括杨晗如、朱金荣、昌成程、罗苇、丁智朗、罗泽琳、李一萌、杨茉萱、李梦瑶、陈越、徐俊杰等。常健负责对翻译初稿进行校对，同时补充翻译了 1949 年以后张彭春在人权委员会第四、五、六届会议上的发言，以及 1949 年之前一些漏译的资料，统一了全书内容的格式，设计了整体布局。

资料翻译是研究工作的重要基础，但也是一项难以达到尽善尽美的工作。本书的翻译只是抛砖引玉，或未达到信、达、雅的翻译要求，欢迎学界同人不吝指正。

　　衷心感谢参加此书翻译的所有人员，感谢南开大学出版社的编辑为此书出版付出的辛勤劳动。

常健

2022 年 11 月于南开大学

目　录

1946 年 1

　联合国经济及社会理事会第二届会议 1

　　在经济及社会理事会二届 6 次会议上的发言 3

1947 年 5

　联合国人权委员会第一届会议 5

　　在人权委员会第 1 次会议上当选人权委员会副主席 7

　　在人权委员会第 3 次会议上的发言 9

　　在人权委员会第 4 次会议上的发言 12

　　在人权委员会第 5 次会议上的发言 13

　　在人权委员会第 6 次会议上的发言 16

　　在人权委员会第 7 次会议上的发言 20

　　在人权委员会第 11 次会议上的发言 23

　　在人权委员会第 12 次会议上的发言 25

　　在人权委员会第 13 次会议上的发言 28

　　在人权委员会第 14 次会议上的发言 30

　　在人权委员会第 16 次会议上的发言 32

　　在人权委员会第 17 次会议上的发言 35

　　在人权委员会第 18 次会议上的发言 37

　　在人权委员会第 19 次会议上的发言 39

　　在人权委员会第 20 次会议上的发言 41

　　在人权委员会第 21 次会议上的发言 43

　　在人权委员会第 22 次会议上的发言 47

　联合国经济及社会理事会第四届会议 51

　　在经济及社会理事会第 69 次会议上的发言 53

　　在经济及社会理事会社会事务委员会第 6 次会议上的发言 ...55

人权委员会之起草委员会第一届会议.........................57
　在人权委员会之起草委员会第 1 次会议上的发言......................59
　在人权委员会之起草委员会第 2 次会议上的发言......................62
　在人权委员会之起草委员会第 3 次会议上的发言......................64
　在人权委员会之起草委员会第 4 次会议上的发言......................69
　在人权委员会之起草委员会第 5 次会议上的发言......................73
　在人权委员会之起草委员会第 6 次会议上的发言......................75
　在人权委员会之起草委员会第 7 次会议上的发言......................78
　在人权委员会之起草委员会第 8 次会议上的发言......................81
　在人权委员会之起草委员会第 9 次会议上的发言......................88
　在人权委员会之起草委员会第 10 次会议上的发言......................91
　在人权委员会之起草委员会第 11 次会议上的发言......................96
　在人权委员会之起草委员会第 12 次会议上的发言......................99
　在人权委员会之起草委员会第 13 次会议上的发言......................103
　在人权委员会之起草委员会第 14 次会议上的发言......................110
　在人权委员会之起草委员会第 15 次会议上的发言......................113
　在人权委员会之起草委员会第 16 次会议上的发言......................117
　在人权委员会之起草委员会第 17 次会议上的发言......................122
　在人权委员会之起草委员会第 18 次会议上的发言......................132
　在人权委员会之起草委员会第 19 次会议上的发言......................136

1948 年.........................139
　人权委员会之起草委员会第二届会议.........................139
　　人权委员会之起草委员会第 20 次会议简要记录......................141
　联合国人权委员会第三届会议.........................143
　　在人权委员会第 48 次会议上的发言......................145
　　在人权委员会第 50 次会议上的发言......................148
　　在人权委员会第 51 次会议上的发言......................152
　　在人权委员会第 52 次会议上的发言......................155
　　在人权委员会第 53 次会议上的发言......................165
　　在人权委员会第 54 次会议上的发言......................171
　　在人权委员会第 55 次会议上的发言......................175
　　在人权委员会第 56 次会议上的发言......................178

在人权委员会第 57 次会议上的发言 181

在人权委员会第 58 次会议上的发言 186

在人权委员会第 59 次会议上的发言 190

在人权委员会第 60 次会议上的发言 191

在人权委员会第 61 次会议上的发言 195

在人权委员会第 62 次会议上的发言 200

在人权委员会第 63 次会议上的发言 202

在人权委员会第 64 次会议上的发言 206

在人权委员会第 65 次会议上的发言 208

在人权委员会第 67 次会议上的发言 212

在人权委员会第 68 次会议上的发言 217

在人权委员会第 69 次会议上的发言 220

在人权委员会第 70 次会议上的发言 223

在人权委员会第 71 次会议上的发言 225

在人权委员会第 72 次会议上的发言 229

在人权委员会第 73 次会议上的发言 231

在人权委员会第 74 次会议上的发言 232

在人权委员会第 75 次会议上的发言 236

在人权委员会第 76 次会议上的发言 242

在人权委员会第 77 次会议上的发言 246

在人权委员会第 78 次会议上的发言 251

在人权委员会第 80 次会议上的发言 257

在人权委员会第 81 次会议上的发言 261

联合国经济及社会理事会第六、七届会议 265

在经济及社会理事会第 128 次会议上的发言 267

在经济及社会理事会第 180 次会议上的发言 270

在经济及社会理事会第 201 次会议上的发言 272

在经济及社会理事会第 202 次会议上的发言 277

第三届联合国大会第三委员会会议 283

在第三委员会第 88 次会议上的发言 285

在第三委员会第 91 次会议上的发言 288

在第三委员会第 95 次会议上的发言 291

在第三委员会第 96 次会议上的发言 294

在第三委员会第 98 次会议上的发言 298

在第三委员会第 99 次会议上的发言 301

在第三委员会第 100 次会议上的发言 305

在第三委员会第 101 次会议上的发言 308

在第三委员会第 103 次会议上的发言 310

在第三委员会第 105 次会议上的发言 315

在第三委员会第 107 次会议上的发言 319

在第三委员会第 113 次会议上的发言 323

在第三委员会第 119 次会议上的发言 326

在第三委员会第 125 次会议上的发言 329

在第三委员会第 127 次会议上的发言 331

在第三委员会第 131 次会议上的发言 334

在第三委员会第 133 次会议上的发言 338

在第三委员会第 134 次会议上的发言 341

在第三委员会第 141 次会议上的发言 344

在第三委员会第 142 次会议上的发言 346

在第三委员会第 143 次会议上的发言 349

在第三委员会第 144 次会议上的发言 352

在第三委员会第 145 次会议上的发言 356

在第三委员会第 146 次会议上的发言 360

在第三委员会第 150 次会议上的发言 363

在第三委员会第 151 次会议上的发言 366

在第三委员会第 152 次会议上的发言 369

在第三委员会第 153 次会议上的发言 372

在第三委员会第 154 次会议上的发言 374

在第三委员会第 156 次会议上的发言 377

在第三委员会第 157 次会议上的发言 382

在第三委员会第 158 次会议上的发言 384

在第三委员会第 166 次会议上的发言 386

在第三委员会第 167 次会议上的发言 389

在第三委员会第 175 次会议上的发言 394

　　在第三委员会第 177 次会议上的发言..........................396

　　在第三委员会第 178 次会议上的发言..........................400

　第三届联合国大会..........................407

　　在联合国大会第 182 次会议上的发言..........................409

1949 年..........................413

　联合国人权委员会第四届会议..........................413

　人权委员会第 82 次会议简要记录..........................415

　联合国人权委员会第五届会议..........................419

　　在人权委员会第 83 次会议上当选第一副主席..........................421

　　在人权委员会第 84 次会议上的发言..........................423

　　在人权委员会第 85 次会议上的发言..........................426

　　在人权委员会第 87 次会议上的发言..........................429

　　在人权委员会第 88 次会议上的发言..........................433

　　在人权委员会第 90 次会议上的发言..........................438

　　在人权委员会第 91 次会议上的发言..........................442

　　在人权委员会第 93 次会议上的发言..........................444

　　在人权委员会第 95 次会议上的发言..........................446

　　在人权委员会第 98 次会议上的发言..........................449

　　在人权委员会第 99 次会议上的发言..........................451

　　在人权委员会第 100 次会议上的发言..........................454

　　在人权委员会第 102 次会议上的发言..........................457

　　在人权委员会第 103 次会议上的发言..........................459

　　在人权委员会第 104 次会议上的发言..........................463

　　在人权委员会第 115 次会议上的发言..........................465

　　在人权委员会第 117 次会议上的发言..........................468

　　在人权委员会第 118 次会议上的发言..........................470

　　在人权委员会第 119 次会议上的发言..........................478

　　在人权委员会第 120 次会议上的发言..........................481

　　在人权委员会第 121 次会议上的发言..........................484

　　在人权委员会第 122 次会议上的发言..........................487

　　在人权委员会第 123 次会议上的发言..........................491

　　在人权委员会第 124 次会议上的发言..........................494

在人权委员会第 126 次会议上的发言……………………496

在人权委员会第 127 次会议上的发言……………………500

在人权委员会第 129 次会议上的发言……………………503

在人权委员会第 131 次会议上的发言……………………506

在人权委员会第 133 次会议上的发言……………………508

在人权委员会第 134 次会议上的发言……………………509

人权委员会第 135 次会议简要记录………………………512

1950 年……………………………………………………………515

联合国人权委员会第六届会议………………………………515

人权委员会第 136 次会议简要记录………………………517

在人权委员会第 137 次会议上的发言……………………527

在人权委员会第 138 次会议上的发言……………………531

在人权委员会第 139 次会议上的发言……………………535

在人权委员会第 140 次会议上的发言……………………538

在人权委员会第 142 次会议上的发言……………………541

在人权委员会第 143 次会议上的发言……………………543

在人权委员会第 145 次会议上的发言……………………546

在人权委员会第 146 次会议上的发言……………………548

在人权委员会第 147 次会议上的发言……………………550

在人权委员会第 148 次会议上的发言……………………554

在人权委员会第 149 次会议上的发言……………………557

在人权委员会第 150 次会议上的发言……………………560

在人权委员会第 151 次会议上的发言……………………562

在人权委员会第 152 次会议上的发言……………………565

在人权委员会第 153 次会议上的发言……………………568

在人权委员会第 155 次会议上的发言……………………571

在人权委员会第 157 次会议上的发言……………………573

在人权委员会第 158 次会议上的发言……………………575

在人权委员会第 159 次会议上的发言……………………577

在人权委员会第 161 次会议上的发言……………………579

在人权委员会第 163 次会议上的发言……………………581

在人权委员会第 164 次会议上的发言……………………585

在人权委员会第 165 次会议上的发言..................................593

在人权委员会第 166 次会议上的发言..................................598

在人权委员会第 167 次会议上的发言..................................601

在人权委员会第 170 次会议上的发言..................................607

在人权委员会第 171 次会议上的发言..................................610

在人权委员会第 173 次会议上的发言..................................613

在人权委员会第 174 次会议上的发言..................................616

在人权委员会第 175 次会议上的发言..................................619

在人权委员会第 182 次会议上的发言..................................624

在人权委员会第 183 次会议上的发言..................................626

在人权委员会第 184 次会议上的发言..................................631

在人权委员会第 186 次会议上的发言..................................633

在人权委员会第 189 次会议上的发言..................................636

在人权委员会第 192 次会议上的发言..................................638

在人权委员会第 193 次会议上的发言..................................640

在人权委员会第 195 次会议上的发言..................................642

在人权委员会第 196 次会议上的发言..................................644

在人权委员会第 197 次会议上的发言..................................646

在人权委员会第 198 次会议上的发言..................................649

在人权委员会第 199 次会议上的发言..................................652

在人权委员会第 201 次会议上的发言..................................655

附录 《世界人权宣言》通过时的中英文原文..................................658

1946 年

联合国经济及社会理事会第二届会议

在经济及社会理事会二届 6 次会议上的发言

1946 年 5 月 31 日星期五下午 2:45
审议人权委员会报告（续）
（第 E/38 号文件，附件 4，第 224 页）

......

张先生（中国）代表中国代表团对人权委员会特别是委员会主席取得的成就表示祝贺。他建议在讨论人权问题时，不仅要考虑眼前工作的细节，而且要谨记那些涉及的更大的问题，这一点很重要。他指出，对于一个委员会来说，人权是一个太大的概念，而且联合国所有其他机构都在关注这一概念的落实。他回顾了人权在过去一百五十年的发展，并认为现在存在着一种新的人文主义激励着人们努力前行。这些激励因素一定是关于人的自由和尊严的理想。

......

——经济及社会理事会二届 6 次会议简要记录（E/SR.20）

杨晗如译，常健校

E/SR.20
31 May 1946

ECONOMIC AND SOCIAL COUNCIL
SECOND SESSION
SUMMARY RECORD OF THE SIXTH MEETING
Friday, 31 May 1946, at 2:45 p.m.

Consideration of the Report of the Commission on Human Rights (Continuation) (Document E/38, annex 4, page 224)

...

Mr. Chang (China) congratulated the Commission on Human Rights on behalf of the Chinese delegation, and especially its Chairman, for the results achieved. He suggested that it was important, during the discussion on human rights, not only to consider details of immediate work, but to keep in mind the larger issues which were involved. He pointed out that human rights were too large a concept for one commission and that all other organs of the United Nations were concerned with the carrying out of this concept. He recalled the development of human rights during the last one hundred and fifty years and felt that there existed now a new humanism, as otherwise there would be no incentive for the efforts that were made. Those incentives must be the ideals of human freedom and human dignity.

...

1947 年

联合国人权委员会第一届会议

在人权委员会第 1 次会议上当选人权委员会副主席

1947 年 1 月 27 日星期一上午 11:00 纽约成功湖

......

2. 选举主席

汉萨·梅塔女士（印度）提议罗斯福夫人担任主席，对她作为人权核心委员会主席的工作表示敬意。

罗穆洛将军（菲律宾）提议提名结束。一致选举罗斯福夫人担任人权委员会主席。

3. 选举副主席

杜克斯先生（英国）提名张彭春博士，特别提及他在人权领域的出色工作。一致选举张彭春博士担任人权委员会副主席。

4. 选举报告员

罗穆洛将军（菲律宾）提名查尔斯·马利克博士为报告员，特别提及他参加联合国在旧金山、伦敦和 1946 年大会的工作。一致选举马利克博士担任人权委员会报告员。

......

——人权委员会第 1 次会议简要记录（E/CN.4/SR.1）

罗苇、常健译，常健校

E/CN.4/SR.1
27 January 1947

COMMISSION ON HUMAN RIGHTS
FIRST SESSION
SUMMARY RECORD OF THE FIRST MEETING

Held at Lake Success, New York, on Monday, 27 January 1947, at 11:00 a.m.

...

2. Election of Chairman

Mrs. Hansa Mehta (India) proposed Mrs. Roosevelt as Chairman, paying tribute to her work as Chairman of the nuclear Commission on Human Rights.

General Romulo (Philippine Republic) moved that nominations be closed and Mrs. Roosevelt was unanimously elected Chairman.

...

3. Election of Vice-Chairman

Mr. Dukes (United Kingdom) proposed Dr. P. C. Chang, mentioning the quality of his work in the field of Human Rights. Dr. Chang was unanimously elected.

4. Election of the Tapporteur

General Romulo (Philippine Republi) nominated Dr. Charles Malik, as Rapporteur, referring to his participation in the work of the United Nations at San Francisco, London, and in the General Asembly of 1946. Dr. Malik was unanimously elected.

在人权委员会第 3 次会议上的发言

1947 年 1 月 28 日星期二上午 11:00 纽约成功湖

1. 通过议事规则

......

张博士（中国）认为，在秘书处提交的文件（E/CN.4/W.7 号文件）第 4 段中建议的三种解决办法中，第二种无疑是最合理的，即只在第一届会议上采纳所建议的《议事规则》，并将审议和修正推迟到第二届会议。

霍奇森上校（澳大利亚）支持中国代表的建议。如果黎巴嫩代表同意在其提案中增加"临时"一词，就可以避免某些困难。关于各委员会《议事规则》的统一性，他建议人权委员会设立一个小型的小组委员会，并要求其与其他委员会取得联系，研究这些委员会对其《议事规则》已经作出的修改。

梅塔女士（印度）支持中国代表的建议，因为她认为没有必要立即通过最后的《议事规则》。

特普利亚科夫先生（苏联）和张博士（中国）敦促在提案案文中增加"第一届会议"字样，黎巴嫩代表同意了这项修正案，该动议付诸表决，未经反对获得通过。

决定：秘书处提议的《议事规则》暂时获得通过，仅适用于第一届会议。

张博士（中国）在罗穆洛将军（菲律宾共和国）的支持下，提议成立一个由三人组成的委员会，研究对议事规则可能作出的修正。

决定：该提案获得通过。主席任命澳大利亚、中国和苏联的代表为该委员会成员。

......

——人权委员会第 3 次会议简要记录（E/CN.4/SR.3）

常健译校

E/CN.4/SR.3
28 January 1947

COMMISSION ON HUMAN RIGHTS
FIRST SESSION
SUMMARY RECORD OF THE THIRD MEETING

Held at Lake Success, New York, on Tuesday, 28 January 1947, at 11:00 a.m.

1. Adoption of the Rules of Procedure

...

Dr. Chang (China) felt that of the three solutions suggested in paragraph 4 of the document submitted by the Secretariat, (E/CN.4/W.7), the second, namely to adopt the proposed Rules of Procedure for the first session only and to postpone examination and amendment to the second session, was certainly the most reasonable.

Colonel Hodgson (Australia) supported the suggestion of the representative of China. Certain difficulties might be avoided if the representative of Lebanon were prepared to agree to the addition of the word "provisionally" to his proposal. As regards the uniformity of the Rules of Procedure of the various commissions, he suggested setting up a small sub-committee of the Commission on Human Rights with instructions to get in touch with the other commissions and to study the changes they had made in their Rules of Procedure.

Mrs. Mehta (India) supported the proposal of the representative of China, for she did not think it necessary to adopt final Rules of Procedure immediately.

...

Mr. Tepliakov (Union of Soviet Socialist Republics) and Dr. Chang (China) having urged the addition of the words "for the first session" to the text of the proposal, and this amendment having been agreed to by the representative of Lebanon, the motion was put to the vote and adopted without opposition.

DECISION: The Rules of Procedure proposed by the Secretariat were adopted provisionally and for the first session only.

Dr. Chang (China), seconded by General Romulo (Philippine Republic), proposed setting up a committee of three persons to study such amendments as might be made to the rules of procedure.

DECISION: This proposal was adopted. The Chairman appointed the representatives of Australia, China and the Union of Soviet Socialist Republics to serve on this committee.

...

在人权委员会第 4 次会议上的发言

1947 年 1 月 28 日星期二下午 2:30 纽约成功湖

2. 审议收到的来函（续）

......

张先生（中国）建议委员会推迟审议关于其临时议程中第 8 项（审议有效落实人权和基本自由的方式和方法——第 E/CN.4/3 号文件）的提案。

......

——人权委员会第 4 次会议简要记录（E/CN.4/SR.4）

常健译校

E/CN.4/SR.4
28 January 1947

COMMISSION ON HUMAN RIGHTS
FIRST SESSION
SUMMARY RECORD OF THE FOURTH MEETING

Held at Lake Success, New York, on Tuesday, 28 January 1947, at 2:30 p.m.

2. Examination of Communications Received (Continued)

…

Mr. Chang (China) suggested that the Commission should postpone consideration of the proposal dealing with item 8 on its provisional agenda (Consideration of ways and means for the effective implementation of human rights and fundamental freedoms - document E/CN.4/3).

…

在人权委员会第 5 次会议上的发言

1947 年 1 月 29 日星期三上午 11:00 纽约成功湖

1. 讨论议程第 2 项（第 E/CN.4/5 号文件）——新闻和出版自由 小组委员会的设立和职权范围

......

罗穆洛将军（菲律宾）说，他希望将第 E/CN.4/W.11 号文件第 15 段记录在案。他提议"人权委员会依据我们的职权范围设立一个新闻和出版自由小组委员会"。

张先生（中国）建议，如果去掉最后一个短语，该动议将更加清晰。

......

罗穆洛将军（菲律宾）同意张先生的意见，并因此动议"人权委员会设立一个新闻和出版自由小组委员会"。

该动议得到杜克斯先生附议，以 10 票对 0 票获得通过。

主席说，在开始讨论该小组委员会的组成和职权范围之前，将分发一份载有美国提出的建议的文件（第 E/CN.4/7 和 E/CN.4/8 号文件）。

张先生（中国）支持黎巴嫩代表的建议，即任命一个由三人组成的小组委员会，审查各项要点，制定职权范围，并向委员会作出报告。他强调新闻责任与新闻自由具有同样的重要性。

......

张先生（中国）说，尽管经济及社会理事会决议中的一般原则是可以接受的，但小组委员会的职权范围也许应该比经济及社会理事会决议中的措辞更明确、更具有启发性和包容性。

......

张先生（中国）建议，小组委员会还应负责确定该小组委员会的组成。

特普利亚科夫先生（苏联）回顾了他先前关于组成问题的动议，并建议现在审议该动议。

张先生（中国）指出，在小组委员会的组成方面，有几个相关问题需要讨论，例如它与专门机构之间的关系。苏联代表也是最近任命的小组委员会成员，他可以向小组委员会提出建议。

张先生的提议以 9 票对 2 票获得通过。

特普利亚科夫先生（苏联）指出，他自己的动议因此被否决，他撤回动议。

下午 1:00 点休会。

——人权委员会第 5 次会议简要记录（E/CN.4/SR.5）

常健译校

E/CN.4/SR.5
29 January 1947

COMMISSION ON HUMAN RIGHTS
FIRST SESSION
SUMMARY RECORD OF THE FIFTH MEETING

Held at Lake Success, New York, on Wednesday, 29 January 1947,

at 11:00 a.m.

1. Discussion of Item 2 of the Agenda (document E/CN.4/5) – Establishment and Terms of Reference of the Sub-Commission on Freedom of Information and the Press.

…

General Romulo (Philippine Republic) said he wished to place on record paragraph 15 of document E/CN.4/W.11. He moved that the "that the Commission on Human Eights establish a Sub-Commission on Freedom of Information and of the Press in accordance with our terms of reference".

…

Mr. Chang (China) suggested that the motion would be more clear if the last phrase were dropped.

…

General Romulo (Philippine Republic) agreed with Mr. Chang, and accordingly moved "that the Commission on Human Rights establish a Sub-Commission on Freedom of Information and of the Press".

This was seconded by Mr. Dukes and carried by 10 votes to nil.

The Chairman said that, before proceeding to discussion of the composition of the Sub-Commission and Terms of Reference, a document incorporating suggestions made by the United States would be circulated (documents E/CN.4/7 and E/CN.4/8).

Mr. Chang (China) supported the proposal of the Lebanese Representative to appoint a sub-committee of three to go over the various points, formulate Terms of Reference, and report back to the Commission. He emphasized the importance of responsibility of the press as well as freedom of the press.

...

Mr. Chang (China) said that perhaps the Sub-Commissions Terms of Reference should be a little more definitive, suggestive, and inclusive than the words of the resolution of the Economic and Social Council, even though the general principles were acceptable.

...

Mr. Chang (China) suggested that the sub-committee also be given the task of determining the composition of the Sub-Commission.

Mr. Tepliakov (USSR) recalled his previous motion on the issue of composition, and suggested that it now be considered.

Mr. Chang (China) pointed out that there were several problems such as relationship with Specialized Agencies to be discussed in relation to the composition of the Sub-Commission. The Representative of the USSR, who was also on the recently appointed sub-committee, could place his suggestions before it.

Mr. Chang's proposal was carried by 9 votes to 2.

Mr. Tepliakov (USSR) pointed out that his own motion was consequently rejected and he withdrew it.

The meeting adjourned at 1:00 p.m.

在人权委员会第 6 次会议上的发言

1947 年 1 月 29 日星期三下午 2:30 纽约成功湖

1. 少数群体问题小组委员会的设立和职权范围（议程项目 11——第 E/CN.4/1Rev.1 号文件）

......

张博士（中国）认为，防止歧视比保护少数群体更具包容性，因此建议修改澳大利亚的提案，将拟议的小组委员会改称为防止歧视和保护少数小组委员会。

霍奇森上校（澳大利亚）同意中国代表提出的修正案。

......

张博士（中国）解释说，这一建议无疑是为了改进歧视的一般定义，他向苏联代表保证，将在讨论小组委员会的职权范围时讨论这一问题。

......

张博士（中国）说，美国文件的许多要点需要详细讨论；苏联代表的建议应当被考虑；有关小组委员会的组成应结合其他小组委员会的构成加以研究。由于委员会已委任一个起草小组委员会来审议另一个小组委员会的职权范围，张博士提议，防止歧视和保护少数小组委员会的职责范围和组成也应提交给该小组委员会。他进一步动议，鉴于小组委员会将被要求开展额外工作，应为其增加两名新成员。

杜克斯先生（英国）支持动议。

主席说，苏联的动议必须首先付诸表决。

特普利亚科夫先生（苏联）撤回了他的提案，支持中国的动议。

......

张博士（中国）建议将他的两项议案分别付诸表决。

主席将中国提出的关于将防止歧视和保护少数小组委员会的职权范围及组成提交起草小组委员会的动议付诸表决。

决定：动议以 10 票对 0 票获得通过。

主席将中国提出的为起草小组委员会增加两名成员的动议付诸表决。

决定：动议以 10 票对 0 票获得通过。

主席随即任命中国和澳大利亚代表作为防止歧视和保护少数小组委员会的新增成员。在回应特普利亚科夫先生（苏联）的请求时，她列举了起草小组委员会的现有成员，该委员会由澳大利亚、中国、黎巴嫩、菲律宾共和国、苏联、英国的代表和委员会主席组成。议事规则委员会由澳大利亚、中国和苏联的代表组成，而处理来文的委员会则由黎巴嫩、英国和乌拉圭的代表组成。

张博士（中国）建议人权委员会休会，以便研究与《国际人权法案》有关的文件。该建议被接受。人权委员会决定，在委员会休会后，起草小组委员会将立即开会。

会议于下午 3:55 结束。

——人权委员会第 6 次会议简要记录（E/CN.4/SR.6）

常健译校

E/CN.4/SR.6
29 January 1947

COMMISSION ON HUMAN RIGHTS
FIRST SESSION
SUMMARY RECORD OF THE SIXTH MEETING

Held at Lake Success, New York, on Wednesday, 29 January 1947, at 2:30 p.m.

1. Establishment and Terms of Reference of Sub-Commission on Minorities (Item 11 of Agenda—E/CN.4/1Rev.1)

...

Dr. Chang (China) considered that the prevention of discrimination was more inclusive than the protection of minorities, and suggested that the Australian proposal should therefore be amended to refer to the contemplated Sub-Commission as the Sub-Commission on the prevention of discrimination and protection of minorities.

Col. Hodgson (Australia) agreed to the amendment submitted by the representative of China.

...

Dr. Chang (China) explaining that this suggestion was no doubt intended to improve the general definition of discrimination, assured the USSR representative that the matter would be taken up during the discussion of the terms of reference of the Sub-Commission.

...

Dr. Chang (China) said that numerous points of the United States document required detailed discussion; the suggestion of the USSR representative should be given consideration; the composition of the Sub-Commission in question should be studied in connection with that of other Sub-Commissions. Inasmuch as the Commission had appointed a drafting sub-committee to consider the terms of reference of another Sub-Commission, Dr. Chang moved that the terms, of reference and the composition of the Sub-Commission on the Prevention of Discrimination and the Protection of Minorities should also be referred to that sub-committee. He further moved that, in view of the added work which the sub-committee would be called upon to perform, two new members should be added to it.

Mr. Dukes (United Kingdom) supported the motion.

The Chairman stated that the USSR motion would have to be put to the vote first.

Mr. Tepliakov (USSR) withdrew his proposal in favour of the Chinese motion.

...

Dr. Chang (China) proposed that his two motions should be put to the vote separately.

The Chairman put to the vote the Chinese motion to refer the terms of reference and composition of the Sub-Commission on the Prevention of Discrimination and the Protection of Minorities to the drafting sub-committee.

DECISION: *The motion was adopted by ten votes to none.*

The Chairman put to the vote the Chinese motion to add two members to the drafting sub-committee.

DECISION: The motion was adopted by ten votes to none.

The Chairman thereupon appointed the representatives of China and Australia as additional members. In reply to a request by Mr. Tepliakov (USSR), she cited the present membership of the drafting sub-committee, which consisted of the representatives of Australia, China, Lebanon, the Philippine Republic, the USSR, the United Kingdom, and the Chairman of the Commission. The Committee on Rules of Procedure consisted of the representatives of Australia, China, and the USSR, while the Committee on the handling of Correspondence was composed of the representatives of Lebanon, the United Kingdom, and Uruguay.

The suggestion of Dr. Chang (China) that the Commission should adjourn to Study documents with respect to the International Bill of Rights was accepted. It was decided that the drafting sub-committee would sit immediately following the Commission's adjournment.

The meeting rose at 3:55 p.m.

在人权委员会第 7 次会议上的发言

1947 年 1 月 31 日星期五上午 11:00 纽约成功湖

讨论第二项议程：《国际人权法案》（第 E/CN.4/4 和 E/CN.4/W.4 号文件）

......

张先生（中国）认为，人权委员会在目前的讨论阶段不应该投票。但是他建议，在接下来的工作中，应当将该法案作为联合国大会决议来起草，并在此预设的基础上讨论该法案的内容。

人权委员会同意遵循中国代表提议的程序。

......

张先生（中国）指出，在美国的提案中，似乎遗漏了在秘书处准备的文件中所建议的序言部分。他强调，法案应该包括一个序言，该序言应提出该法案所依据的哲学基础。

当前，有必要肯定和扩大人与动物之间存在的差别。应当建立一个标准，用以提升人的尊严的概念，并强调对人的尊重：这项原则应体现在《国际人权法案》的序言中。在回答澳大利亚代表提出的关于人权适用标准的性质问题时，张先生继续解释道：无论对于何种层次的人，人权原则应被赋予普遍的适用性。他还提到建立一种最低标准，用来提升人相对于动物的地位。

最后，中国代表敦促委员会在制定这份为将来的《国际人权法案》奠定哲学基础的序言时，谨记人权的历史背景，特别是 16 世纪思想家对人的价值的强调。

......

——人权委员会第 7 次会议简要记录（E/CN.4/SR.7）

杨晗如、罗苇译，常健校

E/CN.4/SR.7
31 January 1947

COMMISSION ON HUMAN RIGHTS
FIRST SESSION
SUMMARY RECORD OF THE SEVENTH MEETING

Held at Lake Success, New York, on Friday, 31 January 1947, at 11:00 a.m.

Discussion of Item 2 of the Agenda: International Bill of Rights
(E/CN.4/4, E/CN.4/W.4)

Mr. Chang (China) considered that the Commission should take no vote at the present stage of discussion; he suggested, however, that it should proceed on the assumption that the bill would be drafted as a General Assembly resolution, and discuss the substance of the bill on that basis.

The Commission agreed to follow the procedure proposed by the representative of China.

...

Mr. Chang (China) pointed out that the preamble suggested in the document prepared by the Secretariat appeared to have been omitted from the United States proposals. He emphasized that the bill should include a preamble propounding the philosophy on which the bill was based.

At the present time it was necessary to affirm and enlarge the difference existing between man and animal. A standard should be established with a view to elevating the concept of man's dignity and emphasizing the respect of man: that principle should be embodied in a preamble to the International Bill of Rights. In reply to a question from the representative of Australia regarding the nature of the standard envisaged for the application of human rights, Mr. Chang went on to explain that the principle of human rights should be given universal application regardless of human level. He had referred to a minimum standard as a means of increasing the stature of man as opposed to animal.

In conclusion, the representative of China urged the Commission to bear in mind the historical background of human rights, particularly the emphasis placed on human values by the 16th century thinkers, in elaborating a preamble propounding the philosophy on which the future International Bill of Rights would be based.

　　…

在人权委员会第 11 次会议上的发言

1947 年 2 月 3 日星期一上午 11:00 纽约成功湖

2. 讨论起草《国际人权法案》应遵循的程序（第 E/CN.4/12 ar.i 13 号文件）

......

张先生（中国）认为，起草《国际人权法案》所遇到的困难，可能需要委员会全体成员坐在一起来解决。主席可以每两周召开一次会议，在纽约的委员会成员或其副手可以出席会议。不需要进行正式表决，但是委员会将对秘书处在专家协助下撰写的草案发表意见。

他认为，达成这种实际的妥协比进行投票表决更为可取，投票表决将给人留下这样的印象：在如此重要的问题上存在着意见分歧。

......

——人权委员会第 11 次会议简要记录（E/CN.4/SR.11）

杨晗如译，常健校

E/CN.4/SR.11
3 February 1947

COMMISSION ON HUMAN RIGHTS
FIRST SESSION
SUMMARY RECORD OF THE ELEVENTH MEETING
Held at Lake Success, New York, on Monday, 3 February 1947, at 11:00 a.m.

2. Discussion of procedure to be followed in the drafting of an International Bill of Rights (Documents E/CN.4/12 ar.i 13)

...

Mr. Chang (China) thought that the difficulty might be solved by the Commission sitting as a whole as a Committee, to draft the International Bill of Human Rights. The Chairman could call a meeting every two weeks, at which those members or their deputies who were in New York could be present. No formal voting would be done, but the Committee would give its views on the drafts prepared by the Secretariat with the assistance of experts.

He considered it was more desirable to arrive at a practical compromise such as that than to take a vote which would give the impression of a difference of opinion on a matter of such vital importance.

...

在人权委员会第 12 次会议上的发言

1947 年 2 月 3 日星期一下午 2:30 纽约成功湖

讨论和表决人权委员会关于拟定《国际人权法案》初稿的决议

第一款

······

张博士（中国）和卡森教授（法国）要求将"在与秘书处的合作中"改为"在与秘书处的合作下"。

······

应张博士（中国）的要求，委员会决定分段进行表决。

······

特普利亚科夫先生（苏联）指出，与这些组织的合作问题已列入委员会的议程，并将在适当时候进行讨论。

他指出，委员会成员应有权在起草宣言的任何阶段发表意见，这一观点得到了张博士（中国）的支持。

他建议将第二段修改如下：

"委员会主席可向经联合国会员国政府同意选出的专家进行咨询。"

他还建议在"任何意见和建议"的表述之前插入"口头或书面"这一修饰语。

——人权委员会第 12 次会议简要记录（E/CN.4/SR.12）

杨晗如译，常健校

E/CN.4/SR.12
3 February 1947

COMMISSION ON HUMAN RIGHTS
FIRST SESSION
SUMMARY RECORD OF THE TWELFTH MEETING

Held at Lake Success, New York, on Monday, 3 February 1947, at 2:30 p.m.

Discussion and Vote on the Resolution of the Commission on Human Rights the Subject of Formulating a Preliminary Draft International Bill of Human Rights

...

First Paragraph

Dr. Chang (China) and Professor Cassin (France) requested that the phrase "in co-operation with the Secretariat" be changed to "with the co-operation of the Secretariat".

...

At the request of Dr. Chang (China), the Commission decided to take a vote by paragraphs.

...

Mr. Tepliakov (Union of Soviet Socialist Republics) stated that the question of co-operation with those organizations was on the Commission's agenda and would come up for discussion in due course.

Supported by Dr. Chang (China), he stated that the members of the Commission should have the right to express their opinion at any stage in the drafting of the declaration.

He suggested amending the second paragraph as follows:

"The Chairman of the Commission may consult with experts chosen with the consent of their Governments, Members of the United Nations."

He also proposed inserting, before the words "any observations and suggestions", the words "orally or in writing".

…

在人权委员会第 13 次会议上的发言

1947 年 2 月 4 日星期二上午 11:00 纽约成功湖

审议第 E/CN.4/W18 号文件

......

张博士（中国）认为，应研究平等原则，并谨记人的尊严的概念。

......

张博士（中国）认为，为了满足法国和菲律宾共和国代表的意愿，可以在简要记录中加上一句话，表示委员会认为有必要强调人类团结或联合这一理念。这样就可以确保人权宣言始终得到正确的理解，确保随时可以在敌人以种族不平等的名义发动战争后迅速明了其所表达的内容。

......

张博士（中国）强调，中国的宪法已经包含了第 2 款所列举的大多数权利。他补充说，他将把中国宪法的副本分发给委员会成员。

......

张博士（中国）提请委员会注意中国宪法第 18 条，该条规定了成为公职人员的公开考试制度。他认为，该权利应在所有国家中存在，并建议在人权法案中提及此项权利。

......

——人权委员会第 13 次会议简要记录（E/CN.4/SR.13）

杨晗如译，常健校

E/CN.4/SR.13
6 February 1947

COMMISSION ON HUMAN RIGHTS
FIRST SESSION

SUMMARY RECORD OF THE THIRTEENTH MEETING

Held at Lake Success, New York, on Tuesday, 4 February 1947, at 11:00 a.m.

Consideration of Document E/CN.4/W18

...

Dr. Chang (China) considered that the principle of equality should be examined, bearing in mind the concept of human dignity.

...

Dr. Chang (China) considered that, in order to comply with the wishes of the Representatives of France and the Philippine Republic, a sentence might be included in the summary record to the effect that the Commission considered it necessary to emphasize this idea of the solidarity or unity of the human race. It would thereby be ensured that the Declaration of Human Rights would always be correctly understood, and that it would be possible at all times to see what had been formulated on the morrow of a war waged by the enemy in the name of racial inequality.

...

Dr. Chang (China) emphasized that his country's Constitution already contained the majority of the rights enumerated in paragraph 2, and he added that he would have copies of the Chinese Constitution distributed among the members of the Commission.

...

Dr. Chang (China) drew the Commission's attention to Article 18 of the Chinese Constitution which prescribed the system of public examinations for the admission to public office. He considered that that right should exist in all countries, and suggested that it be mentioned in the Bill of Human Rights.

...

在人权委员会第 14 次会议上的发言

1947 年 2 月 4 日星期二下午 2:00 纽约成功湖

继续就《国际人权法案（草案）》（第 E/CN.4/W.18 和 E/CN.4/11 号文件）的内容进行辩论

······

张先生（中国）提醒道，应警惕因为与战后时代的精神和气氛脱节而作出一份不合时宜的文件；他希望看到"免于匮乏的自由"这一表述出现在序言或正文的某个地方。

······

张先生（中国）认为，委员会应在起草委员会的协助下首先起草一份纳入决议草案的人权法案。这一建议得到了特普利亚科夫先生（苏联）的支持。

······

——人权委员会第 14 次会议简要记录（E/CN.4/SR.14）

杨晗如译，常健校

E/CN.4/SR.14
5 February 1947

COMMISSION ON HUMAN RIGHTS
FIRST SESSION
SUMMARY RECORD OF THE FOURTEENTH MEETING
Held at Lake Success, New York, on Tuesday, 4 February 1947, at 2:00 p.m.

Continuation of the Debate on the Contents of the Draft
International Bill of Rights (Documents E/CN.4/W.18 and
E/CN.4/11)

...

Mr. Chang (China) warned against the danger of producing a document which would ill accord with the times owing to its being out of time with the spirit and atmosphere of the post war era; he would like to see the expression "freedom from want" appear somewhere, either in the preamble or in the text itself.

...

Mr. Chang (China), supported by Mr. Tepliakov (Union of Soviet Socialist Republics), thought the Commission ought, first of all, with the assistance of the Drafting Committee, to draw up a Bill of Rights incorporated in a draft resolution.

...

在人权委员会第 16 次会议上的发言

1947 年 2 月 5 日星期三下午 2:45 纽约成功湖

澳大利亚代表提交的《国际人权法院决议（草案）》
（第 E/CN.4/15 号文件）

......

张先生（中国）同意，起草小组已受托承担起草一份人权法案的任务。如果有关实施的建议也提交给该小组，这一情况则应予以明确说明。为了顾及所表达的各种不同观点，中国代表建议，黎巴嫩提出的修正案还应规定，应允许起草小组探讨该问题的所有方面，包括实施。

......

张先生（中国）说，人权委员会的主要职能是起草《国际人权法案》。因此，有关该问题的所有来文都应立即提请人权委员会注意。因此，对于所有其他来文，人权委员会应避免产生不当的期望。

因此，张先生建议，报告第 5 款可立即通过，拟议的小组委员会的问题可提交委员会下届会议审议。

......

张先生（中国）说，除非作出澄清，否则公众可能会误解人权委员会的职能。

他建议立即通过第 5 款，以比利时代表建议的方式修改第（d）项，并删除第（a）项中的"在小组委员会每次会议之前"的字样。根据英国代表的建议，报告的其余部分应重新提交小组委员会。

霍奇森先生（澳大利亚）支持中国的提议。他建议在第 5 款（a）节"收到的来文"之后插入"联合国所有机关"。

......

张先生（中国）表示，无论是否有一个特别小组委员会来接收与人权有关的来文，这些来文都将持续发送过来。其中许多来文可能包含有严重错误的叙述。

……

——人权委员会第 16 次会议简要记录（E/CN.4/SR.16）

杨晗如、常健译，常健校

E/CN.4/SR.16
6 February 1947

COMMISSION ON HUMAN RIGHTS
FIRST SESSION
SUMMARY RECORD OF THE SIXTEENTH MEETING
Held at Lake Success, New York, on Wednesday, 5 February 1947, at 2:45 p.m.

Draft Resolution for an International Court of Human Rights, Submitted by the Representative of Australia (Document E/CN.4/15)

…

Mr. Chang (China) agreed that the drafting group had been entrusted with the task of drafting a bill of rights. If suggestions concerning implementation were also to be referred to that group, that fact should be clearly stated. In order to meet the different points of view expressed, the Chinese representative suggested that the Lebanese amendment should also state that the drafting group should be allowed to explore all aspects of the problem, including implementation.

…

Mr. Chang (China) said that the chief function of the Commission was to draft the International Bill of Human Rights. Therefore all communications on that subject should be brought to the Commission's notice immediately. As regards all other communications, the Commission should therefore refrain from raising false hopes.

Mr. Chang accordingly suggested that paragraph 5 of the report might be adopted at once, and that the question of the proposed Sub-Committee might be deferred to the next session of the Commission.

......

Mr. Chang (China) said that the functions of the Commission might be misconstrued by the general public unless the position were clarified.

He proposed that paragraph 5 should be adopted at once, section (d) being amended in the manner suggested by the Belgian representative and the words "before each meeting of the Sub-Committee" in section (a) being deleted. The rest of the report should be referred back to the Sub-Committee in accordance with the suggestion of the United Kingdom representative.

Mr. Hodgson (Australia) supported the Chinese proposal. He suggested that the words "by all organs of the United Nations" should be inserted after the words "communications received" in paragraph 5, section (a).

......

Mr. Chang (China) remarked that communications dealing with human rights would continue to arrive whether or not there was a special sub-committee to receive them. Many of those communications might contain the accounts of serious wrongs.

......

在人权委员会第 17 次会议上的发言

1947 年 2 月 6 日星期四上午 11:00 纽约成功湖

审议原议程第 13—16 项（第 E/CN.4/1 号文件）

......

张先生（中国）称，起草小组将提交一份人权法案草案。小组成员可以根据其常识来考量所有提交给他们的文件。

主席表示，人权委员会面前的动议和修正案将在下午的会议上讨论。

会议于下午 12:50 结束。

——人权委员会第 17 次会议简要记录（E/CN.4/SR.17）

罗苇、常健译，常健校

E/CN.4/SR.17
6 February 1947

COMMISSION ON HUMAN RIGHTS
FIRST SESSION
SUMMARY RECORD OF THE SEVENTEENTH MEETING
Held at Lake Success, New York, on Thursday, 6 February 1947, at 11:00 a.m.

Consideration of Item13 to 16 of Original Agenda (Document E/CN.4/1)

...

Mr. Chang (China) said that the Drafting Group were only submitting a draft Bill of Rights and it could be left to their common sense to consider all documents submitted to them.

The Chairman said that the motion and amendment before the Commission would be discussed at the afternoon meeting.

The meeting rose at 12:50 p.m.

在人权委员会第 18 次会议上的发言

1947 年 2 月 6 日星期四下午 12:45 纽约成功湖

五、日程第 7 项：与其他委员会的协调

特普利亚科夫先生（苏联）指出，经济及社会理事会的主要职责就是协调各委员会的工作，因此他考虑这个任务应当留给该委员会。

副主席张博士（中国）认为，这个问题应留待下届会议来决定，当下的系统应当尽可能简单和实用。

——人权委员会第 18 次会议简要记录（E/CN.4/SR.18）

常健译校

E/CN.4/SR.18
6 February 1947

COMMISSION ON HUMAN RIGHTS
FIRST SESSION
SUMMARY RECORD OF THE EIGHTEENTH MEETING

Held at Lake Success, New York, on Thursday, 6 February 1947, at 12:45 p.m.

...

V. Item 7 on the Agenda: Co-ordination with other Commissions

Mr. Tepliakov (Union of Soviet Socialist Republics) pointed out that the main function of the Economic and Social Council was to co-ordinate the work of the various Commissions, and he therefore considered that this task should be left to the Council.

Mr. Chang (China), Vice-Chairman, thought that this question should be left aside until the next session, and that for the moment the system should be kept as simple and practical as possible.

在人权委员会第 19 次会议上的发言

1947 年 2 月 7 日星期五上午 11:00 纽约成功湖

1. 讨论程序规则委员会的报告（第 E/CN.4/18 号文件）

规则 5：将"主席"修改为"委员会"

······

张先生（中国）评论道，考虑到其政治意义，地点的问题比日期需要得到更大关注。在这方面的任何决定权都应掌握在委员会的手中。同时，他强调委员会的会议应当在总部举行这个基本原则。

······

——人权委员会第 19 次会议简要记录（E/CN.4/SR.19）

常健译校

E/CN.4/SR.20

7 February 1947

COMMISSION ON HUMAN RIGHTS
FIRST SESSION
SUMMARY RECORD OF THE NINETEENTH MEETING

Held at Lake Success, New York, on Friday, 7 February 1947, at 11:00 a.m.

1. Discussion of the Report of the Committee on Rules of Procedure (Document E/CN.4/18)

...

Rule 5: Amend by changing the word "Chairman" to "Commission"

...

Mr. Chang (China) remarked that the question of location required greater attention than the date, in view of its political significance. Any decision in that respect should be in the hands of the Commission. At the same time, he emphasized the basic principle that the Commission should meet at Headquarters.

...

在人权委员会第 20 次会议上的发言

1947 年 2 月 7 日星期五下午 3:00 纽约成功湖

继续讨论人权委员会提交经济及社会理事会的报告
（第 E/CN. 4/19 和 E/CN. 4/Rev. 2 号文件）

1. 对处理来文小组委员会报告的讨论和表决（E/CN.4/14/Rev.2 号文件）

张先生（中国）准备对第 5 段投赞成票，但对第 4 段投反对票，因为它涉及一个原则问题。他认为，现在说委员会有资格正式接收来文还为时过早。

2. 讨论人权委员会提交经济及社会理事会的报告草案
（E/CN.4/19 号文件）

委员会根据张先生（中国）的提议，决定在第一章第 2 段中删除第 2 行中的"替代"一词，并在最后一行中插入"被代表"而不是"被取代"一词。

——人权委员会第 20 次会议简要记录（E/CN.4/SR.20）

杨晗如译，常健校

E/CN.4/SR.20
7 February 1947

COMMISSION ON HUMAN RIGHTS
FIRST SESSION
SUMMARY RECORD OF THE TWENTYTH MEETING

Held at Lake Success, New York, on Friday, 7 February 1947, at 3:00 p.m.

Continuation of the Discussion of the Report of the Commission on Human rights to the Economic and Social Council (Documents E/CN.4/19 and E/CN.4/Rev.2)

1. Discussion and Vote on the Report of the Sub-Committee on the Handling of Communications (Document E/CN.4/14/Rev.2.)

...

Mr. Chang (China) was ready to vote for paragraph 5 but was against paragraph 4 because it raised a question of principle. He thought it premature to say that the Commission was qualified to receive communications officially.

...

2. Discussion of the Draft Report of the Commission on Human Rights to the Economic and Social Council (Document E/CN.4/19)

...

In Chapter I, paragraph 2, the Commission decided, on the proposal of Mr. Chang (China), to delete the word "substitutes" in line 2 and to insert "represented" instead of "replaced" in the last line.

...

在人权委员会第 21 次会议上的发言

1947 年 2 月 10 日上午 10:00 星期一纽约成功湖

1.讨论经济及社会理事会报告草案（第 E/CN.4/19 号文件）、美国关于新闻和出版自由小组委员会（第 E./CN.4/7 号文件）以及保护少数群体及防止歧视的小组委员会（第 E/CN.4/6 号文件）的建议

……

张先生（中国）同意澳大利亚代表的意见，并建议委员会应当将建立小组委员会的事宜推迟到下届会议。但如果认为新闻和出版自由小组委员会更急迫，那么报告员的报告应当被通过，该小组委员会应当马上成立。

……

张先生（中国）说，可能没有时间接收来自某些遥远地区的提名，理事会将面临从大约几百个名字中进行挑选的职责，几个重要的地理区域可能没在提名之中。

……

霍奇森上校（澳大利亚）询问中国代表，由于他也是经济及社会理事会的代表，许多重要政府拒绝提名是否不是因为沟通困难或疏忽，而是因为原则问题，以及因此，如果采用正在讨论的方法，经济及社会理事会是否不可能实现委员会意图。

张先生（中国）说，未收到提名的原因从未被明确说明。

……

主席宣布委员会进入审议成员的任期，在小组委员报告中的建议是两年。

张先生（中国）提出正式修改案，将小组委员会成员的任期从两年改为一年，特别是考虑到该大会的筹备工作。该事项可以在一年结束时重新考虑。

……

　　张先生（中国）指出，小组委员的职权范围是审查"新闻自由"概念应包括哪些权利、义务和做法。应该有可能在一两届会议上就此问题取得一些进展，委员会不妨在一年后修改职权范围。

　　此外，他认为设立常设性的小组委员会不切实际，因为预算使其无法实现。

　　……

　　张先生（中国）提问，这些小组委员会是否已经被选定了，经济及就业委员作出了什么决定？汉弗莱先生回答说，根据他手中的报告草案，其成员尚未被任命。

　　张先生建议，鉴于将该事项提交理事会有困难，不妨在下午的会议前召开一个七人小组委员会会议讨论此事。

　　就此达成一致，会议于下午 1:00 结束。

——人权委员会第 21 次会议简要记录（E/CN.4/SR.21）

常健译校

E/CN.4/SR.21
10 February 1947

COMMISSION ON HUMAN RIGHTS
FIRST SESSION
SUMMARY RECORD OF THE TWENTY-FIRST MEETING

Held at Lake Success, New York, on Monday, 10 February 1947, at 10:00 a.m.

1. Discussion of the Draft Report to the Economic and Social Council (Document E/CN.4/19), United States Proposals regarding a Sub-Commission on Freedom of Information and of the Press (Document E/CN.4/7) and a Sub-Commission on Protection of Minorities and Prevention of Discrimination (Document E/CN.4/6)

…

Mr. Chang (China) agreed with the representative of Australia and suggested that the Commission should postpone the setting up of Sub-Commissions until its next session, but if the Sub-Commission on Freedom of Information and of the Press was considered more urgent, then the report of the Rapporteur should be approved and that Sub-Commission set up immediately.

...

Mr. Chang (China) said there might not be time to receive nominations from certain distant areas, and the Council would be faced with the responsibility of choosing from perhaps some hundred names, while several important geographical sections might not figure among the nominations.

...

Col. Hodgson (Australia) asked the representative of China, since he was also a representative of the Economic and Social Council whether it was a fact that it was not because of difficulties of communications or through inadvertence that many important governments had refused to submit nominations, but as a matter of principle, and whether consequently, if the method under discussion were to be adopted, it would be impossible for the Economic and Social Council to carry out the intentions of the Commission.

Mr. Chang (China) said the reasons for nominations not coming in had never been clearly stated.

...

The Chairman announced that the Commission would proceed to the consideration of the term of office of members, suggested as two years in the report of the Sub-Commission.

Mr. Chang (China) made a formal amendment to change the term of office from two years to one year, especially in view of the preparation for the Conference. The matter could be reconsidered at the end of one year.

...

Mr. Chang (China) pointed out that the terms of reference of the Sub-Commission were to examine what rights, obligations and practices should be included in the concept "Freedom of Information". It should be possible to make some headway on that subject in one or two sessions, and the Commission might wish to change the terms of reference after one year.

Furthermore, he did not consider it practical to set up permanent Sub-Commissions, as the budget might make that impossible.

…

In answer to a question form Mr. Chang (China) as to whether those sub-commissions had been chosen already and what decision had been reached by the Economic and Employment Commission, Mr. Humphrey said that according to the draft report before him the members had not yet been appointed.

Mr. Chang (China) suggested that in view of the difficulty of referring the matter to the Council, it might be advisable to have a meeting of the sub-committee of seven, to talk the matter over before the afternoon meeting.

That being agreed upon, the meeting rose at 1:00 p.m.

在人权委员会第 22 次会议上的发言

1947 年 2 月 10 日星期一下午 2:30 纽约成功湖

讨论和通过人权委员会提交经济及社会理事会的报告草案
（第 E/CN.4/19 号文件）

……

7. 讨论附录（第 E/CN.4/19 号文件）

……

张先生（中国）建议，专门机构和非政府组织的建议应当由报告员口头转达给经济及社会理事会。

决定：对中国代表的提案以 9 票赞成、0 票反对获得通过。

……

8. 讨论和决定人权委员会下届会议的地点和日期

……

张先生（中国）建议，该届会议应当在联合国的所在地举行，会议日期应由经济及社会理事会来确定。理事会议事规则规定每年举行三届会议，理事会已决定在 1947 年举行三至四届会议。为了节省预算资金，他要求该届会议应在联合国所在地举行。

……

在回答张博士（中国）提出的问题时，斯坦奇克先生（秘书处）说，委员会的投票对秘书处只具有指导性。

……

11.人权委员会第一届会议辩论的结论

张博士（中国）要求将下列陈述写入简要记录，以便转达给所有相关人员：

"人权委员会向秘书长表达对其工作人员在筹备和举行第一届会议期间干练的工作方式的赞赏。

"劳吉尔先生不顾个人的不便和健康状况，发表了令人难忘的开幕致辞。委员会还认为应当祝贺秘书长有汉弗莱博士担任其工作人员，他在本届会议期间担任秘书工作。委员会工作的成功在很大程度上归功于汉弗莱博士对这项工作的周密规划、聪明睿智和不懈投入。

"委员会还谨对其主席的尽心竭力和鼓舞人心的领导表示赞赏和感谢，其迷人和不可抗拒的耐心和幽默精神使我们感到由衷的钦佩。"

霍奇森上校（澳大利亚）、卡森教授（法国）、马利克先生（黎巴嫩）、杜克斯先生（英国）、里尼卡尔先生（南斯拉夫）、埃贝德先生（埃及）与中国代表具有同感。

会议于下午 6:30 结束。

——人权委员会第 22 次会议简要记录（E/CN.4/SR.22）

常健译校

E/CN.4/SR.22
10 February 1947

COMMISSION ON HUMAN RIGHTS
FIRST SESSION
SUMMARY RECORD OF THE TWENTY-SECOND MEETING
Held at Lake Success, New York, on Monday, 10 February 1947, at 2:30 p.m.

Discussion and Adoption of the Draft Report of the Commission on Human Rights to the Economic and Social Council (Document E/CN.4/19)

...

7. Discussion on the Annexes (Document E/CN.4/19)

...

Mr. Chang (China) proposed that the suggestions of the specialized agencies and the non-governmental organizations should be transmitted orally to the Economic and Social Council by the Rapporteur.

DECISION: The proposal of the representative of China was adopted by nine votes to none.

...

8. Discussion and Decision on the Place and Date of the Next Session of the Commission on Human Rights

...

Mr. Chang (China) proposed that the session should take place at the seat of the United Nations, and that the Economic and Social Council should fix the date. The rules of procedure of the Council provided for three annual sessions and the Council had decided to hold three or four sessions in 1947. In order to economize in budget funds, he asked that the session should take place at the seat of the United Nations.

...

In reply to a question from Dr. Chang (China), Mr. Stanczyk (Secretariat) said that the Commission's vote was only a guide to the Secretariat.

...

11. Conclusion of the Debates of the First Session of the Commission on Human Rights

Dr. Chang (China) asked that the following statement be included in the summary record for transmission to all concerned:

"The Commission on Human Rights expresses to the Secretary-General its appreciation of the extremely able manner in which the work of his staff was performed, both in preparation for and during the first session of this Commission.

"The opening address of Monsieur Laugier, delivered at real sacrifice to his personal convenience and his health, will not soon be forgotten. The Commission further feels that the Secretary-General is to be congratulated on having on his staff Dr. Humphrey, who acted as Secretary during this session. The success of the Commission's work has been due in no small measure to the careful planning and the high degree of intelligence and tireless devotion which Dr. Humphrey has given to this work.

"The Commission wishes also to express its appreciation and gratitude for the devoted and inspiring leadership of its Chairman, whose charming and irresistible spirit of patience and humor elicits our sincerest admiration."

Colonel Hodgson (Australia), Professor Cassin (France), Mr. Malik (Lebanon), Mr. Dukes (United Kingdom), Mr. Rienikar (Yugoslavia), Mr. Ebeid (Egypt), associated themselves with the sentiments expressed by the representative of China.

The meeting rose at 6:30 p.m.

联合国经济及社会理事会第四届会议

在经济及社会理事会第 69 次会议上的发言

1947 年 3 月 14 日星期五下午 2:45 纽约成功湖

34. 继续讨论人权委员会的报告

......

张先生（中国）希望，在经历了过去一百五十年的短视浅见之后，各国终于可以跨入一个新人文主义的时代。所设想的法案应奠基在这种新人文主义的抱负之上。

世界上有三十五或四十部宪法中包括了人的权利。这一事实表明，尽管存在哲学或意识形态上的差异，但仍有可能在很大程度上达成一致。

在中国制宪国民大会 1946 年 12 月颁布的宪法第 18 条中，增加了一项新权利，即为担任公职而参加公开考试的权利，而它并没有得到整个世界的关注。公职人员公开考试制度和代议制政府制度，对促进真正的自由和平等作出了巨大贡献，并构成了社会民主的基础。他希望在人权法案中提及公职人员公开考试制度。

......

——经济及社会理事会第 69 次会议简要记录（E/SR.69）

杨晗如译，常健校

E/SR.69
14 March 1947

ECONOMIC AND SOCIAL COUNCIL
FOURTH SESSION
SUMMARY RECORD OF THE SIXTY-NINTH MEETING
Held at Lake Success, New York, on Friday, 14 March 1947, at 2:45 p.m.

34. Continuation of the discussion of the report of the Commission of Human Rights

...

Mr. Chang (China) hoped that after the myopia of the last hundred and fifty years, nations were at last on the threshold of a new humanistic period. The bill envisaged should be based on the aspiration for a new humanism.

The fact that rights of men were included in thirty-five or forty of the world's constitutions indicated that a large measure of agreement was possible in spite of differences of philosophy or ideology.

In Article 18 of the Constitution promulgated in December 1946 by the Constituent Assembly in China a new right was included – the right to take public examination for holding public offices-of which little notice had been taken in the world as a whole. The institution of public civil service examinations and that of representative government had contributed greatly to the promotion of true freedom and equality and formed the basis of social democracy. He hoped that some notice would be taken of the former institution in the Bill of Rights.

...

在经济及社会理事会社会事务委员会第 6 次会议上的发言

1947 年 3 月 20 日下午 3:30 纽约成功湖

……

[此时，张先生（中国）代替杨先生参加会议]。

主席将捷克斯洛伐克提交的修正案付诸表决。该修正案以 10 票赞成、5 票反对和 2 票弃权获得通过。

里德尔先生（加拿大）提出如下动议："在起草委员会举行会议之前，人权委员会主席团成员在秘书处的协助下，起草《国际人权法案（草案）》，并将该草案分发给联合国会员国，供其审阅和评论。"

张先生（中国）请里德尔先生接受对其动议的一处修正，修正后的动议如下：

"在起草委员会举行会议之前，秘书处在人权委员会主席团成员的监督下，起草《国际人权法案（草案）》，并将该草案分发给联合国会员国，供其审阅和评论。"

……

> ——经济及社会理事会社会事务委员会第 6 次会议简要
> 记录（E/AC.7/8）

杨晗如译，常健校

E/AC.7/8
20 March 1947

ECONOMIC AND SOCIAL COUNCIL
COMMITTEE ON SOCIAL AFFAIRS
SUMMARY RECORD OF THE SIXTH MEETING

Held at Lake Success, New York, on 20 March 1947, at 3:30 p.m.

...

[At this point Mr. Chang (China) took the place of Mr. Yang].

The Chairman put to a vote the Czechoslovak amendment. The amendment was adopted by 10 votes for, 5 votes against and 2 abstentions.

Mr. Riddle (Canada) moved that "prior to the meeting of the Drafting Committee the officers of the Commission on Human Rights, assisted by the Secretariat, prepare a Draft International Bill of Human Rights and circulate such draft to the Members of the United Nations for their observations and comments."

Mr. Chang (China) asked Mr. Riddle to accept an amendment to his motion which would then read:

"That, prior to the meeting of the Drafting Committee, the Secretariat under the supervision of the officers of the Commission on Human Rights, prepare a Draft International Bill of Human Rights and circulate such draft to the Members of the United Nations for their observations and comments."

...

人权委员会之起草委员会第一届会议

在人权委员会之起草委员会第 1 次会议上的发言

1947 年 6 月 9 日星期一上午 11:00 纽约成功湖

2.选举主席团成员

......

霍奇森上校（澳大利亚）提出，根据人权委员会的决定，其主席团成员——罗斯福夫人（主席）、张博士（副主席）和马利克先生（报告员）应在秘书处的协助下，承担拟订《国际人权法案》初稿的任务。他建议，起草委员会的成员应与人权委员会的成员相同。

圣克鲁兹先生（智利）支持这项动议，并表示，他认为经济及社会理事会的意图是，人权委员会的这些成员应继续以各自的身份在起草委员会中行事。

决定：由于没有其他提名，人权委员会的主席团成员自动当选为起草委员会的主席团成员。

3.采取临时议程（E/CN. 4/AC. 1 号文件）

张博士（中国）提议，将该临时议程采用为起草委员会的议程。卡森教授（法国）支持该动议。霍奇森上校（澳大利亚）指出，实施问题不在临时议程上。他认为，根据人权委员会通过的关于实施情况的决议，起草委员会有义务研究这个问题。

主席解释说，虽然实施问题没有出现在临时议程上，但这并不意味着起草委员会将完全排除该问题的审议。在她看来，起草委员会的首要目标是就应以权利的方式写入法案的内容达成一致，然后可以非常仔细地讨论和考虑实施问题。霍奇森上校（澳大利亚）表示，他愿意投票支持通过临时议程，但有一项保留意见，即如果时间和机会允许，稍后他可能会提出实施问题，尽管该问题没有出现在议程上。

决定：临时议程在无异议的情况下获得一致通过，成为起草委员会的议程。

……

——人权委员会之起草委员会第 1 次会议简要记录
（E/CN.4/AC.1/SR.1）

罗莘、常健译，常健校

E/CN.4/AC.1/SR.1
10 June 1947

COMMISSION ON HUMAN RIGHTS
DRAFTING COMMITTEE
FIRST SESSION
SUMMARY RECORD OF THE FIRST MEETING

Held at Lake Success, New York, on Monday, 9 June 1947, at 11:00 a.m.

…

2. Election of Officers

Col. Hodgson (Australia) referred to the decision of the Commission on Human Rights, that its officers, Mrs. Roosevelt (Chairman), Dr. Chang (Vice-Chairman), and Dr. Malik (Rapporteur) should undertake, with the assistance of the Secretariat, the task of formulating a preliminary draft of an International Bill of Human Rights. He suggested that the officers of the Drafting Committee be the same as those of the Commission on Human Rights.

Mr. Santa Cruz (Chile) supported the motion, and stated that in his opinion it was the intention of the Economic and Social Council that these members of the Commission should continue to act in their respective capacities on the Drafting Committee.

DECISION: As there were no other nominations, the officers of the Commission on Human Bights were automatically elected as officers of the Drafting Cormnittee.

…

3. Adoption of Provisional Agenda (Document E/CN.4/AC.1)

Dr. Chang (China) moved the adoption of the provisional agenda as the agenda of the Drafting Committee. Prof. Cassin (France) supported the motion. Col. Hodgson (Australia) pointed out that the question of implementation was not on the provisional agenda. He said that he felt that the Drafting Committee was obliged, under the resolution relating to implementation adopted by the Commission on Human Rights, to study this question.

The Chairman explained that although the question of implementation did not appear on the provisional agenda, that did not mean that the subject would be ruled out entirely from consideration by the Drafting Committee. She stated that in her opinion the Drafting Committee's first objective was to come to an agreement on what should be included in the Bill in the way of rights and that then the question of implementation might be taken up and considered very carefully. Col. Hodgson (Australia) stated his willingness to vote for the adoption of the provisional agenda subject to the reservation that later, if time and opportunity permitted, he might raise the question of implementation although it did not appear on the agenda.

DECISION: Without objection the provisional agenda was adopted unanimously as the agenda of the Drafting Committee.

...

在人权委员会之起草委员会第 2 次会议上的发言

1947 年 6 月 11 日星期三上午 11:00 纽约成功湖

1. 关于起草程序的讨论

……

张博士（中国）坚持认为，讨论应当从具体到抽象，应从委员会所有成员均会赞同的秘书处草案的条款开始，然后审议在英国草案或某个其他成员提案中出现的条款。他敦促委员会尽可能地扩展视野，并始终意识到制定这项《国际人权法案》的历史背景。他特别力主不要让它成为先前人权法案的陈旧副本。

……

——人权委员会之起草委员会第 2 次会议简要记录
（E/CN.4/AC.1/SR.2）

杨晗如译，常健校

E/CN.4/AC.1/SR.2
13 June 1947

COMMISSION ON HUMAN RIGHTS
DRAFTING COMMITTEE
FIRST SESSION
SUMMARY RECORD OF THE SECOND MEETING

Held at Lake Success, New York, on Wednesday, 11 June 1947, at 11:00 a.m.

1. Discussion of Drafting Procedure

…

Dr. Chang (China) maintained that the discussion should proceed from the concrete to the abstract, that it should start with articles in the Secretariat draft on which all members of the Committee could agree and then go on to consider other articles appearing either in the United Kingdom draft or in a proposal by one of the other members. He urged that the Committee attain as wide a perspective as possible and that it be always conscious of the historical context of the formulation of this International Bill of Rights. He particularly urged that it not be allowed to become a stale duplication of previous Bills of Rights.

......

在人权委员会之起草委员会第 3 次会议上的发言

1947 年 6 月 11 日星期三下午 2:30 纽约成功湖

1.审议第 E/CN.4/AC.1/3/Add3 号文件：英国代表团提交的草案与秘书处编写的草案的文本对比

……

秘书处大纲草案第 14 条和英国草案第二部分第 13 条

……

张博士（中国）评论道，就宗教歧视而言，在他看来中国也许是麻烦最少的国家。他补充说，这一事实在 18 世纪吸引了英国哲学家的关注。他接着说，草案中每项条文的相对简洁程度或所包含的细节内容，应该逐条加以讨论。

……

秘书处草案大纲第 17 条以及英国草案第二部分第 14 条

……

张博士（中国）评论道，英国草案将肯定性理念放在首位，这看起来是一个更好的安排。哈里先生（澳大利亚）同意科瑞斯基教授的说法，即起草委员会应考虑新闻和出版自由小组委员会的报告。他提议，如有必要，可请小组委员会审议拟列入人权法案的条款案文。汉弗莱教授（秘书处）提请注意以下事实：新闻和出版自由小组委员会要到明年冬天才会再次开会，因此，起草委员会可能不得不独立于该小组委员会来审议这个主题。

……

2. 审议人权司起草的《国际人权法案草案大纲》（第 E/CN.4/AC.1/3 号文件）

……

圣克鲁兹先生（智利）说，他目前对第 1 条或第 8 条都没有意见。哈里先生（澳大利亚）认为，相较于对各项一般权利的表述，应当更多关注个人的一般责任。他说，他稍后将就这个问题作出陈述。张博士（中国）

评论道，委员会不应倾向于设定国家与个人之间可以如此截然对立起来。
......

秘书处草案大纲第 2 条

......

张博士（中国）指出，美国提出的修正案表述清晰。在他看来，它包含两个不同意思，可以分别加以论述。在逻辑上可以允许中间的语句独立成句。他正式建议采用美国提出的修正案，但要将其分为两条：一条是关于个人与国家之间关系的陈述，另一条是关于一个人与另一个人之间关系的陈述。
......

秘书处草案大纲第 3 条和美国替代文本

......

张博士（中国）评论道，委员会所有成员显然都会同意将生命权写入人权法案中。但是他建议，对"生命"一词的定义应当作出更多思考——是仅仅用它来指机体的存在，还是意指某些超出机体存在的更多内容？
......

秘书处草案大纲第 4 条

......

张博士（中国）认为该条与上一条相关联，应将两者都纳入委员会的草案中。他认为草案应以某种方式强调生命本身的善。
......

秘书处草案大纲第 5 条

......

张博士（中国）提请委员会成员注意 E/CN.4/AC.1/3/Add.2 号文件，并指出，共有 7 条（第 5 至 11 条）涉及个人自由。他建议，在委员会的草案中，应将涉及这一主题的所有条款归拢在一起。马利克先生（黎巴嫩）支持他的建议，威尔逊先生（英国）说，他也赞成这一安排。
......

——人权委员会之起草委员会第 3 次会议简要记录
（E/CN.4/AC.1/SR.3）

杨晗如译，常健校

E/CN.4/AC.1/SR.3

13 June 1947

COMMISSION ON HUMAN RIGHTS

DRAFTING COMMITTEE

FIRST SESSION

SUMMARY RECORD OF THE THIRD MEETING

Held at Lake Success, New York, on Wednesday, 11 June 1947, at 2:30 p.m.

1. Consideration of Document E/CN.4/AC.1/3/Add.3: Textual Comparison of the Draft Submitted by the United Kingdom Delegation and the Draft Prepared by the Secretariat

...

Article 14 of the Secretariat Draft Outline and Part Ⅱ Article 13 of the United Kingdom Draft

...

Dr. Chang (China) remarked that in his opinion China was perhaps the least bothersome nation insofar as religious discrimination was concerned. This fact, he added, had attracted the attention of the English philosophers in the eighteenth century. He added that the relative brevity or detail to be contained in each article of the draft would have to be discussed article by article.

...

Article 17 of the Secretariat Draft Outline and Part Ⅱ Article 14 of the United Kingdom Draft

...

Dr. Chang (China) remarked that the United Kingdom draft put the affirmative ideas first and that this appeared to be a better arrangement. Mr. Harry (Australia) agreed with the statement made by Professor Koretsky that the Drafting Committee should consider the report of the Sub-Commission on Freedom of Information and of the Press. If necessary, he proposed, the Sub-Commission might be asked to consider the text of an article for inclusion in the

Bill of Rights. Professor Humphrey (Secretariat) drew attention to the fact that the Sub-Commission on Freedom of Information and of the Press would not meet again until next winter and that, therefore, the Drafting Committee might have to consider the subject independently of the Sub-Commission.

...

2. Consideration of the Draft Outline of the International Bill of Rights prepared by the Division of Human Rights (E/CN.4/AC.1/3)

...

Mr. Santa Cruz (Chile) stated that he had no comments to make at the moment on either Article 1 or Article 8. Mr Harry (Australia) felt that attention should be drawn to the general duty of the individual comparing to each general right. He said that he would make a statement on this subject later. Dr. Chang (China) remarked that the Committee should not tend to set up the possibility of the State and the individual being so sharply contrasted.

...

Article 2 of the Secretariat Draft Outline

...

Dr. Chang (China) pointed out that the modification proposed by the United States was clearly worded. In his opinion it contained two different ideas which might be separated. The middle sentence might logically be permitted to stand by itself. He formally suggested using the United States modification by separating it into two articles, one a statement of the relation of individuals to the State and the other a statement of the relation of one individual to another.

...

Article 3 of the Secretariat Draft Outline and the United States Alternate Text

...

Dr. Chang (China) observed that it was obvious that all members of the Committee would agree that the right to life should be included in a Bill of Rights. He suggested, however, that more thought should be put into a definition of the word "life"—was it intended to mean mere physical existence or did it imply something more than that?

…

Article 4 of the Secretariat Draft Outline

…

Dr. Chang (China) felt that the article was tied up with the previous article and that both should be included in the Committee's draft. He felt that the draft somehow should stress the goodness of life itself.

…

Article 5 of the Secretariat Draft Outline

…

Dr. Chang (China) called the attention of the members of the Committee to document E/CN.4/AC.1/3/Add.2 and pointed out that there were seven articles numbered 5 to 11, all dealing with liberty of the person. He suggested that in the Committee's draft all of the articles on this subject should be grouped together. Mr. Malik (Lebanon) supported his suggestion and Mr. Wilson (United Kingdom) said that he also was in favour of this arrangement.

…

在人权委员会之起草委员会第 4 次会议上的发言

1947 年 6 月 12 日星期四上午 10:30 纽约成功湖

1.继续审议秘书处起草的《国际人权法案》大纲草案（第 E/CN.4/AC.1/3 号文件）

第 6 条

……

张博士（中国）指出，有必要澄清秘书处草案中使用的"国家紧急状态"一词。

马利克博士（黎巴嫩）表示同意，认为"国家紧急状态"一词弹性很大，必须仔细定义。

……

第 8 条

……

张博士（中国）也倾向于采用美国草案。他认为"本人权法案禁止"这一措辞不合适，并认为应在另一点提及民生和工作。他认为，由于世界各国关于合同的法律存在差异，因此必须对"合同义务"的概念进行限定。

……

第 10 条

……

张博士（中国）说，他认为迁徙自由是基础性的。他认为，可以作出对该原则的陈述，但其实施只能是各个国家关切的事项。

……

第 21 条

写入第 21 条的内容是由张博士（中国）提议的。

……

第 28 条

写入第 28 条的内容是由张博士（中国）提议的。但是他指出，必须澄清联合国在申诉方面能做些什么。

……

第 31 条

写入第 31 条的内容是由张博士（中国）提议的。但是，他认为可能需要更改措辞。

……

第 34 条

写入第 34 条的内容是由马利克博士（黎巴嫩）和张博士（中国）提议的。

……

第 47 条

张博士（中国）指出，第 47 条涉及实施人权法案的方法。因此，他认为不应立即对此进行讨论。

第 48 条

……

张博士（中国）设想了三份不同的文件：第一份是用简洁的措辞起草的宣言；第二份是对宣言每一条的评论；第三份是一系列实施建议。

……

——人权委员会之起草委员会第 4 次会议简要记录
（E/CN.4/AC.1/SR.4）

杨晗如译，常健校

E/CN.4/AC.1/SR.4
13 June 1947

COMMISSION ON HUMAN RIGHTS
DRAFTING COMMITTEE
FIRST SESSION
SUMMARY RECORD OF THE FOURTH MEETING

Held at Lake Success, New York, on Thursday, 12 June 1947, at 10:30 a.m.

1. Consideration of Secretariat Draft Outline of International Bill of Rights continued (Document E/CN.4/AC.1/3)

Article 6

...

Dr. Chang (China) pointed out that it would be necessary to clarify the term "national emergency" used in the Secretariat draft.

Dr. Malik (Lebanon) agreed that the term "national emergency", being very elastic, would have to be carefully defined.

...

Article 8

...

Dr. Chang (China) also preferred the United States draft. He considered the phrase "prohibited by this Bill of Rights" unsuitable, and felt that reference to livelihood and work should be made at another point. "Contractual obligations", in his opinion, would have to be qualified inasmuch as laws relating to contracts differed throughout the world.

...

Article 10

...

Dr. Chang (China) said he believed liberty of movement to be fundamental. A statement of principle might be drawn up, he felt, but its implementation would have to be the concern of the individual countries.

...

Article 21

The inclusion of the substance of Article 21 was sponsored by Dr. Chang (China).

...

Article 28

The inclusion of the substance of Article 28 was sponsored by Dr. Chang (China). He pointed out, however, that what the United Nations could do about grievances would have to be made clear.

...

Article 31

The inclusion of the substance of Article 31 was sponsored by Dr. Chang (China). He felt, however, that a change of wording might be necessary.

...

Article 34

The inclusion of the substance of Article 34 was sponsored by Dr. Malik (Lebanon) and Dr. Chang (China).

...

Article 47

Dr. Chang (China) pointed out that Article 47 dealt with a method of implementing the Bill of Rights. For this reason he felt that it should not be discussed immediately.

Article 48

...

Dr. Chang (China) envisaged three distinct documents: one a Declaration, drafted in simple phrases; the second a commentary on each Article of the Declaration; the third a series of proposals for implementation.

...

在人权委员会之起草委员会第 5 次会议上的发言

1947 年 6 月 12 日星期四下午 2:30 纽约成功湖

1. 根据秘书处提供的文件起草《国际人权法案》初稿

......

张博士（中国）说，在现阶段，委员会只能希望起草一份关于一般性原则和权利的清单，以宣言草案的形式提交联合国大会审议。可以在该原则和权利清单后附上评注，以简洁的措辞定义术语。之后，委员会可以考虑切实可行的实施方法。他强调，在现阶段不应限制条款的数目。在初始阶段，委员会对条款数目的要求可以是宁多勿少。

......

——人权委员会之起草委员会第 5 次会议简要记录

（E/CN. 4/AC. 1/SR. 5）

李梦瑶译，常健校

E/CN.4/AC.1/SR.5

17 June 1947

COMMISSION ON HUMAN RIGHTS

DRAFTING COMMITTEE

FIRST SESSION

SUMMARY RECORD OF THE FIFTH MEETING

Held at Lake Success, New York, on Thursday, 12 June 1947, at 2:30 p.m.

1. Preparation of a Preliminary Draft of an International Bill of Human Rights on the Basis of Documentation Supplied by the Secretariat

...

Dr. Chang (China) stated that at this stage the Committee could only hope to draw up a list of general principles and rights, putting them into the form of a draft Declaration for consideration by the General Assembly. A commentary might be attached to that list of principles and rights, defining the terms in simple formulations. Later the Committee could consider practical methods of implementation. He emphasized that the number of articles should not be limited at this stage, and that the Committee might, at the first stage, allow itself to err on the side of too many articles rather than too few.

...

在人权委员会之起草委员会第 6 次会议上的发言

1947 年 6 月 13 日星期五上午 10:30 纽约成功湖

1. 审议起草《国际人权法案》初稿应遵循的程序

……

威尔逊先生（英国）建议将委员会分成两组，每组四名成员，每一组负责起草一份文件。他认为让一个代表来起草宣言，负担过重。

卡森教授（法国）提出，或是由一组负责起草宣言，另一组负责起草公约，或者也可以由每一组都负责起草每份文件的特定部分。他认为英国的建议是可行的。张博士（中国）评论道，英国的建议涉及委员会的每一位成员。他认为，这项建议并非不可行，但应明确，这些小组不是起草委员会，而是小型工作组，每个工作组承担起草委员会的部分初期工作。他还认为，分组不应使起草委员会永久分隔。

……

张博士（中国）建议，工作组根据委员会的指令审阅此前所讨论过的材料，并向委员会全体会议作出报告。他认为，工作组只需对先前的讨论作出总结，也许还可以提出一些具体的建议。威尔逊先生（英国）说，确切理解工作组的职责并不十分困难。委员会已经：（1）讨论了秘书处的草案；（2）就应列入该文件的事项基本达成一致；（3）阐明了应当起草两份文件的意见。他认为委员会成员现在应该自己着手起草这些文件，并补充说，两个文件起草的横向分工可能会导致困惑。张博士（中国）说，他希望工作组承担下列工作：（1）对秘书处的草案作出合乎逻辑的重新安排；（2）根据委员会作出的讨论重新起草各项条款的粗稿；（3）划分工作，指明哪些条款需要纳入国际公约，哪些条款不需要纳入国际公约。

决定：委员会决定任命一个由法国、黎巴嫩和英国代表组成的临时工作组，该工作组的职能如下。

（1）就对秘书处提供的大纲草案的条款作出合乎逻辑的重新安排提出建议；

（2）根据起草委员会的讨论，就重新起草各项条款提出建议；

（3）对宣言和公约条款的内容划分向起草委员会提出建议。

会议于下午 1:00 结束。

——人权委员会之起草委员会第 6 次会议简要记录（E/CN. 4/AC. 1/SR. 6）

李梦瑶译，常健校

E/CN.4/AC.1/SR.6

16 June 1947

COMMISSION ON HUMAN RIGHTS
DRAFTING COMMITTEE
FIRST SESSION
SUMMARY RECORD OF THE SIXTH MEETING

Held at Lake Success, New York, on Friday, 13 June 1947, at 10:30 a.m.

1. Consideration of Procedure to Be Followed in Preparing a Preliminary Draft of the International Bill of Human Rights

...

Mr. Wilson (United Kingdom) suggested splitting the Committee into two groups of four members, each group charged with the preparation of one document. He thought it would be too much of a burden for one representative to be called upon to produce the Manifesto.

Prof. Cassin (France) observed that either one group could undertake the writing of the Manifesto and one group the writing of the Convention, or alternatively each group could take responsibility for certain parts of each document. He thought the suggestion of the United Kingdom was a practical one. Dr. Chang (China) remarked that the United Kingdom proposal involved every member of the Committee. He thought the suggestion was not impractical, but that it should be made clear that these were not drafting committees but small working groups, each undertaking a part of the preliminary work of the Drafting Committee. He also thought that the division of groups should not be such that the Drafting Committee would be divided permanently.

...

Dr. Chang (China) suggested that the Committee instruct the working group to go over the material which had been discussed up to that point and to report back to the Committee as a whole. He thought that the group need do no more than summarize the discussions and perhaps produce some concrete suggestions. Mr. Wilson (United Kingdom) said it was not very difficult to understand exactly what the working group was to do. The Committee had (1) discussed the Secretariat draft; (2) agreed in substance regarding matters which should find a place in the document; and (3) expressed the opinion that two documents should be prepared. He thought the members of the Committee should now set about drafting the documents themselves, and added that confusion might result if there was a horizontal division of work between the two documents. Dr. Chang (China) said he would like to have the small group undertake (1) a logical rearrangement of the Secretariat draft; (2) a rough redrafting of the various articles on the basis of discussions which had taken place in the Committee; and (3) a division of the work indicating which articles would require international conventions and which would not.

DECISION: The Committee decided to appoint a Temporary Working Group consisting of the representatives of France, the Lebanon and the United Kingdom, the functions of the Group to be
1. To suggest a logical rearrangement of the articles of the Draft Outline supplied by the Secretariat;
2. To suggest a redraft of the various articles in the light of the discussions of the Drafting Committee;
3. To recommend to the Drafting committee the division of the substance of the articles between a Manifesto and a Convention.

The meeting adjourned at 1:00 p.m.

在人权委员会之起草委员会第 7 次会议上的发言

1947 年 6 月 17 日星期二上午 11:00 纽约成功湖

根据秘书处提供的文件拟订《国际人权法案》初稿

……

张博士（中国）认为，工作组朝着有序的方向迈出了重要的一步。但是他认为，首先应该由委员会全体成员对所提议的每一条款进行审议。

主席指出，张博士显然与美国的主张一致，即认为应该先有一个宣言，然后再有一个或多个公约。

马利克博士（黎巴嫩）指出，起草委员会已经同意起草两份文件：一份是一般性的宣言，另一份是公约，它们将同时被提交给人权委员会。

关于宣言，他认为它应该非常简短，但应该涵盖人权法案的所有基本原则。它应该是一种基本原则的典籍，从中可以衍生出实在的法律；应该是一种为自由和解放而战的呐喊；应该是一种体现联合国关于人权基本理念的信条。从这一宣言出发，会派生出一个或多个公约。世界等待的并不仅仅是一项决议，它要求最大限度地保证人权不被侵犯，期待各项切实可行的公约。他指出，在应立即成为公约主题内容的某些事项上，已经达成了一致。个人自由这一领域——保护人的身体完整——就是这样的主题之一。他同意张博士（中国）的意见，即委员会可以作为一个整体工作一段时间。他认为应当尝试起草两份文件：

1. 一份简短但全面的宣言；

2. 一份总结，总结在哪些内容应当被写入一个或多个公约方面已达成的最大共识。

……

——人权委员会之起草委员会第 7 次会议简要记录
（E/CN. 4/AC. 1/SR. 7）

李梦瑶译，常健校

E/CN.4/AC.1/SR.7

19 June 1947

COMMISSION ON HUMAN RIGHTS
DRAFTING COMMITTEE
FIRST SESSION
SUMMARY RECORD OF THE SEVENTH MEETING

Held at Lake Success, New York, on Tuesday, 17 June 1947, at 11:00 a.m.

Formulation of a Preliminary Draft of an International Bill of Human Rights on the Basis of Documentation Supplied by the Secretariat

...

Dr. Chang (China) said the Working Group had made a significant step towards orderliness. He felt, however, that the entire Committee should go over each of the proposed articles first.

The Chairman stated that Dr. Chang apparently agreed with the position of the United States, that there should be a Declaration, followed by one or more Conventions.

Dr. Malik (Lebanon) pointed out that the Drafting Committee already had agreed that two documents should be prepared, one a general Declaration and the other a Convention, to be submitted simultaneously to the Commission on Human Rights.

Regarding the Declaration, he felt that it should be very brief but should include all the basic principles of a Bill of Human Rights. It should be a fundamental matrix of doctrine from which positive law might be elaborated; a battle cry for freedom, for liberty; a Credo embodying the basic philosophy of the United Nations regarding human rights. From this declaration, there might flow one or more conventions. The world was awaiting more than mere resolutions. It wanted maximum assurance against the infringement of human rights and actual conventions. He pointed out there was already agreement on certain things that should be made the subject of Conventions at once. The field of personal liberties—protection of the bodily integrity of man—was one such subject. He agreed with Dr. Chang (China) that the Committee might work as a whole for some time. He felt it should attempt to draft two documents:

1. a Declaration, brief and all-inclusive, and

2. a summary of the maximum agreement as to what ought to go into one or more Conventions.

…

在人权委员会之起草委员会第 8 次会议上的发言

1947 年 6 月 17 日星期二下午 2:30 纽约成功湖

1. 工作组提交的《国际人权宣言（草案）》，序言和第 1—6 条（第 E/CN. 4/AC. 1/W. 1 号文件）

第 1 条

主席宣读了第 1 条。她指出，美国政府对目前的措辞不满意，并请委员会成员提出可能的修订建议。张博士（中国）认为，应该用一个中国的理念对"理性"的理念作出补充，这个理念的字面翻译为"二人心系"。该理念的英语对应词可能是"sympathy（同情）"或"consciousness of his fellow men"（同胞意识）。他觉得这个新观念很可能被列为人的基本属性。主席同意第 1 条的基本内容可以改为："所有人作为一个家庭的成员，必定自由且在尊严和权利上平等。由于赋有理性，他们必须对自己的同胞的自由和平等有更多的理解。"主席觉得这一条的措辞还需要修改。

……

第 6 条

主席宣读了第 6 条。张博士建议用"尊严"这个词来代替"生命"，这样第一句话就会变为："应当尊重人的尊严。"他还认为，美国觉得第 5 条中不必要的那句话，可以删去。

主席指出，美国建议中的有些想法，可以写入宣言的序言部分。其中包括：（1）"国家是人民为增进其福祉和保护其人权而建立的。每个人在行使自己的权利时，都受到他人权利的限制"；（2）"国家只能对这样的权利施加符合所有人的自由和福祉的限制"。

2. 法国代表就《国际人权宣言》第 7—44 条提出的建议（第 E/CN. 4/AC. 1/W. 2/Rev. 1 号文件）

......

第 8 条

威尔逊先生（英国）建议将第 8、9、10、11、12 和 13 条纳入公约，它们可被视为保护个人自由这一原则的具体适用。

张博士（中国）虽然同意威尔逊先生的建议，但他觉得第 6 至 13 条中的某些短语或句子可以摘取出来用于宣言。他说，把所有这些条款都纳入宣言会使宣言变得过于复杂。

......

第 12 条

......

张先生（中国）回顾了他以前的建议，即除了一个宣言和一个或多个公约之外，还可以有第三类——评注。他认为宣言中的条款应不超过 20 条。评注可以放在那些需要解释但又不能立即在公约中予以处理的条款之后。主席认为他的建议不错。

第 13 条

......

张博士（中国）表示，希望在卡森教授的指导下，能够在第二天准备出一份更简明的宣言，并由秘书处列出一份建议纳入公约的主题清单。

哈里先生（澳大利亚）觉得他的建议是切实可行的。主席认为委员会全体成员应先审阅卡森教授所提交的其余条款。对这一工作流程没有反对意见。

第 14 条

主席宣读了第 14 条。张博士觉得"法律人格"这个词有点太专业了。

卡森教授试图解释第四章"法律地位"中出现的这一条款的哲学基础。他指出，承认所有人的法律人格是废除奴隶制的第二种手段。奴隶曾被认为是工具和个人财产，而不是拥有权利的人。此外，就在战前，还有难民的结婚权利被拒斥的例子，借口是他们没有所有必要的证明和文件，没有居住授权书，没有官方许可等，尽管他们可能已经在那个国家住了几年。就是通过这些琐碎的规定，这些最基本的人权就被剥夺了。

......

第 18 条

主席宣读了第 18 条，认为第 4 款的内容在第 1 款中已有涉及，没有必要再次出现。张博士（中国）认为，前两款可以视为包含了后两款的内容。他建议前两款可作为对原则的宣示，后两款可作为"评注"。威尔逊先生（英国）同意张博士的意见，但认为该条款还可以进一步缩限为第一款，即"人人有权拥有个人财产"这一款。

......

第 20 条

......

张博士（中国）提出草案变更建议，删去"morals"（道德）一词，因为"他人的权利和自由"这一短语中已经隐含了这一概念；该句话的这部分可以修改为："……维护公共秩序和他人的权利和自由。"

......

第 24 条

卡森教授（法国）认为，请愿权可以被纳入人的政治权利之中。他建议第 20、21、22 和 23 条可以在宣言中合并。张博士（中国）同意这一建议，并补充说，第 24 和 25 条也可以合并为政治权利。

......

——人权委员会之起草委员会第 8 次会议简要记录
（E/CN. 4/AC. 1/SR. 8）

李梦瑶译，常健校

E/CN.4/AC.1/SR.8

20 June 1947

COMMISSION ON HUMAN RIGHTS
DRAFTING COMMITTEE
FIRST SESSION
SUMMARY RECORD OF THE EIGHTH MEETING

Held at Lake Success, New York, on Tuesday, 17 June 1947, at 2:30 p.m.

1. Draft International Declaration of Rights Submitted by Working Group, Preamble and Articles 1-6 (Document E/CN.4/AC.1/W.1)

...

Article 1

The Chairman read Article 1. She stated that the United States government was not satisfied with the present wording, and invited the members to suggest possible revisions. Dr. Chang (China) thought that there should be added to the idea of "reason", the idea which in a literal translation from the Chinese would be "two-man-mindedness". The English equivalent might be "sympathy" or "consciousness of his fellow men". This new idea, he felt, might well be included as an essential human attribute. The Chairman agreed that Article 1 might be changed to read in substance: "All men, as members of one family, must be free and equal in dignity and rights. Being endowed with reason, they must have the additional sense of understanding of their fellow men about them." She felt that the wording of this would need revision.

...

Article 6

The Chairman read Article 6. Dr. Chang suggested that the word "dignity" be used instead of "life" so that the first sentence would read: "There shall be respect for human dignity." He also felt that the sentence in Article 5 which the United States considered unnecessary might be eliminated.

The Chairman pointed out that in the United States proposal there appeared certain ideas that might be included in the Preamble of the Declaration. Among these were: (a) "The State is created by the people for the promotion of their welfare and the protection of their human rights. In the exercise of his rights, everyone is limited by the rights of others"; and (b) "The State may impose only such limitations on such rights as are compatible with the freedom and welfare of all."

2. Suggestion submitted by the Representative of France for Articles 7-44 of the International Declaration of Rights (Document E/CN.4/AC.1/W.2/Rev.1)

...

Article 8

Mr. Wilson (United Kingdom) suggested that Articles 8, 9, 10, 11, 12 and 13, which might be considered particular applications of the principle that the liberty of the individual shall be protected, should find a place in a Convention.

Dr. Chang (China), while agreeing with Mr. Wilson's suggestion, felt that certain phrases or sentences appearing in Articles 6 to 13 might be extracted for use in the Declaration. Inclusion of the whole of these articles in the Declaration would make it too complex, he said.

...

Article 12

...

Mr. Chang (China) recalled his previous proposal that in addition to a Declaration and one or more conventions there might be a third category – a commentary. He felt that there should be not more than twenty articles in the Declaration. The commentary would follow those articles which needed to be explained, but which could not be dealt with immediately in a convention. The Chairman agreed that his suggestion was a good one.

Article 13

...

Dr. Chang (China) expressed the hope that by the following day a more concise Declaration could be prepared under the supervision of Professor Cassin, and a proposed list of topics to be included on conventions by the Secretariat.

Mr. Harry (Australia) felt that Dr. Chang's proposal was a practical one. The Chairman expressed the view that the full Committee should first go through the rest of the Articles presented by Professor Cassin. There was no objection to this procedure.

Article 14

The Chairman read Article 14. Dr. Chang felt that the phrase "legal personality" was a little too technical.

Professor Cassin attempted to explain the philosophical basis of the articles appearing in Chapter Ⅳ, headed "Legal Status". The recognition of the juridical personality of all human beings is a second means of abolishing slavery, he pointed out. Slaves were once considered as instruments, as chattels, not as beings who could have rights. Also, just before the war there were instances when the right to marry was refused to refugees under the pretext that they did not have all the necessary papers and documents, that they did not have an authorization of residence, an official permit, and so forth, although they might have been living in a particular country for several years. Through such small detailed regulations the most fundamental human rights were denied.

...

Article 18

The Chairman read Article 18, and suggested that the fourth paragraph, which seemed to her to be included in the first, did not appear to be necessary. Dr. Chang (China) felt that the first two paragraphs might be taken to include the last two. He suggested that the first two might serve as a declaration of principle, the latter two as "commentary". Mr. Wilson (United Kingdom) agreed with Dr. Chang, but felt that the Article might be limited still further, to the first paragraph, "Everyone has a right to own personal property".

...

Article 20

...

Dr. Chang (China) suggested as a drafting change that the word "morals" be eliminated, since it already was implied in the phrase "rights and freedoms of others"; and that the sentence might then read, in part, "... to protect public order and the rights and freedoms of others".

...

Article 24

Professor Cassin (France) felt that the right of petition might be included among the political rights of man. He suggested that Articles 20, 21, 22, and 23 might be grouped together in the Declaration. Dr. Chang (China) agreed, and added that Articles 24 and 25 also might be grouped, as political rights.

...

在人权委员会之起草委员会第 9 次会议上的发言

1947 年 6 月 18 日星期三上午 10:30 纽约成功湖

审议第 E/CN.4/AC.l/W.2/Rev.1 号文件：法国代表就《国际人权宣言》条款提出的建议

......

第 29 条

......

张博士（中国）说，他倾向于将第 29 条的最后一句替换为秘书处大纲草案（E/CN.4/AC.1/3 号文件）第 31 条第 2 部分："公职人员的任命应通过竞争性考试。"他强调，随着公共职能越来越多且越来越重要，所有人都应有权通过担任公职来参与公共生活。他回顾了中国在这方面的经验，指出为担任公职而进行的竞争性考试在中国已经存在了几个世纪。在他看来，"免费的竞争性考试"应被视为通往真正自由民主的路径之一。

......

科瑞斯基教授（苏联）问张博士，是否中国竞争性考试的复杂性和数量在一定程度上使普通人无法担任公职，因为他们无法获得必要的教育以便能够通过这种考试。张博士（中国）解释说，根据他的观点，这不是对中国历史的正确解释。他认为，竞争性考试是在安定的社会生活中给予平等机会担任公职的一种方式。

第 30 条

......

张博士（中国）提请委员会注意第 27 条。该条提到"选举"是实现人权的一种方法。他觉得竞争性考试也是实现人权的一种方式，因此应当被提及。

......

第 32 条

……

张博士（中国）表示希望在宣言中看到个人获得庇护的权利和国家给予庇护的权利。

……

――人权委员会之起草委员会第 9 次会议简要记录
（E/CN. 4/AC. 1/SR. 9）

李梦瑶译，常健校

E/CN.4/AC.1/SR.9

3 July 1947

COMMISSION ON HUMAN RIGHTS
DRAFTING COMMITTEE
FIRST SESSION
SUMMARY RECORD OF THE NINTH MEETING

Held at Lake Success, New York, on Wednesday, 18 June 1947, at 10:30 a.m.

Consideration of document E/CN.4/AC.l/W.2/Rev.1: Suggestions Submitted by the Representative of France for Articles of the International Declaration of Rights

…

Article 29

…

Dr. Chang (China) stated that he would prefer to replace the last sentence of Article 29 by the second part of Article 31 of the Secretariat draft Outline (document E/CN.4/AC.1/3), reading: "Appointments to the Civil Service shall be by competitive examination." He stressed the fact that as public functions grew more and more numerous and important, all men should have the right to participate in the public life by holding public office. He reviewed the experience of China in this matter and pointed out that competitive examination for public jobs had existed in his country for centuries. In his opinion "free competitive examinations" should be considered as one of the ways to a truly free democracy.

...

Prof. Koretsky (Union of Soviet Socialist Republics) asked Dr. Chang whether or not the complexity and the number of competitive examinations in China had not in part eliminated from public office the common man, who was not able to get the education necessary to be able to pass such examinations. Dr. Chang (China) explained that this, in his opinion, was not a correct interpretation of Chinese history. He thought that a competitive examination was one way, in settled community life, to give an equal chance of access to public office.

...

Article 30

...

Dr. Chang (China) called the attention of the Committee to Article 27. In this Article "elections" were mentioned as a method of achieving human rights. He felt that competitive examinations were also a method of achieving human rights, and should therefore be mentioned.

...

Article 32

...

Dr. Chang (China) stated that he would like to see the individual's right to asylum and the State's right to grant asylum stated in the Declaration.

...

在人权委员会之起草委员会第 10 次会议上的发言

1947 年 6 月 18 日星期三下午 3:30 纽约成功湖

2. 审议第 E/CN. 4/AC. 1/4 号文件附件一《国际人权法案》，英国人权委员会代表杜克斯顿勋爵给联合国秘书长的信

......

第 8 条

......

主席读了第 8 条，并要求委员会成员作出评论，并补充说，由于起草委员会正在考虑是否可以将这些条款纳入公约，因此应仔细考虑。

张博士（中国）询问，这是否意味着所包括的所有条款在条约义务方面都是可强制执行的。他认为第 8 条就很难强制执行。

主席表示，委员会成员们在思考过程中，必须考虑某一条款是否可由整个国家强制执行，因为在一个法案中加入那些不可强制执行的条款是没有什么用处的。

......

第 10 条

......

张博士（中国）认为，首先提出宣言是完全正确的，因此秘书处的文件采取了这种一般形式。问题是起草委员会该如何开展工作。所有形式和内容问题都必须由人权委员会来决定，但委员会成员可能希望带上法律专家，这些法律专家可以作为特设法律工作组与人权委员会同时开会。

主席说，她认为起草委员会应着手讨论人权公约的内容，同时注意它只考虑原则而不考虑措辞。她认为，起草委员会可能会作出这样的建议，即一旦这些原则得到了充分的思考，各国的法律专家便可以在下一届会议之前准备新的草案。

......

第 15 条

......

主席说，她假定沉默表示接受正在讨论的原则，并一致同意在公约草案中就该主题应写入某些内容。

科瑞斯基教授（苏联）提醒注意，他的沉默甚至并不意味着他接受应该提及该原则这个事实。

张博士（中国）说，就他而言，沉默往往表明需要成熟的考虑和专家建议。

......

张博士（中国）表示，他希望人权委员会成员能够收到（1）起草委员会会议的所有简要记录，（2）已提交的所有草案，（3）可能被列入宣言的各项条款的综合草案，以及（4）可能被列入公约的各项条款的综合草稿。

......

第 16 条

......

张博士（中国）说，作为一名非技术人员，他觉得英国草案的结构非常重要。他认为，委员会成员也不应忽视该草案的序言和第三部分。

......

张博士（中国）再次强调了英国草案第一部分和第三部分的重要性。

......

——人权委员会之起草委员会第 10 次会议简要记录
（E/CN. 4/AC. 1/SR. 10）

常健译校

E/CN.4/AC.1/SR.10

20 June 1947

COMMISSION ON HUMAN RIGHTS
DRAFTING COMMITTEE
FIRST SESSION
SUMMARY RECORD OF THE TENTH MEETING
Held at Lake Success, New York, on Wednesday, 18 June 1947, at 3:30 p.m.

2. Consideration of Annex I, "International Bill of Human Rights", of Document E/CN.4/AC.1/4, Text of Letter from Lord Dukeston, the United Kingdom Representative on the Commission on Human Rights, to the Secretary-General of the United Nations

...

Article 8

...

The Chairman read Article 8, and asked for Members comments, adding that since the Drafting Committee was considering whether or not these Articles could be incorporated in a convention, careful thought should be given them.

Dr. Chang (China) asked whether that implied that all Articles included were to be enforcible in terms of obligations in a treaty. He thought that Article 8 would be difficult of enforcement.

The Chairman remarked that, in their thinking, Members had to consider whether an Article was enforcible by the nations as a whole, as there was little use in putting unenforcible items into a bill.

...

Article 10

...

Dr. Chang (China) thought it was not far from wrong to say that a Declaration had been envisaged first of all, and therefore the Secretariat document had taken that general form. The question was how the Drafting Committee should proceed. All questions of form and substance would have to be decided by the Commission, but the Members of the Commission might wish to bring legal experts with them, who could meet simultaneously with the Commission as an ad hoc legal working group.

The Chairman said that in her opinion the Committee should proceed to discuss the substance of a Convention on Human Rights, keeping in mind that it was considering only principles and not wording. She felt that the Committee might suggest that once the principles had been thought over, legal experts from the various countries could prepare new drafts before the next session.

...

Article 15

...

The Chairman said she presumed that silence indicated acceptance of the principle under discussion, and general agreement that something should be said on the subject in the draft Convention.

Prof. Koretsky (Union of Soviet Socialist Republics) asked that it be noted that his silence did not even mean his acceptance of the fact that the principle should be mentioned.

Dr. Chang (China) said that in his case silence often indicated the need for mature consideration and expert advice.

...

Dr. Chang (China) said that he hoped the Members of the Commission might receive (1) all summary records of the meetings of the Drafting Committee, (2) all drafts that had been submitted, (3) a composite draft of the Articles which might be included in a Declaration, and (4) a composite draft of the Articles that might be included in a Convention.

Article 16

...

Dr. Chang (China) said that as a non-technician, he was impressed by the importance of the structure of the United Kingdom draft. He felt that Members should not lose sight of its Preamble and of Part III.

...

Dr. Chang (China) emphasized again the importance of Parts I and III of the United Kingdom draft.

......

在人权委员会之起草委员会第 11 次会议上的发言

1947 年 6 月 19 日星期四下午 2:30 纽约成功湖

......

第 7 条：英国草案

......

张博士（中国）称赞了英国和澳大利亚委员关于实施所提出的建议，但他补充说，他认为人权委员会的工作应该更进一步，不能仅限于对违反人权法案的行为规定惩罚措施。关于修改委员会职权的建议，他认为，仅仅将委员会当作一个上诉法庭，用来受理那些向经济及社会理事会或联合国大会提出的申诉，这是错误的。因为这将把委员会的职权范围缩窄至只涉及法律问题。

为了说明他的观点，张博士引用了两句中国谚语，即"徒善不足以为政"，"徒法不能以自行"。他坚持认为：实施宣言的意图和目标应该是为了培养更好的人，而不是仅仅惩罚那些侵犯人权者。权利必须由法律来保护，但法律也需要用来促进人的至善。它们的重点应该是通过教育和道德手段来促进人权的扩展和完善。实施不能仅仅意味着惩罚，而且应该是人全面发展的手段。

......

起草委员会提交人权委员会报告的格式

......

张博士（中国）赞成关于设单独一节来涵盖讨论有关实施内容的建议。会议于下午 5:10 结束。

——人权委员会之起草委员会第 11 次会议简要记录
（E/CN. 4/AC. 1/SR. 11）

罗苇译，常健校

E/CN.4/AC.1/SR.11

3 July 1947

COMMISSION ON HUMAN RIGHTS
DRAFTING COMMITTEE
FIRST SESSION
SUMMARY RECORD OF THE ELEVENTH MEETING
Held at Lake Success, New York, on Thursday, 19 June 1947, at 2:30 p.m.

...

Article 7: United Kingdom Draft

...

Dr. Chang (China) complimented the United Kingdom and Australian members on their proposals for implementation but added that he felt the work of the Commission on Human Rights should go a step further than making provision for the punishment of violations of the Bill of Rights. Concerning the suggestion for revising the terms of reference of the Commission, he felt that it would be a mistake to make the Commission merely a court of appeal for petitions for presentation to the Economic and Social Council or the General Assembly, as that would narrow the scope of the Commission to only legal questions.

In illustration of his point of view, Dr. Chang quoted two Chinese proverbs which he translated as follows: "Good intentions alone are not sufficient for political order," and "Laws alone are not sufficient to bring about results by themselves." The intention and goal should be to build up better human beings, and not merely to punish those who violate human rights, he maintained. Rights must be protected by law, but laws are necessary also to promote the best in men. They should emphasize the promotion of the extension and refinement of human rights through education and moral means. Implementation does not only mean punishment, but also measures for the full development of man.

...

Form of the Report of the Drafting Committee to the Commission on Human Rights

…

Dr. Chang (China) approved of the suggestion for a separate section to cover the discussion on implementation.

The meeting adjourned at 5:10 p.m.

在人权委员会之起草委员会第 12 次会议上的发言

1947 年 6 月 20 日星期五上午 11:00 纽约成功湖

审议法国代表提交的关于《国际人权宣言》条款修订后的建议（第 E/CN.4/AC.1/W.2/Rev.2 号文件）

......

第 1—4 条

......

主席请澳大利亚代表起草一份关于第 1—4 条的更简短的版本，将她本人和卡森教授的意见考虑在内。

张博士（中国）指出，委员会所能支配的时间是有限的，如果每一条都重新起草，那么委员会的工作就无法取得进展。

......

张博士（中国）同意美国提出的建议，即以某种方式将前四条合并。然而，他希望保留第一条的前四个词："All men are brothers"（所有人皆为兄弟）。

......

第 5 条

......

张博士（中国）和卡森教授（法国）赞同美国作出的修正。

......

第 6 条

主席宣读了第 6 条。她说，美国建议将"作出如下宣言"改为"本宣言确认"。张博士（中国）赞成这一改动。他认为，一般性原则可以归入序言部分，而不是被起草为一个单独的条款。马利克博士（黎巴嫩）赞同张博士的观点。

......

第 7 条和第 8 条

……

张博士（中国）认为，关注人的文化发展很重要，只讲身体的存在是不够的，还要涉及"生命本身的发展完善"。

……

第 9 条

……

张博士（中国）指出，第 7 条是一般性原则声明，而第 8 条是法律程序。他认为"正当的法律程序"无法解释清楚。他主张，第 8 条应该保留，但第 9 条和第 10 条可以降级为脚注或评注。

威尔逊先生（英国）认为，鉴于"审议"是比"缩短"更广泛的术语，他所提出的脚注措辞可以涵盖张博士的观点。

主席指出，委员会的普遍感觉是应该保留第 8 条。虽然第 9 条和第 10 条包含重要内容，但它们应放在第 7 条和第 8 条的辅助位置。

张博士（中国）建议，第 8、9、10 条各自的第一句话可以构成新的第 8 条，因为它们阐明了一般性的理念。这些条款的剩余语句是限制条件，可以加为脚注或评注。

主席请张博士重新起草这些条款和脚注，用于下午会议讨论。

会议于下午 1:00 结束。

——人权委员会之起草委员会第 12 次会议简要记录
（E/CN. 4/AC. 1/SR. 12）

李梦瑶译，常健校

E/CN.4/AC.1/SR.12

3 July 1947

COMMISSION ON HUMAN RIGHTS
DRAFTING COMMITTEE
FIRST SESSION
SUMMARY RECORD OF THE TWELFTH MEETING

Held at Lake Success, New York, on Friday, 20 June 1947, at 11:00 a.m.

Consideration of Revised Suggestions Submitted by the Representative of France for Articles of the International Declaration of Rights (Document E/CN.4/AC.1/W.2/Rev.2)

...

Articles 1 to 4

...

The Chairman asked the Representative of Australia to draft a somewhat shortened version of Articles 1 to 4, taking her own and Prof. Cassin's views into consideration.

Dr. Chang (China) pointed out that the time at the disposal of the Committee was limited and that if redrafts were made of each Article, the work of the Committee would not progress.

...

Dr. Chang (China) agreed with the suggestion of the United States, that the first four Articles might be merged in some way. He wished, however, to retain the first four words of Article 1, "All men are brothers".

...

Article 5

...

Dr. Chang (China) and Prof. Cassin (France) were in favour of the United States revision.

...

Article 6

The Chairman read Article 6. She stated that the United States suggested that "hereunder declared" be replaced by "set forth in this Declaration".

Dr. Chang (China) was in favour of this change. He thought the general principle might be included in the Preamble rather than drafted as a separate Article. Dr. Malik (Lebanon) shared the viewpoint of Dr. Chang.

...

Articles 7 and 8

...

Dr. Chang (China) thought it important to take note of the cultural development of man, to include "the better development of life itself", inasmuch as mere physical existence was not sufficient.

...

Article 9

...

Dr. Chang (China) pointed out that Article 7 was a statement of general principle while Article 8 dealt with a process of law. He thought that the "due process of law" could not be spelled out. He believed that Article 8 should remain but that Articles 9 and 10 might be relegated to a footnote or commentary.

Mr. Wilson (United Kingdom) thought that his suggested wording of a footnote would cover Dr. Chang's point inasmuch as "considered" was a broader term than "shortened".

The Chairman stated that the general feeling of the Committee was that Article 8 should be retained. Although Articles 9 and 10 contained important points, they should be included in a subsidiary position to Articles 7 and 8.

Dr. Chang (China) suggested that the first sentences of Articles 8, 9 and 10 might form a new Article 8, as they enunciated ideas of a general character. The remaining sentences of the Articles were qualifications and might be added as footnotes or commentaries.

The Chairman requested Dr. Chang to redraft the Articles and footnote for consideration at the afternoon meeting.

The meeting adjourned at 1:00 p.m.

在人权委员会之起草委员会第 13 次会议上的发言

1947 年 6 月 20 日星期五下午 2:30 纽约成功湖

1. 审议法国代表提交的关于《国际人权宣言》条款的修订后建议（第 E/CN.4/AC.1/W.2/Rev.2 号文件）

......

第 11 条

主席宣读第 11 条，并补充说，美国建议第二句应该删去。

威尔逊先生（英国）支持这一建议，并补充说，废除奴隶制是这项条款的主要目的：关于强迫劳动的内容可以写入公约，但必须非常仔细地对其进行审查。张博士（中国）对此表示赞同。

......

张博士（中国）说，他想知道委员会成员是否应该说明他们对公约意义的看法。这可能无法在公约中加以说明，但可以在评论中进行说明。某些事项可在评论中加以澄清，其余的则需通过公约强制执行。

主席称，张博士在使用"强制实施"一词时，喻示了一些希望被写入公约的内容。

......

第 1、2、3、4 条

......

张博士（中国）赞同黎巴嫩代表的观点，即前几个条款的语句需要简短精炼，但觉得澳大利亚代表的建议很有意思且意义重大。他赞同英国代表的意见，即应增加"良知"一词，但除"理性"外，还应增加一些词来指称某些具有道德意义的内容。他建议将第 1 条改为："所有人皆为兄弟。作为大家庭之成员，他们赋有理性和良知、自由且拥有平等的尊严与权利。"第 2 条、第 3 条和第 4 条应加以合并，成为如下的第 2 条（采纳澳大利亚的建议）："这些权利只受他人拥有的同样权利的限制。人也对社会负有责任，通过履行这种社会责任，他能够在更广泛的自由中发展自身的精神、思想与体魄。"

......

第 13 条

主席宣读第 13 条，并请各位代表提出意见。

威尔逊先生（英国）评论道，该条的主要意蕴是防止出现基于种族、肤色、居住地以及迁徙方式而产生的歧视，因此是"预防歧视和保护少数群体"小组委员会应审议的另一个问题。他指出，这一条款还涉及私有财产权利。

张博士（中国）称，他保留自己的主张，因为他也意识到在资格认定方面的困难。他建议作为一项草案变更将句首由"依据"修改为"应有……自由"。

主席作为委员会成员发言称，美国也保留添加合格脚注的权利。

......

张博士（中国）称，在现阶段继续推进是不明智的。他补充道，他现在关注的是宣言中每一条都附带一条评论这种可能的呈现形式。在这种情况下，并不需要为每个条款都附带一条评论，但他认为，条款本身应该简短，如果文意不清，则应在文后添加评论。他觉得，解释性评论对这种特殊条款是有用的。

......

第 15 条

......

张博士（中国）说，他认为第 15 条第 3 款的第一句话可与正在重新起草的第 8、9、10 条所隐含的一些概念合并。他觉得第 1 款需要划分。

......

主席就关于该条款的建议流程进行了解释。

张博士（中国）说，第三款对普通人来说依旧有点太过专业，普通人要求平等和体谅，希望了解他与法庭的关系。他已经提出过建议，由于第 1 条显得过于专业，如果是要澄清个人与法庭之间的关系，那么这可能会被视为法庭与个人关系考量的一部分。

主席回顾道，在讨论中，设立强调所谓"法律人格"的专门条款被认为具有重要意义，并且法国代表接受了她提出的更为简洁的表述。既然被接受，她认为委员会成员应同意加入第 3 款。

张博士（中国）认为，最后一句话可能仍然是一个评论，而非条款的内容。他想保留他在关于保留这一条款问题上的主张。

……

第 20 条

……

马利克博士（黎巴嫩）建议委员会采用法国代表的措辞，作为一种替代办法，可以将英国的建议附在脚注中。

张博士（中国）表示赞同，认为包括这两种形式是有益的，但认为法国代表的措辞并不清晰。

主席表示同意"良心和信仰自由"意味着一个人可以改变自己的信仰。

马利克博士（黎巴嫩）解释说，他希望两种可能的选择，一是将法国代表的表述根据法国代表的建议和他自己提出的建议进行修改，二是英国代表建议的表述。

张博士（中国）建议将法国代表的原初表述作为第三种选择。

……

——人权委员会之起草委员会第 13 次会议简要记录
（E/CN. 4/AC. 1/SR. 13）

陈越译，常健校

E/CN.4/AC.1/SR.13
8 July 1947

COMMISSION ON HUMAN RIGHTS
DRAFTING COMMITTEE
FIRST SESSION
SUMMARY RECORD OF THE THIRTEENTH MEETING

Held at Lake Success, New York, on Friday, 20 June 1947, at 2:30 p.m.

1. Consideration of Revised Suggestions Submitted by the Representative of France for Articles of the International Declaration of Human Rights (Document E/CN.4/AC.1/W.2/Rev.2)

...

Article 11

The Chairman read Article 11, and added that the United States suggested that the second sentence should be deleted.

Mr. Wilson (United Kingdom) supported this proposal, adding that the abolition of slavery was the main purpose of the Article: the subject of compulsory labour would be included in the Convention, and would then have to be very carefully examined. Dr. Chang (China) agreed with this.

...

Dr. Chang (China) said he wondered whether Members should not clarify their thinking as to what was meant by a Convention. In this case it might not be possible to have it clarified in a Convention, but it might be possible to clarify it in a comment. Certain things could be clarified in a comment and others enforced in a Convention.

The Chairman said that in his use of the word "enforced", Dr. Chang implied what was intended as something to be included in a Convention.

...

Article 1, 2, 3, and 4

...

Dr. Chang (China) said he was in agreement with the Representative of the Lebanon that short, pithy sentences were needed for the first few articles, but he felt the Australian suggestions were interesting and significant. He agreed with the Representative of the United Kingdom that the word "conscience" should be added, but there should also be some word indicating, aside from "reason", something of a moral significance. He suggested that Article 1 should read as it stands: "All men are brothers. Being endowed with reason and conscience, members of one family, they are free and possess equal dignity and rights." Articles 2, 3, and 4 should be combined and become Article 2 (taken from the

Australian proposal) as follows: "These rights are limited only by the equal rights of others. Man also owes duties to society, through which he is enabled to develop his spirit, mind and body in wider freedom."

...

Article 13

The Chairman read Article 13 and asked for comments.

Mr. Wilson (United Kingdom) observed that this was another matter which should be considered by the Sub-Commission on Prevention of Discrimination and Protection of Minorities, since the main implication was the prevention of discrimination, on grounds of race, colour, where people might live and how they might move from place to place. He pointed out that this Article was also subject to the rights of private property.

Dr. Chang (China) said he reserved his position, since he, too, realized the difficulties in qualification. He suggested as a drafting change that instead of the words "Subject to", the sentence should begin "There shall be liberty...".

The Chairman, speaking as a Member of the Committee, said that the United States might also reserve the right to put in a qualifying footnote.

...

Dr. Chang (China) said that it would not be wise at the present stage to go any further. He added that his attention had been drawn to a possible form of presenting a Declaration which included a comment for each Article. In this case, there was no necessity to include a comment to every Article, but he thought that the Articles themselves should be short, and if they were not clear, should then be followed by a comment. For this particular Article, he felt an explanatory comment would be useful.

...

Article 15

...

Dr. Chang (China) said he thought that the first sentence of the third paragraph of Article 15 might be combined with some of the concepts implied in Articles 8, 9, and 10, which were being redrafted. He felt that paragraph 1 required classification

…

The Chairman explained the procedure which had been suggested regarding the Article.

Dr. Chang (China) said that the third paragraph was still a little too technical for the common man, who wanted equality, consideration, and wished to know his relationship with the courts. He had already suggested that inasmuch as the first Article might appear too technical, and if a clarification of the relation of the individual to the tribunals was concerned, it might be considered as a part of the consideration of the tribunal relationship with the individual.

The Chairman recalled that in the discussion it had been held important to have an Article stressing the right to what was called a "legal personality", and the Representative of France had accepted her simpler wording. That being accepted, she thought Members would agree that paragraph 3 should go in.

Dr. Chang (China) said that the last sentence might still be a comment rather than a part of the Article. He would like to reserve his position with regard to retaining this Article.

…

Article 20

…

Dr. Malik (Lebanon) suggested that the Committee adopt the phraseology of the Representative of France and add the United Kingdom proposal in a footnote as an alternative.

Dr. Chang (China) agreed that it would be useful to include the two forms, but thought that the phrase offered by the Representative of France was not clear.

The Chairman agreed that "freedom of conscience and belief" implied that one could change one's beliefs.

Dr. Malik (Lebanon) explained that he wished, as alternatives, the phrasing of the Representative of France with the changes suggested by the Representative of France and by himself, and the phrasing suggested by the Representative of the United Kingdom.

Dr. Chang (China) suggested adding the original wording of the Representative of France as a third alternative.

...

在人权委员会之起草委员会第 14 次会议上的发言

1947 年 6 月 23 日星期一上午 10:30 纽约成功湖

审议法国代表提交的关于《国际人权宣言》条款的修订后建议（第 E/CN.4/AC.1/W.2/Rev.2 号文件）

......

第 26 条

......

张博士（中国）欣赏美国政府的形式，但补充道，"政府"应包括所有形式的政府，而不应像其他方案那样只包括国家的或地域政府。

......

第 28 条

主席宣读第 28 条案文，并提请委员会注意，在此前关于本条内容的讨论中，他们同意用"担任所有公职或在国家机构任职的平等机会"来替换"担任国家所有公职"。

张博士（中国）建议增加"免费参加为担任公职而举行的公开考试"。他赞成该条的其余部分，但提示"公职"一词容易引发误解，因为某些公职是选任的。

圣克鲁兹先生（智利）说，写入这句话将表明：委员会认为应通过竞争性考试来选拔担任公职的人员。他指出，在智利，获得公职只需通过某种程度的考试；最高职位的任命取决于行政机关的意愿或与立法机关商议后作出。他觉得这意味着规定得太过详细了。张博士（中国）觉得，如果去掉"公职"一词，就不会反对他的表述。威尔逊先生（英国）不反对张博士的建议，但他指出，该条旨在防止在担任公职方面的歧视，因此应提交"预防歧视和保护少数群体"小组委员会。

......

——人权委员会之起草委员会第 14 次会议简要记录
（E/CN. 4/AC. 1/SR. 14）

陈越译，常健校

E/CN.4/AC.1/SR.14
3 July 1947

COMMISSION ON HUMAN RIGHTS
DRAFTING COMMITTEE
FIRST SESSION
SUMMARY RECORD OF THE FOURTEENTH MEETING
Held at Lake Success, New York, Monday, 23 June 1947, at 10:30 a.m.

Consideration of Revised Suggestions Submitted by the Representative of France for Articles of an International Declaration on Human Rights (Document E/CN.4/AC.1/W.2/Rev.2)

...

Article 26

...

Dr. Chang (China) was in favour of the United States form, adding that Government included all forms of government, and not only State or territorial government as in the other text.

...

Article 28

The Chairman read the text of Article 28 and drew the attention of the Committee to a previous discussion on the substance of this Article in which they had agreed to substitute "equal opportunity of engaging in all public employment, or offices of the State", in the place of "occupying all public functions of the State".

Dr. Chang (China) proposed the addition of the sentence "There shall be free access to public examinations for public employment". He was in favour of the rest of the Article but suggested that the word "offices" might give rise to misunderstanding as some offices are elective.

Mr. Santa Cruz (Chile) said that to include this sentence would indicate that the Committee was of the opinion that public offices should be filled by competitive examination. He pointed out that in Chile public offices are attained by examination up to a certain point only; the highest appointments are made through the will of the Executive or after consultation with the Legislative power. He felt that this meant too detailed specifications. Dr. Chang (China) felt there would be no objection to his wording if "offices" were omitted. Mr. Wilson (United Kingdom) had no objection to Dr. Chang's proposal but he pointed out that, as the Article aimed at the prevention of discrimination in public office, it should be referred to the Sub-Commission on Prevention of Discrimination and Protection of Minorities.

......

在人权委员会之起草委员会第 15 次会议上的发言

1947 年 6 月 23 日星期一下午 2:30 纽约成功湖

审议法国代表提交的关于《国际人权宣言》条款的修订后建议（第 E/CN.4/AC.l/W.2/Rev.2 号文件）的第 35 至 42 条

……

第 36 条和第 37 条

在等待修正文本的书面版本时，主席宣读了第 36 条。

张博士（中国）认为，公平分享休息和闲暇的权利与从外界获取知识的权利可以分开，后者可以被纳入教育的主题中。

主席说道，第 36 条现在写成这样："每个人拥有平等享有休息和闲暇的权利。"大家一致认为第 37 条应该保留原样，并用脚注说明：该条款的内容会写入序言，而不是在宣言中详细说明。

张博士（中国）要求对第 37 条中的"分享科学的好处"这一表述予以解释。

圣克鲁兹先生（智利）说，智利草案是这样表述的：科学发明应属于社会，应被所有人共享。

第 35 条

回到第 35 条，主席作为美国代表发言，建议增加以下内容：这不排除私人教育设施和机构。

张博士（中国）建议这一条应改为：

"人人享有受教育权利。小学教育应是义务性的，应由其生活所在的国家或社区提供。应该有平等的机会获得国家或社区可以提供的职业教育、文化教育和高等教育，这些教育的提供应以成绩为依据，不因种族、性别、语言或宗教而区别对待。"

主席建议删除"其生活所在的"这一措辞，张博士接受这一修改。

……

主席作为美国代表指出，义务教育不同义务工作。儿童太小，无法捍卫自己的权利，因此他的受教育权利应该受到保护。她觉得私人教育机构应获得认可。

主席宣读修订后的案文：

"人人享有受教育的权利。小学教育应是免费和强制性的。应有平等的机会获得国家或社区可以提供的技术教育、文化教育和高等教育，这些教育的提供应以成绩为依据，不因种族、性别、语言或宗教而区别对待。"

卡森教授（法国）认为，应将"社会状况和地位"加入关于歧视的条款中。

张博士（中国）称，他不反对在条款中提及社会地位或政治信仰。

......

——人权委员会之起草委员会第 15 次会议简要记录

（E/CN. 4/AC. 1/SR. 15）

陈越译，常健校

E/CN.4/AC.1/SR.15
3 July 1947

COMMISSION ON HUMAN RIGHTS
DRAFTING COMMITTEE
FIRST SESSION
SUMMARY RECORD OF THE FIFTEENTH MEETING

Held at Lake Success, New York, on Monday, 23 June 1947, at 2:30 p.m.

Consideration of Articles 35 to 42 of the Revised Suggestions Submitted by the Representative of France for Articles of the International Declaration of Rights (Document E/CN.4/AC.l/W.2/Rev.2)

...

Articles 36 and 37

While waiting for the written version of the amended text, The Chairman read Article 36.

Dr. Chang (China) thought that the right to a fair share of rest and leisure might be separated from the right to the knowledge of the outside world which could be included in the subject of education.

...

The Chairman stated that Article 36 would now read: "Everyone has the right to a fair share of rest and leisure." It was the general consensus of opinion that Article 37 be retained as it stood, with a footnote saying that the substance of the Article might be included in the Preamble instead of being spelt out in the Declaration. Dr. Chang (China) asked for an explanation of the phrase "share in the benefits of science" in Article 37. Mr. Santa Cruz (Chile) said that in the Chilean Draft, it was stated that scientific inventions should belong to society and be enjoyed by all.

...

Article 35

Returning to Article 35, The Chairman, speaking as the Representative of the United States, proposed the addition of the following sentence: "This will not exclude private educational facilities and institutions."

Dr. Chang (China) proposed that the Article should read:

"Everyone has the right to education. Primary education shall be obligatory and shall be provided by the State or community in which he lives. There shall be equal access to technical, cultural and higher education as can be provided by the State or community on the basis of merit and without distinction as to race, sex, language or religion."

The Chairman proposed the deletion of the words "in which he lives" and Dr. Chang accepted this amendment.

...

The Chairman, speaking as the Representative of the United States, said that obligatory education differed from obligatory work. As the child is too young to defend his rights, his right to education should be protected for him. She felt that private institutions of learning should be recognized.

The Chairman read the amended text:

"Everyone has the right to education. Primary education shall be free and compulsory. There shall be equal access for all to technical, cultural and higher education as can be provided by the State or community on the basis of merit and without distinction as to race, sex, language or religion."

Prof. Cassin (France) said that "social conditions and standing" should be added to the clause on discrimination.

Dr. Chang (China) stated that he had no objection to the inclusion of reference to social standing or political belief.

...

在人权委员会之起草委员会第 16 次会议上的发言

1947 年 6 月 24 日星期二上午 10:45 纽约成功湖

审议起草委员会提交人权委员会的报告草案
（第 E/CN.4/AC.1/14 号文件）

......

第 10 段

......

主席解释，委员会将提交一份工作文件，总结在本届会议期间所表达的观点，该文件对任何个人或政府均不具有约束力。

张博士（中国）建议将第 10 条中的"一致同意"删去。他觉得甚至可以删去整条文字。

主席同意删除该条。

科瑞斯基教授（苏联）认为，张博士的建议合乎逻辑，赞成完全删除该条。他说，也许可以在第二章提及这一点。

哈里先生（澳大利亚）同意删去该条。

马利克博士（黎巴嫩）解释道，原来的受托权限要求起草委员会起草《国际人权法案》初稿。但鉴于起草委员会实际上并未起草这样一份初稿，他认为有必要对这种不一致作出解释性提及。然而，如果起草委员会希望删去第 10 条，他也会同意。

主席表示，第 10 条可以被删除，主席或报告员在向人权委员会提交报告时，会解释工作的方式和遇到的困难。

第二章
第 14 段

......

张博士（中国）说，鉴于委员会尚未通过简要记录，因此可能还有机会修改措辞。他提议，在讨论中期所采用的下述表述是合适的："进行工作划分以表明哪些条款需要写入国际公约，哪些不需要写入公约。"

……

第17段

主席表示，她提请关注"美国保留敦促委员会在宣言中写入美国对秘书处草案中的条款重新作出表述的权利。"

科瑞斯基教授（苏联）评论道，在第17条最后一句话中，不用其他的同义词，只用"评论"也许就足够了。他指出，所有代表都保留了自己的主张。

威尔逊先生（英国）认为，最好在17条第六行说"无人发表意见"，而不是"无人采取行动"。鉴于所有代表都保留了稍后作出评论的权利，他提议增加如下这句话：

"起草委员会所有成员都明白，会议期间任何人所说的话都不应被认为对其政府具有约束力，并保留在稍后阶段提出进一步建议的权利。"

马利克博士（黎巴嫩）评论道，在科瑞斯基教授的评论中，"建议"并不是"评论"的同义词，虽然这两个词都应予以保留。

科瑞斯基教授（苏联）表示，他同意将两个词都写入。

在会议的这个时段，副主席张博士（中国）主持会议，亨德里克先生接替罗斯福夫人担任美国代表。

……

—— 人权委员会之起草委员会第16次会议简要记录

（E/CN.4/AC.1/SR.16）

徐俊杰译，常健校

E/CN.4/AC.1/SR.16
3 July 1947

COMMISSION ON HUMAN RIGHTS
DRAFTING COMMITTEE
FIRST SESSION
SUMMARY RECORD OF THE SIXTEENTH MEETING

Held at Lake Success, New York, on Tuesday, 24 June 1947, at 10:45 a.m.

Consideration of the Draft Report of the Drafting Committee to the Commission on Human Rights (Document E/CN.4/AC.1/14)

...

Paragraph 10

...

The Chairman explained that the Committee was submitting the views expressed during the course of its session in a working paper which was not binding upon any individual or Government. Dr. Chang (China) suggested that the words "it was agreed" be deleted. He felt that it might even be possible to omit the entire paragraph.

The Chairman agreed that the paragraph might be omitted. Prof. Koretsky (Union of Soviet Socialist Republics) thought the suggestion of Dr. Chang was a logical one and favoured complete elimination of the paragraph. He said that perhaps some mention might be made of this point in Chapter II. Mr. Harry (Australia) agreed to elimination of the paragraph. Dr. Malik (Lebanon) explained that the original terms of reference had requested the Drafting Committee to prepare a preliminary draft of an International Bill of Human Rights. Inasmuch as the Drafting Committee had not actually prepared such a Preliminary Draft, he felt that an explanatory reference to the discrepancy was necessary. He would, however, agree, should the Drafting Committee so wish, to the deletion of the paragraph.

The Chairman stated paragraph 10 could be deleted and that the Chairman or the Rapporteur, in presenting the Report to the Commission on Human Rights, might explain the manner in which the work was done and the difficulties encountered.

Chapter II

...

Paragraph 14

...

Dr. Chang (China) said that inasmuch as the Summary Record had not been passed by the Committee, there might be opportunity to change the phrasing. He proposed that the terminology used at the intermediate stage of discussions might be appropriate: "to undertake a division of the work indicating which Articles would require International Conventions and which would not."

...

Paragraph 17

The Chairman stated that she wished to have it noted that "The United States reserved the right to urge before the Commission the inclusion, in the Declaration, of the United States rewording of Articles in the Secretariat draft."

Prof. Koretsky (Union of Soviet Socialist Republics) remarked that in the final sentence it might perhaps be sufficient to say "observations", without any additional synonyms. He pointed out that all Representatives had reserved their positions.

In the sixth line of the paragraph, Mr. Wilson (United Kingdom) thought it preferable to say "nothing said by any of them" rather than "no action taken by them". Inasmuch as all Representatives had reserved their right to make comments at a later time, he proposed the following sentence:

"All Members of the Drafting Committee understood that nothing said by any of them during the session was to be considered binding upon their Governments, and reserved the right to make further suggestions at a later stage."

Dr. Malik (Lebanon) observed, in connection with Prof. Koretsky's remarks that "proposals" was not synonymous with "observations" and thought that both words should be retained.

Prof. Koretsky (Union of Soviet Socialist Republics) said he would agree to the inclusion of both words.

At this point in the meeting, Dr. Chang (China) Vice-Chairman, took the chair and Mr. Hendrick replaced Mrs. Roosevelt as Representative of the United States.

......

在人权委员会之起草委员会第 17 次会议上的发言

1947 年 6 月 24 日星期二下午 2:30 纽约成功湖

张彭春博士主持了前半场会议。

继续审议起草委员会提交人权委员会的报告草案
（第 E/CN.4/AC.1/14 号文件）

因主席缺席，由副主席张博士临时主持会议。

……

第 19 段

……

主席也认为，应当明确指出，起草一项公约的决定权在人权委员会。

马利克博士（黎巴嫩）认为，这一点隐含在"人权委员会可能希望详细阐述的"一语中。

主席认为，本段应包括时间紧迫和需要咨询法律专家等内容。他得到威尔逊先生（英国）的支持。

……

主席指出，起草委员会面前的案文中已经隐含了时间紧迫的意思。

……

第三章，第 20 段

……

主席建议删除第 6 页第（f）款第 3 行的"再次"一词，并获得接受。

……

（此时，罗斯福夫人到达并主持了会议的其余部分。）

……

哈里先生（澳大利亚）认为，对既起草宣言又起草公约的讨论，不仅促进了对审议英国草案的讨论，也促进了对实施的讨论。他表示，最重要的是向人权委员会传达所提出的各种不同建议，将其按照逻辑顺序列出。

他认为有必要发表一项声明，表明没有任何建议得到委员会的认可。他建议如下案文：

"1. 在联合国大会决议中的人权和基本自由宣言将具有相当重要的道德意义。

2. 国际法中的各项权利除非载入公约并得到各成员国政府的批准，否则将会是不确定的。

3. 除了承认公约中规定的权利是国际法中的权利外，还需要签署公约，以确保其国内法与公约完全一致，以及这些权利可在国内法院执行。（在这方面，委员会发现，联邦制国家、没有成文宪法的国家以及尚未完成立法的国家需要履行特别职责。）

4. 无论是宣言还是公约，其本身都不足以确保成员国可以去遵守，联合国应该采取进一步措施。

5. 认识到侵犯这些权利或与这些权利不相一致的国内法将会予以曝光，并可能受到国际谴责，这将起到威慑作用；而且可以采取以下措施增加曝光度：

（1）个人和团体向联合国提交申诉书；

（2）由秘书长要求提供相关信息；

（3）在联合国大会上进行讨论。

6. 研究在联合国的框架内是否可能创立一个组织，以便对指控人权侵犯的来函进行接收、筛选、审查和处理。

7. 经济及社会理事会可以重新审议对人权委员会的授权范围，以便赋予委员会在这个领域的更大职责。

8. 公约应承认联合国有权利将持续侵犯人权和基本自由的成员国除名。

9. 应设立国际人权法院，以便对涉及可能侵犯人权和基本自由的国际案件进行司法裁决。"

哈里先生（澳大利亚）提议，应随后发表一份声明，表明上述观点均未获得委员会的认可，但已被提交给人权委员会成员作为参考。

哈里先生（澳大利亚）进一步建议，将报告员报告中的第（b）2款调为最后一款，并改写如下：

"委员会成员普遍认为，人权和基本自由不能仅靠国内或国际的强制执行来予以保障，还需要联合国设法对世界各国人民进行人权教育，并创造社会条件和其他条件来确保尊重和促进人权。"

马利克博士（黎巴嫩）认为，对该主题的详细陈述会过分强调实施，而且这似乎显示对该问题的讨论花费了过多的时间，但实际情况并非如此。他赞成保留委员会面前的简短形式的报告。

圣克鲁兹先生（智利）认为，苏联和智利的评论可能有实际用途。他建议用第3条替换第4条，并将第4条重新起草。应该指出的是，起草一项国际公约已得到了各方代表的支持，此外还有人提议建立一个机构来支持对人权的保护。

威尔逊先生（英国）赞同按哈里先生（澳大利亚）所建议的思路，即在报告中列入所提出的实施意见。他并不觉得当附上附件后报告还会显得不平衡。

主席（罗斯福夫人）觉得保持报告的平衡很重要，她支持哈里先生的提议，但感觉声明应该更简短。

科瑞斯基教授（苏联）认为，实施并不在委员会的职权范围之内，因此该报告应仅列出建议，并说明对其存在反对意见。

张博士（中国）支持哈里先生的案文，并觉得其内容应该被保留，但赞同采用更简短的形式。他提议应该由报告员和哈里先生重新起草这一节。

圣克鲁兹先生（智利）支持他。

奥多瑙先生（法国）支持澳大利亚的提案以及重新起草的建议。

大家同意由报告员和哈里先生（澳大利亚）重新起草第三章第20段。

第 19 段

威尔逊先生（英国）宣读了他对第19段的修改建议："委员会发现，由于可用时间太短，而且大多数代表还没有机会获得专家建议，因此，无法起草一份详细的公约草案提交人权委员会。但是，起草委员会采用附件I英国提案的第2部分作为基础，对公约草案可能的具体内容进行了一般性审查。此次审查的结果体现在本报告附录G中。该附件已作为《国际人权公约》初稿的工作文件提交人权委员会。"

科瑞斯基教授（苏联）反对将缺乏时间和机会咨询法律专家作为起草委员会没有详细审议公约的原因：真正的原因是起草公约的决定必须留给人权委员会作出。

主席指出，大家普遍认为，在最终以任何形式起草公约之前，人权委员会均需要法律咨询。

马利克博士（黎巴嫩）提议，委员会对英国草案的审查结果可以体现在附件中，作为人权委员会的工作文件：他建议附件 B 可以包括原始的英国提案文件，而这些修订可以脚注的形式体现在该附件中。

威尔逊先生（英国）觉得，有必要用一个新的附件来显示对英国草案案文的修改。考虑到一些反对意见，他提议将有关专家建议的表述从他对第 19 段修正建议的案文中删去。

哈里先生（澳大利亚）撤回了他原来的提案，赞成英国的修正案。

张博士（中国）接受英国的修正案，但希望在最后保留"委员会不妨审议并加以详细阐释"的措辞。威尔逊先生同意了。

大家都同意，修正后的英国草案案文应在一个单独的附件中发布。

……

审议起草委员会提交人权委员会的报告草案附件 F

……

第 8 条

报告员宣读了该条的全文和脚注。张博士（中国）要求撤回包含中国修正案的脚注，他打算稍后向人权委员会提交他的修正案。

……

第 11 条

报告员宣读了第 11 条的全文和脚注。

主席说，卡森先生（法国）接受了"一切形式的奴隶制"的表述。她自己还认为，第二句话应被写入脚注，并注明委员会已考虑其内容可以写入公约。张博士（中国）和威尔逊先生（英国）同意主席的意见，该建议被采纳。

因此，第 11 条被改为："禁止一切形式的与人的尊严相悖的奴隶制。"

本次会议于下午 5:05 休会。

——人权委员会之起草委员会第 17 次会议简要记录
（E/CN.4/AC.1/SR.17）

徐俊杰译，常健校

E/CN.4/AC.1/SR.17
3 July 1947

COMMISSION ON HUMAN RIGHTS
DRAFTING COMMITTEE
FIRST SESSION
SUMMARY RECORD OF THE SEVENTEENTH MEETING
Held at Lake Success, New York, on Tuesday, 24 June 1947 at 2:30 p.m.

Dr. P. C. Chang presided over the first part of the meeting

Continuation of the Discussion of the Draft Report of the Drafting Committee to the Commission on Human Rights (Document E/CN.4/AC.1/14)

In the absence of the Chairman, Dr. Chang, the Vice-Chairman, temporarily presided.

...

Paragraph 19

...

The Chairman was also of the opinion that it should be made clear that the decision to draft a Convention rested with the Commission on Human Rights.

Dr. Malik (Lebanon) felt that this was implicit in the words "which the Commission on Human Rights may wish to elaborate".

The Chairman felt that the shortness of time and the need to consult legal experts should be included in this paragraph. He was supported by Mr. Wilson (United Kingdom).

...

The Chairman pointed out that the shortness of time was already implied in the text before the Committee.

...

Chapter III, Paragraph 20

...

The Chairman proposed the deletion of the word "again" on Page 6, paragraph (f), line 3, which was accepted.

...

(At this point Mrs. Roosevelt arrived and presided over the remainder of the meeting.)

...

Mr. Harry (Australia) felt that the discussion of drafting both a Declaration and a Convention had promoted a discussion on implementation as well as consideration of the United Kingdom Draft. He said that it was most important to convey to the Commission on Human Rights the different suggestions that had been made, set out in logical order. He recognized the need for a statement that no suggestion had received the endorsement of the Committee.

He proposed the following text:

"(a) that a declaration of human rights and fundamental freedoms in a resolution of the General Assembly would have considerable moral weight.

(b) that rights in international law would be uncertain unless embodied in a convention and ratified by member governments.

(c) that signatories of a convention, in addition to recognizing the rights specified therein as rights in international law should be required to ensure that their domestic law was in full conformity and that the rights would be enforceable in domestic courts. (The committee found that in this connection the position of federal states, of states without written constitutions and of states where law has not been completely codified would require special duty.)

(d) That neither a declaration nor a convention would in itself be fully adequate to ensure observance by member nations and that the United Nations should take further measures.

(e) That knowledge that violations or inconsistent domestic laws would be given publicity and might be internationally censured would act as a deterrent and that measures should be taken to promote such publicity including:

(i) Petitions by individuals and groups to the United Nations;

(ii) Requests for information by the Secretary-General;

(iii) Discussion in the General Assembly.

(f) That the possibility should be studied of creating, within the framework of the United Nations, an organization to receive, sift, examine and deal with communications alleging the violations of human rights.

(g) That the terms of reference of the Commission on Human Rights might be reexamined by the Economic and Social Council with a view to granting greater responsibility in this field to the Commission.

(h) That a Convention should recognize the right of the United Nations to expel a member who had persistently violated human rights and fundamental freedoms.

(i) That an International Court of Human Rights should be established for judicial determination at the international level of cases involving possible violation of human rights and fundamental freedoms."

Mr. Harry (Australia) proposed that there should then be a statement that none of these views were endorsed by the Committee, but were submitted for the information of the Members of the Commission on Human Rights.

Mr. Harry (Australia) proposed further that paragraph (b) 2, of the Rapporteur's report should be the last paragraph and might be reworded as follows:

"There was general agreement among members of the Committee that human rights and fundamental freedoms could not be secured through enforcement alone, whether nationally or internationally, but that the United Nations should seek to educate the peoples of the world with regard to human rights and to create social and other conditions under which respect for and the promotion of human rights could be secured."

Dr. Malik (Lebanon) felt that such a detailed exposé of the subject would overemphasize implementation and would seem to indicate that more time had been spent on discussion of the problem than was the case. He was in favour of retaining the shorter form of the Report before the Committee.

Mr. Santa Cruz (Chile) thought the Union of Soviet Socialist Republics and Chilean observations might serve a practical purpose. He proposed that paragraph (c) should replace paragraph (d) and (d) be redrafted. It should be stated that the drawing up of an international convention had been supported by various delegates, and it was also suggested that an organ might be established to sponsor the protection of human rights.

Mr. Wilson (United Kingdom) approved the inclusion in the Report of a formulation of views on implementation on the lines suggested by Mr. Harry (Australia) and did not feel that the Report would be thrown off balance when the Annexes were attached.

The Chairman (Mrs. Roosevelt) felt it was important to keep the Report in balance, and supported Mr. Harry's proposal, but felt it should be shorter.

Prof. Koretsky (Union of Soviet Socialist Republics) was of the opinion that as implementation was not in the terms of reference of the Committee, the Report should only list the suggestions and say that there had been objections.

Dr. Chang (China) supported Mr. Harry's text, and felt the substance should be retained, but was in favour of a shorter form. He proposed that the Rapporteur and Mr. Harry should redraft this section.

Mr. Santa Cruz (Chile) supported him.

Mr. Ordonneau (France) supported the Australian proposal and the suggestion that it be redrafted.

It was agreed that the Rapporteur and Mr. Harry (Australia) should redraft Chapter III, paragraph 20.

Paragraph 19

Mr. Wilson (United Kingdom) read his proposed revision of paragraph 19: "The Committee found that owing to the short time available and the fact that most Representatives had not had an opportunity of obtaining expert advice, it could not prepare a detailed draft convention for submission to the Commission on Human Rights. However, the Drafting Committee used Annex I, Part 2 of the United Kingdom proposal as the basis for a general examination of the possible substantive contents of a draft Convention. The result of this examination is embodied in Annex G of this Report which is submitted to the Commission on Human Rights as a working paper for a preliminary draft of an International Convention on Human Rights."

Prof. Koretsky (Union of Soviet Socialist Republics) objected to the reference to lack of time and opportunity of consulting legal experts as being the reason why the Committee had not considered a Convention in detail: the real reason was that the decision to draft a Convention must be left to the Commission on Human Rights.

The Chairman pointed out that it was generally felt that the Commission on Human Rights would need legal advice before the Convention could be drafted in any fifinal form.

Dr. Malik (Lebanon) proposed that the result of the Committee's examination of the United Kingdom Draft might be embodied in the Annex, as a working paper for the Commission on Human Rights: he suggested that these modifications could be presented in the form of footnotes to Annex B, which would contain the original United Kingdom document.

Mr. Wilson (United Kingdom) felt that a new Annex to show the changes in text of the United Kingdom Draft was necessary. He proposed, in order to meet some of the objections, that the phrase concerning expert advice be deleted from his amended text of paragraph 19.

Mr. Harry (Australia) withdrew his original proposal in favour of the United Kingdom amendment.

Dr. Chang (China) accepted the United Kingdom amendment, but wished to retain the phrase "which the Commission may wish to consider and elaborate" at the end. Mr. Wilson agreed.

There was a general consensus of opinion that the modified text of the United Kingdom Draft should be issued in a separate Annex.

......

Consideration of Annex F of the Draft Report of the Drafting Committee to the Commission on Human Rights

......

Article 8

The Rapporteur read the text of the Article and the footnotes. Dr. Chang (China) requested the withdrawal of the footnote containing a Chinese amendment as he intended to present his amendment later to the Commission on

Human Rights.

...

Article 11

The Rapporteur read the text of the Article and footnotes.

The Chairman said that M. Cassin (France) had accepted that "slavery in all its forms" should be stated. It was her opinion also that the second sentence should be included in a footnote with a note stating that the Committee had considered that its substance might be included in a Convention. Dr. Chang (China) and Mr. Wilson (United Kingdom) agreed with the Chairman and the suggestion was adopted.

Article 11 then read: "Slavery, which is inconsistent with the dignity of man, is prohibited in all its forms."

The meeting adjourned at 5:05 p.m.

在人权委员会之起草委员会第 18 次会议上的发言

1947 年 6 月 25 日星期三上午 10:30 纽约成功湖

1. 审议起草委员会提交人权委员会的报告草案第三章 （第 E/CN.4/AC.1/14 号文件）

主席请报告员介绍他和澳大利亚代表修订的第三章案文。

……

哈里先生（澳大利亚）提议采用以下表述："委员会个别成员建议，这种教育应通过联合国现有机构或一个可能的国际机构进行。"

张博士（中国）指出，利用现有机构的想法在先前的会议中并没有被澄清，因此他觉得不应在这里写入。

主席认为，不妨保留第 21 节的原文，在"建议"之后加上"个别成员"。罗斯福夫人（美国）随后建议将第 20 条第二部分中的"国际社会必须确保遵守"改为"应以某种形式落实人权"。

张博士（中国）针对同一条指出，委员会没有就这些原则达成一致。因此，他建议删去第一句。至于第 20 条第一段中的"大会"一词，他认为应该用"会议"一词来代替。

……

2. 审议报告草案附件 F 中的第 12 至 40 条

……

第 15 条

罗斯福夫人说，美国建议，"他应有权咨询律师并由其代表"这句话不应是一个脚注，而应被写入该条。

报告员解释说，由于主席和卡森教授在这一点上没有达成明确的共识，所以这句话被放到了脚注中。张博士（中国）建议将其放在该条的结尾处。报告员接受了这一改动。奥多诺先生（法国）建议用以下法文文本取代该条第 2 款第二句：

"他应有权得到协助，并在法律不要求他亲自出庭的情况下，由律师代理。"

报告员接受了上述建议。

······

第 28 条

主席建议在"公职"之后插入"担任公职"。张博士（中国）建议在第 28 条中增加下述这句话："参加公职考试不应成为特权或优惠。"

报告员说，接受这一建议就需要删除第一个脚注。

······

第 31 条

张博士（中国）认为第 31 条中的"和"字最好改成"或"字。

报告员接受了这一建议，并建议将该条中的"应当"改为"将"。

······

——人权委员会之起草委员会第 18 次会议简要记录

（E/CN.4/AC.1/SR.18）

杨茉萱译，常健校

E/CN.4/AC.1/SR.18

3 July 1947

COMMISSION ON HUMAN RIGHTS
DRAFTING COMMITTEE
FIRST SESSION
SUMMARY RECORD OF THE EIGHTEENTH MEETING

Held at Lake Success, New York, on Wednesday, 25 June 1947, at 10:30 a.m.

1. Consideration of Chapter III of Draft Report of the Drafting Committee to the Commission on Human Rights (Document E/CN.4/AC.1/14)

The Chairman invited the Rapporteur to present the text of Chapter III as revised by him and the Representative of Australia.

...

Mr. Harry (Australia) proposed the following wording: "It was suggested by individual Members of the Committee that such education should be carried out through the existing organs of the United Nations or a possible international organ."

Dr. Chang (China) pointed out that the idea of using existing organs had not been clarified during the previous meetings and that therefore he felt it might not be included here.

The Chairman thought that it might be well to keep the original text of Section 21 with the insertion of "by individual Members" after "It was suggested". Mrs. Roosevelt (United States of America) then suggested substituting "there should be some form of implementation with respect to human rights" for "the international community must ensure the observance of ..." in the second part of Paragraph 20.

Dr. Chang (China) referring to the same paragraph, pointed out that there was no expression of the consensus of opinion of the Committee regarding these principles. Therefore he suggested the deletion of the first sentence. With regard to the word "session" in the first paragraph of Paragraph 20, he thought that the word "meeting" should be substituted.

...

2. Consideration of Articles 12 to 40 in Annex F of the Draft Report

...

Article 15

Mrs. Roosevelt stated that the United States suggested that the phrase "he shall have the right to consult with and to be represented by counsel" should not be a footnote but should be included in the Article.

The Rapporteur explained that because of the lack of clear agreement between the Chairman and Professor Cassin on this point this phrase had been put into a footnote. Dr. Chang (China) suggested putting it at the end of the Article. The Rapporteur accepted the change. Mr. Ordonneau (France) suggested the following text, in French, to replace the Second sentence of the second paragraph of the Article:

"Il aura le droit d'être assisté et, toutes les fois que sa comparution personnelle ne sera pas exigée par la loi, représenté par un conseil."

The Rapporteur accepted these suggestions.

...

Article 28

The Chairman suggested inserting the words "to hold public office" after "public employment". Dr. Chang (China) suggested adding the following sentence to Article 28: "Access to examinations for public employment shall not be a matter of privilege or favour."

The Rapporteur said the acceptance of this suggestion called for the deletion of the first footnote.

...

Article 31

Dr. Chang (China) thought the word "and" in Article 31 might better be changed to "or".

The Rapporteur accepted this suggestion and suggested the substitution of "shall" for "should" in this Article.

...

在人权委员会之起草委员会第 19 次会议上的发言

1947 年 6 月 25 日星期三下午 2:30 纽约成功湖

1.审议将纳入公约的人权和基本自由的拟议定义（人权委员会之起草委员会报告草案附件 C）（第 E/CN.4/AC.1/14 号文件）

张博士（中国）说，他和英国代表认为，这份文件的标题应该是："将考虑纳入公约的人权和基本自由条款草案"。

主席说，由于没有其他意见，这一建议被接受。她指出，附件 C 中的所有项目都取自已经讨论过的其他文件，因此可能不需要进一步讨论。

......

> ——人权委员会之起草委员会第 19 次会议简要记录
> （E/CN.4/AC.1/SR.19）

常健译校

E/CN.4/AC.1/SR.19

3 July 1947

COMMISSION ON HUMAN RIGHTS
DRAFTING COMMITTEE
FIRST SESSION
SUMMARY RECORD OF THE NINETEENTH MEETING

Held at Lake Success, New York, on Wednesday, 25 June 1947, at 2:30 p.m.

1. Consideration of Proposed Definition of Human Rights and Fundamental Freedoms for Inclusion in a Convention (Annex C of the Draft Report of the Drafting Committee to the Commission on Human Rights) (Document E/CN.4/AC.1/14)

Dr. Chang (China) said that he and the Representative of the United Kingdom felt that this document should be headed: "Draft Articles on Human Rights and Fundamental Freedoms to Be Considered for Inclusion in a Convention."

The Chairman said that since there were no comments, this suggestion was accepted. She pointed out that all of the items in Annex C had been taken from other documents which had already been discussed, therefore they might require no further discussion.

...

1948 年

人权委员会之起草委员会第二届会议

人权委员会之起草委员会第 20 次会议简要记录

1948 年 5 月 3 日星期一下午 3:15 纽约成功湖

3. 选举副主席和报告员

主席要求提名委员会副主席的人选。

圣克鲁兹先生（智利）说，他支持澳大利亚代表的建议，即起草委员会的主席团成员应保持不变。但是，由于张彭春博士（中国）无法出席，他考虑副主席和报告员的职能可以合并于一个职位。他随后提名由查尔斯·马利克博士（黎巴嫩）担任这一职务。

奥多诺先生（法国）支持这一提名。

马利克博士（黎巴嫩）当选副主席和报告员。

——起草委员会第 2 届会议第 20 次会议简要记录
（E/CN.4/AC.1/SR.20）

杨茉萱译，常健校

E/CN.4/AC.1/SR.20
3 May 1948

COMMISSION ON HUMAN RIGHTS
DRAFTING COMMITTEE
SECOND SESSION
SUMMARY RECORD OF THE TWENTIETH MEETING

Lake Success, New York, Monday, 3 May 1948, at 3:15 p.m.

…

3. Election of Vice-Chairman and Rapporteur

The Chairman asked for nominations for the Vice-Chairmanship of the

Committee.

Mr. Santa Cruz (Chile) stated that he supported the Representative of Australia in his proposal that the same officers be maintained for the Drafting Committee. However, since Dr. Chang (China) would be unable to be present, he considered that the functions of the Vice-Chairman and Rapporteur could be combined under one office. He then nominated Dr. Charles Malik (Lebanon).

M. Ordonneau (France) supported the nomination.

Dr. Malik (Lebanon) was elected Vice-Chairman and Rapporteur.

联合国人权委员会第三届会议

在人权委员会第 48 次会议上的发言

1948 年 5 月 26 日星期三下午 2:45 纽约成功湖

......

应主席的要求，汉弗莱先生（秘书处）解释说，根据议事规则第 31 条的规定，英文和法文是经济及社会理事会的工作语言。议事规则第 38 条规定，理事会的所有决议、建议和其他正式决定，都应以官方语言传达。这些规定适用于理事会的所有机构。

因此，各代表团有权要求将起草委员会的报告翻译成官方语言，因为这是该机构的一项"正式决定"。关于工作文件，诸如各代表团提交的决议草案，秘书处可以只分发英文版和法文版，但其已向讲俄语的代表团保证，其将尽最大努力，让他们得到这些文件的俄文版本。

莫拉先生（乌拉圭）不坚持要求将委员会的所有文件翻译成西班牙语，但他保留在某些情况下要求翻译成西班牙语的权利。

张先生（中国）说，在讨论中需要中文翻译版本时，中国代表团也保留要求将任何决议、建议或正式决定翻译成中文的权利。

他随后询问，法国提案中的"实施"是否像适用于宣言那样也适用于公约。

......

主席回顾说，委员会在其第二届会议上就实施问题已经提出了一些建议。这些建议已提交给经济及社会理事会，理事会在其第 116F（VI）号决议中请人权委员会就这一问题提出最后建议，以便尽快向成员国政府提交有关实施问题的条款草案。正是由于这个问题的紧迫性，法国代表建议委员会在审查宣言之后和审议公约之前，立即审议实施问题。

......

——人权委员会第 48 次会议简要记录（E/CN.4/SR.48）

杨茉萱译，常健校

E/CN.4/SR.48
4 June 1948

COMMISSION ON HUMAN RIGHTS
THIRD SESSION
SUMMARY RECORD OF THE FORTY-EIGHTH MEETING
Held at Lake Success, New York, Wednesday, 26 May 1948, at 2:45 p.m.

...

At the Chairman's request Mr. Humphrey (Secretariat) explained that under the terms of rule 31 of the rules of procedure English and French were the working languages of the Economic and Social Council. Rule 38 of the rules of procedure provided that all resolutions, recommendations and other official decisions of the Council should be communicated in the official languages. Those provisions applied to all the bodies of the Council.

Consequently, the delegations were entitled to request the translation into the official languages of the report of the Drafting Committee, since it was an "official decision" of that body. With regard to working documents, such as draft resolutions submitted by the various delegations, the Secretariat could just distribute them in English and French, but it had assured the Russian-speaking delegations that it would do its utmost to let them have those documents in Russian.

Mr. Mora (Uruguay) would not insist on a Spanish translation of all the Commission's documents, but he reserved the right to ask for it in certain cases.

Mr. Chang (China) said that his delegation also reserved the right to ask for a Chinese translation of any resolution, recommendation or official decision if it considered that it needed that translation for the discussion.

He then asked whether "implementation" in the French proposal applied to the Covenant as well as to the Declaration.

...

The Chairman recalled that the Commission had made certain suggestions concerning implementation at its second session. These suggestions had been submitted to the Economic and Social Council, which, by its resolution 116F(VI), had invited the Commission on Human Rights to submit final recommendations on the question so that the draft articles dealing with implementation could be submitted to the Member Governments as soon as possible. It was because of the urgency of that question that the French representative had proposed that the Commission should consider the question of implementation immediately after examining the Declaration and before considering the Covenant.

...

在人权委员会第 50 次会议上的发言

1948 年 5 月 27 日星期四下午 2:30 纽约成功湖

......

审议起草委员会提交的《国际人权宣言（草案）》（第 E/CN.4/95 号文件附件 A）

......

张先生（中国）提请注意中国代表团提交的较短的宣言草案，它载于起草委员会报告的附件 A。委员会正在处理联合国和整个世界面临的最严肃的问题之一。宣言的主要目的是唤起世界对某些基本人权的关注，以期促进教育的进步。"教育"一词在这里是广义使用的，是指如何提高生活质量。宣言应尽可能简单，并采用易于理解的形式。他敦促那些没有在起草委员会任职的委员会成员，仔细研究中国的草案。

......

第 1 条

......

张先生（中国）对英国和印度代表提交的案文进行了修正，删除了第一句之后的句号，以及"自然本性赋予他们理性和良知"这一表述。

......

第 2 条

......

张先生（中国）提请委员会注意第 2 条的中国草案，它将起草委员会案文中的第 2 条和第 3 条合并为一段。如果委员会希望达成一个简短的宣言文本，他建议用该段的第二句话作为第 2 条。然而他认为，最好将关于限制个人权利的条款放在宣言的最后，因为在还没有讲权利本身之前就宣布对其的限制，这是不符合逻辑的。

威尔逊先生（英国）同意智利代表的意见，也同意中国代表关于简洁性的提议。但是，中国草案的缺点是不够具体，他倾向于用"确保应有的尊重等所需的限制"来代替"承认他人的权利"。

　　巴甫洛夫先生（苏联）要求有更多的时间，使委员会成员能够充分考虑提交给他们的所有草案。他还赞同法国代表希望在该条中提及"民主国家"的愿望。

　　张先生（中国）再次强调，委员会正在起草的宣言，旨在被广大人民群众阅读和理解，因此应尽可能简短易懂。他敦促委员会成员，考虑中国代表团提交的载于 E/CN.4/95 号文件第 14 和 15 页的草案。

　　......

——人权委员会第 50 次会议简要记录（E/CN.4/SR.50）

杨茉萱译，常健校

E/CN.4/SR.50
4 June 1948

COMMISSION ON HUMAN RIGHTS
THIRD SESSION
SUMMARY RECORD OF THE FIFTIETH MEETING
Lake Success, New York, Thursday, 27 May 1948, at 2:30 p.m.

...

Consideration of Draft International Declaration on Human Rights, Submitted by the Drafting Committee (Annex A of Document E/CN.4/95)

...

　　Mr. Chang (China) drew attention to the shorter draft Declaration submitted by his delegation, and contained in Annex A of the report of the Drafting Committee. The Commission was dealing with one of the most serious questions before the United Nations and the whole world. The principal aim of the Declaration was to call the attention of the world to certain fundamental human rights, with a view to educational advancement. The term "education" was here used in the broad sense of how to improve the quality of life. The Declaration should be as simple as possible and in a form which was easy to grasp. He urged those members of the Commission who had not served on the Drafting Committee to examine carefully the Chinese Draft.

...

Article 1

...

Mr. Chang (China) amended the text submitted by the representatives of the United Kingdom and India by deleting the full stop after the first sentence and the words "They are endowed by nature with reason and conscience".

...

Article 2

...

Mr. Chang (China) drew the Commission's attention to the Chinese draft of Article 2, which condensed Articles 2 and 3 of the Drafting Committee's text in one paragraph. If the Commission desired to arrive at a brief text for the Declaration, he would suggest using the second sentence of that paragraph for Article 2. However, in his opinion, it would be preferable to place the Article on the restrictions of the rights of the individual at the very end of the Declaration, for it was not logical to proclaim the restrictions before the rights themselves had not been stated.

Mr. Wilson (United Kingdom) agreed with the representative of Chile and with the Chinese representative's plea for brevity. However, the Chinese draft had the disadvantage of being insufficiently specific and he would prefer the phrase "restrictions necessary to secure due regard, etc." to "recognition of the rights of others".

Mr. Pavlov (Union of Soviet Socialist Republics) requested further time to enable members of the Commission to give due consideration to all the drafts submitted to them. He also felt in sympathy with the French representative's wish to see a reference to the "democratic State" in the article.

Mr. Chang (China) once more stressed the fact that the Declaration which the Commission was drafting was intended to be read and understood by large masses of people, and should therefore he as brief and intelligible as possible. He urged the members of the Commission to give consideration to the draft submitted by his delegation, appearing on pages 14 and 15 of document E/CN.4/95.

...

在人权委员会第 51 次会议上的发言

1948 年 5 月 28 日星期五上午 10:45 纽约成功湖

审议宣言第 2 条（第 E/CN.4/95、E/CN.4/99、E/CN.4/102、E/600 号文件）

......

阿兹库勒先生（黎巴嫩）评论道，宣言的前三条为其后列举的各项权利奠定了基础；因此，在前三条中提及个人义务是可以的。在第 1 条中，委员会阐述了人权的基础；第 2 条应当写入限制这些权利的基础。因此，他接受法国修正案的第一部分。

在修正案的第二部分，"国家"一词受到质疑。所有国家都不认为国家本身是一个享有可能与个人权利相冲突的权利的理想实体。无论委员会各成员对这一问题持何种观点，"国家"一词都应当被删除；因为它代表了一种所有人都不同意的观点。另外，"所有人的福利和安全"这句话，对每个人来说都是可以接受的。他同意智利代表的意见，认为"民主"一词不应被使用。如果国际文书先前对一个民主国家的各项权利进行了界定，他倒是愿意谈论民主国家的这些权利；但国际文书并没有作出这种界定。

因此，他建议将法国修正案的第一部分与印度和英国修正案的第二部分合并，以"仅受……"作为开头。

张先生（中国）建议，他的修正案应改为如下内容："行使这些权利需要承认他人的权利和所有人的福利。"福利包括了安全的理念，而承认所有人的权利包括了民主的理念。他强调了"承认"这个词所包含的自愿因素的价值。重点不应放在对人民的约束，而应放在对人民的教育。所有社会的和政治的教育，其目的是对他人权利的自愿承认。委员会的理想不应该是施加限制，而是使所有人自愿承认他人的权利。这就是宣言应该表达的理想。

威尔逊先生（英国）说，虽然中国代表的提议在许多方面都是慷慨的，但也确实存在一些危险。印度和英国修正案规定的限制包括自愿接受的限制，但在任何形式的人类社会中，国家都必须为所有人的利益施加某些限制。"承认"一词只是表达了一种理想，不足以确保人权委员会任务的完成。

......

——人权委员会第 51 次会议简要记录（E/CN.4/SR.51）

杨茉萱译，常健校

E/CN.4/SR.51

9 June 1948

COMMISSION ON HUMAN RIGHTS
THIRD SESSION
SUMMARY RECORD OF THE FIFTY-FIRST MEETING

Lake Success, New York, Friday, 28 May 1948, at 10:45 a.m.

CONSIDERATION OF ARTICLE 2 OF THE DECLARATION
(Documents E/CN.4/95, E/CN.4/99, E/CN.4/102, E/600)

...

Mr. Azkoul (Lebanon) observed that the first three articles of the Declaration laid the foundation for the rights subsequently enumerated; for that reason it was permissible to mention in them the duties of the individual. In the first article, the Commission had stated the basis for human rights; the second article should include the bases for the limitation of those rights. He therefore accepted the first part of the French amendment.

In the second part of the amendment the word "State" was open to question. All countries did not consider the State as a desirable entity in itself, with rights that might conflict with the rights of the individual. Whatever opinion the various members of the Commission might hold on the subject the word "State" should be deleted, since it stood for an idea on which all did not agree. On the other hand the words "the welfare and security of all" were acceptable to everybody. He agreed with the representative of Chile that the word "democracy" should not be used. He would be willing to speak of the rights of a democratic State if those rights had been previously defined by an international instrument, but that had not been done.

He therefore proposed that the first part of the French amendment should be combined with the second part of the Indian and United Kingdom amendment beginning with the words "subject only ...".

Mr. Chang (China) suggested that his amendment should be changed to read as follows: "The exercise of these rights requires recognition of the rights of others and the welfare of all." Welfare included the idea of security: and recognition of the rights of all included the idea of democracy. He stressed the value of the voluntary element in the word "recognition". Emphasis should be placed not on restraining people, but on educating them. The purpose of all social and political education was the voluntary recognition of the rights of others. The Commission's ideal should not be the imposition of restrictions but rather the voluntary recognition by all of the rights of others. That was the ideal which the Declaration should express.

Mr. Wilson (United Kingdom) remarked that while the Chinese representative's proposal was in many ways a generous one it did contain some dangers too. The limitations provided for in the Indian and United Kingdom amendment included those voluntarily accepted, but in any form of human society it was imperative that the State should impose certain limitations in the interest of all. The word "recognition" merely expressed an ideal and was inadequate to ensure the fulfilment of the Commission's task.

……

在人权委员会第 52 次会议上的发言

1948 年 5 月 28 日星期五下午 2:30 纽约成功湖

继续审议《国际人权宣言（草案）》（第 E/CN.4/95 号文件附件 A）

......

第 3 条第 1 款

张先生（中国）说，鉴于委员会显然希望起草一份在形式上比中国代表团设想的更详细的宣言，他撤回对相关段落的修正案。（参考第 E/CN.4/102 号文件）

......

克莱科夫金先生（乌克兰）接受张先生（中国）的建议，即在"财产"和"地位"之间插入"或其他"字样，这可以满足他想表达的观点。

乌克兰的修正案以 13 票赞成、0 票反对、1 票弃权获得通过。

阿兹库勒先生（黎巴嫩）提议，第 2 款中出现的"职位"一词应从该款中删除，放在第 1 款"财产或其他地位"之后。

卡森先生（法国）支持该提议。他反对在第 2 款中使用"无论职位或地位如何"的措辞。法律面前人人平等；提及应避免的具体例外情形只会削弱这一表述。

维尔凡先生（南斯拉夫）觉得"职位"一词不属于第 1 款，而属于第 2 款。第 1 款列出了不应存在歧视的各种理由，而第 2 款则是针对不公平的特权。

张先生（中国）认为增加"职位"一词是不必要的；"财产或其他地位"的措辞已经涵盖了这一概念。

阿兹库勒先生（黎巴嫩）说，既然委员会接受了中国代表的解释，他愿意撤回其修正案。

修改后的第 3 条第 1 款获得一致通过。

第 3 条第 2 款

主席回顾说，对于第 2 款，有英国和印度的修正案以及法国的修正案（文件 E/CN.4/99 和 E/CN.4/82/Add.3）。所有这些代表团都强调法律面前的平等，以及需要平等保护以防止任意的歧视；法国的修正案还包括防止煽动这种歧视。这三点将被分别付诸表决。

她作为美国代表发言指出，美国代表团更倾向于 E/CN.4/95 号文件中的更简单措辞。

克莱科夫金先生（乌克兰）建议作进一步修正。他认为原始文本（E/CN.4/95 号文件）中的"任意的"一词应当被删除。

阿兹库勒先生（黎巴嫩）说，他认为英国和印度的修正案中不需要使用"不论职位或地位"这一短语。只提到两种例外情形是很危险的；如果删除这一短语，表述会更加有力。

张先生（中国）指出，那些不希望使用该短语的人，可以投票支持不包含该短语的法国修正案。

威尔逊先生（英国）希望在其修正案中保留这一短语。身居高位或拥有一定社会地位的人，很容易认为自己可以凌驾于法律之上；指出他们不能凌驾于法律之上是有益的。

卡森先生（法国）认为他的修正案是有用的；他同意黎巴嫩代表的观点，即只列举某些例外情形会削弱案文。

洛佩兹先生（菲律宾）希望黎巴嫩的修正案被接受；这将使他能够投票支持英国和印度的修正案，他更喜欢法国的提案，因为"法律面前人人平等"这句话的英文比法国提案中的相应短语听起来更响亮。

张先生（中国）支持菲律宾代表的意见。为了达成一致意见，他还准备接受删除"任意的"一词。

……

洛佩兹先生（菲律宾）提出，"不受任何歧视"的措辞，是否比"反对任何歧视"的措辞可以更好地表达该条的真正意图。

圣克鲁兹先生（智利）不同意菲律宾代表的观点。该条的意图是明确法律有责任保护人们不受任何歧视；委员会第二届会议通过的草案中，该句的最后部分证明了这一论断。菲律宾的修正案将改变该条的主要思想。

他同意"任意的"一词可以被删除。为避免对该条中"歧视"的含义产生任何误解，可以参考第 1 款的做法，将"任何任意的歧视"改为"这种歧视"。

阿兹库勒先生（黎巴嫩）同意智利代表的意见。

张先生（中国）提议将菲律宾的建议纳入该条，这样将该短语改为"不受并反对任何歧视"。"歧视"一词并不适用于有用的区别。

……

卡森先生（法国）赞赏英国的论点，针对所提出的问题，他建议在第二行"任何歧视"之前加上"违反本宣言"的限定词。

勒博先生（比利时）同意法国代表的意见。

……

主席以美国代表的身份发言，她认为困难在于对"歧视"一词的含义存在不同意见。形容词"任意的"可以澄清所要表达的意思。不过，她不反对法国的建议。

威尔逊先生（英国）也愿意接受法国的建议，但他担心"法律的平等保护"这一概念是否会因为补充提及宣言中规定的那些权利而有所窄化。

张先生（中国）同意英国代表的意见，即所建议的补充可能会产生限制法律平等保护理念的效果，并建议对该条款进行进一步审议。说"反对违反本宣言的任何歧视"也许是可以接受的，但肯定不如"不受或反对任何歧视"这样的短语更有力。

"歧视"的含义并不构成问题，因为该词无疑用于贬义。

……

威尔逊先生（英国）指出，该条第 1 款已经提到了"不加区别"。因此，"不受或反对任何歧视"这一短语似乎是不必要的重复，为了简洁起见，应该避免这种重复。

张先生（中国）不同意说该短语是重复的，因为在该条第 2 款中，它被用于描述法律的平等保护。

……

卡森先生（法国）再次建议在第二行增加"违反本宣言的原则"的字样，既然"任意的"一词已被删除，加上这个短语似乎是必要的。

威尔逊先生（英国）担心，如果第 2 款讲宣言的原则，而该条第 1 款却提到"本宣言规定的权利和自由"，会造成混乱。

巴甫洛夫先生（苏联）和斯捷潘年科先生（白俄罗斯）认为，对违反本宣言的提及，只应放在"煽动这种歧视"之后。

张先生（中国）同意英国代表的意见，认为法国的建议是不明智的。他建议在第二行"歧视"一词之后结束该句。

······

在回答巴甫洛夫先生（苏联）提出的问题时，威尔逊先生（英国）同意英国的奥斯瓦德·莫斯利爵士犯有反犹太主义宣传之罪。但他强调说，他并不是想说他的国家不存在煽动歧视的行为，而是想表明，英国可以用自己的方式最好地处理这种情况。

威尔逊先生询问"法律的平等保护"这一短语的确切含义：它是指应该有平等适用的法律，还是指所有人都有平等的权利获得法律可能提供的任何保护？如果是后一种情况，他的反对意见就会基本得到解决。

张先生（中国）认为，如果以适当的语气重点来解读这句话，其含义是清楚的。既然它已经被委员会投票接受，就不再开放讨论了。

······

应勒博先生（比利时）的要求，主席将中国代表建议删除的第一部分付诸表决。

删除"或反对任何煽动歧视的行为"的提案以 8 票反对、7 票赞成、1 票弃权被否决。

谈到其建议的最后一部分，即删除"违反本宣言"，张先生（中国）指出，逗号应该省略，因为它影响了文本的含义。如果没有逗号，这句话只适用于句子的最后一部分，这是可以接受的。

卡森先生（法国）要求对他之前提出的在第二行"歧视"之后插入"违反本宣言的原则"的建议进行表决。这里所说的歧视要严重得多，也更经常发生，提及违反本宣言不仅适用于第三行，而且适用于这一行。

张先生（中国）认为，法国的修正案会不恰当地削弱"不受并反对任何歧视"的说法。最后的短语已经足够了。

主席任命了一个由中国、法国和英国代表组成的小型起草委员会，负责在已进行的讨论基础上，起草一份案文或多个备选案文。

会议于下午 6:20 结束。

——人权委员会第 52 次会议简要记录（E/CN.4/SR.52）

杨茉萱译，常健校

E/CN.4/SR.52
8 June 1948

COMMISSION ON HUMAN RIGHTS
THIRD SESSION
SUMMARY RECORD OF THE FIFTY-SECOND MEETING
Lake Success, New York, Friday, 28 May 1948, at 2:30 p.m.

Continuation of the Consideration of the Draft International Declaration on Human Rights (Document E/CN.4/95 Annex A)

...

Article 3, Paragraph 1

Mr. Chang (China) stated that, in view of the fact that the Commission apparently preferred to draft the Declaration in a more detailed form than the Chinese delegation had envisaged, he withdrew his amendment to the paragraph in question. (Cf. Document E/CN.4/102)

...

Mr. Klekovkin (Ukrainian Soviet Socialist Republics) accepted the suggestion of Mr. Chang (China) to insert the words "or other" between the words "property" and "status", which would meet the point he wished to make.

The Ukrainian amendment was adopted by thirteen votes to none, with one abstention.

Mr. Azkoul (Lebanon) proposed that the word "office" which appeared in paragraph 2 should be removed from that paragraph and inserted in paragraph 1, after the words "property or other status".

Mr. Cassin (France) supported the proposal. He was opposed to the use of the words "regardless of office or status" in paragraph 2. All men were equal before the law; mentioning specific exceptions to be avoided merely weakened the statement.

Mr. Vilfan (Yugoslavia) felt that the word "office" belonged not in paragraph 1, which contained a list of grounds on which there should be no discrimination, but in paragraph 2, which was directed against unfair privileges.

Mr. Chang (China) considered the addition of the word "office" unnecessary; the concept was covered by the words "property or other status".

Mr. Azkoul (Lebanon) said that, on the understanding that the Commission accepted the Chinese representative's interpretation, he would withdraw his amendment.

Article 3, paragraph 1 as amended, was approved unanimously.

Article 3, Paragraph 2

The Chairman recalled that there was a United Kingdom and Indian amendment and a French amendment to paragraph 2 (documents E/CN.4/99 and E/CN.4/82/ Add.3). All those delegations had stressed equality before the law and the need of equal protection against arbitrary discrimination; the French amendment also included protection against the incitement to such discrimination. Those three points would be put to the vote separately.

Speaking as the representative of the United States, she said that her delegation preferred the simpler wording contained in document E/CN.4/95.

Mr. Klekovkin (Ukrainian Soviet Socialist Republic) proposed a further amendment. He thought the word "arbitrary" in the original text (document E/CN.4/95) should be deleted.

Mr. Azkoul (Lebanon) said that he saw no need in the United Kingdom and Indian amendment for the phrase "regardless of office or status". It was dangerous to mention only two exceptions; the statement would be stronger if the phrase were deleted.

Mr. Chang (China) pointed out that those who wished to avoid use of that phrase could vote for the French amendment which did not contain it.

Mr. Wilson (United Kingdom) wished to maintain the phrase in his amendment. Persons holding high office or possessed of a certain social status were apt to consider themselves above the law; it was useful to state that they were not.

Mr. Cassin (France) considered his amendment useful; he agreed with the Lebanese representative that citing only certain exceptions weakened the text.

Mr. Lopez (Philippines) hoped that the Lebanese amendment would be accepted; that would enable him to vote for the United Kingdom and Indian amendment, which he preferred to the French proposal because the words "All are equal before the law" sounded better in English than the corresponding phrase in the French proposal.

Mr. Chang (China) supported the observations of the Philippine representative. In the interest of unanimity he was also ready to accept the deletion of the word "arbitrary".

...

Mr. Lopez (Philippines) wondered whether the true intention of the Article would not be better expressed by the words "without any discrimination" than by "against any discrimination".

Mr. Santa Cruz (Chile) did not agree with the Philippine representative. The intention of the Article was to state that it was the duty of the law to protect men against any discrimination; the last part of that sentence in the draft adopted at the Second Session of the Commission proved that assertion. The Philippine amendment would alter the main idea of the article.

He agreed that the word "arbitrary" might be deleted. To avoid any misunderstanding of the meaning of "discrimination" as used in the Article, it might be advisable to refer to the first paragraph by changing the words "any arbitrary discrimination" to "such discrimination".

Mr. Azkoul (Lebanon) agreed with the Chilean representative.

Mr. Chang (China) proposed to incorporate the Philippine suggestion in the article so that the phrase would read "without and against any discrimination". The word "discrimination" did not apply to useful distinction.

...

Mr. Cassin (France) was impressed by the United Kingdom argument and proposed to meet the point raised by the addition of the words "in violation of this Declaration" after the words "any discrimination" in the second line.

Mr. Lebeau (Belgium) agreed with the French representative.

...

The Chairman speaking as the United States representative thought the difficulty lay in the differences of opinion concerning the meaning of the word "discrimination". The adjective "arbitrary" would make clear what was intended. She did not, however, oppose the French suggestion.

Mr. Wilson (United Kingdom) was also willing to accept the French suggestion but he wondered whether the concept of "equal protection of the law" would be somewhat narrowed by the added reference to the rights laid down in the Declaration.

Mr. Chang (China) agreed with the United Kingdom representative that the suggested addition might have the effect of limiting the idea of equal protection of the law and advised further consideration of the article. To say "against any discrimination in violation of this Declaration" was perhaps acceptable but was certainly less strong than the phrase "without or against any discrimination".

The meaning of "discrimination" did not present a problem, for the word was unquestionably used in a derogatory sense.

...

Mr. Wilson (United Kingdom) pointed out that "without distinction" had already been mentioned in paragraph 1 of the article. The phrase "without or against any discrimination" seemed therefore an unnecessary repetition which should be avoided in the interest of brevity.

Mr. Chang (China) did not agree that the phrase was repetitious since in paragraph 2 of the article it was used to describe equal protection of the law.

...

Mr. Cassin (France) proposed again the addition of the words "in violation of the principles of this Declaration" in the second line which seemed necessary now that the word "arbitrary" had been deleted.

Mr. Wilson (United Kingdom) feared that confusion would result if paragraph 2 spoke of the principles of the Declaration whereas paragraph 1 of the article had mentioned "rights and freedoms set forth in this Declaration".

Mr. Pavlov (Union of Soviet Socialist Republics) and Mr. Stepanenko (Byelorussian Soviet Socialist Republic) thought that reference to violation of the present Declaration should be made only at the end of the sentence after the words "incitement to such discrimination".

Mr. Chang (China) agreed with the United Kingdom representative that the

French suggestion was unwise. He proposed that the sentence should end after the word "discrimination" in the second line.

...

In reply to a point raised by Mr. Pavlov (Union of Soviet Socialist Republics), Mr. Wilson (United Kingdom) agreed that Sir Oswald Mosley of the United Kingdom was guilty of anti-Semitic propaganda. He stressed however that he had not intended to say that there was no incitement to discrimination in his country, but rather to show that the United Kingdom could best deal with such a situation in its own way.

Mr. Wilson asked the exact meaning of the phrase "equal protection of the law". Did it mean that there should be laws which should be applied equally or did it mean that all were equally entitled to whatever protection the law might provide? In the latter case his objections would be largely resolved.

Mr. Chang (China) thought the meaning of the phrase was clear if it were read with the proper emphasis. Since it had already been accepted by a vote of the Commission it was no longer open to question.

...

At the request of Mr. Lebeau (Belgium), the Chairman put to the vote the first part of the deletion proposed by the Chinese representative.

The proposal to delete "or against any incitement to discrimination" was rejected by eight votes to seven, with one abstention.

Referring to the last part of his proposal, namely, the deletion of the words "in violation of this Declaration", Mr. Chang (China) pointed out that the comma should be omitted as it affected the meaning of the text. Without the comma the phrase would apply only to the last part of the sentence and would be acceptable.

Mr. Cassin (France) asked for a vote on his earlier proposal to insert the words "in violation of the principles of this Declaration" after "discrimination" in the second line. The discrimination spoken of there was much more serious and more frequently practised and there should be no doubt that reference to violation of the Declaration applied in that line as well as in the third line.

Mr. Chang (China) thought the French amendment would unduly weaken the words "without and against any discrimination". The phrase at the end was sufficient.

The Chairman appointed a small drafting committee made up of the representatives of China, France and the United Kingdom to draw up a text, or alternative texts, on the basis of the discussion that had taken place.

The meeting rose at 6:20 p.m.

在人权委员会第 53 次会议上的发言

1948 年 5 月 27 日星期二下午 2:30 纽约成功湖

审议人权宣言草案

……

第 5 条

张先生（中国）提请注意中国的第 5 条草案，其第一部分与英国和印度草案中所采用的措辞相同。他认为目前的讨论应限于第 5 条，将第 5 条和第 8 条的合并问题留待以后讨论。

……

第 3 条第 2 款

主席提请委员会注意第 3 条第 2 款下述新草案，它是由上次会议为此目的成立的小型起草小组起草的：

"法律面前人人平等，并有权享受法律的平等保护，不受任何歧视，以免受违反本宣言的任何歧视以及煽动这种歧视之害。"

胡德先生（澳大利亚）反对说，措辞上的过度阐释影响了清晰度，而且"歧视"一词的使用涉及两种不同的含义。他建议用"区别"一词代替第一次使用的"歧视"一词，这样，措辞将是"……没有区别，以免受任何歧视……"

张先生（中国）解释说，起草小组对最后的措辞并不特别满意；不过，该案文的优点是符合委员会在上次会议上作出的决定，因此委员会可以通过该案文，无须重新审议已作出的表决。

……

主席指出，鉴于澳大利亚修正案只作了很小的草案变更，它可以被接受，无须重新审议先前的表决结果。

巴甫洛夫先生（苏联）提出抗议，认为由起草小组来决定"违反本宣言"的短语放在该款的何处，这超越了其职权范围。澳大利亚修正案只是使位置问题更加复杂，因为委员会已经就"歧视"一词作出了决定。

主席指出，起草小组没有超越其任务范围，因为新的草案与上次会议作出的决定相比并没有实质性的变化。

张先生（中国）回顾说，委员会在上次会议上进行了两次表决，决定将"不受和反对任何歧视"这一短语写入，并决定提及对歧视的煽动。唯一没有决定的问题，是关于宣言原则的短语的恰当位置，法国代表建议将其写入。起草小组决定，也征得法国代表同意，"违反本宣言"这一短语应该是对"反对任何歧视"这一短语的限定，而不是对"不受任何歧视"这一短语的限定。

张先生争辩道，起草小组在作出这一决定时，绝没有超越其职权范围。然而如果有任何成员感到措辞不当，委员会可以恢复原来的案文。在这种情况下，中国代表团将放弃妥协的案文，并像以前一样，敦促段落缩短，用"和反对任何歧视"的措辞作为结尾。

至于澳大利亚的修正案，对它的接受需要重新审议先前会议的表决结果。

卡森先生（法国）肯定中国代表的陈述。起草小组严格遵守委员会的指示来执行任务，并一致决定"违反本宣言"的限制语只能放在"反对任何歧视"之后。在他看来，澳大利亚修正案主要是风格问题，是要避免"歧视"一词的重复使用。

主席裁定，起草小组提交的案文体现了先前的表决结果所要表达的意思，澳大利亚的建议只是对起草小组案文措辞的修正，对它的接受并不需要对先前表决的结果进行重新审议。

巴甫洛夫先生（苏联）提出反对，认为裁定是不正确的。主席宣布她愿意将裁定诉诸表决。

斯捷潘年科先生（白俄罗斯）不能同意澳大利亚修正案只是一个形式问题；就其俄文译本来说，它肯定改变了该条的实质内容。

他反对对先前表决结果进行任何重新审议，并认为应该对起草小组起草的案文进行表决。

主席提议，由于在目前阶段显然没有达成一致，唯一的程序就是由起草小组与澳大利亚和白俄罗斯的代表一起再次讨论该案文，并提出备选方案供委员会表决。

张先生（中国）支持这一提议。

……

　　主席要求起草小组考虑这样的事实："区分"一词在《联合国宪章》中从头到尾被使用，使用"歧视"一词构成一项重要的变动。因为澳大利亚代表已经撤回了他的修正案，他就不再需要参加起草小组的讨论，现在起草小组是由中国、法国、英国、白俄罗斯和菲律宾组成。

　　会议于下午 1:00 结束。

——人权委员会第 53 次会议简要记录（E/CN.4/SR.53）

杨茉萱译，常健校

E/CN.4/SR.53
4 June 1948

COMMISSION ON HUMAN RIGHTS
THIRD SESSION
SUMMARY RECORD OF THE FIFTY-THIRD MEETING

Held at Lake Success, New York, on Tuesday, 27 May 1948, at 2:30 p.m.

Consideration of the Draft Declaration of Human Rights

…

Article 5

Mr. Chang (China) drew attention to the Chinese draft for article 5, the first part of which was the same as that used in the United Kingdom and Indian draft. For the present, he thought discussion ought to be limited to article 5, leaving the question of merging articles 5 and 8 to a later stage.

…

Article 3, Paragraph 2

The Chairman drew the attention of the Commission to the following new draft of article 3, paragraph 2, which had been prepared by the small drafting group set up for that purpose at the previous meeting:

"All are equal before the law and are entitled to equal protection of the law without any discrimination, and against any discrimination in violation of this Declaration or incitement to such discrimination."

Mr. Hood (Australia) objected that there was over-elaboration of the wording at the expense of clarity, and that the word "discrimination" had been used with two different shades of meaning. He proposed that the word "distinction" should be substituted for the first use of the word "discrimination", so that the wording would then be "…without distinction, against any discrimination…"

Mr. Chang (China) explained that the small drafting group had not been particularly satisfied with the final wording; the text had, however, the advantage of being in conformity with the decisions taken by the Commission at the previous meeting, and could therefore be adopted without the Commission reconsidering the votes already taken.

   …

The Chairman stated that, as the Australian amendment was only a minor drafting change, it could be accepted without reconsidering earlier votes.

Mr. Pavlov (Union of Soviet Socialist Republics) protested that the drafting group had gone beyond its terms of reference, which had been to decide where the phrase "in violation of this Declaration" was to appear in the paragraph.

The Australian amendment only made the position more complicated, since the Commission had decided upon the word "discrimination".

The Chairman pointed out that the drafting group had not exceeded its mandate, since the new draft contained no substantive changes from the decisions which had been taken at the previous meeting.

Mr. Chang (China) recalled that by the two votes taken at the previous meeting, the Commission had decided that the phrase "without and against any discrimination" was to be included, and that mention was to be made of incitement to discrimination. The only question not decided had been the position of the phrase concerning the principles of the Declaration, the inclusion of which had been suggested by the representative of France. The drafting group had decided, with the agreement of the French representative, that the phrase "in violation of this Declaration" should qualify the phrase "against any discrimination" and not the phrase "without any discrimination".

Mr. Chang contended that in making that decision, the drafting group had in no way overstepped its terms of reference. If, however, any members felt that an unwarranted liberty had been taken with the wording, the Commission could revert to the original text, in which case the Chinese delegation would abandon the compromise text and urge, as before, a shorter paragraph, ending with the words "and against any discrimination".

With regard to the Australian amendment, its acceptance would necessitate a reconsideration of the votes taken at the previous meeting.

Mr. Cassin (France) confirmed the statement of the Chinese representative. The drafting group had carried out its mandate in strict observance of the instructions of the Commission, and had unanimously decided that the qualifications "in violation of this Declaration" could only be placed after the phrase "against any discrimination".

The Australian amendment seemed to him to be chiefly a question of style, to avoid the repetition of the word "discrimination".

The Chairman ruled that the text submitted by the drafting group embodied the meaning of the votes taken previously, and that the Australian proposal was simply an amendment to the wording of the text of the drafting group, the acceptance of which would not necessitate any reconsideration of those votes.

Mr. Pavlov (Union of Soviet Socialist Republics) objected to that ruling as incorrect. The Chairman declared herself willing to have the ruling put to a vote.

Mr. Stepanenko (Byelorussian Soviet Socialist Republic) could not agree that the Australian amendment was merely a question of form; as far as the Russian translation was concerned, it certainly changed the substance of the article.

He was opposed to any reconsideration of the votes already taken, and thought a vote should be taken upon the text prepared by the drafting group.

The Chairman proposed that since it was obvious that there would be no agreement at the present stage, the only procedure was for the drafting group, together with the representatives of Australia and the Byelorussian Soviet Socialist Republic, to discuss the text again, and present alternative formulas for the Commission to vote upon.

Mr. Chang (China) supported that proposal.

…

The Chairman asked the drafting group to take into account the fact that the word "distinction" was used throughout the Charter, and that the use of the word "discrimination" would constitute an important change. Since the Australian representative had withdrawn his amendment, he would not need to take part in the discussions of the drafting group which would now be composed of the representatives of China, France, the United Kingdom, the Byelorussian Soviet Socialist Republic and the Philippines.

The meeting rose at 1:00 p.m.

在人权委员会第 54 次会议上的发言

1948 年 6 月 1 日星期二下午 2:30 纽约成功湖

继续审议《国际人权宣言（草案）》（第 E/CN.4/95 号文件）

第 3 条

张先生（中国）报告说，在第 53 次会议上任命的起草小组委员会商定了经最初修订的第 3 条第 2 款案文。

……

第 7 条

张先生（中国）接受印度-英国的草案（第 E/CN.4/99 号文件），但建议将其修改如下："每个人在确定对其的任何刑事指控或确定其权利和义务时都有权……"他解释说，他建议作出此改动，是因为委员会第二届会议通过的案文遵循的就是这个词序。

……

威尔逊先生（英国）接受中国代表关于从句换位的建议。

……

威尔逊先生（英国）觉得，中国-印度-英国的草案是最短的，与日内瓦案文相差最大。关于苏联对公约第 13 条的修正案的第一句话，在英国，法庭面前平等的概念是包含在法律面前平等的原则之中的。因此，他反对苏联的提案，认为它重复了前面已经阐述的原则。

张先生（中国）也认为，法律面前平等的原则和法庭面前平等的原则是同样的。

……

卡森先生（法国）呼吁尽可能就草案达成一致意见，并敦促委员会接受以下修正："每个人都有权完全平等地参加由一个独立且公正不倚的法庭组织的公正的听证会来裁定其权利……"

威尔逊先生（英国）不反对添加"独立且"，但觉得"完全平等地"这一表达是重复的，因此是不可取的。

张先生（中国）与英国代表有相同的看法。

......

主席将法国代表修改后的中国-印度-英国的草案进行投票表决。

修改后的中国-印度-英国的草案以 13 票同意、0 票反对、4 票弃权获得通过。

第 8 条

......

张先生（中国）指出，清晰且简明的第 3 款草案获得了普遍的认可。对于其他段落，可能会产生分歧，不是针对所涉及的原则，而是涉及其在目前语境下的适当性。他赞成保留第 1 款第 1 句，删除第 2 句，对第 3 和第 4 句不作表态。第 2 款可以删除，第 3 款保留。

......

——人权委员会第 54 次会议简要记录（E/CN. 4/SR. 54）

朱金荣译，常健校

E/CN.4/SR.54
10 June 1948

COMMISSION ON HUMAN RIGHTS
THIRD SESSION
SUMMARY RECORD OF THE FIFTY-FOURTH MEETING

Held at Lake Success, New York, on Tuesday, 1 June 1948, at 2:30 p.m.

Continuation of Consideration of Draft International Declaration on Human Rights (Document E/CN.4/95)

Article 3

Mr. Chang (China) reported that the drafting sub-committee appointed at the fifty-third meeting had agreed on the text of paragraph 2, Article 3 as originally amended.

...

Article 7

Mr. Chang (China) accepted the India-United Kingdom text (E/CN.4/99) but suggested that it should be changed as follows: "Everyone in the determination of any criminal charge against him and of his rights and obligations is entitled ..." He explained that he suggested the change because the text adopted at the second session of the Commission followed that order.

...

Mr. Wilson (United Kingdom) was ready to accept the Chinese representative's suggestion concerning the transposition of the clauses.

...

Mr. Wilson (United Kingdom) felt that the Chinese-Indian-United Kingdom draft, being the shortest, was farthest removed from the Geneva text. As regards the first sentence of the USSR amendment to Article 13 of the Covenant, in the United Kingdom the concept of equality before tribunals was included in the principle of equality before the law. He therefore opposed the USSR proposal as repetitious of previously stated principles.

Mr. Chang (China) also felt that the principles of equality before the law and before the tribunal were the same.

...

Mr. Cassin (France) appealing for the greatest possible measure of agreement on the text, urged the Commission to accept the following amendment:

"Everyone is entitled in full equality to a fair hearing by an independent and impartial tribunal in the determination of his rights..."

Mr. Wilson (United Kingdom) was not opposed to the addition of the words "independent and", but felt that the expression "in full equality" was repetitious, and therefore inadvisable.

Mr. Chang (China) shared the United Kingdom representative's opinion.

...

The Chairman put to the vote the Chinese-Indian-United Kingdom draft, as amended by the representative of France.

The Chinese-Indian-United Kingdom draft, as amended, was adopted by thirteen votes to none, with four abstentions.

...

Article 8

...

Mr. Chang (China) noted general agreement on the clear and simple drafting of paragraph 3. As regards the other paragraphs, disagreement might arise, not on the principles involved, but with regard to their appropriateness in the present context. He favoured retention of the first sentence of paragraph 1, deletion of the second sentence, and would abstain from voting on the third and fourth sentences. Paragraph 2 could be deleted, and paragraph 3 maintained.

...

在人权委员会第 55 次会议上的发言

1948 年 6 月 2 日星期三上午 11:00 纽约成功湖

继续审议起草委员会提交人权委员会的报告（第 E/CN.4/95 号文件）
审议宣言的条款和各代表团提出的修正案（第 E/CN.4/82/Add.8 号、第 E/CN.4/99 号、第 E/CN.4/102 号文件）

第 9 条

······

张先生（中国）提请注意，在中国代表团建议的案文中，第 9 条的措辞采取的是否定形式。"任何人不得受到无理干涉……"的措辞含蓄地申明了每个人都有权受到法律的保护，避免了由于在起草委员会案文中删除了"法律的"一词所可能导致的模糊不清。

此外他认为，中国代表团案文中各项规定的呈现顺序更符合逻辑，即从对个人的干涉开始，再到对其家庭、住宅、通信和声誉的干涉。

······

第 8 条

主席宣读了前一天专门成立的小组委员会起草的第 8 条草案，分发的草案文本如下：

"1. 任何人在被依法证明有罪之前（在他享有为其辩护所需的一切保障的公开审判中），都被推定为无罪。

2. 任何人的任何行为或不行为，在其发生时依国家法律或国际法均不构成犯罪时，不得被判有罪。"

张先生（中国）代表小组委员会解释说，"在他享有为其辩护所需的一切保障的公开审判中"这一表述被放在括号里，是表明小组委员会在这一问题上存在意见分歧。小组委员会仅就第 1 款的第一部分达成了一致。因此，他建议将括号内的从句付诸表决。

......

——人权委员会第 55 次会议简要记录（E/CN. 4/SR. 55）

朱金荣译，常健校

E/CN.4/SR.55
15 June 1948

COMMISSION ON HUMAN RIGHTS
THIRD SESSION
SUMMARY RECORD OF THE FIFTY-FIFTH MEETING
Held at Lake Success, New York, on Wednesday, 2 June 1948, at 11:00 a.m.

Continuation of the Consideration of the Report of the Drafting Committee to the Commission on Human Rights (Document E/CN.4/95);
Consideration of the Articles of the Declaration and the Amendments Presented by Various Delegations (Documents E/CN.4/82/Add.8; E/CN.4/99; E/CN.4/102)

Article 9

…

Mr. Chang (China) drew attention to the negative form in which article 9 was worded in the text proposed by his delegation. The wording "No one shall be subjected to unreasonable interference..." affirmed implicitly everyone's right to protection under the law and avoided the ambiguity which might arise as a result of the deletion of the words "under the law" from the Drafting Committee's text.

He thought, moreover, that the order of presentation of the provisions was more logical in his delegation's text beginning as it did with interference with the individual and from there going on to cover interference with his family, home, correspondence and reputation.

...

Article 8

The Chairman read the draft of article 8 prepared by the Sub-Committee set up for the purpose on the previous day, the text of which had just been distributed:

"1. Everyone is presumed to be innocent until proved guilty according to law (in a public trial at which he has had all guarantees necessary for his defence).

2. No one shall be held guilty of any offence on account of any act or omission which did not constitute an offence, under national or international law, at the time when it was committed."

Mr. Chang (China) explained on behalf of the Sub-Committee that the phrase "in a public trial at which he has had all guarantees necessary for his defence" had been placed in brackets to indicate that there had been a difference of opinion on the subject in the Sub-Committee. The Sub-Committee reached a unanimous decision with regard to the first part of paragraph 1 only. He therefore suggested that first the clause in brackets be put to the vote.

...

在人权委员会第 56 次会议上的发言

1948 年 6 月 2 日星期三下午 2:30 纽约成功湖

继续讨论人权宣言草案（E/CN.4/95 号文件）

第 8 条第 1 款

主席宣读起草小组委员会起草的下列案文：

"每一个被控刑事犯罪者，在他享有为其辩护所需的一切保障的审判中被证明有罪之前，应被推定为无罪。审判应公开进行，除根据公共道德或安全的利益认定的例外情况。"

张先生（中国）提议将小组委员会的案文改为：

"每一个被控刑事犯罪者，在依据法律被证明有罪之前，应被推定为无罪。"

"依据法律"一词在英文译文中被无意地遗漏了。

……

第 11 条（第 E/CN.4/104 号、第 E/CN.4/102 号、第 E/CN.4/99 号、第 E/CN.4/97 号文件）

森德女士（美国劳工联合会）对起草小组建议的措辞感到极不满意。"可以获得庇护"这一表述的含糊性，使该条款失去了任何实际价值。

……

在回答主席的问题时，张博士（中国）同意将其提案修改如下："人人有权在其他国家寻求并获得临时庇护，以免遭受迫害。"

……

张博士（中国）说，第 11 条处理的是使难民免受迫害的问题，因此不会牵涉到在中国的日本战犯问题。

……

——人权委员会第 56 次会议简要记录（E/CN.4/SR.56）

朱金荣译，常健校

E/CN.4/SR.56
4 June 1948

COMMISSION ON HUMAN RIGHTS
THIRD SESSION
SUMMARY RECORD OF THE FIFTY-SIXTH MEETING
Held at Lake Success, New York, Wednesday, 2 June 1948, at 2:30 p.m.

Continuation of the Discussion of the Draft Declaration of Human Rights
(Document E/CN.4/95)

Article 8, Paragraph 1

The Chairman read out the following text prepared by the drafting sub-committee:

"Everyone charged with a penal offence is presumed to be innocent until proved guilty in a trial at which he will have had all the guarantees necessary to his defence. Trials shall be public subject to exceptions made in the interests of public morals or security."

Mr. Chang (China) proposed to replace the sub-committee's text by the following:

"Everyone charged with a penal offence is presumed to be innocent until proved guilty according to law."

The phrase "according to law" had been inadvertently omitted in the English translation.

...

Article 11 (Documents E/CN.4/104, E/CN.4/102, E/CN.4/99, E/CN.4/97)

Miss Sender (American Federation of Labor) felt that the wording proposed by the drafting group was highly unsatisfactory. The permissive character of the phrase "may be granted asylum" deprived the article of any real value.

....

In reply to the Chairman, Dr. Chang (China) agreed to amend his proposal to read as follows: "Everyone has a right to seek and shall be granted temporary asylum from persecution in other countries."

...

Dr. Chang (China) said that the question of Japanese war criminals in China did not arise, because article 11 dealt with refugees from persecution.

...

在人权委员会第 57 次会议上的发言

1948 年 6 月 3 日星期四上午 10:45 纽约成功湖

第 11 条——继续审议

主席指出，起草小组委员会草拟了第 11 条第 1 款的下列两个版本，二者仅略有不同。

1. "基于人道要求，人人有权在其他国家寻求和获得庇护，以免遭受迫害。"

2. 人人有权在其他国家寻求并获得基于人道要求使其免遭迫害的庇护。"

······

马利克先生（黎巴嫩）希望知道第 1 款的两个拟议案文之间是否有任何实质上的差异。如果没有，那么他更喜欢第二个版本的风格。"基于人道要求"这一短语似乎非常宽泛和模糊；因此，他建议对这一限定短语单独进行表决。他希望删除该条款，代之以先前被拒绝的法国建议案，即委托联合国来处理庇护问题。如果可以的话，他准备提议重新审议该建议案。

······

勒博先生（比利时）与黎巴嫩代表有同感，对先前法国修正案遭到拒绝感到遗憾。他希望表明，对一位不熟悉的读者来说，其与英国代表的看法相反，第 1 款的两个备选版本之间存在本质性差别。在法文文本中，第一个版本意味着给予庇护要根据有关国家的人道主义考量，而第二个版本则确定了庇护的一般哲学概念。他喜欢第一个版本，并提议修改如下："人人有权在其他国家寻求和获得庇护，以免遭受迫害。"

······

张先生（中国）同意比利时代表对两个版本的解释，强调在这一问题上文本的明确而无歧义最为重要。第一个版本的确赋予移入国在给予庇护方面的一定控制权。中国原先的修正案包括了各国控制移民的权利。他支持已被拒绝的法国建议案，因为事实上安理会正在审议一个类似的问题。

如果没有可能恢复这一建议案，人权委员会可以表明考虑由一个联合国机构处理这一问题。他同意黎巴嫩代表的意见，即资格条款含糊不清，未能在给予庇护的国家和寻求庇护的人的权利之间达成妥协。人权委员会应明确和坦率地说明各国是否可以控制对庇护的给予。如果没有列入资格条款，可能会产生一个问题，即各国是否有义务在收到庇护要求时给予庇护。有两种可能性：人权委员会可以接受没有保留条款的第一版，在这种情况下，最好回到法国的提案，或者至少记录在案，法国的提案是解决问题的最理想的办法；或者人权委员会应该明确地让各国决定是否给予庇护。第一个备选方案应首先付诸表决，因为它与起草委员会案文的差距最大。

主席在提到中国代表的发言时解释说，人权委员会对法国提案采取的行动是基于这样一个事实，即经济及社会理事会要求对国籍问题进行单独研究，其中可能包括庇护问题。她还指出，起草小组委员会引入了资格条款，部分原因是中国代表指出了寻求和获得庇护作为无条件权利的危险。这样的规定可能会使许多国家无法作出这样的承诺，从而无法批准该公约。

……

在有卡森先生（法国）、张先生（中国）、胡德先生（澳大利亚）和威尔逊先生（英国）参加的简短讨论之后，主席将第 11 条第 1 款的修正案付诸表决。

人权委员会以 12 票对 1 票、4 票弃权通过了第 1 款的以下版本："每个人都有权在其他国家寻求和获得庇护，免受迫害。"

会议于下午 1:20 结束。

——人权委员会第 57 次会议简要记录（E/CN.4/SR.57）

朱金荣、常健译，常健校

E/CN.4/SR.57

7 June 1948

COMMISSION ON HUMAN RIGHTS
THIRD SESSION
SUMMARY RECORD OF THE FIFTY-SEVENTH MEETING

Held at Lake Success, New York, on Thursday, 3 June 1948, at 10:45 a.m.

Article 11-Continuation of consideration.

The Chairman pointed out that the drafting sub-committee had prepared the two following versions of article 11, paragraph 1, which differed only slightly from each other.

1. "Everyone has the right to seek and be granted in other countries asylum from persecution as humanity requires."

2. Everyone has the right to seek and be granted in other countries such asylum from persecution as humanity requires."

...

Mr. Malik (Lebanon) wished to know whether there was any difference of substance between the two proposed versions of paragraph 1. If not, then he would prefer the better style of the second version. The phrase "as humanity requires" seemed very broad and vague; he therefore suggested that a separate vote should be taken on that qualification clause which he would rather see deleted and replaced by the previously rejected French proposal to entrust the United Nations with the problem of asylum. He was prepared, if in order, to propose reconsideration of that proposal.

...

Mr. Lebeau (Belgium) shared the Lebanese representative's regrets at the previous rejection of the French amendment. He wished to show that to an uninitiated reader, contrary to the United Kingdom representative's view of the matter, there was a substantial difference between the two alternative versions of paragraph 1. In the French text, the first version implied granting of asylum subject to the humanitarian considerations of the country concerned, while the second version laid down the general philosophical concept of asylum. He favoured the first version with the following amendment: "Everyone has the right to seek and be granted in other countries asylum from persecution."

...

Mr. Chang (China), agreeing with the Belgian representative's interpretation of the two versions, noted the importance of a clear and unambiguous text on the matter. It was true that the first version gave the country of immigration certain control over the granting of asylum. The original Chinese amendment had included that right of states to control immigration. He supported the French proposal which had been rejected in view of the fact that a similar question was under consideration by the Council. Should it be impossible to revert to that proposal, the Commission might go on record as considering that a United Nations organ should deal with that problem. He agreed with the representative of Lebanon regarding the vagueness of the qualification clause which could not be a compromise between the rights of states granting, and persons seeking, asylum. The Commission should state clearly and frankly whether or not countries had control over the granting of asylum. If no qualification clause was included, the question might arise whether countries were obliged to grant asylum whenever asked for it. There were two possibilities, the Commission could either accept the first version without the qualification clause, and in that case it would be well to revert to the French proposal or at least go on record that the French proposal constituted the most desirable solution to the problem; or the Commission should clearly leave it to countries to decide whether they would grant asylum. The first alternative should be put to the vote first as being farthest removed from the Drafting Committee's text.

The Chairman, referring to the Chinese representative's remarks, explained that the Commission's action with regard to the French proposal had been based on the fact that the Council had called for a separate study of the question of nationality which would probably include the problem of asylum. She also pointed out that the qualification clause had been introduced by the drafting sub-committee partly because the Chinese representative had indicated the danger of an unqualified right of persons to seek and be granted asylum. Such a provision might keep many countries unable to make such a commitment from ratifying the Convention.

　　…

After a short discussion in which Mr. Cassin (France), Mr. Chang (China), Mr. Hood (Australia) and Mr. Wilson (United Kingdom) took part, the Chairman put the amended version of paragraph 1, article 11 to the vote.

The Commission adopted by twelve votes to one with four abstention, the following version of paragraph 1: "Everyone has the right to seek and be granted in other countries asylum from persecution".

The meeting rose at 1:20 p.m.

在人权委员会第58次会议上的发言

1948 年 6 月 3 日星期四下午 2:30 纽约成功湖

继续审查起草委员会提交人权委员会的报告（第 E/CN.4/95 号文件）

第 12 条

......

卡森先生（法国）指出了将"droits civils fondamentaux"这一短语翻译成英语的困难。英文对应的表达是指作为整体的人权——基本自由。在法国法律以及所有以罗马法为基础的法律中，"droits civils fondamentaux"被理解为由规范私人关系的法律所保护的所有权利。因此，他建议"droits civils fondamentaux"应翻译为"fundamental rights in domestic relations"（家庭关系中的基本权利）。这不是字对字的翻译，但是更为准确。

......

主席以美国代表的身份发言说，第 12 条目前形式的含义在盎格鲁-撒克逊法中还不够明确，其代表团无法接受。

......

针对主席的建议，卡森先生（法国）同意，如果"fundamental private rights"（基本私权）似乎更容易为讲英语的代表团所接受，那么将"droits civils fondamentaux"这一短语修改为"droits privés fondamentaux"。

勒博先生（比利时）无法相信盎格鲁-撒克逊的法律术语不能表达罗马法中的"civil rights"（公民权利）这一概念。

......

张先生（中国）指出，中国的法律也没有明确定义这一概念。

......

第 13 条

主席宣读由起草委员会起草的第 13 条案文，以及由英国和印度代表团（E/CN.4/99 号文件）、比利时代表团（3/CN.4/103 号文件）和黎巴嫩代表团（E/CN.4/105 号文件）提交的修正案。她回顾道，中国代表团倾向于不在宣言中写入这一条款。

主席以美国代表的身份指出，美国代表团坚决赞成通过由英国和印度代表团提交的案文，她认为该案文不仅包括了缔结婚姻的权利，而且包括了解除婚姻的权利。

……

张先生（中国）指出，中国代表团将投票赞成最简洁的文本，即由印度和英国代表团建议的文本。

……

张先生（中国）正式提议暂停讨论。

……

——人权委员会第 58 次会议简要记录（E/CN.4/SR.58）

朱金荣译，常健校

E/CN.4/SR.58
16 June 1948

COMMISSION ON HUMAN RIGHTS
THIRD SESSION
SUMMARY RECORD OF THE FIFTY-EIGHTH MEETING

Lake Success, New York, Thursday, 3 June 1948, at 2:30 p.m.

Continuation of the Examination of the Report of the Drafting Committee to the Commission on Human Rights (Document E/CN.4/95)

Article 12

…

Mr. Cassin (France) pointed out the difficulty of translating the term "droits civils fondamentaux" into English. The corresponding expression in English meant human rights as a whole—the fundamental liberties. In French law, and generally in all legislation based on Roman Law, "droits civils fondamentaux" were understood as all the rights protected by laws governing private relations. He therefore suggested that "droits civils fondamentaux" should be translated by "fundamental rights in domestic relations". Such a translation would not be literal, but it would be accurate.

...

The Chairman, speaking as representative of the United States of America, said that the meaning of Article 12 in its present form was not sufficiently precise in Anglo-Saxon law for her delegation to accept it.

...

On the Chairman's suggestion, Mr. Cassin (France) agreed to amend the term "droits civils fondamentaux" to read "droits privés fondamentaux", if "fundamental private rights" seemed more acceptable to the English speaking delegations.

Mr. Lebeau (Belgium) was unable to believe that Anglo-Saxon legal terminology could not express the Roman concept of "civil rights".

...

Mr. Chang (China) stated that the law of his country, too, did not clearly define the concept.

...

Article 13

The Chairman read out the text of Article 13 proposed by the Drafting Committee and the amendments submitted by the United Kingdom and Indian delegations (document E/CN.4/99), the Belgian delegation (document 3/CN.4/103) and the Lebanese delegation (document E/CN.4/105). She recalled that the Chinese delegation would prefer not to include such a provision in the Declaration.

Speaking as representative of the United States of America, the Chairman stated that her delegation was strongly in favour of adopting the text submitted by the United Kingdom and Indian delegations, which she understood to cover not only the right to contract marriage but also the right to dissolve it.

　　…

　　Mr. Chang (China) stated his delegation would vote in favour of the most concise text, namely, that proposed by the delegations of India and the United Kingdom.

　　…

　　Mr. Chang (China) formally proposed the adjournment of the discussion.

　　…

在人权委员会第 59 次会议上的发言

1948 年 6 月 4 日星期五上午 10:45 纽约成功湖

继续讨论人权宣言草案（第 E/CN.4/95 号文件）

......

第 15 条

......

张先生（中国）支持第 15 条的英国文案（第 E/CN.4/99 号文件）。

......

——人权委员会第 59 次会议简要记录（E/CN.4/SR.59）

常健译校

E/CN.4/SR.59
10 June 1948

COMMISSION ON HUMAN RIGHTS
THIRD SESSION
SUMMARY RECORD OF THE FIFTY-NINTH MEETING

Lake Success, New York, Friday, 4 June 1948, at 10:45 a.m.

Continuation of the Discussion on the Draft Declaration of Human Rights (Document E/CN.4/95)

...

Article 15

...

Mr. Chang (China) supported the United Kingdom text of article 15 (document E/CN.4/99).

...

在人权委员会第 60 次会议上的发言

1948 年 6 月 4 日星期五下午 3:00 纽约成功湖

继续讨论人权宣言草案第 15 条（第 E/CN.4/95、E/CN.4/99 和 E/CN.4/102 号文件）

第 15 条（续）

卡森先生（法国）指出，委员会通过了印度和英国对第 15 条的修正案，但尚未就日内瓦会议期间通过的、由起草委员会重新提交的并在法国修正案中再次提及的案文作出任何决定，即"人人有权获得国籍"这句话。他不想质疑委员会关于印度和英国修正案的决定，但认为起草委员会案文中的第 15 条应在讨论下一条之前付诸表决。

……

张先生（中国）不反对法国代表的表决请求，但担心写入他提议的措辞会出现重复。

……

第 16 条

……

主席指出，委员会可以首先就中国的修正案进行表决，该修正案似乎是最深远的。

张先生（中国）指出，中国的修正案同时适用于第 16、17、18 和 19 条，建议不应在现阶段予以审议。

巴甫洛夫先生（苏联）说，苏联的修正案是中国提议的案文与起草委员会案文之间的折中，前者过于简单，后者过于冗长。

……

马利克先生（黎巴嫩）（报告员）同意在其案文中提及思想自由权，并将其修正案分为如下两款：

"人人有权享有宗教、良心、信仰和思想自由，包括改变其宗教或信仰的自由。"

"人人有权享有单独或在与其他有同样精神的人组成的共同体中，通过公开或私下的方式，以教义、实践、礼拜和戒律来表明其宗教或信仰的自由。"

……

张先生（中国）倾向于后一种修正。第 16 条应只涉及保护宗教和信仰自由；保护思想自由在第 17 条和第 18 条中处理。

他建议将"单独或在与其他有同样精神的人组成的共同体中"改为"和他人一起"。

他将投票赞成印度和英国的修正案。

……

洛佩兹先生（菲律宾）赞成在第 16 条而不是第 17 条中提及思想自由权，第 17 条是要保障言论自由。

此外，由于第 16 条主要是保护宗教自由，他认为该条中列举自由的逻辑顺序应当是"宗教、良心、思想和信仰自由"——思想自由应该放在宗教和良心自由之后。

张先生（中国）表示赞同，他认为根据欧洲的观念，思想自由是信仰自由的基础。信仰虽然隐含着思想，但在历史进程中，思想自由实际上先于信仰自由。但享有这些自由的权利意味着也享有改变它们的权利。因此，他建议简单地写成"思想、宗教和信仰自由的权利"。

……

——人权委员会第 60 次会议简要记录（E/CN.4/SR.60）

朱金荣译，常健校

E/CN.4/SR.60
23 June 1948

COMMISSION ON HUMAN RIGHTS
THIRD SESSION
SUMMARY RECORD OF THE SIXTIETH MEETING

Lake Success, New York, Friday, 4 June 1948, at 3:00 p.m.

Continuation of the Discussion of Article 15 of the Draft Declaration on Human Rights (Documents E/CN.4/95, E/CN.4/99, E/CN.4/102)

Article 15 (Continued)

Mr. Cassin (France) pointed out that the Commission had adopted the Indian and United Kingdom amendment to article 15, but had not yet taken any decision on the text adopted during the session at Geneva, re-submitted by the Drafting Committee and taken up again in the French amendment, namely the sentence: "Everyone has the right to a nationality." He did not wish to question the Commission's decision on the Indian and United Kingdom amendment, but thought that article 15 of the Drafting Committee's text should be put to the vote before the next article was discussed.

...

Mr. Chang (China) did not oppose the French representative's request for a vote, but feared that the inclusion of the words he proposed would amount to a repetition.

...

Article 16

...

The Chairman said the Commission could begin by voting on the Chinese amendment, which seemed to be the most far-reaching.

Mr. Chang (China) pointed out that the Chinese amendment applied simultaneously to articles 16, 17, 18 and 19, and suggested that it should not be considered at present.

Mr. Pavlov (Union of Soviet Socialist Republics) said that the USSR amendment was a compromise between the Chinese text, which was an over-simplification, and the Drafting Committee's text, which was too long.

...

Mr. Malik (Lebanon) (Rapporteur) agreed to insert in his text a mention of the right to freedom of thought, and to divide his amendment into two paragraphs as follows:

"Everyone has the right to freedom of religion, conscience, belief and thought, including freedom to change his religion or belief."

"Everyone has the right to freedom, either alone or in community with other persons of like mind, and in public or private, to manifest his religion or belief in teaching, practice, worship and observance."

...

Mr. Chang (China) preferred the latter amendment. Article 16 should treat only of the protection of freedom of religion and belief; the protection of freedom of thought was dealt with in Articles 17 and 18.

He suggested replacing "either alone or in community with other persons of like mind" by "with others".

He would vote for the Indian and United Kingdom amendment.

...

Mr. Lopez (Philippines) was in favour of mentioning the right to freedom of thought in Article 16, and not in Article 17, which was intended to guarantee freedom of expression.

Moreover, since Article 16 was intended essentially to protect religious freedom, the logical order in which the freedoms should be enumerated in that article were, in his opinion, "freedom of religion, of conscience, of thought and of belief", freedom of thought thus following freedom of religion and conscience.

Mr. Chang (China) agreed that according to European ideas freedom of thought was the basis of freedom of belief. Although belief implied thought, freedom of thought had in the course of history actually preceded freedom of belief. But the right to those freedoms implied the right to change them. He therefore suggested simply saying: "the right to freedom of thought, religion and belief".

...

在人权委员会第 61 次会议上的发言

1948 年 6 月 7 日星期一上午 11:00 纽约成功湖

继续审议起草委员会的报告（第 E/CN.4/95 号文件）

……

第 19 条

主席宣读起草委员会建议的第 19 条案文（第 E/CN.4/95 号文件）和中国代表团建议的备选案文（第 E/CN.4/102 号文件）、法国代表团建议的备选案文（第 E/CN.4/88/Add.8 号文件）以及英国和印度代表团建议的备选案文（第 E/CN.4/99 号文件）。

张先生（中国）说，在研究了被提交的不同提案之后，他希望强调，中国代表团草案的优点是既完整又简洁。

印度和英国代表团提出的联合案文在中国的提案中加入了起草委员会案文中的一个条件："为了促进、防卫和保护等……"。这一相当长的保留似乎没有必要，因为民主社会的普遍利益是这份拟议宣言的一贯目的。

起草委员会的案文还列举了个人有权加入的各种社团。但任何列举都是危险的。例如，有人可能认为，宗教协会与工会组织有同样的权利被写入第 19 条。他不明白为什么后者比前者更应该被提及。第 19 条的目的应该是给予每个人组织或加入任何社团的自由，但前提是这是在民主利益的框架内进行的。中国代表团提倡的简化草案最能实现这一目的。

方泰纳先生（乌拉圭）赞同中国代表的发言。人权委员会的任务是确立结社权和集会权。对宣布该权利作出的任何补充都将构成对它的限制。

特别是美国的修正案提出了一个有些奇怪的限制，因为它只提到了一种类型的结社。

乌拉圭代表团将投票支持中国代表团提出的案文。

洛佩兹先生（菲律宾）说，菲律宾代表团认为中国案文不仅最简单，而且最令人满意。限制集会和结社自由的理由，莫过于宗教自由或言论自由；然而，第 17 条和第 18 条没有这类规定，菲律宾代表团认为唯一可取的限制是宣言第 2 条所载的一般性保留。

......

主席将中国提出的备选案文（E/CN.4/102 号文件）付诸表决。

关于第 19 条的中国草案以 7 票对 4 票、3 票弃权获得通过。

......

第 21 条和第 22 条

主席宣读起草委员会提出的第 21 条和第 22 条草案（第 E/CN.4/95 号文件），以及法国代表团提出的草案（第 E/CN.4/82/Add.8 号文件）、印度和英国代表团提出的草案（第 E/CN.4/99 号文件）与中国代表团提出的草案（第 E/CN.4/102 号文件）。

张先生（中国）撤回其修正案，并表示中国代表团赞赏并接受印度和英国代表团的措辞。

......

方泰纳先生（乌拉圭）支持法国代表关于在宣言中提及国家对个人之义务具有重要意义的评论。

他还指出，担任公职的概念和参与政府管理工作的概念是不同的。因此，他建议将印度和英国的案文修改如下："人人有权担任公职并直接或通过其自由选出的代表参与本国的政府管理工作。"

......

张先生（中国）建议，在英文案文中恢复起草委员会的措辞，即改为"获得公共就业机会"。

主席请中国、印度和英国代表一起拟定一个表述，供人权委员会在下次会议上进行表决。

会议于下午 1:15 结束。

——人权委员会第 61 次会议简要记录（E/CN.4/SR.61）

朱金荣、常健译，常健校

E/CN.4/SR.61
23 June 1948

COMMISSION ON HUMAN RIGHTS
THIRD SESSION
SUMMARY RECORD OF THE SIXTY-FIRST MEETING

Held at Lake Success, New York, on Monday, 7 June 1948, at 11:00 a.m.

Continuation of Consideration of the Report of the Drafting Committee (Document E/CN.4/95)

...

Article 19

The Chairman read the text proposed by the Drafting Committee for article 19 (document E/CN.4/95) and the alternative text proposed by the Chinese delegation (document E/CN.4/102), the French delegation (document E/CN.4/88/Add.8) and the United Kingdom and Indian delegations (document E/CN.4/99).

...

Mr. Chang (China) said that after studying the different proposals submitted, he wished to stress that his delegation's draft had the advantage of being both complete and concise.

The Joint text proposed by the delegations of India and the United Kingdom added to the Chinese proposal a condition taken from the Drafting Committee's text: "for the promotion, defence and protection etc..." That rather long reservation did not seem necessary, for the general interest of the democratic societies was the constant aim of the proposed Declaration.

The Drafting Committee's text enumerated moreover the kinds of associations to which a person had a right to belong. But any enumeration was dangerous. It might be argued that religious associations, for example, had the same right to be included in article 19 as trade union organizations. He did not see why the latter should be mentioned any more than the former. The purpose of article 19 should be to grant to every one freedom to organize or join any association provided only that that was done within the framework of democratic interests. The simplified draft advocated by the Chinese delegation best fulfilled that purpose.

Mr. Fontaina (Uruguay) associated himself with the remarks made by the Chinese representative. The Commission's task was to establish the right of association and of assembly. Anything added to the declaration of that right would amount to a limitation.

The amendment proposed by the United States of America in particular, was a somewhat peculiar limitation, as it mentioned only one type of association.

The uruguayan delegation would vote for the text proposed by the Chinese delegation.

Mr. Lopez (Philippines) said his delegation considered the Chinese text not only the simplest but the most satisfactory. There was no more reason to limit freedom of assembly and of association than religious freedom or freedom of expression; yet articles 17 and 18 contained no provisions of that sort. The only limitation which the Philippine delegation considered desirable was the general reservation contained in article 2 of the Declaration.

...

The Chairman put to the vote the variant proposed by China (document E/CN.4/102).

The Chinese draft for article 19 was adopted by seven votes to four with three abstentions.

...

Articles 21 and 22

The Chairman read out the drafts proposed by the Drafting Committee for article 21 and 22 (document E/CN.4/95) and the variants proposed by the French delegation (document E/CN.4/82/Add.8), the Indian and United Kingdom delegations (document E/CN.4/99) and the Chinese delegation (document E/CN.4/102).

Mr. Chang (China) withdrew his amendment and said the Chinese delegation preferred and accepted the wording proposed by the Indian and United Kingdom delegations.

...

Mr. Fontaina (Uruguay) supported the remarks made by the French representative on the importance of mentioning the duties of the State to the individual in the Declaration.

He would also point out that there was a difference between the notions of access to public office and participation in the government, and he suggested, amending the Indian and United Kingdom text as follows: "Everyone has the right to access to public office and to take part in the government of his country directly or through his freely chosen representatives."

...

Mr. Chang (China) proposed, as regards the English text, to revert to the Drafting Committee's wording and say "access to public employment".

The Chairman asked the representatives of China, India and of the United Kingdom to work out a formula on which the Commission would vote at its next meeting.

The meeting rose at 1:15 p.m.

在人权委员会第 62 次会议上的发言

1948 年 6 月 7 日星期一下午 2:30 纽约成功湖

审议起草委员会提交的《国际人权宣言（草案）》（第 E/CN.4/95 号文件附件 A）

第 21 和 22 条

……

张先生（中国）提出，考虑到宣言的总体结构，更简单的形式是否更可接受。他提出了一些简单的表达，诸如"政府应顺应民意"。

胡德（澳大利亚）支持中国代表的意见。委员会可能在审议第 21 条时进展得太快，应该在宣言的某处写入提及民意的内容。他希望比中国代表更进一步，建议委员会重新审议第 21 条，在该条第 1 句的末尾处加入如下表述："……人人有权担任公职并直接或通过自由选择的代表参与本国的政府管理工作，以使政府顺应民意。"

……

在简短的讨论中，张先生（中国）指出，如果该案文作为一条条款被否决，在讨论序言时，各成员仍有权重新提出它。随后，方泰纳先生（乌拉圭）撤回了他的建议。

……

——人权委员会第 62 次会议简要记录（E/CN.4/SR.62）

朱金荣译，常健校

E/CN.4/SR.62
11 June 1948

COMMISSION ON HUMAN RIGHTS
THIRD SESSION

SUMMARY RECORD OF THE SIXTY-SECOND MEETING

Held at Lake Success, New York, on Monday, 7 June 1948, at 2:30 p.m.

Consideration of Draft International Declaration on Human Rights, Submitted by the Drafting Committee (Annex A of Document E/CN.4/95)

Articles 21 and 22

...

Mr. Chang (China) wondered whether a simplified form would be acceptable, taking into consideration the general structure of the Declaration. He proposed some such simple formula as "The Government shall conform to the will of the people".

Mr. Hood (Australia) supported the representative of China. It was possible that the Commission had proceeded too rapidly in its consideration of Article 21 and that some mention of the will of the people should be included somewhere in the declaration. He would go even further than the Chinese representative, and would suggest that the Commission might go back to Article 21 with a view to including that phrase at the end of the first sentence, along the following lines: "... freely chosen representatives, to the end that the Government shall conform to the will of the people."

...

After a short discussion, in which Mr. Chang (China) pointed out that if the text was rejected as an article, members would still have the right to reintroduce it when the Preamble was discussed, Mr. Fontaina (Uruguay) withdrew his suggestion.

...

在人权委员会第 63 次会议上的发言

1948 年 6 月 8 日星期二上午 10:45 纽约成功湖

第 17 条和第 18 条

主席指出，起草委员会已将联合国新闻自由会议通过的第 17 条和第 18 条案文转交委员会。法国、中国和苏联对该案文提出了修正案（第 E/CN.4/82/Add.8 号、第 E/CN.4/102 号和第 E/CN.4/95 号文件）。然后，她开始主持讨论苏联的修正案，将其作为与日内瓦草案差异最大的案文。

……

主席以美国代表的身份发言说，她支持联合国新闻自由会议提交的措辞。

张先生（中国）也支持联合国新闻自由会议提交的案文，但提出，鉴于先前已商定将日内瓦草案第一句中的"思想"一词替换为"意见"，该条可以重新措辞如下："人人有权享有主张和发表意见的自由。此项权利包括不分国界和不受干涉地寻求、接收和传递信息和观点的自由。"日内瓦案文中第三行的"以任何方式"这一表达似乎是多余的。然而，他不会反对写入这样一个概念，但建议将这几个词改为："通过所有表达媒介"。

……

对于中国代表提出的这一修改建议，威尔逊先生（英国）指出，将联合国新闻自由会议案文第一行中的"思想"一词改为"意见"，仅仅是前一条修改的逻辑后果。他也愿意接受用"通过所有表达媒介"的措辞来替换"以任何方式"这种草案变更，以便澄清原来措辞中可能模棱两可的含义。但是，他希望委员会明白所受到的约束，不要引入任何新的观念或剔除案文中已经包含的任何观点。

……

胡德先生（澳大利亚）同意英国代表的意见，即委员会不应对所提交的案文作出任何实质性改动。但是，他赞同中国提出措辞修改，认为将第一行中的"思想"一词替换为"意见"一词所带来的草案变更是必要且适当的。

张先生（中国）并不认为联合国新闻自由会议的建议必然对委员会具有约束力，但他同意对该会议案文中的重要观点应予保留。但是，如果意见自由已经在第一行中被提到，第二行中保留"持有意见"这一短语似乎就多余了。

马利克先生（黎巴嫩）指出，会议案文的第一个从句是一般性的原则陈述，第二个从句对其作出了解释。如果"持有意见"这一短语被省略，那么在第一个从句中所阐述的享有该权利的部分过程就会缺失。因此，在第二部分保留这一短语并非多余。他准备接受用"通过所有表达媒介"来替代"以任何方式"。

洛佩兹先生（菲律宾）指出，传递信息的自由必然意味着持有意见的自由，因此他支持中国代表的建议，省略第二行的"持有意见"。他也赞同将第一行中的"思想"改为"意见"，以及将"不受干涉"放在"不分国界"之前，因为这两个短语放在一起会构成一个更和谐且更符合逻辑的陈述。

……

张先生（中国）建议黎巴嫩、菲律宾、英国和中国的代表为下午的会议起草一份委员会可以接受的案文。

主席要求按照中国的建议执行。

会议于下午 1:00 结束。

——人权委员会第 63 次会议简要记录（E/CN.4/SR.63）

朱金荣译，常健校

E/CN.4/SR.63
22 June 1948

COMMISSION ON HUMAN RIGHTS
THIRD SESSION
SUMMARY RECORD OF THE SIXTY-THIRD MEETING
Held at Lake Success, New York, on Tuesday, 8 June 1948, at 10:45 a.m.

Articles 17 and 18

The Chairman pointed out that the Drafting Committee had transmitted to the Commission the text of articles 17 and 18 as adopted by the United Nations Conference on Freedom of Information. Amendments to that text had been presented by France, China and the Union of Soviet Socialist Republics (documents E/CN.4/82/Add.8, E/CN.4/102, and E/CN.4/95). She then opened discussion of the USSR amendment as the most removed text from the Geneva draft.

...

The Chairman, as representative of the United States of America, stated that she supported the wording submitted by the United Nations Conference on Freedom of Information.

Mr. Chang (China) also supported the text submitted by the United Nations Conference on Freedom of Information, but proposed, in view of the previously agreed substitution of the word "opinion" for the word "thought" in the first line of the Geneva text, the following re-arrangement of the article: "Everyone shall have the right to freedom of opinion and expression; this right shall include freedom to seek, receive and impart information and ideas without interference and regardless of frontiers." The word "by any means" in the third line of the Geneva text seemed superfluous. He would not oppose, however, the inclusion of such an idea, but suggested that the words should be changed to: "through all media of expression".

...

Referring to certain Chinese amendments, Mr. Wilson (United Kingdom) pointed out that changing the word "thought" to the word "opinion" in the first line of the Conference text, was merely a logical result of changes that had been made in the previous article. He was also willing to accept as a drafting change the substitution of the words "through all media of expression" for "by any means", in order to clarify a meaning which might have been ambiguous in the original wording. He hoped, however, that the Commission would feel bound not to introduce any new ideas or to exclude any ideas which were already contained in the text.

...

Mr. Hood (Australia) agreed with the United Kingdom representative that the Commission should not make any substantive changes in the text submitted. However, he approved the Chinese wording as a necessary and proper drafting change resulting from the substitution of the word "opinion" for the word "thought" in the first line.

Mr. Chang (China) did not think that the suggestions of the Conference on the Freedom of Information were necessarily binding on the Commission but he agreed that the important ideas in the Conference text should be retained. It seemed redundant, however, to keep the phrase "to hold opinions" in the second line, if freedom of opinion had already been mentioned in the first line.

Mr. Malik (Lebanon) pointed out that the first clause of the Conference text was a general statement of principle, which was explained in the second clause. If the phrase "to hold opinions" were omitted, then part of the process of enjoying the right stated in the first clause, would be missing. It was not, therefore, redundant to retain the phrase in the second part. He was prepared to accept the substitution of "through all media of expression" for "by any means".

Mr. Lopez (Philippines) observed that freedom to impart information necessarily implied freedom to hold opinions and he therefore supported the Chinese suggestion to omit "to hold opinions" in the second line. He also favoured changing "thought" to "opinion" in the first line and placing the phrase "without interference" before "regardless of frontiers", as the two phrases taken together would make for a more harmonious and logical statement.

...

Mr. Chang (China) suggested that the representatives of Lebanon, Philippines, the United Kingdom and China should try to prepare for the afternoon meeting a text that would be acceptable to the Commission.

The Chairman stated that the Chinese suggestion would be followed.

The meeting rose at 1:00 p.m.

在人权委员会第 64 次会议上的发言

1948 年 6 月 8 日星期二下午 2:30 纽约成功湖

继续审议人权宣言条款

第 17 条和第 18 条（继续）

主席请中国代表介绍起草小组委员会关于第 17 条和第 16 条的结论。

张先生（中国）说，起草小组委员会并不打算改变这些条款的实质内容，仅限于对草案提出几处小的修改建议：将第二行中的"意见自由"改为"思想自由"，将英语译本中的"任何方式"改为"任何媒介"。

……

张先生（中国）回顾说，中国代表团曾建议将第二条放在宣言的末尾。此外，大多数成员显然都赞成重新审议该条款，但他认为，在知晓将以何种方式修改该条款之前就对是否重新审议进行投票表决，这是不适当的。因此，他建议委员会仅在会议记录中提及这两项建议。

第 23 和第 24 条

……

张先生（中国）认为，应该接下来审议中国提交的案文，因为它体现了一种关于应当如何起草宣言的不同概念。

……

——人权委员会第 64 次会议简要记录（E/CN.4/SR.64）

朱金荣译，常健校

E/CN.4/SR.64
17 June 1948

COMMISSION ON HUMAN RIGHTS

THIRD SESSION
SUMMARY RECORD OF THE SIXTY-FOURTH MEETING

Held at Lake Success, New York, on Tuesday, 8 June 1948, at 2:30 p.m.

Continuation of Consideration of the Articles of the Declaration of Human Rights

Articles 17 and 18 (Continuation)

The Chairman requested the representative of China to present the conclusions of the Drafting Sub-Committee on articles 17 and 16.

Mr. Chang (China) said that the Drafting Sub-Committee had not intended to change the substance of the articles and had limited itself to proposing slight drafting modifications: replacing "freedom of opinion", in the second line, by "freedom of thought", and in the English text, replacing "any means" by "any media".

...

Mr. Chang (China) recalled that his delegation had suggested placing article 2 at the end of the Declaration. In addition, since it was apparent that the majority of members favoured a reconsideration of that article, he did not think it appropriate to vote for its reconsideration before it was known, in what way it would be modified. He therefore proposed that the Commission should merely mention those two suggestions in its minutes.

...

Articles 23 and 24

...

Mr. Chang (China) thought that the Chinese text would have to be considered subsequently, for it embodied a different conception of how the Declaration should be set out.

...

在人权委员会第 65 次会议上的发言

1948 年 6 月 9 日星期三上午 10:15 纽约成功湖

继续讨论人权宣言草案（第 E/CN.4/95 号文件）

第 23 条

　　……

　　卢特菲（埃及）建议，第 23 条第 2 款应成为单独一条，放在专门论述经济和社会权利一节的开头，从而确立一项一般原则。

　　……

　　马利克先生（黎巴嫩）认为，失业保护权可以写入第 23 条第 1 款。这并不妨碍通过一项涵盖所有经济和社会权利的一般性条款。

　　……

　　张先生（中国）认为，是否将这项规定写入第 23 条是难以决定的。因为并没有一个全体成员一致同意的可用案文。他同意黎巴嫩代表的意见，即应在第 23 条中提及失业问题，并应在专门讨论经济和社会权利的这一节末尾写入一个一般性条款。

　　他提议将第 23 条第 1 款和第 2 款合并形成如下案文。

　　"人人享有工作权，有权享有公正和适宜的工作条件及薪酬；这项权利包括采取各种措施创造尽可能广泛的有价值工作的机会，并防止失业。"

　　他要求将他的提案付诸表决。

　　维尔凡先生（南斯拉夫）对中国代表提交的案文提出一项修正：在"采取各种措施"前加上"由国家或社会"。

　　卡森先生（法国）也提出了一项修正；他建议：在"各种措施"后加上"由各个国家采取或通过国际合作"。

　　张先生（中国）不能接受这两项修正。

　　巴甫洛夫先生（苏联）询问黎巴嫩代表是否已经撤回了其修正案；他倾向于黎巴嫩案文而不是中国案文，因为前者的表述方式更有气势。

洛佩兹先生（菲律宾）说，他支持黎巴嫩的修正案；但是，由于中国的案文更符合他本人的意愿，他会支持后者，并对黎巴嫩的修正案投反对票。

主席宣读经中国代表修正后的第 1 款。她说她将对该修正案投反对票。

马利克先生（黎巴嫩）觉得自己的草案更好些；与英国代表的意见相反，他认为"保护"一词是完全无歧义的，并包括了为解决失业问题而应采取的所有措施。

马利克先生要求对其修正案进行表决。如果该修正案被否决，他将提议用"适足"代替"尽可能广泛"，作为对中国案文的修正。他指出，虽然法国代表的意图是好的，但他的修正案可能会因引入一个需要进一步研究的新因素而增加难度。

张先生（中国）接受黎巴嫩代表对其案文的修正。

……

巴甫洛夫先生（苏联）提议对中国草案进行修改，将"包括"改为"提供"。

威尔逊先生（英国）说，如果印度代表接受黎巴嫩的修正案，他也会接受。他同意"保护"一词不会造成误解。

威尔逊先生不能接受中国修正案，因为它掩盖了分歧而没有解决它，这很难作出解释。

张先生（中国）认为他的案文是一个折中的方案。他指出，处理失业问题不可能不提及需要采取的措施。

……

——人权委员会第 65 次会议简要记录（E/CN.4/SR.65）

朱金荣译，常健校

E/CN.4/SR.65
24 June 1948

COMMISSION ON HUMAN RIGHTS
THIRD SESSION
SUMMARY RECORD OF THE SIXTY-FIFTH MEETING

Held at Lake Success, New York, on Wednesday, 9 June 1948, at 10:15 a.m.

Continuation of the Discussion of the Draft Declaration on Human Rights (Document E/CN.4/95)

Article 23

…

Mr. Loutfi (Egypt) suggested that paragraph 2 of article 23 should become a separate article to be placed at the beginning of the section devoted to economic and social rights, thus establishing a general principle.

…

Mr. Malik (Lebanon) thought that the right to protection against unemployment could be included in the first paragraph of article 23. That would in no way interfere with the adoption of a general article covering all economic and social rights.

…

Mr. Chang (China) thought that it was difficult to decide whether or not the provision should be included in article 23, since no text was available on which all members agreed. He agreed with the Lebanese representative that reference to unemployment should be made in article 23 and that a general article should be placed at the end of the section devoted to economic and social rights.

He proposed the following text combining the provisions of paragraphs 1 and 2 of article 23:

"Everyone has the right to work and to just and favourable conditions of work and pay; that right includes the adoption of such measures as would create the widest possible opportunities for useful work and prevent unemployment."

He asked that his proposal be put to the vote.

Mr. Vilfan (Yugoslavia) proposed an amendment to the text submitted by the representative of China; involving the addition of the words "taken by the State or society" after the word "measures".

Mr. Cassin (France) also proposed an amendment; he suggested the addition of the words "taken by the various States, and with international co-operation" after the word "measures".

Mr. Chang (China) could accept neither of the two amendments.

Mr. Pavlov (Union of Soviet Socialist Republics) asked whether the representative of Lebanon had withdrawn his amendment; he preferred the Lebanese to the Chinese text in view of its more energetic formulation.

Mr. Lopez (Philippines) stated that he had supported the Lebanese amendment; but, since the Chinese text corresponded more to his own wishes, he would support the latter and vote against the Lebanese amendment.

The Chairman read out paragraph 1 as amended by the representative of China. She said that she would vote against that amendment.

Mr. Malik (Lebanon) felt that his own draft was better; the word "protection", contrary to the views of the United Kingdom representative, was completely unambiguous and included all measures to be taken against unemployment.

Mr. Malik asked for a vote on his amendment. If that amendment were rejected, he would propose, as an amendment to the Chinese text, replacing the words "the widest possible" by the word "adequate". He pointed out that, while the French representative's intentions were excellent, his amendment might raise difficulties in introducing a new element which would require further study.

Mr. Chang (China) accepted the Lebanese representative's amendment to his text.

...

Mr. Pavlov also proposed that the Chinese draft should be amended by replacing the word "includes" by the word "provides".

Mr. Wilson (United Kingdom) stated that if the Indian representative accepted the Lebanese amendment, he would do the same. He agreed that the words "protection" would not cause misunderstanding.

Mr. Wilson could not accept the Chinese amendment; it would be difficult to interpret since it concealed the disagreement without settling it.

Mr. Chang (China) considered that his was a compromise formula; he pointed out that it was impossible to deal with the question of unemployment without mentioning measures to be taken against it.

...

在人权委员会第 67 次会议上的发言

1948 年 6 月 10 日星期四上午 11:00 纽约成功湖

继续审议起草委员会提交人权委员会的报告（第 E/CN.4/95 号文件）

新条款

……

张先生（中国）建议不应立即决定新条款的位置。同意在宣言的末尾增加这些条款就足够了。

他支持这样的观点，即宣言应包括一项一般性原则的条款，确立人人有权享有良好的社会和国际秩序，但他认为委员会应该更进一步，应当确定所有人都有责任为建立和维护这一秩序作出贡献。

他强调这一问题十分重要，但认为没有必要立即就小组委员会提出的案文进行表决。委员会应反思在这方面可以作出怎样的改进。因此，他建议对这个问题的审议推迟到以后。

但是，如果委员会决定立即讨论这两个新的条款，他建议在第一个案文中增加一个短语来表达他刚才提出的想法，即需要在确认国家的义务的同时，确认个人也有义务对他所要求的良好社会秩序作出贡献。因此，他建议在"人人有权"后面加上"并有义务协助实现"或"并有义务实现"。

马利克先生（黎巴嫩）完全同意张先生希望在宣言中写入的观点，并认为这十分重要。不过，这一观点应在序言中加以陈述，因为序言中将提及国家的权利以及个人的义务。在一个条款中引入个人义务的观念，将偏离宣言其他条款的表述形式。委员会应决定，该条款是否足够重要，使其能够允许这种偏离。

张先生（中国）在回答主席的一个问题时说，第 2 条并不完全符合他希望通过新条款所表达的想法。第 2 条提及的个人义务是他对其所属国家或该国其他国民所负的义务。小组委员会建议增加的这一条款引入了一个新的概念，即个人享有良好社会秩序的权利。但是根据该条规定，个人有权要求的社会秩序，首先取决于他对建立和维护它所作的贡献。因此，这项权利取决于该义务的充分履行，而这项义务应当被清晰阐明。

......

张先生（中国）要求对体裁委员会的职能有所说明。他认为，委员会主要处理体裁问题和翻译的一致性，但竟然要委托它作出条款位置这样的重要决定，这让他感到十分惊讶。

主席说，体裁委员会将只处理形式和结构问题，而不会作出实质性决定。这一观点得到了威尔逊先生（英国）的支持。

......

第 27 条和第 28 条

......

张先生（中国）提议通过以下案文：

"1. 人人有受教育的权利，包括免费基础教育和根据成绩平等接受高等教育的权利。

2. 教育的目的应是充分发展人的人格，并加强对人权及基本自由之尊重。"

张先生指出，这个单独条款的第 1 款保留了英国-印度联合案文中所包含的两个观点，而第 2 款则以压缩的形式阐明了第 28 条的实质内容，中国代表团多次强调了它的重要性。

......

——人权委员会第 67 次会议简要记录（E/CN.4/SR.67）

朱金荣译，常健校

E/CN.4/SR.67
25 June 1948

COMMISSION ON HUMAN RIGHTS
THIRD SESSION
SUMMARY RECORD OF THE SIXTY-SEVENTH MEETING
Held at Lake Success, New York, on Thursday, 10 June 1948, at 11:00 a.m.

Continuation of the Consideration of the Report of the Drafting Committee to the Commission on Human Rights (Document E/CN.4/95)

New article

...

Mr. Chang (China) suggested that the place to be given to the new articles should not be decided upon immediately. It was sufficient to agree that the articles would be added towards the end of the Declaration.

While supporting the idea that an article of general principle establishing everyone's right to a good social and international order should be included in the Declaration, he thought that the Commission should go further, and should affirm that it was the duty of all to contribute towards the establishment and maintenance of that order.

While stressing the importance of the question, he thought that there was no need for an immediate vote on the text proposed by the Sub-Committee. The Commission should reflect on what improvements might be made in it. He, therefore, suggested that the consideration of the question should be postponed till a later date.

If, however, the Commission decided on an immediate discussion of the two new articles, he would propose the inclusion in the first text of a phrase expressing the idea he had just set forth, namely, the need to affirm, side by side with the duties of the State, the individual's duty to contribute to the good social order he demanded. He therefore suggested adding after the words "everyone has the right" either "and the duty to assist in the realization of" or "and the duty to bring about".

Mr. Malik (Lebanon) entirely agreed with the idea Mr. Chang wished to have included in the Declaration, and realized its importance. That idea should, however, be stated in the Preamble which would mention the rights of States as well as the duties of the individual. To introduce the idea of the individual's duties into an article would be a departure from the form given to the other articles of the Declaration. The Commission should decide whether it considered such a departure Justified by the importance of the article in question.

Mr. Chang (China) said in answer to a question by the Chairman that article 2 did not fully meet the idea he wished to express by the new article. The duties of the individual mentioned in article 2 were those which he owed to the State of which he was a national, or to other nationals of that State. The article, the addition of which had been recommended by the Sub-Committee, introduced a new idea, namely the individual's right to a good social order. As, however, the social order which the individual was entitled to demand, under the terms of that article, depended in the first instance on the individual's contribution to its establishment and maintenance, that right was dependent on the fulfilment of a duty which should be clearly stated.

...

Mr. Chang (China) asked for some enlightenment on the functions of the Style Committee. He thought that that Committee would deal mainly with questions of style and with the uniformity of translations, and he was surprised that it should be entrusted with important decisions such as the placing of articles.

The Chairman, supported by Mr. Wilson (United Kingdom) said that the Style Committee would only deal with questions of form and construction, and would take no decisions of substance.

...

Articles 27 and 28

...

Mr. Chang (China) proposed the adoption of the following text:

"1. Everyone has the right to education, including free fundamental education and equal access on the basis of merit to higher education.

2. Education shall be directed to the full development of the human personality and to the strengthening of respect for human rights and fundamental freedoms."

Mr. Chang pointed out that the first paragraph of that single article retained the two ideas contained in the joint United Kingdom-India text, while the second paragraph set forth, in condensed form, the substance of article 28, the importance of which the Chinese delegation had stressed time and again.

　…

在人权委员会第 68 次会议上的发言

1948 年 6 月 10 日星期四下午 3:30 纽约成功湖

继续讨论人权宣言草案（第 E/CN.4/95 号文件）

第 27—28 条

……

莱巴尔先生（联合国教科文组织）想知道人权委员会是否能够将义务教育的概念与基础教育的概念结合起来。"基础"一词包括了晚近更广泛的成人教育，代表了过去几十年教育工作者思想上的巨大进步。莱巴尔先生特别赞成用"基础"取代"初级"。

……

张先生（中国）呼吁支持教科文组织代表阐述的"基础"教育概念。这些新的现代概念特别适用于那些急需对没有机会享受小学教育的人进行成人教育的国家。张先生同意英国代表的意见，即"义务的"一词应被删除。

……

张先生（中国）觉得，在这一短语中省略"基础"一词将是可悲的。他敦促委员会在"初级"之后插入"和基础"，从而涉及成人教育。

中国代表的修正案以 10 票赞成、1 票反对、5 票弃权获得通过。

主席请人权委员会关注"根据成绩平等接受高等教育"这句话。

巴甫洛夫先生（苏联）对"根据成绩"的措辞质疑。他对现在拿到的俄文译本不满意。为了避免如财富这样的因素可能对成绩造成的影响，他建议改用"根据个人的能力和知识"。

主席指出，"根据成绩"的措辞明确表达了巴甫洛夫先生所寻求的保障。它们排除了诸如财富、个人或政治偏好这样的因素，并确保高等教育向有能力接受它的人开放。卡森先生（法国）和张先生（中国）支持主席的意见。

......

张先生（中国）指出，在第 1 款中，"义务的"一词仅涉及初级和基础教育。他认为其不应被用于这个也适用于高等教育的段落。

巴甫洛夫先生（苏联）同意中国代表的意见。他质疑目前将高等教育定为义务教育的实际可行性。

......

——人权委员会第 68 次会议简要记录（E/CN.4/SR.68）

丁智朗译，常健校

E/CN.4/SR.68
14 June 1948

COMMISSION ON HUMAN RIGHTS
THIRD SESSION
SUMMARY RECORD OF THE SIXTY-EIGHTH MEETING
Held at Lake Success, New York, Thursday, 10 June 1948, at 3:30 p.m.

Continuation of the Discussion on the Draft Declaration of Human Rights (Document E/CN.4/95)

Articles 27-28

...

Mr. Lebar (UNESCO) wondered whether the Commission might be able to combine the concept of compulsory education with that of fundamental education. The word "fundamental" contained the more recent and much broader concept of adult education and represented great progress in the thinking of the past educators over several decades. Mr. Lebar strongly favoured "fundamental" to replace "elementary".

...

Mr. Chang (China) pleaded for support of the concept of "fundamental" education as elucidated by the representative of UNESCO. That new and modern concept was particularly well adapted to countries where adult education became imperative for those persons who had not enjoyed the opportunities of grade-school instruction. Mr. Chang agreed with the representative of the United Kingdom that the word "compulsory" should be deleted.

...

Mr. Chang (China) felt that it would be tragic to omit the word "fundamental" from that phrase. He urged the Commission to insert the words "and fundamental" after "elementary", thus making a reference to education for adults.

The Chinese representative's amendment was approved by ten votes to one, with five abstentions.

The Chairman directed the Commission's attention to the phrase, "and equal access on the basis of merit to higher education".

Mr. Pavlov (Union of Soviet Socialist Republics) questioned the words, "on the basis of merit". The Russian translation which he had before him was unsatisfactory. To avoid the possibility that such factors as wealth might be included, he suggested, instead, the words "on the basis of personal capabilities and knowledge."

The Chairman, supported by Mr. Cassin (France) and Mr. Chang (China) stated that the words "on the basis of merit" represented precisely the safeguard sought by Mr. Pavlov. They excluded such factors as wealth, personal or political favour, and ensured that higher education would be open to those who had the ability to receive it.

...

Mr. Chang (China) pointed out that in the first paragraph the word "compulsory" referred only to elementary and fundamental education. He did not think it should be used in a paragraph which applied also to higher education.

Mr. Pavlov (Union of Soviet Socialist Republics) agreed with the Chinese representative. He questioned the practical possibility of making higher education compulsory at the present time.

...

在人权委员会第 69 次会议上的发言

1948 年 6 月 11 日星期五上午 11:00 纽约成功湖

继续审议《人权宣言》第 27 和 28 条

......

主席以美国代表的身份发言，她指出，很难断言美国维护的是有利于盎格鲁-撒克逊种族的种族理论，因为美国的人口是由如此不同的众多族群组成的，因此无法为任何种族理论提供根据。但美国确实甚至过于频繁地发布有关其科学发现的信息，而苏联政府却对苏联的类似研究守口如瓶。公开发表的东西对和平的威胁肯定不会高于被保密的东西。

威尔逊先生（英国）同意主席的意见。英方的案文意在取代第 27 和 28 条，实际上等于完全删除第 28 条。该提案还在等待人权委员会审议，由于它是最早提出的，因此应该是第一个付诸表决的提案。他认为仅用三四行文字来概括所有关于教育目的的理论是危险的。

......

张先生（中国）回顾说，人权委员会在上次会议上终于讨论了教育问题，重要的是宣言不应在这方面保持沉默。在他看来，起草小组委员会重新起草的第 2 款充分表达了积极教育应当追求的目标。

......

张先生（中国）建议英方代表修改其提案，使其不仅适用于第 26 条，而且适用于第 27 条整个第 2 款，因为该款体现了第 28 条所包含的思想。

......

张先生（中国）提议删除词语"并促进国际谅解"，以避免同一观点在同一款中重复两次。

投票结果为 4 票赞成、4 票反对、5 票弃权，决定保留以下措辞："并促进国际谅解"。

......

张先生（中国）提出以下案文："教育应旨在充分发展人的人格，加强对人权及基本自由之尊重，并促进国际善意。"

　　……

中国代表提交的案文经修正后以 7 票对 5 票、2 票弃权获得通过。

　　……

　　——人权委员会第 69 次会议简要记录（E/CN.4/SR.69）

丁智朗译，常健校

E/CN.4/SR.69

25 June 1948

COMMISSION ON HUMAN RIGHTS
THIRD SESSION
SUMMARY RECORD OF THE SIXTY-NINTH MEETING

Lake Success, New York, Friday, 11 June 1948, at 11:00 a.m.

Continuation of the Consideration of Articles 27 and 28 of the Declaration on Human Rights

…

The Chairman, speaking as United States representative, pointed out that it would be difficult to assert that the United States upheld racial theories favouring the Anglo-Saxon race, since its population was made up of groups which differed so much that any racial theory would be devoid of any basis. It was true that the United States published, perhaps even too often, information about its scientific discoveries, while the government of the Soviet Union was rigorously silent on similar research in the Soviet Union. What was published was certainly no more of a threat to the peace than what was kept secret.

Mr. Wilson (United Kingdom) agreed with the Chairman. The United Kingdom text which was meant to replace articles 27 and 28 actually amounted to the complete deletion of article 28. That proposal was still before the Commission and, as it was the earliest, it should be the first to be put to the vote. He thought it dangerous to try to summarize in three or four lines all the theories on the aims of education.

...

Mr. Chang (China) recalled that the Commission had discussed the question of education at length at its last meeting, and that it was essential that the declaration should not be silent on that point. Paragraph 2, as re-drafted by the Drafting Sub-Committee, appeared to him to express adequately the aim which positive education should pursue.

...

Mr. Chang (China) suggested that the United Kingdom representative should modify his proposal by applying it not only to article 26, but to the whole of paragraph 2 of article 27, since that paragraph embodied the ideas contained in article 28.

...

Mr. Chang (China) proposed the deletion of the words: "and foster international understanding", in order to avoid two repetitions of the same idea in a single paragraph.

It was decided to retain the words: "and foster international understanding" by 4 votes to 4, with 5 abstentions.

...

Mr. Chang (China) proposed the following text:

"Education shall be directed to the full development of the human personality, to the strengthening of respect for human rights and fundamental freedoms and to the promotion of international goodwill."

...

The text submitted by the representative of China was adopted in its amended form by 7 votes to 5, with 2 abstentions.

...

在人权委员会第 70 次会议上的发言

1948 年 6 月 11 日星期五下午 2:30 纽约成功湖

继续审议《国际人权宣言（草案）》（E/CN.4/95 号文件）

……

审议第 30 条

张先生（中国）提议将该句"分享"一词后面的内容改为"在科学进步中"，并回顾说，该短语源自培根。

……

张先生（中国）提请人权委员会注意，委员会全体会议原计划的开会时间已过，卡森先生（法国）提议继续讨论，直到就该条内容作出决定。

……

张先生（中国）坚持认为，他的修正案与原案文相差最大，因此应首先被表决。

……

> ——人权委员会第 70 次会议简要记录（E/CN.4/SR.70）

丁智朗译，常健校

E/CN.4/SR.70
21 June 1948

COMMISSION ON HUMAN RIGHTS
THIRD SESSION
SUMMARY RECORD OF THE SEVENTIETH MEETING
Held at Lake Success, New York, on Friday, 11 June 1948, at 2:30 p.m.

Continuation of Consideration of the Draft International Declaration on Human Rights (Document E/CN.4/95)

...

Consideration of Article 30

...

Mr. Chang (China) proposed the replacement of the last part of the sentence after "share" by "in scientific advancement" and recalled that the phrase was derived from Bacon.

...

After Mr. Chang (China) had drawn the Commission's attention to the fact that the time originally set aside for the plenary meeting of the Commission had elapsed, Mr. Cassin (France) moved that the discussion should be continued until a decision on the Article could be reached.

...

Mr. Chang (China) maintained that his amendment was furthest removed from the original text and consequently should be voted first.

...

在人权委员会第 71 次会议上的发言

1948 年 6 月 14 日星期一上午 10:30 纽约成功湖

继续讨论《国际人权宣言（草案）》（第 E/CN.4/95 号文件）

......

第 25 条和第 26 条（续）

......

巴甫洛夫先生（苏联）指出，苏联代表团所捍卫的社会保险概念与其他代表团坚持的概念有本质不同。在苏联代表团看来，仅以从雇员工资中扣除的缴款为基础的社会保险制度并不构成真正的社会保险，而仅仅是强加于雇员的强制储蓄制度。他认为，社会保险应由国家或雇主缴纳。

苏联代表团意识到社会保险的方法在各地并不相同。考虑到这一事实，其案文中加入了"根据各国立法"一语。此外，苏联案文的第一部分在涉及社会保障时，规定要保护每一个人，包括那些非雇员。因此，苏联的修正案涵盖了所有需要考虑的要点。

最后，巴甫洛夫先生重申，让工人为其社会保险全部买单的制度是反民主的，不能算是真正的社会保险。他建议其他国家特别是英国应当考虑这个问题。

......

张先生（中国）希望在对第 1 款第一部分进行表决之前指出，其规定与劳工组织案文所包含的规定基本相同。因此，对苏联的案文投反对票只意味着不同意其措辞，而不是其所依据的原则。

......

张先生（中国）看不出在全世界数百万人都缺衣少食的情况下，对该短语还有什么可能的反对意见。

巴甫洛夫先生（苏联）表示惊讶，因为中方代表对苏联修正案的最后一款竟然投了反对票，而该款规定的那些手段正是要确保他希望保障的那些权利。

张先生（中国）指出，该款中提出的问题，应作为一个单独的"总括"条款的主题，或将其内容插入序言中。他补充说，他投票反对苏联案文的原因是其措辞问题。

......

张先生（中国）认为"生活水准"一词不够精确。所涉及的问题不仅包括食物产量，而且包括食物质量。中国代表不理解，为何要回避提及适当生活水准的这两个主要因素。

主席建议在"生活水准"之后插入"包括食宿、住房和医疗"的词语。

张先生（中国）同意这一建议。

主席要求就是否应当将"衣食"写入该文本进行投票。

以 11 票对 3 票的表决结果决定写入这些措辞。

主席将中国修正案整体付诸表决。

中国修正案以 12 票对 0 票、2 票弃权获得通过。

......

——人权委员会第 71 次会议简要记录（E/CN.4/SR.71）

丁智朗译，常健校

E/CN.4/SR.71
28 June 1948

COMMISSION ON HUMAN RIGHTS
THIRD SESSION
SUMMARY RECORD OF THE SEVENTY-FIRST MEETING

Held at Lake Success, New York, on Monday, 14 June 1948, at 10:30 a.m.

Continuation of the Discussion on the Draft International Declaration on Human Rights (Document E/CN.4/95)

...

Articles 25 and 26(Continued)

....

Mr. Pavlov (Union of Soviet Socialist Republics) pointed out that the concept of social insurance which his delegation defended was fundamentally different from that upheld by the others. In the eyes of the USSR delegation, a system of social insurance based only on contributions deducted from the employee's wages did not constitute real social insurance but merely a system of compulsory savings imposed on the employee. Contributions to social insurance should, in his opinion, be made either by the State or by the employer.

The USSR delegation was aware of the fact that methods of social insurance were not identical everywhere and had included the phrase "in accordance with the legislation of each country" in its text with that fact in mind. Moreover, the first part of the USSR text, in referring to social security, provided for the protection of everyone, including those who were not employees. The USSR amendment thus covered all the points which could be considered necessary.

In conclusion, Mr. Pavlov repeated that a system under which the worker paid the entire contribution towards his insurance was antidemocratic and did not constitute real social insurance. He suggested that other countries, and especially the United Kingdom, should ponder that question.

...

Mr. Chang (China) wished to point out before a vote was taken on the first part of paragraph 1 that its provisions were fundamentally the same as those contained in the ILO text. To vote against the USSR text would, therefore, signify disagreement with its wording only, but not with the principles on which it was based.

...

Mr. Chang (China) did not see what possible objection there could be to that phrase when millions of people throughout the world were deprived of food and clothing.

Mr. Pavlov (Union of Soviet Socialist Republics) was surprised that the representative of China should have voted against the last paragraph of the USSR amendment which made provision for the means to ensure those very rights which he wished to safeguard.

Mr. Chang (China) stated that the question raised in that paragraph would form the subject either of a separate "umbrella" clause or of a paragraph to be inserted in the Preamble. He added that his reasons for voting against the USSR text were connected with its wording.

...

Mr. Chang (China) did not agree that the term "standard of living" was sufficiently precise. The question involved concerned not only the quantity but also the quality of food. The Chinese representative did not understand the wish to avoid reference to the two principal factors of an adequate standard of living.

The Chairman suggested that the words "including food and lodging, housing and medical care" should be inserted after the words "standard of living".

Mr. Chang (China) agreed to that proposal.

The Chairman called for a vote on the question as to whether the words "food and clothing" should be included in the text.

It was decided to include those words by 11 votes to 3.

The Chairman put to the vote the Chinese amendment as a whole.

The Chinese amendment was adopted by 12 votes to none with 2 abstentions.

...

在人权委员会第 72 次会议上的发言

1948 年 6 月 14 日星期一下午 2:30 纽约成功湖

继续讨论人权宣言草案（第 E/CN.4/95 号文件）

……

张先生（中国）评论道，原先的短语"经济、社会和文化权利列举如下"似乎更可取。它包括一个一般性陈述，含义比"社会保障"更为广泛。如果委员会觉得有必要在宣言中使用"社会保障"一词，可以在修订有关社会权利的条款时写入。张先生的评论得到马利克先生（黎巴嫩）的支持。

……

张先生（中国）想知道，人权委员会是否打算通过将涵盖性条款置于处理经济和社会权利条款的开始处来为这些权利起一个"社会保障条款"的名称。他建议对两项提案中涉及社会保障的条款应分别进行表决。

……

——人权委员会第 72 次会议简要记录（E/CN.4/SR.72）

丁智朗译，常健校

E/CN.4/SR.72
24 June 1948

COMMISSION ON HUMAN RIGHTS
THIRD SESSION
SUMMARY RECORD OF THE SEVENTY-SECOND MEETING

Held at Lake Success, New York, on Monday, 14 June 1948, at 2:30 p.m.

Continuation of the Discussion of the Draft Declaration of Human Rights (Document E/CN.4/95)

...

Mr. Chang (China), supported by Mr. Malik (Lebanon), remarked that the original phrase, "economic, social and cultural rights enumerated below", appeared preferable. It contained a general statement, the meaning of which was wider than social security. If the Commission felt it necessary to use the term in the Declaration, it could do so when it revised the articles dealing with social rights.

...

Mr. Chang (China) wondered whether it was the intention of the Commission, by placing the covering article at the head of the articles dealing with economic and social rights, to create for them the name of "social security articles". He suggested that the clause referring to social security should be voted upon separately in both proposals.

...

在人权委员会第 73 次会议上的发言

1948 年 6 月 15 日星期二上午 10:45 纽约成功湖

......
继续讨论人权宣言草案（第 E/CN.4/95 号文件）（第 31 条）

主席概述了人权委员会下一步的工作流程，然后转向审议涉及少数群体权利的第 31 条。中国、印度和英国提议删除该条。

......

——人权委员会第 73 次会议简要记录（E/CN.4/SR.73）

朱金荣译，常健校

E/CN.4/SR.73
24 June 1948

COMMISSION ON HUMAN RIGHTS
THIRD SESSION
SUMMARY RECORD OF THE SEVENTY-THIRD MEETING

Held at Lake Success, New York, on Tuesday, 15 June 1948, at 10:45 a.m.

…

Continuation of Discussion on the Draft Declaration on Human Rights (Document E/CN.4/95) (Article 31)

The Chairman then outlined the Commission's further procedure and turned to the consideration of article 31 dealing with the rights of minorities. China, India and the United Kingdom had proposed the deletion of the article.

…

在人权委员会第 74 次会议上的发言

1948 年 6 月 15 日星期二下午 2:30 纽约成功湖

继续审议起草委员会提交人权委员会的报告（第 E/CN.4/95 号文件）：
审议宣言草案和各国代表团提出的修正案

第 30 条

......

胡德先生（澳大利亚）指出，"自由地自我发展"这个表述更是模棱两可。它指的是文化发展还是民族解放？

张先生（中国）评论道，造成这种模棱两可的原因是"文化"一词可以有两种含义；它既可以指科学实践和艺术，也可以指一个共同体的种族渊源。毫无疑问，第 30 条中的"文化"一词指的是前者，根据该词的上下文语境，"文化团体"指的只能是"文化组织"。将该条插入黎巴嫩代表提议的案文中也许不是最好的位置安排。

......

第 31 条

......

张先生（中国）指出，委员会不应给人以完全忽视特殊宗教或族裔群体保护问题的印象。在关于受教育权的条款中，就有一项有利于宗教少数群体的规定。

......

序言

张先生（中国）强调序言的重要性，起草序言时必须极为谨慎，并建议将对提交人权委员会的两个案文的审议推迟到第二天。

......

第 2 条第 2 款

洛特非先生（埃及）提交了埃及代表团与法国和英国代表团协商起草的第 2 条第 2 款的如下案文：

"在行使本宣言所列举的一切权利和自由时，每个人仅受为确保充分承认和尊重他人权利以及在民主社会中道德、公共福利和公共秩序要求所必需的限制。"

……

张先生（中国）支持这一建议。他指出，在涉及人权所受限制的条款中，最好避免任何列举，因为它会给人以人权委员会倾向过度设限的印象。

……

——人权委员会第 74 次会议简要记录（E/CN.4/SR.74）

丁智朗译，常健校

E/CN.4/SR.74
28 June 1948

COMMISSION ON HUMAN RIGHTS
THIRD SESSION
SUMMARY RECORD OF THE SEVENTY-FOURTH
MEETING

Held at Lake Success, New York, on Tuesday, 15 June 1948, at 2:30 p.m.

Continuation of the Consideration of the Report of the Drafting Committee to the Commission on Human Rights (Document E/CN.4/95):
Consideration of the Draft Declaration and Amendments Submitted by Various Delegations

Article 30

…

Mr. Hood (Australia) pointed out that the words "free self-development" were even more ambiguous. Did they refer to cultural development or to national emancipation?

Mr. Chang (China) remarked that the ambiguity was caused by the fact that the word "cultural" could have two meanings: it could refer either to the practice of science and the arts, or the ethnical origin of a community. There could be no doubt that in article 30 the word "cultural" was used in the former sense, and in the context of the words "cultural groups" could mean nothing but "cultural organizations". That article was perhaps not the best place to insert the text proposed by the Lebanese representative.

...

Article 31

...

Mr. Chang (China) pointed out that the Commission should not give the impression that it had completely ignored the question of the protection of special religious or ethnical groups. In the article relating to the right to education there was a provision in favour of religious minorities.

...

Preamble

...

Mr. Chang (China) stressed the importance of the Preamble and the necessity of taking the utmost care in drafting it, and suggested that the consideration of the two texts submitted to the Commission should be deferred until the following day.

...

Article 2, Paragraph 2

Mr. Loutfi (Egypt) submitted the following text for article 2, paragraph 2, which his delegation had drafted in consultation with the delegations of France and the United Kingdom:

" In the exercise of all the rights and freedoms enumerated in this Declaration, everyone shall be subject only to such limitations as are necessary to secure due recognition and respect for the rights of others and to the requirements of morality, of general welfare and of public order in a democratic society."

...

Mr. Chang (China) supported that suggestion. He pointed out that, in the article which dealt with limitations to which human rights were to be subject, it would be well to avoid any enumeration which might give the impression that the Commission was inclining towards too much restriction.

...

在人权委员会第 75 次会议上的发言

1948 年 6 月 16 日星期三上午 10:45 纽约成功湖

继续讨论人权宣言草案：继续讨论体裁委员会报告

······

张先生（中国）建议条款顺序应作如下改动。（1）修订后的第 2 条应直接放在上次会议通过的第 33 条之前，黎巴嫩代表提议的条款应放在第 2 条之前。（2）组成第 3 条的两款可分成单独两条：第 1 款成为第 2 条，第 2 款成为第 5 条，置于有关法律权利的规定之前。（3）第 4 条和第 5 条将分别成为第 3 条和第 4 条。第 6、7、8 条保持不变。

······

张先生（中国）指出，他的建议应作为对体裁委员会报告的修正，因此应与该报告同时审议。

······

主席宣读了第 1 款案文。

威尔逊先生（英国）对草案提出了一个措辞修正，但它不会影响法文文本：在 "the equal" 语词之前插入 "of" 一词。

该提案被通过。

张先生（中国）希望该款获得通过，因为它具有特殊的重要性和内在价值。

第 1 款以 11 票对 0 票、5 票弃权获得通过。

······

主席将有关省略这些词语的提案付诸表决。

该提案以 6 票反对、3 票赞成、5 票弃权被否决。

第 2 款最后一句被保留。

张先生（中国）指出，在英文文本中添加 "of" 一词会缩小 "无知" 一词的含义。体裁委员会的大多数成员所想说的是一般意义上的无知，而不仅仅是对人权的无知。

......

张先生（中国）解释了他为什么不认可这一款的案文。诚然，德国人和日本人因蔑视人权而受到谴责，但不能说他们对这些权利一无所知。英文文本中的"无知"一词并不是一个恰当的词汇，他提议在英文文本中用"无视"来取代。

......

张先生（中国）提议，对用"无视"替换"无知"一事应付诸表决。**该修正案以 10 票对 1 票、2 票弃权获得通过。**

......

胡德先生（澳大利亚）再次就第二款的措辞发言。虽然委员会决定保留其中过于武断的说法，但他想知道，即便如此，更准确地界定其范围是否为更明智的做法，即在英文文本中这一句的最后处用"the"来替代"a"，使"并向所有人表明基本自由是冲突唯一最重要问题"变为"并向所有人表明基本自由是冲突的一个最重要问题"。

张先生（中国）指出，由于这句话背后的思想得到了保留，因此提交对该句的修正案是完全没有问题的。

主席表示同意。

......

张先生（中国）指出，序言没有按照委员会所有成员都能接受的观点来起草。这是第二段没有得到一致支持的原因。

......

张先生（中国）也希望提及改善经济和社会条件的需要。可以借用《联合国宪章》中有关这一问题的措辞来表述这种需要。

他建议成立一个小型委员会，负责从《联合国宪章》中选择适当内容进行引用。

主席同意中国代表的要求，并为此设立了一个专门委员会，由中国、英国、澳大利亚、美国和南斯拉夫代表组成，将于下午早些时候举行会议。

维尔凡先生（南斯拉夫）拒绝了这一提议，因为序言作为一个整体，无论是有意还是无意，都是基于一个他无法认同的观念；他无法对起草一个基于他不认同的观念的案文作出任何具体贡献。

在回答张先生（中国）的问题时，他指出，序言只提到了个人的权利，而它也可以作为一种妥协，并尊重委员会成员的想法，提到国家和人民的权利。

提交的序言没有承认个人对国家和国家的义务。

主席请菲律宾代表代替南斯拉夫代表参加专门委员会，从《联合国宪章》中选择可以在序言中提及的段落。

会议于下午 1:05 结束。

——人权委员会第 75 次会议简要记录（E/CN.4/SR.75）

丁智朗、常健译，常健校

E/CN.4/SR.75
30 June 1948

COMMISSION ON HUMAN RIGHTS
THIRD SESSION
SUMMARY RECORD OF THE SEVENTY-FIFTH MEETING
Held at Lake Success, New York, on Wednesday, 16 June 1948, at 10:45 a.m.

Continuation of the Discussion on the Draft Declaration of Human Rights: Continuation of the Report of the Style Committee

...

Mr. Chang (China) suggested that the order of the articles should be altered as follows: (a) the revised article 2 should be placed immediately before article 33 which had been adopted at the previous meeting; the article proposed by the representative of Lebanon should be placed before article 2; (b) the two paragraphs which made up article 3 might become two separate articles: the first paragraph would become article 2 and the second paragraph would become article 5 preceding the provisions concerning legal rights; (c) articles 4 and 5 would then become respectively articles 3 and 4; articles 6, 7 and 8 would remain unchanged.

...

Mr. Chang (China) pointed out that his proposal should be taken as an amendment to the report of the Style Committee and should, therefore, be considered at the same time as that report.

...

The Chairman read the text of paragraph 1.

Mr. Wilson (United Kingdom) proposed a drafting amendment which would not affect the French text: that the word "of" should be inserted before the words "the equal".

The proposal was adopted.

Mr. Chang (China) hoped this paragraph would be adopted in view of its special importance and intrinsic value.

Paragraph 1 was adopted by 11 votes to none, with 5 abstentions.

...

The Chairman put the proposal for the omission of these words to the vote.

The proposal was rejected by 6 votes to 3 with 5 abstentions.

The last sentence of paragraph 2 was retained.

Mr. Chang (China) pointed out that the addition of the word "of" in the English text would narrow the meaning of the word "ignorance". Most of the members of the Style Committee had had in mind ignorance in general and not simply ignorance of human rights.

...

Mr. Chang (China) explained that he had not approved the drafting of this paragraph. It was true that the Germans and the Japanese were to blame for their contempt of human rights, but it could not be said that they had been ignorant of those rights. The word "ignorance" in the English text was not the right word, and he would propose that it should be replaced in the English text by the words "indifference to".

...

Mr. Chang (China) proposed that the substitution of the words "disregard of" for "ignorance" should be put to the vote.

The amendment was adopted by 10 votes to 1 with 2 abstentions.

...

Mr. Hood (Australia) spoke again on the wording of the second paragraph.

Although the Commission had decided to retain the much too dogmatic statement it contained, he wondered whether, in spite of that, it would not be wiser to define its scope more precisely by saying, in the English text, at the end of the sentence "and made it apparent to all that the fundamental freedoms were a (instead of 'the') supreme issue of the conflict".

Mr. Chang (China) pointed out that as the idea underlying the sentence was saved, it would be perfectly in order to submit amendments to that sentence.

The Chairman agreed.

...

Mr. Chang (China) pointed out that the Preamble had not been drafted in accordance with a concept acceptable to all the members of the Committee. That was why the second paragraph had not been unanimously supported.

...

Mr. Chang (China) also wanted the need for an improvement in economic and social conditions mentioned. It could be done by borrowing the words of the Charter on that subject.

He suggested setting up a small committee to choose the appropriate quotations from the Charter.

The Chairman agreed with the Chinese representative's request and appointed a committee for that purpose, consisting of the representatives of China, the United Kingdom, Australia, the United States and Yugoslavia, which would meet in the early afternoon.

Mr. Vilfan (Yugoslavia) declined the offer as the Preamble as a whole, either wittingly or unwittingly, was based on a conception to which he could not subscribe; he could not make any concrete contributions to the preparation of a text based on a conception he did not share.

In reply to a question by Mr. Chang (China), he pointed out that the Preamble spoke only of the rights of the individual, whereas it could also have mentioned, as a compromise, and in deference to the ideas of as the members of the Commission, the rights of the Nation and of peoples.

The Preamble as submitted failed to recognize the duty of the individual to his Nation and to his State.

The Chairman asked the representative of the Philippines to take the place of the Yugoslav representative on the Committee to choose the paragraphs from the Charter to be mentioned in the Preamble.

The meeting rose at 1:05 p.m.

在人权委员会第 76 次会议上的发言

1948 年 6 月 16 日星期三下午 10:45 纽约成功湖

……

小组委员会关于研究种族灭绝公约草案的报告（E/CN.4/l36 号文件）

……

张先生（中国）强调，种族灭绝问题对中国具有极为重要的意义，在中国，日本人通过各种方法，特别是通过毒品犯下了这一罪行。

这个问题在联合国已经审议了两年多；世界舆论期待采取具体行动。即使人权委员会没有足够的时间彻底研究该公约，其仍然可以就此发表意见。他建议将"研究"一词改为"审议"，并将最后一句改为："委员会认为，公约草案是经济及社会理事会和联合国大会在即将举行的届会上紧急审议和采取决定性行动的适当基础。"

……

张先生（中国）指出，人权委员会现在面临两项提案：小组委员会起草并根据智利和中国的建议修改的决议草案，以及苏联代表提交的修正案草案。

显然，人权委员会所有成员都同意种族灭绝是一种罪行，因此应当找到打击这一罪行的手段。诚然，公约草案并不完美，但如果人权委员会未能就这一问题发表意见，那将是可悲的。因此，应表明人权委员会的意见；此外，可以指出，某些成员认为公约草案并不令人满意。

……

张先生（中国）动议结束辩论。

结束辩论的动议以 11 票对 4 票、2 票弃权获得通过。

由被指定重新起草序言部分第四段的小组委员会提出的建议
（第 E/CN.4/138 号文件）

......

张先生（中国）提交了小组委员会起草的两项提案，并指出这些提案的内容取自《联合国宪章》的序言部分。

......

张先生（中国）承认，起草委员会的工作过于匆忙，此事项在下次会议处理更为妥当。

在黎巴嫩、法国、英国、中国和苏联代表参加了讨论之后，主席要求起草委员会在会议结束后立即开会。

会议于下午 5:45 结束。

——人权委员会第 76 次会议简要记录（E/CN.4/SR.76）

丁智朗、常健译，常健校

E/CN.4/SR.76
1 July 1948
Original Text: French

COMMISSION ON HUMAN RIGHTS
THIRD SESSION
SUMMARY RECORD OF THE SEVENTY-SIXTH MEETING

Held at Lake Success, New York, on Wednesday, 16 June 1948, at 10:45 a.m.

...

Report of the Sub-Commission Studying the Draft Convention on Genocide (Document E/CN.4/l36)

...

Mr. Chang (China) emphasized that the question of genocide was of cardinal importance for China, where the Japanese had committed that crime by various methods, in particular by means of narcotic drugs.

The question had been under consideration in the United Nations for over two years; world public opinion was expecting concrete action. Even though the Commission had not had sufficient time to study the Convention thoroughly, it could still express an opinion. He suggested that the word "study" should be replaced by "consider" and that the last sentence should be changed as follows: "The Commission is of the opinion that the draft Convention represents an appropriate basis for urgent consideration and decisive action by the Economic and Social Council and the General Assembly during their forthcoming sessions."

…

Mr. Chang (China) noted that the Commission was now faced with two proposals: the draft resolution drawn up by the Sub-Committee and amended in accordance with the suggestions of Chile and China, and the draft amendment submitted by the representative of the USSR.

It was apparent that all the members of the Commission agreed that genocide was a crime and that means should be found to combat that crime. True, the draft of Convention was not perfect, but it would be deplorable if the Commission were to fail to state its views on the subject. The opinion of the Commission should therefore be indicated; in addition, it could be stated that certain members considered the draft Convention unsatisfactory.

…

Mr. Chang (China) moved the closure of the debate.

Closure of debate was accepted by 11 votes to 4, with 2 abstentions.

…

Proposals Worked Out By The Sub-Committee Appointed To Redraft the Fourth Paragraph of the Preamble (Document E/CN.4/138)

Mr. Chang (China) submitted the two proposals drawn up by the Sub-Committee and pointed out that the text of those proposals was taken from the preamble of the Charter.

…

Mr. Chang (China) admitted that the work of the Drafting Committee had been unduly hurried and that it might be desirable to refer the matter to the next meeting.

Following a discussion in which the representatives of Lebanon, France, the United Kingdom, China and the Union of Soviet Socialist Republics took part, the Chairman requested the Drafting Committee to meet immediately after the meeting.

The meeting rose at 5:45 p.m.

在人权委员会第 77 次会议上的发言

1948 年 6 月 17 日星期四上午 11:00 纽约成功湖

审议中国代表团提交的关于宣言条款顺序的提案

张先生（中国）提议将第 2 条作为宣言的倒数第二条。处理宣言所宣布的各项权利和自由行使限制的条款，不应在阐释这些权利和自由之前就写在宣言的开始部分。

……

主席以美方代表的身份发言，她认为关于对享受权利的一般限制的条款，放在宣言的结尾会更好。

中国代表的提案以 8 票赞成、7 票反对、1 票弃权获得通过。

张先生（中国）提议将宣言前 5 条的顺序改动如下：第 1 条保持原位；第 3 条第 1 款（非歧视原则）变为第 2 条；第 3 条第 2 款（法律面前人人平等原则）变为第 5 条；第 4 条（生命权）变为第 3 条；第 5 条（尊重人的尊严）变为第 4 条。

中国代表的提案以 9 票赞成、1 票反对、6 票弃权获得通过。

张先生（中国）提议将关于婚姻的第 13 条放在关于家庭的第 9 条之后。

卢特菲先生（埃及）指出，第 9 条并不只涉及家庭。因此，他反对所提议的修改。

中国代表的提案以 5 票反对、4 票赞成、7 票弃权被否决。

张先生（中国）提议将关于国籍的第 15 条放在第 12 条之后，后者涉及在法律面前被承认为人的权利。

卢特菲先生（埃及）支持该提议。

洛佩兹先生（菲律宾）指出，第 12 条本身的位置并不适当，应置于关于生命权和自由权的第 3 条之后。

张先生（中国）认为最好将第 12 条放在关于法律面前人人平等的第 5 条之后。

……

继续审议人权宣言序言（第 E/CN.4/138 和 E/CN.4/139 号文件）

……

马利克先生（黎巴嫩）和张先生（中国）也认为，只要《联合国宪章》的措辞未经联合国大会正式修改，就不能对其作出任何改动。

……

巴甫洛夫（苏联）希望删除第 6 款，因为他认为其引入了一个不仅是错误的而且是危险的概念。使人权宣言依赖于对权利和自由性质的共同理解，会破坏其宗旨。人权委员会的讨论已清楚表明委员会成员之间在哲学和意识形态领域存在分歧；而这种分歧并没有妨碍其富有成效的合作，因为尽管对权利的性质观点不一，但人权委员会仍然就各项权利实际可行的适用达成了令人满意的一致意见。

第 6 款目前的措辞似乎要求思想与观点的统一，而这是不可能实现的。然而苏联代表团认为，尽管存在哲学上的分歧，但由于诸如宣言所确立的那些最低限度权利可以被所有国家完全适用，国际合作仍然可能。宣言的适用不应受到目前提交委员会审议的第 6 款所含规定的威胁，该规定是不可接受的。

……

张先生（中国）说，苏联代表的解释是有些道理的：该款所起草的内容可能意味着，如果不能就一个公认概念达成一致的理解，联合国会员国所承担的义务将不具有约束力。

……

主席和张先生（中国）一致认为，第 6 款并非必不可少，因此可以被删除。张先生指出，对根据《联合国宪章》作出的承诺的任何保留意见，都会削弱该承诺。

……

张先生（中国）建议任命一个小型委员会，根据会议期间提出的各种评论，起草一份大家都能接受的方案。

……

——人权委员会第 77 次会议简要记录（E/CN.4/SR.77）

丁智朗译，常健校

E/CN.4/SR.77
28 June 1948

COMMISSION ON HUMAN RIGHTS
THIRD SESSION
SUMMARY RECORD OF THE SEVENTY-SEVENTH
MEETING

Lake Success, New York, Thursday, 17 June 1948 at 11:00 a.m.

Consideration of the Proposal Submitted by the Chinese Delegation Regarding the Order of the Articles of the Declaration

Mr. Chang (China) proposed making article 2 the penultimate article of the Declaration. An article which dealt with the limitations on the exercise of the rights, and freedoms proclaimed in the Declaration should not appear at the beginning of the Declaration before those rights and freedoms themselves had been set forth.

...

The Chairman, speaking as United States representative, thought that the article regarding the general limitations on the enjoyment of rights would be better placed towards the end of the Declaration.

The Chinese representative's proposal was adopted by 8 votes to 7 with 1 abstention.

Mr. Chang (China) proposed changing the order of the first five articles of the Declaration as follows: article 1 to remain where it was; article 3, paragraph 1 (principles of non-discrimination) to become article 2; article 3, paragraph 2 (principles of equality before the law) to become article 5; article 4 (right to life) to become article 3; article 5 (respect for human dignity) to become article 4.

The Chinese representative's proposal was adopted by 9 votes to 1 with 6 abstentions.

Mr. Chang (China) proposed placing article 13, which dealt with marriage, after article 9 which dealt with the family.

Mr. Loutfi (Egypt) pointed out that article 9 did not deal exclusively with the family. He was, therefore, opposed to the proposed change.

The Chinese representative's proposal was rejected by 5 votes to 4, with 7 abstentions.

Mr. Chang (China) proposed placing article 15, on nationality, after article 12, which dealt with the right to recognition as a person before the law.

Mr. Loutfi (Egypt) supported the proposal.

Mr. Lopez (Philippines) pointed out that article 12 itself had not been properly placed; it should follow article 3 which dealt with the right to life and freedom.

Mr. Chang (China) thought it would be better to place article 12 after article 5 which dealt with equality before the law.

…

Continuation of the Consideration of the Preamble to the Declaration on Human Rights (Documents E/CN.4/138 and E/CN.4/139)

…

Mr. Malik (Lebanon) and Mr. Chang (China) also thought that, as long as the wording of the Charter had not been officially modified by the General Assembly, no changes could be made to it.

…

Mr. Pavlov (Union of Soviet Socialist Republics) wished paragraph 6 to be deleted, as he thought it introduced not only an erroneous but a dangerous conception. To make the Declaration on Human Rights dependent on the application of a common conception of the nature of rights and freedoms would destroy its very purpose. The Commission's discussions had clearly shown the divergences which existed between the members in the fields of philosophy and ideology; that difference of ideas had not prevented fruitful co-operation, because even though there had been disagreement on the nature of the rights, the Commission has, nevertheless, come to a satisfactory agreement as to their practicable application.

Paragraph 6 in its present wording seemed to require a unity of thought and ideas which was impossible to achieve. His delegation, however, held that, in spite of philosophical differences, international co-operation was possible, as it considered that the minimum of rights, as set forth in the Declaration, could be applied in every detail by all. Its application should not be threatened by an unacceptable provision such as was contained in paragraph 6, at present submitted for the Commission's consideration.

...

Mr. Chang (China) said that there was something to be said for the USSR representative's interpretation: the paragraph, as drafted could mean that the obligation assumed by the Members of the United Nations would not be binding should agreement on a common conception not be reached.

...

The Chairman and Mr. Chang (China) agreed that paragraph 6 was not essential and could, therefore, be deleted. Mr. Chang pointed out that any reservation regarding the pledge taken under the Charter would weaken that pledge.

...

Mr. Chang (China) proposed appointing a small committee to draft a formula acceptable to all, bearing in mind the various comments made during the meeting.

...

在人权委员会第 78 次会议上的发言

1948 年 6 月 17 日星期四下午 2:30 纽约成功湖

继续审议《国际人权宣言（草案）》（第 E/CN.4/95 号文件）

第 20 条

……

张先生（中国）说，他更喜欢"定义"而非"共识"，更喜欢"必要的"而非"具有最重要意义"。

他进一步建议将"履行"改为"充分实现"。

人权委员会以 9 票对 1 票、4 票弃权决定赞成"共识"。

委员会以 6 票对 4 票、4 票弃权决定赞成"具有最重要意义"。

委员会以 8 票对 2 票、4 票弃权决定赞成"充分实现"。

委员会以 13 票对 0 票、1 票弃权通过了修正后的法案。

……

张先生（中国）赞同苏联提案背后的观点，即目前尚未享有自治权的人民无疑应被纳入宣言。但是，他认为在"所有国家"之后，加上"和人民"的措辞，会消除任何可能的误解。

……

威尔逊先生（英国）将投票支持中国代表的提议，他认为这是更清楚地表明宣言适用于所有人民——无论其地位如何——的最简单方式。他认为苏联的提案使委员会的工作超出了序言的范围，进入了实施的范围。

……

巴甫洛夫先生（苏联）反对中国的修正案，认为该修正案太不明确。非自治领土人民的问题应当得到正视，而不是以含糊的一般性陈述来回避。

张先生（中国）同意苏联代表关于应当正视该问题的观点，但认为不该在序言部分处理这一问题。如果在宣言通过后，苏联在联合国大会上提议采纳这样一个条款，他将予以支持。

关于苏联的提案，他指出，当今世界上独立的人民比非自治的人民多得多。因此，纯粹从起草的角度来看，这两个短语并不平衡。此外，增补苏联提议的这句话，会导致该段过长。

……

苏联提案的第一部分以 9 票反对、4 票赞成、1 票弃权被否决。
苏联提案的第二部分以 6 票反对、5 票赞成、3 票弃权被否决。
埃及提案以 9 票对 3 票、2 票弃权获得通过。
中国提案以 8 票对 0 票、5 票弃权获得通过。

……

张先生（中国）提请注意两个起草要点。第一，他对将"社会"和"国际"并列提出疑问，因为这两个词并不是对比词。"国家和国际的社会秩序"可能更可取。第二，因为"权利"一词在该条中重复使用，他提出可以在第一行中用"有资格"取代"有权利"。

……

主席以美国代表的身份发言，支持拟议的条款，并对中国代表提到的措辞进行了修改。

她恢复主席的身份，将苏联提出的用"这样"代替"好"的建议付诸表决。

苏联的提案以 6 票反对、4 票赞成、3 票弃权被否决。

……

主席提请注意法国代表团在第 E/CN.4/82/Add.8 号文件提出的条款，它将作为宣言第 28 条。

张先生（中国）指出，所建议的这一条更适合作为执行措施。

……

主席将是否在宣言中插入该拟议条款付诸表决。委员会以 8 票对 3 票、2 票弃权决定不插入该条款。

……

讨论审议报告员报告的程序

……

主席要求审议法国和美国的提案，即在向经济及社会理事会提交人权委员会报告时附上以下声明：

"人权委员会认识到，批准这一宣言，并没有完成其起草人权法案的任务。该法案包括宣言、公约和执行措施。

"宣言只构成人权法案的一部分。关键是要完成包括执行措施在内的公约。

"人权委员会建议经济及社会理事会，在理事会 1949 年第八届会议之后，立即就完成公约和执行措施举行一次人权委员会会议。"

……

张先生（中国）认为，法国和美国提案的前两段是不必要的。

他还建议修正第三段，将"在理事会 1949 年第八届会议之后"改为"1949 年初"，因为理事会第八届会议的日期尚未确定。

主席解释说，提案的前两段是为了明确表明，人权委员会并不认为宣言构成完整的人权法案。

张先生认为，这一想法可以被写入报告员的报告中。

……

——人权委员会第 78 次会议简要记录（E/CN.4/SR.78）

丁智朗译，常健校

E/CN.4/SR.78
24 June 1948

COMMISSION ON HUMAN RIGHTS
THIRD SESSION
SUMMARY RECORD OF THE SEVENTY-EIGHTH
MEETING

Held at Lake Success, New York, on Thursday, 17 June 1948 at 2:30 p.m.

Continuation of the Consideration of the Draft International Declaration on Human Rights (Document E/CN.4/95)

Article 20

…

Mr. Chang (China) stated that he preferred "definition" to "common understanding" and "necessary" to "of the greatest importance".

He further suggested replacing "fulfilment" by "full realization".

The Commission decided, by 9 votes to 1 with 4 abstentions, in favour of the words "common understanding".

The Commission decided, by 6 votes to 4 with 4 abstentions, in favour of the words "of the greatest Importance".

The Commission decided, by 8 votes to 2 with 4 abstentions, in favour of the words "full realization".

The Commission adopted the amended teat by 13 votes to none, with 1 abstention.

...

Mr. Chang (China) concurred in the idea behind the USSR proposal, i.e. there should be no doubt that peoples who did not at present enjoy self-government should be included in the Declaration. He thought, however, that the addition of the words "and peoples" after "all nations" would remove any possibility of misunderstanding.

...

Mr. Wilson (United Kingdom) would vote for the proposal of the Chinese representative, which appeared to him the simplest way of making even clearer that the Declaration applied to all peoples, whatever their status. With regard to the USSR proposal, he considered it took the Commission outside the scope of the Preamble and into the sphere of implementation.

...

Mr. Pavlov (Union of Soviet Socialist Republics) opposed the Chinese amendment, which he considered too indefinite. The question of the populations of non-self-governing territories should be faced squarely and not evaded by vague general statements.

Mr. Chang (China) agreed with the USSR representative that the problem should be faced, but thought the Preamble was not the place to deal with it. If the USSR would propose the adoption of such a clause at the General Assembly, after the adoption of the Declaration, he would support it.

With regard to the USSR proposal, he pointed out that there were many more independent peoples than Non-Self-Governing peoples in the world today. From a purely drafting point of view, therefore, the two phrases did not balance. Furthermore, the addition of the sentence proposed by the USSR made the paragraph unduly long.

...

The first part of the USSR proposal was rejected by 9 votes to 4 with 1 abstention.

The second part of the USSR proposal was rejected by 6 votes to 5 with 3 abstentions.

The Egyptian proposal was adopted by 9 votes to 3 with 2 abstentions.

The Chinese proposal was adopted by 8 votes to none with 5 abstentions.

...

Mr. Chang (China) drew attention to two drafting points. Firstly, he questioned the juxtaposition of "social" and "international", which were not contrasting terms. "Social order, national and international" might be preferable. Secondly, he raised the point that "is entitled" might be substituted in the first line for "has the right" since the word "rights" was used further on in the article.

...

The Chairman, speaking as the United States representative, supported the proposed article, with the drafting changes mentioned by the Chinese representative.

Reverting to her position as Chairman, she put to the vote the USSR proposal to substitute "such" for "good".

The USSR proposal was rejected by six votes to four with three abstentions.

The Chairman drew attention to the article proposed by the French delegation and contained in document E/CN.4/82/Add.8 as article 28.

...

Mr. Chang (China) pointed out that the proposed article belonged more properly with measures for implementation.

...

The Chairman put to the vote the question of whether or not the proposed article should be inserted in the Declaration.

It was decided not to insert the article eight votes to three, with two abstentions.

Discussion of Procedure for Considering the Rapporteur's Report

...

The Chairman asked for consideration of the French-United States proposal to transmit the Commission's report to the Council with the following statement:

"The Commission recognizes that in approving this Declaration it has not completed its task of preparing a Bill of Human Rights. The Bill consists of a Declaration, a Covenant and measures of implementation.

"The Declaration forms part only of the Bill of Rights. Completion of a Covenant including measures of implementation is essential.

"The Commission recommends to the Economic and Social Council that a meeting of the Commission be held immediately after the eighth session of the Council in 1949 for the completion of the Covenant and the measures of implementation."

...

Mr. Chang (China) considered the first two paragraphs of the French-United States proposal unnecessary.

He further suggested an amendment to the third paragraph so that "after the eighth session of the Council in 1949" would be changed to "early in 1949". The date of the Council's eighth session was not as yet fixed.

The Chairman explained that the first two paragraphs of the proposal were designed to ensure that there should be no doubt of the fact that the Commission did not consider the Declaration a complete Bill of human rights.

Mr. Chang (China) thought that idea might be included in the Rapporteur's report.

...

在人权委员会第 80 次会议上的发言

1948 年 6 月 18 日星期五上午 10:45 纽约成功湖

审议报告员提交的报告草案（第 E/CN.4/148 号文件）

张先生（中国）回顾说，他缺席了第一次会议，但他的替补者吴先生提议将第二次会议推迟到 5 月 26 日。该建议的目的不是等待白俄罗斯和乌克兰代表的到来，而是使委员会成员能够仔细审阅提交给他们的各项文件。

　　……

张先生（中国）指出，第 46 次会议中吴先生的发言记录显示，根据中国代表的提议，人权委员会将其工作推迟到 5 月 26 日，这不是因为乌克兰和白俄罗斯的代表尚未到达，而是因为委员们没有足够的时间审阅必要的文件。

巴甫洛夫先生（苏联）指出，根据议事规则，各代表团必须在 24 小时内提交对简要记录的更正。如果在这段时间内没有收到任何更正，则将简要记录作为辩论的客观记录。

张先生（中国）引用了记录中一段相关内容，根据该记录，主席表达了她的意愿，即会议的意义和讨论的内容应当告知秘书长。除此之外，只有一项正式决定被记录在案，而它涉及中国的提案。

张先生提议，报告员应着手重新起草报告第 6 段。

无人反对，这项建议被接受。

克莱科夫金先生（乌克兰）在答复张先生的发言时引述了秘书长给他的一封信，根据这封信，人权委员会决定将关于议程的讨论推迟到 5 月 26 日，等待两个代表团的到来。

　　……

讨论有关《国际人权宪章》的工作计划中的第 12 段

张先生（中国）想知道，是否最好在该段中对委员会起草公约及其执行措施的工作进程作出一些解释。

奥多诺先生（法国）也持同样意见。

······

张先生（中国）接受报告员的建议。

他接着问，委员会某些成员不希望联合国大会在下届会议上就宣言作出决定，是否有任何特殊原因？或是否因为他们希望将公约和执行措施的草案与宣言同时提交，以便一并审议？此外，一些成员赞成立即向联合国大会提交宣言的主张。他认为，宣言的发布刻不容缓。委员会至少应建议今年将宣言提交给联合国大会。

······

——人权委员会第 80 次会议简要记录（E/CN.4/SR.80）

丁智朗译，常健校

E/CN.4/SR.80
29 June 1948

COMMISSION ON HUMAN RIGHTS
THIRD SESSION
SUMMARY RECORD OF THE EIGHTIETH MEETING

Held at Lake Success, New York, on Friday, 18 June 1948, at 10:45 a.m.

Consideration of the Draft Report Presented by the Rapporteur (Document E/CN.4/148)

...

Mr. Chang (China) recalled that he had been absent from the first meeting but that his alternate, Mr. Wu, had proposed the postponement of the second meeting until 26 May. The aim of that proposal had not been to await the arrival of the Byelorussian and Ukrainian representatives but to enable the members of the Commission to consider the various documents submitted to them.

...

Mr. Chang (China) pointed out that it appeared from the speech made by Mr. Wu as recorded in the summary record of the forty-sixth meeting that the Commission had postponed its work until 26 May following a proposal of the Chinese representative, not because the representatives of the Ukrainian and Byelorussian Soviet Socialist Republics had not yet arrived, but because members had not had sufficient time to examine the necessary documents.

Mr. Pavlov (Union of Soviet Socialist Republics) pointed out that under the rules of procedure the delegations were required to submit corrections to summary records within twenty-four hours. If no corrections were sent in within that period, the summary records were taken to he objective accounts of the debates.

Mr. Chang (China) quoted a passage of the summary record concerned, according to which the Chairman had expressed her willingness that the Secretary-General should be informed of the sense of the meeting and of the substance of the discussion. Apart from that, only one formal decision-that relating to the Chinese proposal-had been recorded.

Mr. Chang proposed that the Rapporteur should proceed to redraft paragraph 6 of the report.

There being no objection, that proposal was accepted.

Mr. Klekovkin (Ukrainian Soviet Socialist Republic), replying to Mr. Chang's statement to the effect that the meeting had been postponed to 26 May in order to enable members to study the documents, quoted a letter sent to him by the Secretary General, according to which the Commission had decided to postpone the discussion on the agenda until 26 May pending the arrival of the two delegations.

...

Discussion of paragraph 12 of the plan of work in regard to the International Charter on Human Rights

Mr. Chang (China) wondered whether it would not be better to include in that paragraph some explanation on the stage of the Commission's work on the Covenant and the measures to implement it.

Mr. Ordonneau (France) was of the same opinion.

…

Mr. Chang (China) accepted the Rapporteur's proposal.

He went on to ask whether there was any special reason why certain members of the Commission did not wish a decision to be taken on the Declaration by the General Assembly at its next session, or whether the reason was that they preferred to present the drafts of the Covenant and the measures of implementation at the same time as the Declaration, so that they could be considered together. On the other hand, some members favoured the idea of submitting the Declaration to the Assembly at once. He was of the opinion that the Declaration should be proclaimed without delay. The Commission should at least recommend that the Declaration should come before the General Assembly this year.

…

在人权委员会第 81 次会议上的发言

1948 年 6 月 18 日星期五下午 2:30 纽约成功湖

继续讨论人权委员会提交经济及社会理事会的报告草案
（第 E/CN.4/148 号文件）

......

第 6 段

马利克先生（黎巴嫩）提醒委员会，对报告第 6 段提出了两修正案。(1) 中国代表要求加入以下措辞：在" 5 月 26 日"后加上"因为委员们需要有充裕的时间审阅各种文件"；(2) 美国代表要求将"并且违反协议"的措辞替换为"并且某些委员认为延误违反了协议"。需要委员会对这两项修正案作出决定。

主席首先对中国修正案开放讨论。

维尔凡先生（南斯拉夫）说，中国修正案不尊重日程安排。中国代表建议在 5 月 26 日下午召开委员会第二次会议，"因为委员们需要有充裕的时间审阅各种文件"。委员会刚刚在原则上同意将白俄罗斯和乌克兰代表的迟到通知秘书长，中国代表就提出了这项动议。

张先生（中国）提醒委员会，他的动议是在讨论苏联代表的提案时提出并通过的。

人权委员会以 11 票赞成、4 票反对、1 票弃权通过了中国的修正案。

主席随后将美国的修正案付诸表决。

......

第 11 段

......

张先生（中国）说，一般来说，人权宣言可以说代表着对《联合国宪章》的适用，而人权公约又是对人权宣言的适用。设立调解委员会或法庭以处理侵权案件则是进一步的执行。尽管人权委员会已经认可该问题的重要性，但还没有时间对其进行详细研究。在这方面提出的各种建议，特别是卡森教授提出的建议，值得经济及社会理事会注意。鉴于这些事实，张先生支持报告员的建议，即应将收到的各种提案转交经济及社会理事会，并说明人权委员会当时没有时间进行研究。

......

来文特设委员会的报告（E/CN.4/148/Add.2 号文件）

......

张先生（中国）回顾说，处理其他段落的其他小组委员会成员的姓名并没有被提及。因此，他建议省略来文特设委员会成员的姓名。

......

宣言序文

张先生（中国）认为，投票的实际票数应写入委员会的报告。全世界应该知道，历时两年严谨认真的工作而形成的宣言，获得了 12 名委员的支持，4 名委员弃权，无委员反对。

......

张彭春先生对主席所做的出色工作表示赞赏。

在人权委员会第三届会议闭幕时，主席感谢人权委员会耐心和辛勤的工作，并对取得的成果表示满意。她代表人权委员会感谢秘书处成员，他们的工作为本届会议的成功作出了贡献。

会议于下午 7:20 结束。

——人权委员会第 81 次会议简要记录（E/CN. 4/SR. 81）

罗泽琳、常健译，常健校

E/CN.4/SR.81

1 July 1948

COMMISSION ON HUMAN RIGHTS
THIRD SESSION
SUMMARY RECORD OF THE EIGHTY-FIRST MEETING

Held at Lake Success, New York, on Friday, 18 June 1948, at 2:30 p.m.

Continuation of Discussion of the Draft Report of the Commission on Human Rights to the Economic and Social Council (Document E/CN.4/148)

...

Paragraph 6

Mr. Malik (Lebanon) reminded the Commission that two amendments had been proposed to paragraph 6 of the report: (1) the Chinese representative had requested the insertion of the words "because of the necessity for members to have ample time to examine the various documents" after the words "of 26 May"; (2) the United States representative had requested that the words: "and in violation of the agreement" be replaced by the words "and that certain members felt the delay was in violation of the agreement". It was for the Commission to decide on those two amendments.

The Chairman opened the discussion on the Chinese amendment first.

Mr. Vilfan (Yugoslavia) said that the Chinese amendment did not respect the chronological order of events. The Chinese representative's proposal to convene the second meeting of the Commission for the afternoon of 26 May "because of the necessity for members to have ample time to examine the various documents" had been moved only after the Commission had agreed in principle to inform the Secretary-General of the Byelorussian and Ukrainian representatives' delay in arriving.

Mr. Chang (China) reminded the Commission that his proposal had been moved and adopted during the discussion on the USSR representative's proposal.

The Commission adopted the Chinese amendment by 11 votes to 4, with one abstention.

The Chairman then put to the vote the United States amendment.

...

Paragraph 11

...

Mr. Chang (China) stated that, generally speaking, the Declaration on Human Rights could be said to represent the application of the Charter, while the Covenant was the application of the Declaration. The creation of committees of conciliation or of tribunals to deal with case of violation was a further degree of implementation. Though the Commission had agreed on the importance of the problem, it had not yet had time to study it in detail. The various proposal which had been submitted in that connection, and in particular the one submitted by Professor Cassin, deserved the Economic and Social Council's attention. In view of those facts, Mr. Chang supported the Rapporteur's proposal that the various proposals received should be transmitted to the Council with the explanation that the Commission had not had time to study then.

...

Report of the Ad Hoc Committee on Communications (Document E/CN.4/148/Add.2)

...

Mr. Chang (China) recalled that the names of members of other Sub-Committees dealing with other paragraphs had not been mentioned. He proposed therefore that the names of members of the Ad Hoc Committee on Communications should be omitted.

...

Preamble of the Declaration

Mr. Chang (China) thought that the actual figures of the vote should be included in the Commission's report. The world should know that the Declaration produced after two years of serious work had obtained the support of twelve members, with four abstentions and no one opposed.

...

Mr. Chang (China) expressed his appreciation for the great work of the Chairman.

In closing the third session of the Commission on Human Rights, the Chairman thanked the Commission for its patience and hard work, and expressed her satisfaction at the results achieved. On behalf of the Commission, she thanked the members of the Secretariat whose work had contributed to the success of the session.

The meeting rose at 7:20 p.m.

联合国经济及社会理事会第六、七届会议

在经济及社会理事会第 128 次会议上的发言

1948 年 2 月 5 日星期四上午 11:00 纽约成功湖

15. 人权委员会的报告（第二届会议）（第 E/600 号文件）

......

张先生（中国）就此项工作向人权委员会表示祝贺，并感谢秘书处对这项工作的贡献，他强调中国对制订宣言和公约给予了极高的重视。

......

主席邀请就美国代表的正式动议发表评论，该动议提出，有关在经济及社会理事会会议召开前六周收到报告的规定应当被延后。

张先生（中国）附议该动议。

动议获得通过。

......

张先生（中国）提议休会。整个报告应该交给起草委员会，澳大利亚的决议案可以一并进行审议。

主席指出，经济及社会理事会已经同意第一章至第四章以及附件 A 和附件 B 不应提交起草委员会。

戴维森先生（加拿大）反对休会动议。他提议将第六至十一章连同澳大利亚的决议案一起提交起草委员会，第五章在现阶段不作进一步审议。

张先生（中国）撤回了休会动议，并支持加拿大的提案。

加拿大的提案获得一致通过。

会议于下午 1:30 结束。

——经济及社会理事会第 128 次会议简要记录（E/SR.128）

杨茉萱、常健译，常健校

E/SR.128
5 February 1948

ECONOMIC AND SOCIAL COUNCIL
SIXTH SESSION
SUMMARY RECORD OF THE ONE HUNDRED AND
TWENTY-EIGHTH MEETING

Held at Lake Success, New York, on Thursday, 5 February 1948, at 11:00 a.m.

15. Report of the Commission on Human Rights (Second Session) (E/600)

...

Mr. Chang (China) congratulated the Commission on Human Rights on its work and thanked the Secretariat for its contribution to that work, emphasizing the great importance given to the formulation of the declaration and covenant by his country.

...

The president invited comments on the formal motion of the United States representative that the rule concerning the receipt of reports six weeks before sessions of the Council should be waived.

Mr. Chang (China) seconded the motion.

The motion was adopted.

...

Mr. Chang (China) proposed the adjournment of the meeting. The whole report should then be handed to the Committee, and the Australian resolution could be considered there.

The president pointed out that the Council had already agreed that chapters I to IV, together with annexes A and B, should not go to the committee.

Mr. Davidson (Canada) opposed the motion for adjournment. He proposed that chapters VI to XI, together with the Australian resolution, should be sent to the committee, and that chapter V should have no further consideration at the current stage.

Mr. Chang (China) withdrew his motion for adjournment, and supported the Canadian proposal.

The Canadian proposal was adopted unanimously.

The meeting rose at 1:30 p.m.

在经济及社会理事会第 180 次会议上的发言

1948 年 7 月 21 日星期三下午 3:00 日内瓦万国宫

9. 继续讨论本届会议的工作安排

人权事务委员会

……

迪阿斯克里先生（委内瑞拉）认为，人权事务委员会必须审议重要的事项，在讨论这些重要事项时，所有代表团都应有代表参加；因此，它应该是一个全体委员会。

张彭春先生（中国）和威格尼斯先生（加拿大）支持委内瑞拉代表的观点。

在阿鲁提乌尼安先生（苏联）和兰格先生（波兰）表达了类似的意见之后，麦克尼尔先生（英国）撤回了他的建议。

经济及社会理事会以 12 票对 3 票、2 票弃权决定设立人权事务委员会作为全体委员会。

……

——经济及社会理事会第 180 次会议简要记录
（E/SR. 180）

罗泽琳译，常健校

E/SR.180
21 July 1948

ECONOMIC AND SOCIAL COUNCIL
SEVENTH SESSION
SUMMARY RECORD OF THE ONE HUNDRED AND
EIGHTIETH MEETING

Held at the Palais des Nations, Geneva, on Wednesday, 21 July 1948, at 3:00 p.m.

9. Continuation of the Discussion on Working Arrangements for the Session

Human Rights Committee

...

Mr. D'Ascoli (Venezuela) felt that the Human Rights Committee would have to consider important items, in the discussion of which all delegations should be represented; it should therefore be a committee of the whole.

Mr. P. C. Chang (China) and Mr.Wilgress (Canada) supported the Venezuelan representative's view.

After Mr. Arutiunian (Union of Soviet Socialist Republics) and Mr. Lange (Poland) had expressed themselves in a similar sense, Mr. Mcenil (United Kingdom) withdrew his proposal.

The Council decided, by 12 votes to 3, with 2 abstentions, to set up a Human Rights Committee as a committee of the whole.

...

在经济及社会理事会第 201 次会议上的发言

1948 年 8 月 17 日星期二上午 9:30 日内瓦万国宫

47. 继续讨论本届会议的工作安排（第 E/965 和 E/979 号文件）

......

张彭春先生（中国）说，人权事务委员会已对该委员会遵循的程序进行了讨论，但这并没有减少对正在审议的公约的众多修正和大量评论。在预定的会议结束日期 8 月 20 日之前完成审议工作是不可能的。鉴于大量修正案被提交，他非常怀疑人权委员会即便在每天举行三次会议的情况下，是否能于 8 月 27 日前完成对第 17、18 和 19 条的审议工作。他希望看到经济及社会理事会的工作得到妥善开展，而不是被过于仓促的行动所破坏，该项工作不能在现有的有限时间内妥善完成。

他并没有正式提议再举行另一届会议，但他指出，由于今年只举行了两届会议，因此经济及社会理事会很可能会再举行一届。

他无法对经济及社会理事会的各委员会直接向大会提交文件的建议置之不理。虽然他赞赏英国代表提出这一建议的理由，但考虑到宪章规定，加之通过该建议会削弱经济及社会理事会的尊严，他对是否接受这一建议犹豫不决。

由于似乎不可能在 8 月 27 日之前充分完成工作，经济及社会理事会只能采取方案 A。许多成员希望看到有关人权事项的公约提交给即将举行的下届联合国大会，而方案 A 并不排除这种可能性。虽然方案 A 不尽如人意，但它似乎是最理想和可行的。他同意荷兰代表关于新闻自由的第 39 号决议的建议。经济及社会理事会应就其提交联合国大会的有关公约草案的决议作出决定。

......

张彭春先生（中国）同意法国代表的意见，即本届会议不应迟于 8 月 25 日休会，并强调其他几位代表似乎也表示希望会议结束日期早于主席建议的日期。如果将经济及社会理事会届会延期几周而不是几天，这将是一个危险的先例。

他大体同意加拿大代表的建议，但建议在其他事务完成后继续召开人权事务委员会会议。每天举行两次全体会议当然是可取的，他认为继续推迟审议不断堆积的项目是危险的。他认为，法国代表以及所有其他代表都开始意识到，在最后一刻如此不体面地推迟议程项目可能会对经济及社会理事会造成损害，并意识到迫切需要决定每年举行多少届会议以及会议应持续多久。

美国代表说，联合国大会的行动不应受到限制，提交人权委员会的不同事项应得到同等尊重。主席建议的方案 A 并没有违反这些原则。这将导致将有关新闻自由、人权和种族灭绝的三个事项重新提交经济及社会理事会全体会议审议，这三个事项均不同程度地准备不足，无一作好了充分的准备。然而，准备不足的程度并不影响案文的地位。如果指示人权事务委员会接下来用 10 天时间来审议关于新闻自由的各种公约草案、人权宣言草案和种族灭绝公约草案，可能会准备得更加充分；但也不可能寄希望于在 10 天之内就能对这五份文件作出充分审议并提出建议。

他同意智利代表的意见，即人权事务委员会面临最重要的问题是人权。如果没有一篇人权宣言，《联合国宪章》特别是其第 55 条的意蕴就不可能被清晰和全面地表达出来。种族灭绝和信息自由是极其重要的主题，但它们与《联合国宪章》的关系并不像人权问题那样密切。如果通过了方案 A，经济及社会理事会应首先处理人权问题，其次处理种族灭绝问题，最后处理新闻自由问题，而无论该事项在人权事务委员会那里已经取得了多大的进展。在这方面，他觉得过于严格地限制人权事务委员会每天只能举行一次会议是不明智的。

……

——经济及社会理事会第 201 次会议简要记录

（E/SR. 201）

罗泽琳译，常健校

E/SR.201

17 August 1948

ECONOMIC AND SOCIAL COUNCIL
SEVENTH SESSION
SUMMARY RECORD OF THE TWO HUNDRED AND FIRST MEETING

Held at the Palais des Nations, Geneva, on Tuesday, 17 August 1948,

at 9:30 a.m.

47. Continuation of the Discussion on Working Arrangements for the Session (E/965 and E/979)

...

Mr. P. C. Chang (China) said that the procedure to be followed by the Human Rights Committee had been discussed by the Committee itself, but that had not resulted in any reduction of the numerous amendments and copious comments on the conventions under consideration. There was no chance of finishing the work by 20 August, which was still the scheduled date for closing the session. In view of the large number of amendments already submitted, he greatly doubted whether the Committee would be able to finish its work on items 17, 18 and 19 by 27 August, even if three meetings a day were held. He wished to see the Council's work properly carried out, not spoiled by over hasty action, and it could not be completed properly in the limited time available.

He was not formally proposing that there should be another session, but he pointed out that the Council could well hold one, as there had only been two sessions during the current year.

He could not pass over, without comment, the suggestion that Committees of the Council should transmit documents directly to the Assembly. While appreciating the reasons for which the United Kingdom representative had made that suggestion, he hesitated to accept it, both on constitutional grounds and because its adoption would lower the dignity of the Council.

Since it did not seem possible to complete the work adequately by 27

August, the Council could only adopt course A. Many members wished to see the conventions on matters relating to human rights submitted to the forthcoming session of the General Assembly, and course A did not preclude that possibility. Although course A was unsatisfactory, it seemed the most desirable and practicable one. He agreed with the Netherlands representative's suggestion regarding resolution No.39 on freedom of information. The Council should take a decision on resolutions concerning the draft conventions which it submitted to the General Assembly.

…

Mr. P. C. Chang (China) agreed with the French representative that the session should be adjourned not later than 25 August, and said that several other representatives also appeared to have indicated their preference for an earlier date than that suggested by the President. It would be a dangerous precedent if extensions of Council sessions were to be reckoned in weeks rather than days.

He was in general agreement with what had been suggested by the Canadian representative, except for the proposal to keep the Human Rights Committee in session after the completion of other business. It would certainly be desirable to hold two plenary meetings daily, and he agreed that it would be dangerous to go on piling up items to be deferred. The French representative and, he thought, all other representatives were beginning to realize the damage that might be done to the Council by such undignified last-minute deferment of items on the agenda, and to appreciate the urgent need to decide how many sessions should be held each year and how long they should last.

The United States representative had said that the action of the General Assembly should not be restricted and that the different items referred to the Human Rights Committee should be treated with equal respect. Those principles were not contravened by course A suggested by the President, which would have the effect of returning to the plenary Council the three items relating to freedom of information, human rights and genocide, perhaps in different degrees of unpreparedness but none of them fully prepared. But the degree of unpreparedness did not affect the status of the texts. If the Human Rights Committee were instructed to consider the three draft conventions on freedom of information, the Draft Declaration of Human Rights and the Draft Convention on the Crime of Genocide over the next ten days, their state of preparedness might be improved; but it could not be hoped that, within ten days, the five documents could be fully examined and recommendations made on them.

He agreed with the representative of Chile that human rights was the most important question before the Committee. The implications of the Charter, and especially of Article 55, could not be clearly and comprehensively brought out without a declaration on human rights. Genocide and freedom of information were subjects of great importance, but they had not the same close connexion with the Charter. If course A were adopted, the Council should deal first with human rights, then with genocide, and finally with freedom of information, however far that item had advanced in the Human Rights Committee. In that connexion, he felt that it would be unwise to limit the Human Rights Committee too strictly to one meeting per day.

...

在经济及社会理事会第 202 次会议上的发言

1948 年 8 月 17 日星期二下午 3:00 日内瓦万国宫

49.继续讨论本届会议的工作安排（第 E/979、E/984、E/Conf.6/79 号文件）

……

张彭春先生（中国）解释说，他提出了两项非正式建议：（1）在全体会议而不是在人权事务委员会上，首先审议人权宣言草案，然后审议种族灭绝公约草案；（2）决定人权事务委员会应以正常速度工作，每天举行一次或两次会议。在他提到的两个项目被撤出议程后，人权事务委员会应努力完成对《新闻自由会议最终文件》所载公约草案初稿的审查；如果它成功地完成了此项工作，那么它就应着手审议第二和第三项公约草案，并且无论其进展到了哪个阶段，均应在届会结束前两天或至少一天，即 8 月 23 日或 24 日，将其提交经济及社会理事会。经济及社会理事会将在全体会议上以与灭绝种族公约草案和人权宣言草案相同的方式处理这些公约草案，并将其提交联合国大会。经济及社会理事会不应晚于 8 月 26 日开会。

阿鲁提乌尼安先生（苏联）认为，中国代表的建议不符合主席说明中概述的方案 A，即新闻自由、人权和种族灭绝这三个议题将得到同等的考虑。如果将人权和种族灭绝问题从人权事务委员会的议程中删除，那么该委员会就应该更名，这样公众舆论就不会受到误导。人权事务委员会应审议与人权有关的事项；苏联代表团认为将这些议题从人权事务委员会的议程中删除是不恰当的。

张彭春先生（中国）指出，他主要关注的是人权事务委员会完成其承诺审查的公约草案初稿。他不反对人权事务委员会若有时间可以考虑其他问题。

……

张彭春先生（中国）想知道，加拿大的提案是否应被视为对第 E/979 号文件所述方案 C 的修正，而不是对整个文件的修正。

他对加拿大提案的实质内容发表评论。有些事情被拖得太晚了；这意味着经济及社会理事会可能在 8 月 25 日上午决定重新审议加拿大最初的提议（第 E/965 号文件），并延长人权事务委员会的会议时长。经济及社会理事会和秘书处都不能用这种工作方法工作。会议的闭幕日期必须立即确定。一周或更长的时间都未作出任何决定是不可以的。此外，加拿大代表建议，人权事务委员会应继续按照以前的进程开展工作；他（张先生）认为，遵循这种方法不可能取得任何成就。很明显，目前困难是迄今进展缓慢导致的。

他建议首先对方案 A 进行表决，然后对方案 B 进行表决，再对被视为方案 C 修正案的加拿大的新提案（第 E/984 号文件）进行表决，最后对方案 C 本身进行表决。

……

主席指出，辩论的目的是在本次会议上就工作安排作出决定。若将这一决定推迟到一周后，将给他本人、报告的起草以及秘书处带来困扰。

随后，他将加拿大决议草案（第 E/984 号文件）付诸表决。

加拿大决议草案以 12 票反对、3 票赞成、3 票弃权被否决。

……

主席轮流将方案 A、B 和 C 付诸投票表决，只计算对每个工作进程的赞成票；他解释说，此时只决定原则，细节稍后安排。

投票结果如下：方案 A 获得 11 票赞成；方案 B 获得 3 票赞成；方案 C 获得 4 票赞成。

无人反对，主席宣布经济及社会理事会将采用与方案 A（E/979 号文件）所规定的原则相符合的工作方法。

……

张彭春先生（中国）建议，人权事务委员会提交给经济及社会理事会全体会议的项目应按以下顺序审议：（1）人权；（2）种族灭绝；（3）关于新闻自由的三项公约草案。

他建议，给人权事务委员会的指示应措辞如下："人权事务委员会应尽最大努力在三到四次会议内完成对《新闻收集和国际传播公约（草案）》的审议"。

索普先生（美国）建议用"在本周末之前"取代"在三到四次会议内"。

主席将中国代表向人权事务委员会提出的指示付诸表决；该指示的案

文经美国代表修正，并有一项非正式谅解，即将由主席来安排适当的会议
日程。

该提案以 15 票对 0 票、3 票弃权获得通过。

……

——经济及社会理事会第 202 次会议简要记录
（E/SR. 202）

罗泽琳、常健译，常健校

E/SR.202

17 August 1948

ECONOMIC AND SOCIAL COUNCIL
SEVENTH SESSION
SUMMARY RECORD OF THE TWO HUNDRED AND
SECOND MEETING

Held at the Palais des Nations, Geneva, on Tuesday, 17 August 1948, at 3:00 p.m.

49. Continuation of the Discussion on Working Arrangements for the Session (E/979, E/984 and E/Conf.6/79)

…

Mr. P. C. Chang (China) explained that he had made two informal proposals: (1) to examine in plenary, and not in the Human Rights Committee, first the Draft Declaration on Human Rights and then the Draft Convention on the Crime of Genocide; (2) to decide that the Human Rights Committee should work at a normal pace, holding one or two meetings a day. After the two items he had mentioned had been withdrawn from its agenda, the Committee should endeavour to complete its examination of the first draft convention contained in the Final Act of the Conference on Freedom of Information; if it succeeded in so doing, it should then proceed to the second and third draft conventions and should transmit them to the Council two days, or at least one day, before the end of the session, irrespective of the stage reached. That would be on 23 or 24

August. The Council, in plenary, would then deal with those draft conventions in the same way as with the draft Convention on the Crime of Genocide and the draft Declaration on Human Rights, and transmit them to the General Assembly. The Council should not sit later than 26 August.

Mr. Arutiunian (Union of Soviet Socialist Republics) did not consider that the Chinese representative's proposals were in conformity with course A as outlined in the President's note, which implied that the three subjects of freedom of information, human rights and genocide would receive the same amount of consideration. If human rights and genocide were to be removed from the agenda of the Human Rights Committee, that Committee should be renamed, so that public opinion would not be misled. A Committee on Human Rights should consider matters pertaining to human rights; the Soviet Union delegation did not consider it proper for those items to be taken out of the hands of the Committee.

Mr. P. C. Chang (China) observed that he was mainly concerned to see the Committee finish the first draft convention which it had undertaken to examine. He would not object to a ruling that it might consider theother questions if it had time to do so.

...

Mr. P. C. Chang (China) wondered whether the Canadian proposal should not be considered as an amendment to course C described in document E/979 rather than an amendment to the whole of the document.

He had comments to make on the substance of the Canadian proposal. It left some matters to a rather late hour; indeed it implied that the Council might decide, on the morning of 25 August, to revert to the original Canadian suggestion (E/965) and prolong the meetings of the Human Rights Committee. The Council could not work by such methods of work, nor could the Secretariat. The closing date of the session must be determined forthwith. A week or more could not be allowed to pass without any decision. Moreover, the Canadian representative had suggested that the Human Rights Committee should continue to work at its previous pace; he (Mr. Chang) did not think it would be likely to accomplish anything by following that method. It was clear that the difficulties which had arisen were due to the slow progress so far achieved.

He suggested that a vote should be taken first on course A, then on course B, then on the new Canadian proposal (E/984), to be considered as an amendment to course C, and, finally, on course C itself.

...

The President observed that the purpose of the debate was to reach a decision at that meeting on working arrangements. To postpone the decision until one week later would cause difficulties both to himself, in the preparation of the Report, and also to the Secretariat.

He then put the Canadian draft resolution (E/984) to the vote.

The Canadian draft resolution was rejected by 12 votes to 3, with 3 abstentions.

...

The President put courses A, B and C to the vote in turn, counting only votes cast in favour of each course; he explained that only the principle was to be decided at that stage, details being arranged later.

The result of the vote was as follows: Course A, 11; Course B, 3; Course C, 4.

There being no objection, the President announced that the Council would adopt a method of work conforming to the principle laid down in course A (E/979).

...

Mr. P. C. Chang (China) suggested that the items returned to plenary from the Human Rights Committee should be considered in the following order: (1) human rights; (2) genocide; (3) the three draft conventions on freedom of information.

He proposed that the directive to the Human Rights Committee should be worded as follows: "The Human Rights Committee should do its utmost to finish consideration of the Draft Convention on the Gathering and International Transmission of News within three to four meetings".

Mr. Thorp (United States of America) suggested that the words "by the end of this week" should replace the words "within three to four meetings".

The President put to the vote the directive to the Human Rights Committee proposed by the Chinese representative; as amended by the United States representative, with the informal understanding that he would arrange an appropriate schedule of meetings.

The proposal was adopted by 15 votes to none, with 3 abstentions.

...

第三届联合国大会第三委员会会议

在第三委员会第88次会议上的发言

1948 年 9 月 30 日星期四上午 11:45 巴黎夏乐宫

......

9.《国际人权宣言（草案）》（第 E/800 号文件）

......

张先生（中国）建议，可以选择一个折中的办法，即立即开始对序言的讨论，由于序言对宣言所依据的原则已作出规定，每位成员在讨论中均可阐述其原则。他提议将讨论分为两部分：一部分是关于原则的讨论，另一部分是关于草案的讨论。据此可以确定何种措辞最能表达为委员会所接受的原则。

......

张先生（中国）说，由于委员会成员赞成进行一般性讨论，他将撤回关于委员会应立即开始研究序言的建议。但他请求主席询问代表们，是希望只讨论宣言草案，还是希望讨论包括公约和执行建议在内的整个报告。

......

张先生（中国）询问委员会要审议的究竟是哪个提案，以及究竟要对什么问题进行表决。

主席将该提案陈述如下：

"第三委员会决定立即进行对其日程的第 2 项[《国际人权宣言（草案）》：经济及社会理事会提交事项]进行一般性讨论，它包括人权委员会报告全文。"

......

——第三委员会第 88 次会议简要记录（A/C. 3/SR. 88）

罗泽琳译，常健校

A/C.3/SR.88
30 September 1948

GENERAL ASSEMBLY
THIRD SESSION
THIRD COMMITTEE
SUMMARY RECORD OF THE EIGHTY-EIGHTH MEETING

Held at the Palais de Chaillot, Paris, on Thursday, 30 September 1948,
at 11:45 a.m.

...

9. Draft International Declaration of Human Rights (E/800)

...

Mr. Chang (China) suggested, as a compromise, that the discussion on the preamble might begin immediately, a procedure which would permit every member to state his principles, since the preamble set out the principles on which the declaration was based. He proposed that the discussion should be divided into two parts, a discussion on principles and a discussion on drafting, so as to ascertain what wording would best express the principles accepted by the Commission.

...

Mr. Chang (China) said that as his colleagues were in favour of a general discussion he would withdraw his proposal that the Committee should start immediately by studying the preamble. He would request the President, however, to ask the representatives whether they wished the discussion to deal solely with the draft declaration or with the whole report, including the covenant and the suggestions for implementation.

...

Mr. Chang (China) asked what exactly was the proposal before the Committee and upon what question would the vote be taken.

The Chairman stated the proposal in the following terms:

"The Third Committee "decides to proceed immediately to a general discussion of item 2 of its agenda (Draft International Declaration of Human Rights: item submitted by the Economic and Social Council), which includes the report of the Commission on Human Rights in its entirety."

在第三委员会第 91 次会议上的发言

1948 年 10 月 2 日星期六上午 10:30 巴黎夏乐宫

12.《国际人权宣言（草案）》（第 E/800 号文件）（续）

……

张先生（中国）说道，联合国大会即将通过的《国际人权宣言（草案）》，是一份及时和崇高的文件，是被迫切需要的一份文件。《联合国宪章》要求所有会员国承诺遵守人权，而宣言明确阐述了这些权利。法国是现代自由思想的诞生地，因此，宣言最后的制定工作理应在法国完成。

在 18 世纪，当关于人权的进步思想首先在欧洲被提出时，对中国哲学作品的译本，已经被像伏尔泰、魁奈和狄德罗这样的思想家知晓，并启发他们对封建观念开展人文主义反抗。早在近代欧洲首次探讨人权问题的时候，中国的思想已经与欧洲关于人权的思想和感情相互融合。人权的重点应放在"人"上，一个人必须时刻意识到他所生活的社会中的其他人。唯有经历一个漫长的教育过程，使所有人都能认识到宣言赋予他们的全部价值和义务，这些权利才能在实践中得以实现。因此，需要尽快通过该宣言，使其成为人的人性化的基础和教育方案。

人权宣言应简明扼要，易于被所有人理解。这份文件的对象应该是世界各地所有人，而不仅仅是律师和学者。正是本着这一目标，中国代表团在人权委员会第三届会议上，提出了一份包含 10 条内容的简洁宣言，并认为该文件有助于使现在的宣言草案更加清晰和相对简短。中国代表团将对宣言草案的现存形式给予总体上的支持，并保留在详细审议该文件时提出建议的权利。

……

——第三委员会第 91 次会议简要记录（A/C. 3/SR. 91）

罗泽琳译，常健校

A/C.3/SR.91
2 October 1948

GENERAL ASSEMBLY
THIRD SESSION
THIRD COMMITTEE
SUMMARY RECORD OF THE NINETY-FIRST MEETING

Held at the Palais de Chaillot, Paris, on Saturday, 2 October 1948, at 10:30 a.m.

12. Draft International Declaration of Human Rights (E/800) (Continued)

...

Mr. Chang (China) stated that the Draft International Declaration of Human Rights which the General Assembly was about to adopt was a timely and noble document, for which there was urgent need. The Charter committed all Member States to the observance of human rights; the declaration stated those rights explicitly. It was only proper that their final formulation should take place in France, the birthplace of modern ideas of freedom.

In the eighteenth century, when progressive ideas with respect to human rights had been first put forward in Europe, translations of Chinese philosophers had been known to and had inspired such thinkers as Voltaire, Quesnay and Diderot in their humanistic revolt against feudalistic conceptions. Chinese ideas had been intermingled with European thought and sentiment on human rights at the time when that subject had been first speculated upon in modern Europe. Stress should be laid upon the human aspect of human rights. A human being had to be constantly conscious of other men, in whose society he lived. A lengthy process of education was required before men and women realized the full value and obligations of the rights granted to them in the declaration; it was only when that stage had been achieved that those rights could be realized in practice. It was therefore necessary that the declaration should be approved as soon as possible, to serve as a basis and a programme for the humanization of man.

Declaration of Human Rights should be brief and readily understandable by all. It should be a document for all men everywhere, not merely for lawyers and scholars. It was with that object in mind that the Chinese delegation had introduced, at the third session of the Commission on Human Rights, a brief declaration containing ten articles and it was gratified by the fact that the document had aided in making the present draft declaration clear and relatively brief. The Chinese delegation would give its general support to the draft declaration in its existing form, and reserved the right to present suggestions during the detailed examination of that document.

...

在第三委员会第 95 次会议上的发言

1948 年 10 月 6 日星期三下午 3:15 巴黎夏乐宫

16.《国际人权宣言（草案）》（第 E/800 号文件）（续）

······

张先生（中国）对促使埃及代表提出建议的情感表示理解。仅仅诉诸委员会权限之类的形式考量，不足以解决这个问题。中国代表觉得，伦理考量应在这场讨论中发挥更大的作用。这个问题不是纯粹的政治问题。联合国的目的不是确保个人的私利，而是努力提高人的道德地位。有必要宣布个人的义务。因为正是意识到自己的义务才能使人达到更高的道德标准。

······

17. 第三委员会会议记录

······

圣克鲁兹先生（智利）正式提议，今后应逐字记录第三委员会的会议内容，如果不可行，则应要求提供更完整的简要记录。

张先生（中国）指出，智利代表在其请求中的措辞是明智的，因为他要求秘书处尽可能提供会议的逐字记录，如果无法提供逐字记录的话，则保留要求简要记录的可能性。

······

张先生（中国）预计，第三委员会更倾向于采纳智利提案的第二部分，而不是第一部分。由于有成员要求分别投票，他将对提案的第一部分投反对票，对第二部分投赞成票。如果代表们想知道会议上所说的确切言辞，他们可以听录音。

······

——第三委员会第 95 次会议简要记录（A/C.3/SR.95）

罗泽琳、常健译，常健校

A/C.3/SR.95
6 October 1948

GENERAL ASSEMBLY
THIRD SESSION
THIRD COMMITTEE
SUMMARY RECORD OF THE NINETY-FIFTH MEETING
Held at the Palais de Chaillot, Paris, on Wednesday, 6 October 1948,
at 3:15 p.m.

16. Draft International Declaration of Human Rights (E/800) (Continued)

...

Mr. Chang (China) expressed his sympathy with the feelings which had motivated the proposal of the Egyptian representative. It was not sufficient to resolve the question by invoking formal considerations such as that of the Committee's terms of reference. The Chinese representative felt that ethical considerations should play a greater part in the discussion. The question was not purely political. The aim of the United Nations was not to ensure the selfish gains of the individual but to try and increase man's moral stature. It was necessary to proclaim the duties of the individual for it was a consciousness of his duties which enabled man to reach a high moral standard.

...

17. Records of The Meetings of the Committee

...

Mr. Santa Cruz (Chile) formally proposed that the meetings of the Third Committee should be recorded verbatim in future or, if that were not possible, that a request should be made for fuller summary records.

Mr. Chang (China) observed that the representative of Chile had been wise in the wording of his request inasmuch as he had asked the Secretariat to provide verbatim records of meetings if possible, reserving the possibility of requesting summary records if it were impossible to have verbatim records.

...

Mr. Chang (China) had anticipated that the Committee would be more inclined to adopt the second part of the Chilean proposal than the first. Since a request had been made for separate votes, he would vote against the first part of the proposal and in favour of the second. If representatives wished to know the exact words spoken at a meeting, they could listen to the sound recordings.

...

在第三委员会第 96 次会议上的发言

1948 年 10 月 7 日星期四上午 10:30 巴黎夏乐宫

18.《国际人权宣言（草案）》（第 E/800 号文件）（续）

......

第 1 条（续）

......

张先生（中国）觉得，宣言第 1 条应保持不变，构成该条的两句话不应分开。第一句对权利的概括表述和第二句对义务的意指相得益彰。如果将第 1 条从宣言正文中删除，就不会引起读者应有的注意；此外，如果不在各种权利前面提到"兄弟情谊"，就会显得只注重私人利益。类似的推理也适用于包含义务陈述的第 27 条。关于权利和义务的陈述，应成为宣言的内在组成部分。

张先生支持按照比利时代表的建议，删除第一条中的"根据自然本性"的措辞。这一改动将消除所有神学问题，神学问题不能也不应在一篇旨在普遍适用的宣言中提出。

尽管该宣言无疑将得到绝大多数会员国的赞成票而被接受，但在人权领域不应忘记人口的大多数。中国代表回顾说，其国家人口构成了人类人口的很大一部分。中国人民有着不同于西方基督教国家的理想和传统。这些理想包括良好的举止、礼仪、礼节和为他人着想。然而，尽管中国文化最重视作为道德组成部分的礼仪，但中国代表会尽量不提出在宣言中提及礼仪的建议。他希望委员会成员能表现出同样的深思熟虑，撤回对第 1 条提出的那些会产生形而上学问题的修正案。对西方文明来说，宗教不容忍的时代也已经结束了。

张先生同意黎巴嫩代表的意见，即应删去英文文本第 1 条第一句中的"生而"一词，如果没有这一修正，这句话就会让人想起卢梭和人性本善的理论。就宣言而言，最好不涉及这样的内容。

他还欢迎南非代表团撤回其对第 1 条的修正案（第 A/C.3/226 号文件）。

第 1 条第二句呼吁人们以兄弟情谊的精神彼此相待。这种态度与中国人对于礼貌的态度和重视善待他人是完全一致的。只有当人的社会行为上升到这一水平时，他才是真正的人。在维护这些崇高原则的斗争中，礼仪是一种不应忽视的理想——不幸的是，它经常被忽视。

最后，张先生强烈呼吁第 1、2、3 条应保持原样。

……

张先生（中国）说，没有必要将该修正案付诸表决，因为他可以提出另一种处理方式。他希望保留稍后提出这一建议的权利。

……

——第三委员会第 96 次会议简要记录（A/C.3/SR.96）

罗泽琳译，常健校

A/C.3/SR.96
7 October 1948

GENERAL ASSEMBLY
THIRD SESSION
THIRD COMMITTEE
SUMMARY RECORD OF THE NINETY-SIXTH MEETING

Held at the Palais de Chaillot, Paris, on Thursday, 7 October 1948,

at 10:30 a.m.

18. Draft International Declaration of Human Rights (E/800) (Continued)

…

Article 1 (Continued)

…

Mr. Chang (China) felt that article 1 of the declaration should remain where it was, and that the two sentences which made up that article should not be separated. A happy balance was struck by the broad statement of rights in the first sentence and the implication of duties in the second. Should article 1 be taken out of the body of the declaration, it would not claim as much of the reader's attention as it deserved to do; moreover, the various rights would appear more selfish if they were not preceded by the reference to "a spirit of brotherhood". Similar reasoning applied to Article 27, which contained a statement of duties. Statements of rights and duties should form an integral part of the declaration.

Mr. Chang supported the deletion of article 1 of the words "by nature", as suggested by the Belgian representative. That measure would obviate any theological question, which could not and should not be raised in a declaration designed to be universally applicable.

While the declaration would no doubt be accepted by a majority vote of Member States, in the field of human rights popular majority should not be forgotten. The Chinese representative recalled that the population of his country comprised a large segment of humanity. That population had ideals and traditions different from those of the Christian West. Those ideals included good manners, decorum, propriety and consideration for others. Yet, although Chinese culture attached the greatest importance to manners as a part of ethics, the Chinese representative would refrain from proposing that mention of them should be made in the declaration. He hoped that his colleagues would show equal consideration and withdraw some of the amendments to article 1 which raised metaphysical problems. For Western civilization, too, the time for religious intolerance was over.

Mr. Chang agreed with the Lebanese representative that the word "born" in the first sentence of the English text of article 1 should be deleted; without that amendment, the sentence was reminiscent of Rousseau and the theory that man was naturally good. For the purposes of the declaration it was better to start with a clean slate.

He also welcomed the fact that the delegation of the Union of South Africa had withdrawn its amendment to article 1 (A/C.3/226).

The second sentence of article 1 called upon men to act towards one another in a spirit of brotherhood. That attitude was perfectly consistent with the Chinese attitude towards manners and the importance of kindly and considerate treatment of others. It was only when man's social behaviour rose to that level that he was truly human. Decorum was an ideal which should not be lost sight of – as unfortunately it often was-in the struggle to uphold noble principles.

In conclusion, Mr. Chang urged that articles 1, 2 and 3 should be left where they were.

...

Mr. Chang (China) said that it would not be necessary to put that amendment to a vote because he could suggest another way of dealing with it. He wished to reserve the right to make that suggestion later.

...

在第三委员会第 98 次会议上的发言

1948 年 10 月 9 日星期六上午 10:30 巴黎夏乐宫

20.《国际人权宣言（草案）》（第 E/800 号文件）（续）

第 1 条（续）

......

张先生（中国）认为，第 1 条的基本案文，加上比利时代表提出的修正案（第 A/C.3/234 号文件）和黎巴嫩代表提出的修正案（第 A/C.3/235 号文件），如果基于 18 世纪哲学加以理解的话，委员会是可以接受的。

18 世纪的哲学是建立在人性本善基础之上的。其他学派或是说人的本性是中性的，可以变好也可以变坏，或是说人的本性都是坏的。18 世纪的思想家们认识到，虽然人在很大程度上是动物，但有一部分是与动物区别开来的。这一部分是真正的人，是善的。因此，这一部分应当得到更大的重视。这些思想家的工作导致在法国宣布自由、平等和博爱的原则，并在美国导致了《独立宣言》的发布。18 世纪关于人的本性为善的观念，与上帝赋予人以灵魂的观念，彼此并不矛盾，因为上帝的观念特别强调人本性中人的部分，而不是动物的部分。

张先生敦促委员会不应再争论人的本性问题，而应以 18 世纪哲学家的工作为基础。他认为委员会应同意黎巴嫩代表团提议的以"所有人都是自由的……"作为开头的案文，用"人"来指人的非动物部分，并应进一步同意比利时代表团的提议，删除"依据自然本性"的措辞。如果删除"依据自然本性"这几个字，相信上帝的人仍然可以在本条有力的开篇陈述中找到上帝的理念，同时，其他有不同观念的人也能够接受该文本。

张先生希望巴西代表团根据他的解释愿意撤回其修正案（第 A/C.3/215 号文件），从而使委员会成员不必就一项事实上超出人类判断能力的原则进行表决。

张先生特别赞扬法国代表卡森教授对起草宣言草案工作所作的贡献，

并认为他精妙地阐释了 18 世纪的法国学说。

关于苏联代表指出的现实实际问题，张先生说，所有人都承认存在着各种不义行为，纠正这些不义行为的最有效路径，就是制定一个共同标准，而这正是宣言草案试图确立的。然而，承认世界所面临的严酷事实，不应被称为现实主义，而应被称为自然主义，因为现实主义意味着它是真正真实的，并且是可以用心灵的全部力量来加以肯定的。

……

——第三委员会第 98 次会议简要记录（A/C.3/SR.98）

罗泽琳译，常健校

A/C.3/SR.98
9 October 1948

GENERAL ASSEMBLY
THIRD SESSION
THIRD COMMITTEE
SUMMARY RECORD OF THE NINETY-EIGHTH MEETING

Held at the Palais de Chaillot, Paris, on Saturday, 9 October 1948, at 10:30 a.m.

20. Draft international Declaration of Human Rights (E/800)
(Continued)

Article 1 (Continued)

...

Mr. Chang (China) thought that the basic text of article 1, with the amendments proposed by the Belgian (A/C.3/234) and Lebanese (A/C.3/235) representatives, would be acceptable to the Committee if it were understood on the basis of eighteenth century philosophy.

That philosophy was based on the innate goodness of man. Other schools of thought had said that man's nature was neutral and could be made good or bad, or again that his nature was all bad. The eighteenth century thinkers, whose work had led to the proclamation of the principles of liberty, equality and fraternity in France and, in the United States, to the Declaration of Independence, had realized that although man was largely animal, there was a part of him which distinguished him from animals. That part was the real man and was good, and that part should therefore be given greater importance. There was no contradiction between the eighteenth century idea of goodness of man's essential nature and the idea of a soul given to man by God, for the concept of God laid particular stress on the human, as opposed to the animal, part of man's nature.

Mr. Chang urged that the Committee should not debate the question of the nature of man again but should build on the work of the eighteenth century philosophers. He thought the Committee should agree to a text beginning "all human beings are free..."—using "human beings" to refer to the non-animal part of man—as proposed by the Lebanese delegation and should further agree to delete the words "by nature", as proposed by the Belgian delegation. If the words "by nature" were deleted, those who believed in God could still find in the strong opening assertion of the article the idea of God, and at the same time others with different concepts would be able to accept the text.

Mr. Chang hoped that in the light of his explanation the Brazilian delegation would be willing to withdraw its amendment (A/C.3/215) and so spare the members of the Committee the task of deciding by vote on a principle which was in fact beyond the capacity of human judgment.

Mr. Chang paid a particular tribute to the contribution to the work of preparing the draft declaration made by Professor Cassin, the representative of France, who had so ably exposed French doctrines of the eighteenth century.

Concerning practical reality a point raised by the USSR representative, Mr. Chang said that all recognized the existence of wrongs, but the most efficacious way of correcting those wrongs was to set a common standard such as the draft declaration sought to establish. Recognition of the stark facts with which the world was faced should not, however, be termed realism but naturalism, for realism meant that which was truly real and which could be affirmed with the full force of the soul.

...

在第三委员会第 99 次会议上的发言

1948 年 10 月 11 日星期一下午 3:00 巴黎夏乐宫

21.《国际人权宣言（草案）》（第 E/800 号文件）（续）

……

第 1 条（续）

……

格鲁姆巴赫先生（法国）说……关于巴西的修正案，他尊重激发提出该修正案的宗教情感，但他认为在第 1 条中列入一项所有代表都无法同意的关于人类起源的声明是不合适的。宗教自由是一项基本人权，但他同意中国代表（第 98 次会议）的观点，即试图就人类起源达成一致是没有用的，应避免此类有争议的问题。委员会的基本目标是就可付诸实施的基本原则达成一致。这种态度将得到信徒和非信徒的赞同。伟大的天主教徒雅克·马里坦曾就这个问题表示，各国应该努力就人权宣言达成一致，但试图就这些权利的起源达成一致是没有用的。正是由于达成了关于实际基本权利的协议，在被占领的可怕岁月里，他的国家领导人坚强和团结一致。

他支持人权委员会提交的草案中出现的简单声明，但他同意中国代表的意见，即"依据自然本性"一词应从第 1 条第二句中删除。

他请求巴西代表撤回他的修正案，以便该条获得一致通过。

……

纽兰夫人（新西兰）……也同意中国代表的意见，即该条应包含一个肯定的断言：所有人在尊严和权利上都是自由和平等的。然而，她的代表团希望保留"生而"一词。

……

根据比利时、中国和南斯拉夫代表所表达的观点，"依据自然本性"一词被省略。

巴格达迪先生（埃及）……他同意比利时和中国代表的意见，即应删除第 1 条第二句中的"依据自然本性"一词。

卡亚利先生（叙利亚）……同意中国代表的意见，即"赋有理性和良知"一词应当保留，因为它们有助于区分人与动物。在他看来，世界上出现的大多数罪恶和大多数国际误解都是由于人类的理性和良知受到损害。

……

张先生（中国）赞成采纳一个没有限定条件的有力度的肯定陈述。如果"生而"一词被删去，人权始于出生还是始于受孕的问题就不会产生。但是，如果委员会大多数成员希望保留"生而"一词，他建议就插入"并保持"的措辞进行进一步表决。

主席要求对中国提出的删除"生而"一词的提案进行表决。

该提案以 20 票反对、12 票赞成、5 票弃权被否决。

……

——第三委员会第 99 次会议简要记录（A/C.3/SR.99）

罗泽琳、常健译，常健校

A/C.3/SR.99

11 October 1948

GENERAL ASSEMBLY
THIRD SESSION
THIRD COMMITTEE
SUMMARY RECORD OF THE NINETY-NINTH MEETING

Held at the Palais de Chaillot, Paris, on Monday, 11 October 1948, at 3:00 p.m.

21. Draft International Declaration of Human Rights (E/800) (Continued)

…

Article 1 (Continued)

…

Mr. Grumbach (France) …With regard to the Brazilian amendment, he respected the religious sentiments which had inspired it, but he did not think it would be appropriate to include in article 1 a statement on man's origin to which all representatives could not agree. Freedom of religion was a fundamental human right, but he agreed with the representative of China (98th meeting) that it was useless to attempt to reach agreement with regard to man's origin, and such controversial issues should be avoided. The Committee's essential aim was to reach agreement on fundamental principles which could be put into practice. That attitude would be endorsed by believers and non-believers alike. The great Catholic, Jacques Maritain, had stated in relation to that very question that the nations should try to reach agreement on a declaration of human rights, but that it was useless to try to reach agreement on the origin of those rights. It had been that agreement on practical fundamental rights which had kept the leaders of his country strong and united during the terrible years of the occupation.

He supported the simple statement as it appeared in the draft submitted by the Commission Human Rights but he agreed with the representative of China that the words "by nature" should be deleted from the second sentence of article 1.

He appealed to the representative of Brazil to withdraw his amendment, so that the article could be adopted unanimously.

　…

Mrs. Newlands (New Zealand)... She also agreed with the representative of China that the article should contain an affirmative assertion that all men were free and equal in dignity and rights. Her delegation wished, however, to retain the word "born".

　…

The words "by nature" had been omitted in accordance with the views expressed by the representatives of Belgium, China, and Yugoslavia.

Mr. Bagdadi (Egypt) …He agreed with the representatives of Belgium and China that the words "by nature" should be deleted from the second sentence of article 1.

Mr. Kayaly (Syria) …He agreed with the representative of China that the words "endowed with reason and conscience" should be retained as they served to differentiate man from the animals. In his opinion, most of the evils apparent in the world and most international misunderstandings were due to the fact that man's reason and conscience had been impaired.

　…

Mr. Chang (China) was in favour of the adoption of a strong affirmative statement without qualifications. If the word "born" were deleted, the question of whether human rights began at birth or at conception would not arise. However, if the majority of the Committee wanted the word "born" to be retained, he suggested a further vote on the insertion of the words "and remain".

...

The Chairman called for a vote on the Chinese proposal to delete the word "born".

The proposal was rejected by 20 votes to 12, with 5 abstentions.

...

在第三委员会第 100 次会议上的发言

1948 年 10 月 12 日星期二上午 10:45 巴黎夏乐宫

22.《国际人权宣言（草案）》（第 E/800 号文件）（续）

……

第 2 条

……

主席表示，他首先将古巴修正案（第 A/C.3/224 号文件）付诸表决，它是与原草案差别最大的，因为它提议用一个新案文取代现有案文。然后委员会将确定对苏联代表团所提修正案（第 E/800 号文件，第 32 页）的立场。

……

张先生（中国）希望强调，人权委员会是经过深思熟虑之后，才决定将其提交给联合国大会的人权宣言草案中的平等原则和自由原则用两个条目来分别加以阐述。

事实上，第 2 条旨在确保每个人都应享有宣言所规定的一切权利和自由，不受任何歧视。

第 6 条旨在通过给予每个人法律保护，使其不受违反该宣言的歧视，将这一原则变为现实。

中国代表团与人权委员会的观点完全一致，并希望第三委员会特别注意使第 2 条保持现有形式。

关于古巴代表团的修正案，张先生发言指出，由于宣言没有像述及权利那样具体提到义务，最好从建议案文中删除"并在义务的约束下"的表述。事实上各方已达成一致，只在第 27 条和第 1 条中涉及义务，第 27 条随后还须进一步界定和扩充，第 1 条则弘扬激励所有人行动的兄弟情谊。

……

张先生（中国）提议，为了简化程序，应将古巴代表团提交的第 2 条新案文付诸表决。通过投票决定赞成或反对该案文，第三委员会将含蓄地表明它是赞成还是反对案文融合原则。

然而，反对任何形式歧视对世界广大人口的重要性，中国代表团再怎么强调也不过分。对这些人民来说，至关重要的是，不仅其国家立法应保护他们不受歧视，而且应庄严宣布在享有人类所有基本自由和权利方面的平等原则。

……

——第三委员会第100次会议简要记录（A/C.3/SR.100）

罗泽琳、常健译，常健校

A/C.3/SR.100

12 October 1948

GENERAL ASSEMBLY
THIRD SESSION
THIRD COMMITTEE
SUMMARY RECORD OF THE HUNDREDTH MEETING

Held at the Palais de Chaillot, Paris, on Tuesday, 12 October 1948,

at 10:45 a.m.

22. Draft International Declaration of Human Rights (E/800) (Continued)

…

Article 2

…

The Chairman said that he would first put to the vote the Cuban amendment (A/C.3/224), which was the furthest removed from the original draft since it proposed to substitute a new text for the existing one. The Committee would then take a stand with respect to the amendment proposed by the USSR delegation (E/800, page 32).

…

Mr. Chang (China) wished to stress that it was only after mature consideration that the Commission on Human Rights had decided to state the principles of equality and liberty in two separate articles of the draft declaration of human rights which it was submitting to the General Assembly.

Article 2 did, in fact, aim at ensuring that everyone, without distinction of any kind, should enjoy all the rights and freedoms set forth in the declaration.

Article 6 aimed at translating that principle into practical reality by granting everyone protection of the law against discrimination in violation of that declaration.

The Chinese delegation was in whole-hearted agreement with the Commission on Human Rights and hoped that the Third Committee would make a point of retaining article 2 in its existing form.

Speaking on the Cuban delegation's amendment Mr. Chang pointed out that, as the declaration did not make specific mention of duties as well as rights, it would be preferable to delete the words "and subject to the duties" from the proposed text. It had indeed been agreed that duties would be referred to only in article 27 which had to be further defined and amplified at a later date, and in the general declaration of article 1 on the spirit of brotherhood which should inspire the actions of all men.

　…

Mr. Chang (China) proposed, in order to simplify the procedure, that the new text submitted by the Cuban delegation for article 2 should be put to the vote. By voting for the adoption or rejection of that text, the Committee would show by implication whether it was for or against the principle of the fusion of texts.

The Chinese delegation could not, however, stress too much the importance which the fight against discrimination of any kind had for vast sections of the world's population. It was essential for those peoples that they should not only be protected within their national legislation against discrimination, but that the principle of equality in respect of all the fundamental freedoms and rights of mankind should be solemnly proclaimed.

　…

在第三委员会第 101 次会议上的发言

1948 年 10 月 13 日星期三下午 3:00 巴黎夏乐宫

23.《国际人权宣言（草案）》（第 E/800 号文件）（续）

第 2 条（续）

......

希梅内斯·德·阿雷查加先生（乌拉圭）说，所建议的各种词汇当翻译成西班牙文时都是不可接受的。例如，"阶级"具有经济的含义。需要一个表述来说明不应在各群体间存在歧视。"出生"这个词更灵活，而"阶级"或"种性"都不够准确。

......

张先生（中国）指出，这个问题已经被人权委员会充分讨论过了。种族、肤色、社会出身，以及最经常出现的性别，这些概念都涉及出生问题；而社会出身也包含阶级或种姓的概念。

在他看来，人权委员会的案文是最清晰、最少混淆的。他希望第三委员会的大多数成员予以支持。

......

——第三委员会第 101 次会议简要记录（A/C.3/SR.101）

昌成程译，常健校

A/C.3/SR.101
13 October 1948
GENERAL ASSEMBLY
THIRD SESSION
THIRD COMMITTEE
SUMMARY RECORD OF THE HUNDRED AND FIRST MEETING

Held at the Palais de Chaillot, Paris, on Wednesday, 13 October 1948, at 3:00 p.m.

23. Draft International Declaration of Human Rights (E/800)
(Continued)

Article 2 (Continued)

...

Mr. Jiménez de Aréchaga (Uruguay) said that the various words suggested were not altogether acceptable when translated into Spanish. The word "class", for example had an economic meaning. What was wanted was an expression to the effect that no discrimination should exist between groups. The word "birth" was more flexible, but neither "class" nor "caste" was accurate.

...

Mr. Chang (China) pointed out that the question had been discussed fully in the Human Rights Commission. The concept of race, colour, social origin, and in most cases sex, involved the question of birth, while social origin also embraced the idea of class or caste.

The Commission's text seemed to him the clearest and least confused and he hoped that a large majority of the Committee would support it.

...

在第三委员会第 103 次会议上的发言

1948 年 10 月 15 日星期五上午 10:45 巴黎夏乐宫

25. 《国际人权宣言（草案）》（第 E/800 号文件）（续）

第 3 条（续）

......

张先生（中国）评论道，所有已提交的修正案，甚至包括那些未获大多数赞成的修正案，都对起草一个共同宣言作出了建设性贡献。

但是，委员们不应忽视宣言草案本身，它是提交给第三委员会的基本文件。该草案是孜孜不倦努力的结果，已经经过了细致严谨的审议。在日内瓦起草的最初文本，已提交各国政府征求意见。人权委员会对该文本进行了审议，并根据提出的各种评论和建议对其进行了修改。委员会现在看到的宣言草案是所有这些工作的最终产物，其内容只是日内瓦最初草案的三分之二。实际上我们已经意识到，宣言越清晰、越简洁，就会越有效、越持久。宣言并非为法律专家或学者而写，而是要写给一般公众。因此，它应尽可能醒目，且尽可能简洁。最好将宣言限于 10 条；但如不能做到，则至少应限于正在接受审议的草案所包括的 28 条。

张先生接着说，第三委员会尚未研究宣言的整体结构。他认为，这种研究是必不可少的，因此，在审议宣言时，他想特别谈谈其逻辑结构。

第 1、2、3 条表达了 18 世纪哲学的三个主要理念：第 1 条表达了博爱的理念，第 2 条表达了平等的理念，第 3 条表达了自由的理念。

第 3 条对自由的理念进行了分析，并将其适用于人类。第 3 条提出了基本原则，该原则在随后的 9 条中被界定和阐明。第 4 条涉及奴隶制；第 5 条涉及对法律人格权的承认；第 6 条涉及法律面前的平等；第 7 条涉及需要确认逮捕合法性；第 8 条涉及获得公正审判的权利；第 9 条涉及无罪推定的权利；第 10 条禁止干涉个人隐私；第 11 条确认迁徙自由。

在这一系列条款中，自由的理念被逐步扩大：它首先被适用于个人，然后被适用于家庭，最后被适用于国家。因此，这一系列条款有助于发展和澄清自由的理念。

第 13 至 20 条分别涉及各类社会体制。

第 20 条也像第 3 条一样表达了一个总体理念，并在以下各条中对其进行了解释和发展。第 20 条提出了社会保障的理念，该理念在第 21 至 25 条中被界定和发展。

因此，宣言草案的结构是十分清晰和合乎逻辑的。黎巴嫩代表团、乌拉圭代表团和古巴代表团联合提交的修正案，特别是其表达了与第 20 条相同想法的第二部分，与该结构不符。正是出于这个原因，张先生认为宣言草案应该保留原样，因为它具有合乎逻辑、清晰和简洁的特性，这些特性对于证明该宣言的有效性是必不可少的。

……

科罗米纳斯先生（阿根廷）表示，……正如中国代表所说，人权宣言的主要目的是简洁、清晰和明确，以便每个人都能理解。这不是一项供法律专家专用的公约。

……

卡亚利先生（叙利亚）完全同意中国和法国代表的意见：第 3 条的案文涉及人，应严格限于列举人权。保护个人自由和安全的立法是这个问题的另一个方面。目前，委员会的任务是界定个人的基本权利。因此，叙利亚代表团认为，苏联的修正案与所涉条款格格不入；此外，它提出了刑法范围内的问题。该修正案可在稍后阶段加以研究，如有必要，可形成单独的建议。

……

德乌斯先生（比利时）说，他将投票支持苏联代表团提交的修正案的第一句，但不会投票支持最后一句。

他同意中国代表的意见，即第三委员会没有对宣言草案作者迄今所完成的工作给予充分的重视。虽然联合国大会拥有决定权，并非必须要认可提交给它的草案，但同样正确的是，人权宣言草案已经经过了长期和详细的研究。此外，人权委员会的组成考虑到了地域分配原则；因此，提交联合国大会的案文很可能已经是妥协的结果，很难加以改进。

……

——第三委员会第 103 次会议简要记录（A/C.3/SR.103）

昌成程、常健译，常健校

A/C.3/SR.103
15 October 1948

GENERAL ASSEMBLY
THIRD SESSION
THIRD COMMITTEE
SUMMARY RECORD OF THE HUNDRED AND THIRD
MEETING

Held at the Palais de Chaillot, Paris, on Friday, 15 October 1948, at 10:45 a.m.

25. Draft International Declaration of Human Rights (E/800) (Continued)

Article 3 (Continued)

...

Mr. Chang (China) observed that all the amendments that had been submitted, even including those which had not been favourably received by the majority, had made a constructive contribution towards the preparation of a common declaration.

Members should not, however, lose sight of the draft declaration itself, which was the basic document before the Committee. That draft was the result of assiduous efforts and it had been reviewed with meticulous care. The original text prepared at Geneva had been submitted to the various Governments for their comments. It had then been examined by the Commission on Human Rights and had been altered in the light of the various comments and suggestions to which it had given rise. The draft declaration before the Committee was the final product of all that work, and it constituted only two-thirds of the original Geneva draft. It had, in fact, been realized that the clearer and the more concise the declaration was, the more effective and lasting it would be. The declaration was not intended for legal experts or scholars but for the general public; it should therefore be as striking as possible, and, accordingly, as concise as possible. It would be best if the declaration were limited to ten articles, but, if that were not possible, it should at least be limited to the twenty-eight articles which composed the draft under consideration.

Mr. Chang then stated that the Third Committee had not studied the structure of the declaration as a whole. In his opinion, such a study was essential and therefore, in examining the declaration, he would refer specially to its logical structure.

Articles 1, 2 and 3 expressed the three main ideas of eighteenth century philosophy: article 1 expressed the idea of fraternity, article 2 that of equality, and article 3 that of liberty.

The idea of liberty was then analysed and applied to the human being in article 3. Article 3 set forth a basic principle, which was then defined and clarified in the nine following articles. Article 4 dealt with slavery, article 5 with the right to recognition as a person before the law, article 6 with equality before the law, article 7 with the need to establish the legality of arrest, article 8 with the right to a fair trial, article 9 with the right to be presumed innocent until proved guilty, article 10 forbade interference with a person's privacy and article 11 affirmed the right to freedom of movement.

In that series of articles the idea of liberty was gradually and progressively enlarged; it was applied first to the individual, then to the family, and finally to the country. That series of articles therefore served to develop and clarify the idea of liberty.

Articles 13 to 20 dealt individually with the various social institutions.

Article 20, like article 3, expressed a general idea which was explained and developed in the following articles. Article 20 set forth the idea of social security and that idea was defined and developed in articles 21 to 25.

The structure of the draft declaration was, therefore, perfectly clear and logical. The joint amendment submitted by the delegations of Lebanon, Uruguay and Cuba and especially its second part, which expressed the same idea as article 20, was not in harmony with that structure. It was for that reason that Mr. Chang thought that the draft declaration should be left as it was, since it possessed the qualities of logic, clarity and brevity, qualities which were indispensable if the declaration was to prove effective.

...

Mr. Corominas (Argentina)...As the representative of China had said the chief aim of the declaration of human right was to be brief, clear and explicit, so that every one would be able ta understand it. It was not to be a convention for the exclusive use of legal experts.

...

Mr. Kayaly (Syria) was in complete agreement with the representatives of China and France: the text of article 3 was concerned with the human being and should be strictly limited to an enumeration of human rights. The legislation for the protection of the liberty and security of the individual was quite a different aspect of the problem. For the moment, the Committee's task was to define the fundamental rights of the individual. Consequently, the Syrian delegation felt that the USSR amendment was quite out of place in connexion with the article in question; moreover, it raised questions which were within the scope of the penal code. That amendment could be studied at a later stage and might, if necessary, form a separate recommendation.

...

Mr. Dehousse (Belgium) said that he would vote for the first sentences of the amendment submitted by the USSR delegation, but would not vote on the last sentence.

He agreed with the Chinese representative that the Third Committee had not attached sufficient importance to the work so far accomplished by the authors of the draft declaration. Although the General Assembly was sovereign and in no way obliged to confirm drafts submitted to it, it was none the less true that the draft declaration of human rights had already been the subject of long and detailed study. Moreover, the composition of the Commission on Human Rights had taken into account the principle of geographical distribution; it was therefore probable that the text submitted to the Assembly already constituted a compromise, which it would be difficult to improve upon.

...

在第三委员会第 105 次会议上的发言

1948 年 10 月 18 日星期一上午 10:30 巴黎夏乐宫

27. 《国际人权宣言（草案）》（第 E/800 号文件）（续）

第 3 条（续）

……

张先生（中国）说，对比利时代表提到的中国谚语，他愿意提供正确版本，即："各人自扫门前雪，莫管他人瓦上霜。"这有助于形成良好的邻里关系。

他希望重点强调，需要细心审议摆在委员会面前的这些修正案。另一句中国谚语说："事宽则圆。"这就是起草第 3 条应当采取的态度。

他不反对乌拉圭、古巴和黎巴嫩提交的联合修正案修订版（第 A/C.3/274/Rev.1 号文件）中作出的草案变更。但是，他同意比利时代表的建议，即该修正案中的"荣誉"一词还不够具体。对该修正案的表决应当在深思熟虑之后进行。但是如果决定立即进行表决，他将反对写入"荣誉"一词，并赞成保留在基本宣言草案中使用的措辞。

他还会提出一项正式修正案，建议将第 3 条和第 20 条合并，因为联合修正案中所包含的理念已经在该条中讲过。在一个一般概括性条款中进行表达似乎更为可取。但是他坚持认为，新的案文应作为单独一款，以彰显其重要性。他的建议是保留宣言草案第 3 条的案文措辞，将其作为第 1 款，并增加第 20 条的案文作为第 2 款，但要删除"享有社会保障的权利和"的措辞，并用"充分发展人格所必需"取代"下文所列"。"充分发展人格所必需"取自联合修正案，但删去了"人的"一词。

他对联合修正案投反对票，是因为他认为在同一款中表达两组理念是不恰当的。

尽管他不打算讨论苏联修正案的内容，但他会对其投反对票，因为其涉及的是执行问题，这并不属于宣言的范围。

卡森先生（法国）赞同中国代表的发言。苏联关于在宣言中提及国家义务的提案（第 A/C.3/265 号文件）如果获得通过，将引入关于执行的全部问题。法国代表团一直认为，义务的主题应写入人权公约，而不是宣言。

......

圣克鲁兹先生（智利）认为，中国代表的建议可能会被委员会大多数成员接受。因此，他想知道联合修正案的作者是否愿意与该代表合作起草新的案文。

......

——第三委员会第 105 次会议简要记录（A/C.3/SR.105）

昌成程、常健译，常健校

A/C.3/SR.105

18 October 1948

GENERAL ASSEMBLY
THIRD SESSION
THIRD COMMITTEE
SUMMARY RECORD OF THE HUNDRED AND FIFTH MEETING

Held at the Palais de Chaillot, Paris, on Monday, 18 October 1948, at 10:30 p.m.

27. Draft International Declaration of Human Rights (E/800) (Continued)

Article 3 (Continued)

...

Mr. Chang (China) said he wished to give the correct version of the Chinese proverb mentioned by the representative of Belgium. It was: "Sweep the snow in front of one's own door. Overlook the frost on others' roof-tiles." That made for good neighbours.

He wished to lay great stress upon the need for careful consideration of the amendments before the Committee. Another Chinese proverb ran: "Matters allowed to mature slowly are free from sharp corners." That was the spirit in which the drafting of article 3 should be approached.

He had no objection to the drafting changes made in the revised version of the joint amendment submitted by Uruguay, Cuba and Lebanon (A/C.3/274/Rev.1). He agreed with the representative of Belgium, however, that the word "honour" in that amendment was not sufficiently concrete. The vote on that amendment should be taken only after mature consideration. If, however, it were decided to take an immediate vote, he would vote against inclusion of the word "honour" and in favour of the retention of the wording used in the basic draft declaration.

He would also make a formal amendment combining article 3 with article 20, since the ideas contained in the joint amendment were already stated in that article. It might be desirable to express them in a general covering article. He would insist, however, that the new text should be placed in a separate paragraph in order to bring out its importance. His proposal would be to retain as a first paragraph the text of article 3 as worded in the draft declaration and to add the text of article 20 as a second paragraph, deleting, however, the words "has the right to social security and", and substituting for the words "set out below" the words "necessary to the full development of the personality", that phrase being taken, with the omission of the word "human", from the joint amendment.

He would vote against the joint amendment because he considered it incorrect to express two sets of ideas in a single paragraph.

While he would abstain from discussing the substance of the USSR amendment, he would vote against it because it dealt with implementation; that did not come within the scope of the declaration.

Mr.Cassin (France) agreed with much that had been said by the Chinese representative. The USSR proposal (A/C.3/265) to include a reference to the obligations of States would, if adopted, introduce the whole question of implementation. The French delegation had always been of the opinion that the subject of obligations should be included in the covenant on human rights and not in the declaration.

......

Mr. Santa Cruz (Chile) felt that the Chinese representative's proposal might prove to be acceptable to a large majority of the Committee. He wanted to know, therefore whether the authors of the joint amendment would be prepared to collaborate with that representative in the preparation of a new text.

…

在第三委员会第 107 次会议上的发言

1948 年 10 月 19 日星期二下午 3:00 巴黎夏乐宫

29.《国际人权宣言（草案）》（第 E/800 号文件）（续）

第 3 条（续）

……

巴甫洛夫先生（苏联）对这一程序提出抗议……中国代表曾表示，苏联的修正案等同于从条款中删除任何个人的人身自由和安全的权利，但这项权利已写入基本案文，而且他也对写入该权利表示了赞成。巴甫洛夫先生说，苏联提交的修正案并不打算排除这一权利；它只是为了确保生命权得到保护。如果相应条款获得通过，并且如果中国代表希望在苏联修正案中增加一款，申明每个人都有人身自由和安全的权利，巴甫洛夫先生将投票赞成该修正案。

……

巴甫洛夫先生（苏联）要求对该草案的各部分分别付诸表决。委员会应从第一句开始表决，然后再处理后两句，最后再表决最后几句。他要求对这部分进行唱名表决。

他重述了他向中国代表提出的建议，即中国代表应修改草案，增加一款，其内容大致为：每个人都享有人身自由和安全的权利。

张先生（中国）在回答苏联代表时指出，他评论的唯一目的，是提出一个更便捷的表决程序。苏联修正案的第一句话与基本案文是相同的，但删除了"人身自由和安全"等字样。因此张先生建议，新的草案应被视为一项要求删除这几个词的修正案。

瓦特先生（澳大利亚）赞同中国代表的发言。即使修正案的第一部分是以肯定的形式提交的，而不是删除一句话，每个成员都会将提案解释为试图删除规定每个人都有人身自由和安全权利的条款。

……

关于程序问题，张先生（中国）质疑是否需要对比利时代表团的修正案（第 A/C. 3/282 号文件）进行表决，因为委员会刚刚投票反对增加"身体完整性"一词，而该词也出现在比利时代表团的修正案中。

......

张先生（中国）赞同法国和美国代表就"人身安全"一词的定义所表达的观点。由于这些观点将被记录在案，他认为延长关于这一点的辩论是没有意义的。

......

——第三委员会第 107 次会议简要记录（A/C.3/SR.107）

昌成程、常健译，常健校

A/C.3/SR.107

19 October 1948

GENERAL ASSEMBLY
THIRD SESSION
THIRD COMMITTEE
SUMMARY RECORD OF THE HUNDRED AND SEVENTH MEETING

Held at the Palais de Chaillot, Paris, on Tuesday, 19 October 1948, at 3:00 p.m.

29. Draft International Declaration of Human Rights (E/800) (Continued)

Article 3 (Continued)

...

Mr. Pavlov (Union of Soviet Socialist Republics) protested against that procedure... The Chinese representative had expressed the opinion that the USSR amendment would be tantamount to deleting from the articles the right of any individual to liberty and security of person, which right was included in the basic text and he had been in favour of the inclusion of that right. Mr. Pavlov said that the amendment submitted by the Soviet Union did not intend to exclude that right; it was meant simply to ensure protection of the right to life. Should the corresponding clauses be adopted, and should the Chinese representative wish to add to the USSR amendment a paragraph affirming that every individual had a right to liberty and security of person, Mr. Pavlov would vote in favour of that amendment.

...

Mr. Pavlov (Union of Soviet Socialist Republics) requested that this draft should be put to the vote in parts. The Committee should begin with the first sentence, should then deal with the two following sentences, and finally with the last sentences, for which he requested a vote by roll-call.

He repeated the proposal he had made to the Chinese representative that the latter should amend the draft by adding a paragraph to the effect that every individual had the right to liberty and security of person.

Replying to the USSR representative, Mr. Chang (China) pointed out that the sole object of his remarks had been to propose a more convenient voting procedure. The first sentence of the Soviet Union amendment was identical with the basic text, but it omitted the words "liberty and security of person". Mr. Chang therefore proposed that the new draft should be considered as an amendment calling for the deletion of those words.

...

Mr. Watt (Australia) approved the remarks of the Chinese representative. Even if the first part of the amendment were submitted in an affirmative form and not as a deletion of a phrase, every member would interpret the proposal as an attempt to delete the clause which stated that every individual had the right to liberty and security of person.

...

On a point of order, Mr. Chang (China) questioned the desirability of voting on the Belgian delegation's amendment (A/C.3/282), since the Committee had just voted against the addition of the words "physical integrity", which also appeared in that amendment.

...

Mr. Chang (China) endorsed the views expessed by the French and United States representatives regarding the definition of the words "security of person". As those views would be recorded, he thought it useless to prolong the debate on that point.

在第三委员会第 113 次会议上的发言

1948 年 10 月 26 日星期二下午 3:00 巴黎夏乐宫

37.《国际人权宣言（草案）》（第 E/800 号文件）（续）

第 6 条（续）

......

张先生（中国）就程序问题发言时建议，墨西哥修正案可以分部分付诸表决，表决是选择采用短语"有效的司法补救"（第 A/C.3/308 号文件）还是"由合格的国家法院作出的有效补救"（第 A/C.3/309 号文件）。

他表示更喜欢前者。"国家的"一词可能不是普遍适用的，因为一些国家有州和省法院，这些法院不能被认为是国家法院。

......

张先生（中国）表示，他的建议只是为了节省时间和产生更完美的案文。这一目的显然没有达到，因此他撤回该建议。

......

张先生（中国）表示，正在讨论的草案远不够完善。草案应该被修改得更具体、更清楚、更明确。应当认识到，该文本旨在使人类的地位得到改善。用某些被提议的词汇来代替"任意"一词，会打乱该条的平衡。他认为，毫无疑问，可以在其他条款中加入补充内容。

关于流放的建议可写入第 13 条，并可加上这样一句话，即任何人都不应被任意禁止进入自己的国家。

会议于下午 6:15 结束。

——第三委员会第 113 次会议简要记录（A/C.3/SR.113）

昌成程译，常健校

A/C.3/SR.113

26 October 1948

GENERAL ASSEMBLY
THIRD SESSION
THIRD COMMITTEE
SUMMARY RECORD OF THE HUNDRED AND
THIRTEENTH MEETING

Held at the Palais de Chaillot, Paris, on Tuesday, 26 October 1948, at 3:00 p.m.

37. Draft International Declaration of Human Rights (E/800) (Continued)

Article 6 (Continued)

...

Mr. Chang (China), speaking on a point of order, suggested that the Mexican amendment might be put to the vote in parts and that the vote might be taken alternatively on the phrase "an effective judicial remedy" (A/C.3/308) or the phrase "an effective remedy by the competent national tribunals" (A/C.3/309).

He expressed a preference for the former; the word "national" might not be universally applicable, as a number of countries had state and provincial courts, which could not be considered national.

...

Mr. Chang (China) stated that his suggestion had been made solely with a view to saving time and producing a more perfect text. As it did not appear to have achieved its purpose, he withdrew it.

...

Mr. Chang (China) declared that the draft in question was far from perfect. It should be rendered more definite, clearer and more clear cut. It should be realized that the text was intended to achieve improvement in the status of mankind. The adoption of certain substitutes proposed for the word "arbitrary" would disturb the balance of the article. He submitted that additions could doubtless be inserted in other articles.

The suggestion regarding exile might be included in article 13, and a sentence might be added to the effect that no person should be arbitrarily barred from entering his own country.

The meeting rose at 6:15 p.m.

在第三委员会第 119 次会议上的发言

1948 年 10 月 30 日星期六下午 3：00 巴黎夏乐宫

43.《国际人权宣言（草案）》（第 E/800 号文件）（续）

第 10 条（续）

张先生（中国）支持英国修正案。

他同意美国代表的建议，即限定词"任意"比"不合理"或"不可侵犯"要全面得多。

古巴修正案（第 A/C.3/232 号文件）令人感兴趣，因为它将对隐私、家庭和通信的保护扩大到荣誉和名誉，从而涵盖了个人的主观和客观方面。如果将古巴关于保护名誉和荣誉的规定作为单独的一款，就会得到更多重视。

虽然关于法律保护的条款放在宣言中可能显得不合适，但考虑到如果省略它，可能会给决斗等保护荣誉的法外方法留下漏洞，那么就可以将其插入。不过，他认为英国修正案在这方面是最令人满意的。

......

张先生（中国）就程序问题发言，他说，委员会面前有一份不同于其所接受的英文文本。他以及其他可能的代表投票反对第一个版本，因为它似乎没有意义。不能要求委员会就一项修正案的全部内容进行表决，因为该修正案的措辞部分与所表决的案文不同。相反，它应该对第一款进行第二次投票，并有机会予以否决。

科贝特女士（英国）支持中国代表。

主席不能同意中国代表的意见。两个文本之间存在的差异必须消除。包括美国代表在内的几位代表表示，荣誉和名誉应在单独的条款中提及；事实上，法文文本就是这样做的。此外，一些其他代表要求对法文文本进行表决，多数人似乎对法文文本感到满意。由于有两种工作语言，因此可以两种文本为基础。委员会面前的法文文本没有任何改动；但英文文本已与之相对应。

······

——第三委员会第 119 次会议简要记录（A/C.3/SR.119）

昌成程译、常健，常健校

A/C.3/SR.119
30 October 1948

GENERAL ASSEMBLY
THIRD SESSION
THIRD COMMITTEE
SUMMARY RECORD OF THE HUNDRED AND
NINETEENTH MEETING

Held at the Palais de Chaillot, Paris, on Saturday, 30 October 1948, at 3:00 p.m.

43. Draft International Declaration of Human Rights (E/800) (Continued)

Article 10 (Continued)

…

Mr. Chang (China) supported the United Kingdom amendment.

He agreed with the United States representative that the qualification "arbitrary" was far more comprehensive than "unreasonable" or the concept of "inviolability".

The Cuban amendment (A/C.3/232) was interesting in that it extended the protection accorded to privacy, home, family and correspondence to honour and reputation, thus covering the subjective and social aspects of the human individual. Greater weight would attach to the Cuban provision to protect reputation and honour if it were placed in a separate paragraph.

Although the provision for legal protection might appear out of place in the declaration it might be inserted in the case under consideration since its omission might leave a loop-hole for such extra-legal methods of protecting honour as duelling. He thought, however, that the United Kingdom amendment would be most satisfactory in the case in point.

……

Mr. Chang (China), speaking on a point of order, stated that the Committee had before it an English text different from that which it had accepted. He and possibly other representatives had voted against the first version because it had not appeared to make sense. The Committee could not be asked to vote on the whole of an amendment the wording of which was different from the text on which the vote had been taken, in parts. Rather, it should take a second vote on the first paragraph, and be given an opportunity to reject it.

Mrs. Corbet (United Kingdom) supported the Chinese representative.

The Chairman could not agree with the Chinese representative. The discrepancy which existed between the two texts had to be removed. Several representatives, including the representative of the United States, had said that honour and reputation should be mentioned in a separate clause; which had in fact been done in the French text. Moreover, a number of other representatives had requested that the vote might be taken on the French text, which appeared to be satisfactory ta the majority. Since there were two working languages, either text could be taken as a basis. The French text before the Committee had not been altered in any way; but the English text had been made to correspond to it.

……

在第三委员会第 125 次会议上的发言

1948 年 11 月 8 日星期一上午 10:45 巴黎夏乐宫

49. 《国际人权宣言（草案）》（第 E/800 号文件）（续）
第 14 条（续）

……

张先生（中国）说，中国代表团放弃参加对第 14 条的最后表决，因为该条的漏洞太过严重，不容忽视。

这一事实再次表明，在起草过程中避免过于仓促是非常重要的；像这样一份必须由委员会起草的文件，必须经过深思熟虑。

中国代表团认为，应提请联合国大会注意这一问题。

……

——第三委员会第 125 次会议简要记录（A/C.3/SR.125）

昌成程译，常健校

A/C.3/SR.125
8 November 1948

GENERAL ASSEMBLY
THIRD SESSION
THIRD COMMITTEE
SUMMARY RECORD OF THE HUNDRED AND TWENTY-FIFTH MEETING

Held at the Palais de Chaillot, Paris, on Monday 8 November 1948,
at 10:45 a.m.

49. Draft International Declaration of Human Rights (E/800)
(Continued)

Article 14 (Continued)

...

Mr. Chang (China) stated that his delegation had abstained from taking part in the final vote on article 14 because the gaps in that article were too serious to be overlooked.

That fact demonstrated once again the importance of avoiding undue haste in drafting; a document such as the one the Committee had to prepare must be the outcome of long reflection and thorough study.

The Chinese delegation thought that the General Assembly's attention should be drawn to the matter.

...

在第三委员会第 127 次会议上的发言

1948 年 11 月 9 日星期二上午 10∶50 巴黎夏乐宫

51. 《国际人权宣言（草案）》（第 E/800 号文件）（续）

第 16 条

　　张先生（中国）表示，在对第 16 条的讨论中，委员会处理的是宣言中最重要的原则之一。自 18 世纪人权思想在西欧诞生以来，思想自由被认为是人类的基本自由之一，并涵盖了宗教自由的理念。此外他认为，思想自由既包括良心自由，也包括宗教自由。但是，由于宣言是为世界上广大人民而写的，绝不会因直白而遭受批评。

　　他指出，1869 年达尔文论文的公开发表，实际标志着宗教与科学之间所谓冲突的开始。人类这种精神现象令人悲叹，其影响已经延续 80 年了，在委员会内部也可以感受到这种影响。因此他强调，必须从真实的视角来研究宗教表达的问题。

　　为了对这个问题有更多了解，他愿意首先向委员会说明中国人是如何处理宗教问题的。中国哲学本质上基于对一元论本原的坚定信念，但在人文层面上却表现为多元宽容。中国哲学将人的行为看得比形而上学更重要。生活的艺术应高于对生命本原的认知。人证明神灵伟大的最好办法，就是去证明在这个世界上存在着一种典范的人生态度。在中国哲学家眼中，如果人们希望在仁与义的基础上来建立他们之间的关系，就应该受到这种多元宽容精神的启发。这种多元宽容精神体现在思想、良心和宗教的每一个领域。

　　关于第 16 条，张先生说，他理解并尊重沙特阿拉伯代表提出的反对意见。随着西方工业主义扩张，对于远东国家来说，19 世纪并非总是友善的，他也认为传教士的使命始终不只限于传教。

　　不过他表示，人权委员会所建议的案文充分保护了思想自由。人权委员会在讨论中一致认为，信仰自由是思想和良心自由的内在组成部分，如果对保护信仰自由的必要性予以特别强调，那是为了确保思想和良心的这一深刻部分不受侵犯，因为宗教信仰一旦情绪化，就容易使人类陷入无理性的冲突。

——第三委员会第 127 次会议简要记录（A/C.3/SR.127）

昌成程译，常健校

A/C.3/SR.127
9 November 1948

GENERAL ASSEMBLY
THIRD SESSION
THIRD COMMITTEE
SUMMARY RECORD OF THE HUNDRED AND TWENTY-SEVENTH MEETING

Held at the Palais de Chaillot, Paris, on Tuesday, 9 November 1948, at 10:50 a.m.

51. Draft International Declaration of Human Rights (E/800) (Continued)

Article 16

…

Mr. Chang (China) declared that in discussing article 16, the Committee was dealing with one of the most important principles in the declaration. From the eighteenth century, when the idea of human rights was born in Western Europe, freedom of thought had figured among the essential human freedoms and had covered the idea of religious freedom. He felt, moreover, that freedom of thought included freedom of conscience as well as religious freedom, but, as the declaration was destined for the vast mass of the world's population, it should never be criticized for being too explicit.

He declared that 1869, the date of the publication of Darwin's treatises, really marked the beginning of the so-called conflict of religion and science. The effects, already eighty years old, of that manifestation of the human spirit could not be sufficiently deplored, and its influence could be felt in the Committee itself. For that reason he stressed the necessity of studying the problem of religious expression in its true perspective.

In order to throw more light on the question, he wished first of all to explain to the Committee how the Chinese approached the religious problem. Chinese philosophy was based essentially on a firm belief in a unitarian cause, expressed on the human plane by a pluralistic tolerance. That philosophy considered that man's actions were more important than metaphysics, that the art of living should be placed above knowledge of the causes of life, and that the best way for man to testify to the greatness of the Divinity was to give proof of an exemplary attitude in this world. In the eyes of Chinese philosophers, it was pluralistic tolerance, manifesting itself in every sphere of thought, conscience and religion, which should inspire men if they wished to base their relations on benevolence and justice.

Returning to article 16, Mr. Chang said he had heard with sympathy and respect the objections raised by the representative of Saudi Arabia. For the countries of the Far East, the nineteenth century, with its expansion of Western industrialism, had not always been very kind and he admitted that missionaries had not always limited themselves to their religious mission.

He expressed the opinion, however, that freedom of thought was well protected by the text proposed by the Commission on Human Rights. During the discussions in the latter, it had been agreed that freedom of belief was an integral part of freedom of thought and conscience, and if special emphasis was laid on the necessity of protecting it, that was to ensure the inviolability of that profound part of thought and conscience which, being largely emotional, was apt to lead mankind into unreasoned conflict.

...

在第三委员会第 131 次会议上的发言

1948 年 11 月 11 日星期四下午 3:00 巴黎夏乐宫

56.《国际人权宣言（草案）》（第 E/800 号文件）（续）

第 18 条（续）

......

主席指出，在他看来，波兰修正案（第 A/C.3/331 号文件）涉及该问题的实质内容。因此，如果委员会的任何成员提出反对，该修正案就不能被认为是可接受的。

......

瓦特先生（澳大利亚）回顾了序言的措辞，并指出波兰代表建议在第18 条中补充的措辞，最好放在宣言的序言部分。

......

希梅内斯·德·阿雷查加先生（乌拉圭）指出，波兰修正案的设想是，第 18 条所规定的权利只能在《联合国宪章》的宗旨和原则的框架下行使。因此，《联合国宪章》是区分合理使用还是滥用这些权利的标准。各国政府应确保社会组织及其成员遵守这些原则。

......

张先生（中国）表示，他同意澳大利亚和乌拉圭代表的建议。对《联合国宪章》的任何解释，都不能成为干涉会员国内政的理由，这一点在联合国各机构中被频频提及。因此他担心，如果波兰的修正案被接受，集会和结社自由的权利就可以被解释为或是对国家立法的限制，或是其行使可以无视各国法律。

......

张先生（中国）指出，与古巴修正案相差最大的修正案，就是与基本案文最接近的修正案。

他询问，如果比利时修正案获得通过，是否应该取代基本案文？他认为，应该对这两个案文进行比较。

……

张先生（中国）对乌拉圭修正案的通过表示满意。该修正案确立了一项重要的原则。但他不太满意第 18 条的措辞，因为他认为英文文本是有歧义的，不能确定"和平的"这个形容词是仅适用于"集会"这个词，还是适用于"集会"和"结社"这两个词。

……

希梅内斯·德·阿雷查加先生（乌拉圭）感谢中国代表对委员会通过的条款案文所作的明智和恰当的发言，但对他无法改变条款表示遗憾。

……

——第三委员会第 131 次会议简要记录（A/C.3/SR.131）

昌成程译，常健校

A/C.3/SR.131
11 November 1948

GENERAL ASSEMBLY
THIRD SESSION
THIRD COMMITTEE
SUMMARY RECORD OF THE HUNDRED AND THIRTY-FIRST MEETING

Held at the Palais de Chaillot, Paris, on Thursday, 11 November 1948, at 3:00 p.m.

56. Draft International Declaration of Human Rights (E/800) (Continued)

Article 18 (Continued)

...

The Chairman pointed out that the Polish amendment (A/C.3/331), in his opinion, related to the substance of the question. If any member of the Committee, therefore, raised an objection, that amendment could not be considered acceptable.

...

Mr. Watt (Australia) recalled the terms of the preamble, and pointed out that the words which the Polish representative proposed to add to article 18 would be better placed in the preamble of the declaration.

...

Mr. Jiménez de Aréchaga (Uruguay) pointed out that the Polish amendment envisaged that the rights laid down in article 18 could only be exercised within the framework of the aims and principles of the Charter. The latter was therefore a criterion for distinguishing between the use and the abuse of those rights. It would be for Governments to ensure that associations and their members conformed to those principles.

...

Mr. Chang (China) expressed his agreement with the representatives of Australia and Uruguay. It had so often been mentioned in the organs of the United Nations that the Charter could not be interpreted in any way which could justify interference in the internal affairs of Member States, that he feared that, if the Polish amendment were accepted, the right to freedom of assembly and association might be interpreted as either restricting national legislation, or as being capable of exercise in defiance of the laws of the various States.

...

Mr. Chang (China) pointed out that the amendment furthest removed from the Cuban amendment was the nearest to the basic text.

He asked whether the Belgian amendment, if adopted, should replace the basic text. He thought that the two texts should be compared.

...

Mr. Chang (China) expressed his satisfaction at the adoption of the Uruguayan amendment, which established an important principle. But he was not too happy about the wording of article 18, because he considered the English text to be ambiguous on account of the fact that it was not certain whether the adjective "peaceful" was applicable only to the word "assembly", or to the two words "assembly" and "association".

...

Mr. Jiménez de Aréchaga (Uruguay) thanked the Chinese representative for his wise and apposite remarks on the text of the article adopted by the Committee, but regretted that he was unable to change its terms.

...

在第三委员会第 133 次会议上的发言

1948 年 11 月 12 日星期五上午 10:55 巴黎夏乐宫

58.《国际人权宣言（草案）》（第 E/800 号文件）（续）

第 19 条（续）

......

张先生（中国）说，他非常认真地听取了各代表团对宣言第 19 条的意见，并根据各代表团的建议提出了该条的新案文（第 A/C. 3/333 号文件）。

他首先谈到第 3 款。他说，宣言应宣告人权，而不应像法国代表团的修正案那样强调政府的权威。因此，中国代表团在其修正案的第 3 款中提议，"人民的意愿"应成为第 1 分句的主题。该款内容应如下：

"3. 人民的意志是政府权威的源泉；它应在普遍、平等、定期和无记名投票的选举中予以表达，或以同等的自由投票程序加以体现。"

在第 19 条第 1 款中，中国代表团建议在"每个人"之后加上"作为公民"一词。这一增补考虑了古巴和乌拉圭代表团提出的修正案。此外，人权委员会在第 20 条中也采用了类似的措辞，该条以"每个人作为社会的一员"开头。该款的法文可以简化，删去"qu'elle a"（她有）等词。

在中国，公职人员已经存在了很长时间。他强调，公职人员应以竞争的方式录用，以确保只有合格的人才能直接在国家从事公务，这一理念非常重要，但却还没有在西方世界实现。因此，他提议将第 19 条第 2 款修改如下：

"2. 人人有权自由和平等地在其国家从事公务。"

......

——第三委员会第 133 次会议简要记录（A/C.3/SR.133）

昌成程译，常健校

A/C.3/SR.133

12 November 1948

GENERAL ASSEMBLY
THIRD SESSION
THIRD COMMITTEE
SUMMARY RECORD OF THE HUNDRED AND THIRTY-
THIRD MEETING

Held at the Palais de Chaillot, Paris, on Friday, 12 November 1948,

at 10:55 a.m.

58. Draft International Declaration of Human Rights (E/800) (Continued)

Article 19 (Continued)

...

Mr. Chang (China) said that he had listened very carefully to comments by the different delegations on article 19 of the declaration and proposed a new version of that article based on the suggestions of various delegations (A/C.3/333).

Dealing first with paragraph 3, he said that the declaration should proclaim human rights and not stress the authority of Government, as the French delegation's amendment did. For that reason his delegation in paragraph 3 of its amendment proposed that "the will of the people" should become the subject of the first clause. The paragraph would read as follows:

"3. The will of the people is the source of the authority of government; this will shall be expressed in elections, universal, equal, periodic and by secret ballot, or manifested in equivalent free voting procedures."

In the first paragraph of article 19 his delegation proposed adding the words "as a citizen" immediately after the word "everyone". That addition took account of the amendments proposed by the delegations of Cuba and Uruguay. Moreover, the Human Rights Commission had adopted a similar wording in article 20, which began with the words "Everyone, as a member of society". The French text of this paragraph might be simplified by the omission of the words "qu'elle a".

In his country the civil service had been in existence for a long time and he emphasized the importance of the idea, not yet realized in the Western world, that civil servants should be recruited by the competitive method to make sure that only qualified persons took a direct part in the public service of their country. Hence he proposed paragraph 2 of article 19 should be amended to read as follows:

"2. Everyone has the right of free and equal access to public service in his country."

......

在第三委员会第 134 次会议上的发言

1948 年 11 月 12 日星期五下午 4:30 巴黎夏乐宫

59. 《国际人权宣言（草案）》（第 E/800 号文件）（续）

第 19 条（续）

······

张先生（中国）建议对他为第 3 款（第 A/C. 3/333 号文件）所提议的折中文本作几处修改。该款内容如下：

"人民的意志是政府权威的基础；它应在定期选举中表达，这种定期选举应是普遍的、真实的、平等的，并以无记名投票方式进行，或以同等的自由投票程序表示。"

······

张先生（中国）认为，"人民的意志是······权威的源泉"是一个肯定事实的陈述；相反，"应为基础"则表示在某些国家并非总是如此。正是因为这个原因，他倾向于"应为基础"。人们普遍认为，人民的意志在任何情况下都应该是政府权威的基础。

这种措辞也应该使阿根廷代表感到满意，因为它不再是一个简单的事实陈述，而是对一项权利的宣告。

他建议将第 3 款的措辞修改如下：

"人民的意志应是政府权威的基础；它应以定期和真正的选举予以表达，这种选举应是普遍和平等的，并应以无记名投票或同等的自由投票程序进行。"

······

主席将中国代表就第 3 款提出的最后案文付诸表决。

该案文以 39 票对 3 票、3 票弃权获得通过。

······

——第三委员会第 134 次会议简要记录（A/C.3/SR.134）

昌成程、常健译，常健校

A/C.3/SR.134

12 November 1948

GENERAL ASSEMBLY
THIRD SESSION
THIRD COMMITTEE
SUMMARY RECORD OF THE HUNDRED AND
THIRTY-FOURTH MEETING

Held at the Palais de Chaillot, Paris, on Friday, 12 November 1948, at 4:30 p.m.

59. Draft International Declaration of Human Rights (E/800) (Continued)

Article 19 (Continued)

…

Mr. Chang (China) suggested a few changes in the compromise text which he had proposed for paragraph 3 (A/C.3/333). The paragraph would read as follows:

"The will of the people is the basis of the authority of government; this will shall be expressed in periodic elections, which shall be universal, genuine, equal, and held by secret ballot, or manifested in equivalent free voting procedures."

…

Mr. Chang (China) thought the expression "the will of the people is the source of the authority..." was a positive statement of fact; "shall be the basis", on the contrary, would indicate that such was not always the case in certain countries. It was for that reason that he preferred "shall be the basis", it being generally understood that the will of the people should in all cases be the basis of the authority of the Government.

That wording should also satisfy the Argentine representative, since it was no longer a simple statement of fact, but the proclamation of a right.

He proposed the following wording for paragraph 3:

"The will of the people shall be the basis of the authority of government; this will shall be expressed in periodic and genuine elections, which shall be universal and equal, and shall be held by secret vote, or by equivalent free voting procedures."

…

The Chairman put to the vote the last text proposed by the Chinese representative for paragraph 3.

That text was adopted by 39 votes to 3, with 3 abstentions.

…

在第三委员会第 141 次会议上的发言

1948 年 11 月 16 日星期二下午 8:30 巴黎夏乐宫

66.《国际人权宣言（草案）》（第 E/800 号文件）（续）

第 21 条（续）

……

张先生（中国）认为，对整个条款作出否决，并不表示委员会无意写入一项保障劳工权利的条款，而可能是提供一个机会来起草某个同等条款来取代它。对第 1 款一致赞同的表决和对第 3 款几乎一致赞同的表决表明，委员会并非希望将第 21 条完全从宣言中剔除。再者，正如古巴代表所提出的，该修订案文缺乏成熟的考虑，它在措辞上的确存在一定缺陷。考虑到第 2 款的案文，第 1 款中的"并支付"等字样似乎是多余的，可以将其删除。某些款目在表决中仅获得微弱多数赞同，这表明委员会对这些款目并非完全满意。关于生活水准权的第 22 条与薪酬问题密切相关，两者或许可以合并。他支持秘鲁的动议，但认为在委员会商议第 21 条的改进草案时，讨论第 22 条或许是更好的选择。

……

——第三委员会第 141 次会议简要记录（A/C.3/SR.141）

昌成程译，常健校

A/C.3/SR.141
16 November 1948

GENERAL ASSEMBLY
THIRD SESSION
THIRD COMMITTEE
SUMMARY RECORD OF THE HUNDRED AND FORTY-
FIRST MEETING
Held at the Palais de Chaillot, Paris, on Tuesday, 16 November 1948,
at 8:30 p.m.

66. Draft International Declaration of Human Rights (E/800)
(Continued)

Article 21 (Continued)

...

Mr. Chang (China) thought that the adverse vote on the whole article did not indicate that the Committee had no intention of including an article guaranteeing the rights of labour, but might provide an opportunity for drafting some equivalent article to replace it. The unanimous vote in favour of paragraph 1 and the almost unanimous vote for paragraph 3 showed that it could not be said that the Committee wished to exclude article 21 altogether from the declaration. The amended text, in any case, had certain drafting defects due as the representative of Cuba had suggested to lack of mature consideration. The words "and pay" appeared to be redundant in paragraph 1 in view of the text of paragraph 2; they might be deleted. The narrow majority obtained in the vote on certain paragraphs suggested that the Committee had not been wholly satisfied with them. Article 22, which dealt with the right to a standard of living, was closely connected with the question of pay; it might be possible to merge the two. He supported the Peruvian motion, but believed it might be better to take up article 22 while the Committee meditated an improved draft for article 21.

...

在第三委员会第 142 次会议上的发言

1948 年 11 月 17 日星期三上午 10:10 巴黎夏乐宫

67.《国际人权宣言（草案）》（第 E/800 号文件）（续）

第 21 条（续）

……

主席提请委员会注意秘鲁关于重新审议第 21 条的建议，以及英国提出在 11 月 18 日晚之前提交该条新的修正案的建议。还有建议认为委员会应将对该条的重新审议推迟到讨论宣言草案的后期。

……

张先生（中国）敦促将秘鲁的提案付诸表决，但基于一项谅解，即不以任何特定案文作为讨论的基础，但任何可以使案文令人满意且可普遍接受的建议尽可提出。

……

张先生（中国）说，通过秘鲁提案，将意味着要重新审议有关第 21 条的先前所有草案。A/C.3/298/Rev.1 号文件所阐述的修正案，以及上次会议上提出的修正案，都可以被重新引入，还可以仅就起草风格的改变提出新的建议。与此不同，苏联的提案将使委员会仅限于重新审议已被上次会议通过的该条款的各个部分，对其只能提出补充意见。

……

——第三委员会第 142 次会议简要记录（A/C.3/SR.142）

昌成程译，常健校

A/C.3/SR.142

17 November 1948

could be suggested. The USSR proposal, on the other hand, committee in reconsidering the separate parts of the adoption of the very meeting, so which our adoption could...

GENERAL ASSEMBLY
THIRD SESSION
THIRD COMMITTEE
SUMMARY RECORD OF THE HUNDRED AND FORTY-SECOND MEETING

Held at the Palais de Chaillot, Paris, on Wednesday, 17 November 1948, at 10:10 a.m.

67. Draft International Declaration of Human Rights (E/800) (Continued)

Article 21 (Continued)

...

The Chairman drew the Committee's attention to the Peruvian proposal that article 21 should be reconsidered and to the United Kingdom suggestion that new drafting amendments to the article could be received until the evening of 18 November. It had also been suggested that the Committee should postpone reconsideration of the article until some later point in its discussion of the draft declaration.

...

Mr. Chang (China) urged that the Peruvian proposal should be put to the vote on the understanding that no particular text would be used as a basis for discussion but that any suggestion might be made which would lead to a satisfactory and generally acceptable text.

...

Mr. Chang (China) said that the adoption of the Peruvian proposal would mean reconsideration of all the previous drafts of article 21. The amendments set forth in document A/C.3/298/Rev.1, as well as those put forward at the previous meeting, could be reintroduced and new changes of a purely drafting character could be suggested. The USSR proposal, on the other hand, would limit the Committee to reconsidering the separate parts of the article which had been adopted at the previous meeting, to which only additions could be suggested.

...

在第三委员会第 143 次会议上的发言

1948 年 11 月 17 日星期三下午 3:30 巴黎夏乐宫

68.《国际人权宣言（草案）》（第 E/800 号文件）（续）

第 21 条（续）

……

张先生（中国）认为，对委员会在上一次会议作出的决定，不能有多种解释。比利时代表的建议已被接受，但有一项明确的除外，即委员会将立即成立一个起草委员会。

……

张先生（中国）要求结束对乌拉圭代表所作提案的讨论。希梅内斯·德·阿雷查加先生（乌拉圭）要求结束一般性辩论。

结案动议以 26 票赞成、7 票反对、3 票弃权获得通过。

……

第 22 条

张先生（中国）提议对第 22 条第 1 款采用以下措辞：

"人人有权享有足以满足其家庭和自身需求的生活标准，包括食物、衣服、住房、医疗和社会服务；并有权在失业、疾病、残疾、鳏寡、年老或其他因不可控情况而失去生计时获得保障。"

会议于下午 6:15 结束。

——第三委员会第 143 次会议简要记录（A/C.3/SR.143）

李一萌译，常健校

A/C.3/SR.143
17 November 1948

GENERAL ASSEMBLY
THIRD SESSION
THIRD COMMITTEE
SUMMARY RECORD OF THE HUNDRED AND FORTY-
THIRD MEETING

Held at the Palais de Chaillot, Paris, on Wednesday, 17 November 1948,
at 3:30 p.m.

68. Draft International Declaration of Human Rights (E/800) (Continued)

Article 21 (Continued)

...

Mr.Chang (China) thought that the decision taken by the Committee at its previous meeting could not lend itself to more than one interpretation. The Belgian representative's suggestion had been accepted on the clear understanding that the Committee would immediately set up a drafting committee.

...

Mr. Chang (China) asked that the discussion on the Uruguayan representative's proposal should be closed, and Mr. Jiménez De Aréchaga (Uruguay) asked for closure of the general debate.

The motion for closure was adopted by 26 votes to 7, with 3 abstentions.

Article 22

...

Mr.Chang (China) proposed the following wording for the first paragraph of article 22:

"Everyone has the right to a standard of living adequate for the needs of his family and himself, including food, clothing, housing, medical care and social services, and to security in the event of unemployment, sickness, disability, widowhood, old age or other loss of livelihood owing to circumstances beyond his control."

The meeting rose at 6:15 p.m.

在第三委员会第 144 次会议上的发言

1948 年 11 月 18 日星期四上午 10:30 巴黎夏乐宫

69.《国际人权宣言（草案）》（第 E/800 号文件）（续）

第 22 条（续）

......

张先生（中国）说，他可以接受对其修正案的某些措辞上的修改。他同意法国和智利代表的建议，即应该恢复"健康与福祉"一词，用其来替代"各项需要"。然而，他并不完全赞成法国代表的意见，社会服务当然意味着对适当生活水准的支持，但它们不是在同一层次上。但是，可以在这些词前面加上"必要"一词来强调社会服务，它指的是食物、衣服、住房等等。随后用"和"一词来取代"住房"后的逗号。

他不同意新西兰关于在"保障"一词前插入"社会"一词的提议。第 20 条已提到社会保障，旨在涵盖随后的条款。在当前语境中，重复该词会缩窄其含义。他同意乌拉圭代表的意见，认为西班牙文 seguros 意味着保险，而 seguridad 才是对英文 security（保障）一词更为准确的翻译。

他不反对挪威的提议，即应对"在不可控情况下"的短语进行单独表决。但是，最好保留该措辞，因为它有助于激励人们自力更生。

澳大利亚对第 2 款的修改也许是可以接受的。他自己的抽象术语"为母"和"童年"不能与"有权利"一词共同使用；因此，英文文本中的"有资格享有"一词应被替换。

他在答复多米尼加共和国代表时指出，"童年"一词涵盖所有婚生或非婚生儿童。他很高兴地注意到，苏联代表认为南斯拉夫的修正案需要修改措辞。该修正案将通过唱名的方式进行表决，但他建议，应首先对其原则进行表决，如果这一原则被接受，则可以对草案进行修改。他同意多米尼加共和国和法国代表的意见，即南斯拉夫目前的修正案不适合第 22 条，而是属于关于保护社会地位的某一条款。

　　罗斯福夫人（美国）撤回她的修正案（第 A/C.3/343 号文件），赞成中国的修正案。

　　贝尔纳迪诺小姐（多米尼加共和国）不同意中国代表的意见，即第 2 段的英文文本中应保留"有权利"一词。如果将中文文本付诸表决，她将提出一项修正案，将这些词语替换为"有资格享有"。

　　下午 1:20 会议结束。

——第三委员会第 144 次会议简要记录（A/C.3/SR.144）

李一萌、常健译，常健校

A/C.3/SR.144
18 November 1948

GENERAL ASSEMBLY
THIRD SESSION
THIRD COMMITTEE
SUMMARY RECORD OF THE HUNDRED AND FORTY-FOURTH MEETING

Held at the Palais de Chaillot, Paris, on Thursday, 18 November 1948,
at 10:30 a.m.

69. Draft International Declaration of Human Rights (E/800)
(Continued)

Article 22 (Continued)

...

　　Mr.Chang (China) said that he could accept certain drafting changes to his amendment. He agreed with the French and Chilean representatives that the words "health and wellbeing" should be restored; they should be substituted for the word "needs". He could not, however, wholly agree with the representative of France; social services certainly implied a support for an adequate standard of living, but they were not on the same level. It would, however, be possible to give emphasis to social services by inserting the word "necessary" before those words; it would refer to food, clothing, housing, etc. The word "and" would then be substituted for the comma after the word "housing".

He did not agree with the New Zealand proposal to insert the word "social" before the word "security". Social security had been mentioned in article 20, which had been intended to cover the subsequent articles. To repeat the words again in the present context would narrow their meaning. He agreed with the representative of Uruguay that the word *seguridad* was a more accurate translation of the word "security" than the word *seguros*, which implied insurance.

He did not object to the Norwegian proposal that the phrase "in circumstances beyond his control" should be voted separately. It might be well to include the words, however, because they would tend to encourage self-reliance.

The Australian alteration of paragraph 2 might be acceptable. His own abstract terms "motherhood" and "childhood" could not be used with the words "have the right"; the words "are entitled" should therefore be substituted in the English text.

Replying to the representative of the Dominican Republic, he pointed out that the word "childhood" covered all children born in or out of wedlock. He was glad to note that the USSR representative believed that the Yugoslav amendment needed drafting changes. That amendment would be voted on by roll-call, but he suggested that a vote should first be taken on its principle and, if that were accepted, the drafting changes could then be made. He agreed with the representatives of the Dominican Republic and France that the Yugoslav amendment in its present form was inappropriate to article 22 and belonged rather in some article dealing with the protection of social status.

Mrs. Roosevelt (United States of America) withdrew her amendment (A/C.3/343) in favour of the Chinese amendment.

Miss Bernardino (Dominican Republic) disagreed with the representative of China: the words "have the right" should be retained in the English text of paragraph 2. If the Chinese text were put to the vote, she would move an amendment to substitute those words for the words "are entitled".

The meeting rose at 1:20 p.m.

在第三委员会第 145 次会议上的发言

1948 年 11 月 18 日星期四下午 3:15 巴黎夏乐宫

70.《国际人权宣言（草案）》（第 E/800 号文件）（续）

第 22 条（续）

主席提醒委员会，关于第 22 条的一般性讨论已结束，并请委员会就已提交的各项修正案进行表决。

张先生（中国）为了避免程序困难，撤回了他在上一次会议上的提议，以便能够就包含婚生子女和非婚生子女绝对平等理念的原则进行投票表决。

……

张先生（中国）注意到法国代表团提交的案文与中国代表团提交的案文在内容上有所不同。它包含了三个新理念：个人资源，由社会服务来补充这些资源的需要，以及对个人及其家庭的福祉和健康的保障。

罗斯福夫人（美国）、科贝特夫人（英国）和瓦特先生（澳大利亚）同意中国代表的发言，并提请注意在法语修正案的英文翻译中的某些缺陷。

……

主席将中国代表团就第 22 条第 1 款提出的案文（第 A/C.3/347/Rev.1 号文件）付诸表决。

伦德先生（挪威）要求对案文进行部分表决，并要求将"在他无法控制的情况下"一语与该段其余部分分开表决。

案文第一部分，包括"生计"一词在内，以 40 票对 0 票、3 票弃权获得通过。

包括"在他无法控制的情况下"等字样在内的案文最后一部分，以 29 票对 3 票、6 票弃权获得通过。

中国代表团提出的案文以 41 票对 0 票、3 票弃权获得通过，成为第 22 条第 1 款。

......

主席将中国代表团就第 2 段提出的案文（第 A/C.3/347/Rev.1 号文件）付诸表决。

巴甫洛夫先生（苏联）指出，案文措辞不当；诸如"为母和童年"这样的抽象概念不可能成为法律实体。

巴洛迪先生（沙特阿拉伯）支持这一观点；由于案文的措辞，他无法对其投赞成票。

案文以 25 票对 7 票、12 票弃权获得通过。

......

——第三委员会第 145 次会议简要记录（A/C.3/SR.145）

李一萌、常健译，常健校

A/C.3/SR.145
18 November 1948

GENERAL ASSEMBLY
THIRD SESSION
THIRD COMMITTEE
SUMMARY RECORD OF THE HUNDRED AND FORTY-FIFTH MEETING

Held at the Palais de Chaillot, Paris, on Thursday, 18 November 1948, at 3:15 p.m.

70. Draft International Declaration of Human Rights (E/800) (Continued)

Article 22 (Continued)

The Chairman reminded the Committee that the general discussion of article 22 was closed, and asked the Committee to vote on the various amendments which had been submitted.

Mr.Chang (China), with a view to avoiding procedural difficulties, withdrew the proposal he had made at the preceding meeting, in order to enable a vote to be taken on the principle of including the idea of the absolute equality of legitimate and illegitimate children.

...

Mr.Chang (China) observed that the text presented by the French delegation differed in substance from the text submitted by his delegation. It contained three new ideas: individual resources, the need to supplement those resources by social services, and the guarantee to the individual of wellbeing and health for himself and his family.

Mrs. Roosevelt (United States of America), Mrs. Corbet (United Kingdom) and Mr. Watt (Australra) agreed with what had been said by the representative of China and drew attention to certain defects in the English translation of the French amendment.

...

The Chairman put ta the vote the text proposed by the Chinese delegation for article 22, paragraph 1 (A/C.3/347/Rev.l).

Mr. Lunde (Norway) requested that the text be voted upon in parts and that the words "in circumstances beyond his control" be voted upon separately from the remainder of the paragraph.

The first part of the text, up to and including the word "livelihood", was adopted by 40 votes to none, with 3 abstentions.

The last part of the text, containing the words "in circumstances beyond his control", was adopted by 29 votes to 3, with 6 abstentions.

The text proposed by the Chinese delegation was adopted as paragraph 1 of article 22, by 41 votes to none, with 3 abstentions.

...

The Chairman put to the vote the text proposed by the Chinese delegation for paragraph 2 (A/C.3/347/Rev.l).

Mr. Pavlov (Union of Soviet Socialist Republics) pointed out that the text was poorly worded; abstract ideas such as "motherhood and childhood" could not be legal entities.

Mr. Baroody (Saudi Arabia) supported that view; he could not vote in favour of the text because of its drafting.

The text was adopted by 25 votes to 7, with 12 abstentions.

...

在第三委员会第 146 次会议上的发言

1948 年 11 月 19 日星期五上午 10:30 巴黎夏乐宫

71.《国际人权宣言（草案）》（第 E/800 号文件）（续）

第 22 条（续）

......

贝尔纳迪诺小姐（多米尼加共和国）表示，虽然在上次会议上，她接受了中国修正案（第 A/C.3/347/Rev.1 号文件）第 2 款，而非自己提出的修正案（第 A/C.3/217/Corr.2 号文件）；但是她后来发现前者的英文文本有缺陷。因此，她希望委员会重新审议第 2 款，或根据她的修正案的基本精神重新起草，或直接用她的修正案来取代。

她同意主席的意见，重新审议的问题推迟到整个宣言的审议完成之后。

......

张先生（中国）在回答多米尼加共和国代表时说，他此前和现在都没有在第 2 款英文文本中坚持使用"有权利"一词。

他指出，挪威先前的修正案的第 3 款与宣言中大多数条款在风格上有所不同；它首先提到少数群体，而非广泛的一般群体。此外，它是对第 2 款陈述的扩充。他希望挪威代表同意将第 2 款和第 3 款合并，并在第 3 款开头加上以下文字："所有儿童，包括非婚生儿童"。

该建议可与多米尼加共和国代表的建议同时处理。

......

——第三委员会第 146 次会议简要记录（A/C.3/SR.146）

李一萌译，常健校

A/C.3/SR.146
19 November 1948

GENERAL ASSEMBLY
THIRD SESSION
THIRD COMMITTEE
SUMMARY RECORD OF THE HUNDRED AND FORTY-SIXTH MEETING

Held at the Palais de Chaillot, Paris, on Friday, 19 November 1948,

at 10:30 a.m.

71. Draft International Declaration of Human Rights (E/800) (Continued)

·

Article 22 (Continued)

Miss Bernardino (Dominican Republic) remarked that, although at the previous meeting she had accepted paragraph 2 of the Chinese amendment (A/C.3/347/Rev.1) in lieu of her own (A/C.3/217/Corr.2), she had since discovered a drafting imperfection in the English text of the former. She consequently hoped that the paragraph in question might be reconsidered by the Committee and either redrafted in the spirit of her amendment or replaced by it.

She agreed with the Chairman that the question of reconsideration might be postponed until the whole declaration had been dealt with.

...

Mr.Chang (China) said, in reply to the representative of the Dominican Republic, that he had not insisted and did not insist on the use, in the English text of paragraph 2, of the words "have the right".

He pointed out that paragraph 3—the former Norwegian amendment—was different in style from most articles in the declaration in that it began with a reference to a minority rather than to a broad general group. Moreover, it represented an enlargement of the statement in paragraph 2. He hoped that the Norwegian representative would agree to combine paragraphs 2 and 3 and to begin the latter with some such words as: "All children, including those born out of wedlock."

That suggestion might be dealt with at the same time as the suggestion of the representative of the Dominican Republic.

　　…

在第三委员会第 150 次会议上的发言

1948 年 11 月 20 日星期六下午 3:15 巴黎夏乐宫

75. 《国际人权宣言（草案）》（第 E/800 号文件）（续）
第 24 条（续）

......

主席请委员会成员审议新西兰代表团提出的第 24 条备选案文（第 A/C.3/359 号文件）。

张先生（中国）提出了一个新的修正案，内容如下：

"人人都有休息和闲暇的权利，包括规定诸如合理的限定工时和定期带薪休假等。"

由于纽兰夫人（新西兰）不接受中国代表提出的修正案，主席请委员会对第 A/C.3/359 号文件中的新西兰修正案进行表决。

......

该修正案以 25 票对 4 票，10 票弃权获得通过。

......

张先生（中国）考虑到新西兰修正案的措辞，对其投了反对票，但中国代表团并不反对该修正案所依据的原则。闲暇权是一个抽象概念，限制工时是一个涉及具体现实的抽象概念，而带薪休假则是一个具体概念。因此，他认为新西兰修正案的措辞对性质迥异的概念赋予同等的重要性，在表述中没有明确阐述它们之间的逻辑关系，这不甚恰当。

他呼吁新西兰代表团同意修改其修正案的措辞。

......

——第三委员会第 150 次会议简要记录（A/C.3/SR.150）

李一萌译，常健校

A/C.3/SR.150
20 November 1948

GENERAL ASSEMBLY
THIRD SESSION
THIRD COMMITTEE
SUMMARY RECORD OF THE HUNDRED AND FIFTIETH
MEETING

Held at the Palais de Chaillot, Paris, on Saturday, 20 November 1948,
at 3:15 p.m.

75. Draft International Declaration of Human Rights (E/800) (Continued)

Article 24 (Continued)

…

The Chairman asked the members of the Committee to consider the alternative text of article 24 proposed by the New Zealand delegation (A/C.3/359).

Mr. Chang (China) proposed a new version of the amendment, as follows:

"Everyone has the right to rest and leisure, including such provisions as reasonable limitation of working hours and periodical holidays with pay."

As Mrs. Newlands (New Zealand) did not accept the revision submitted by the Chinese representative, the Chairman asked the Committee to vote on the New Zealand amendment as it appeared in document A/C.3/359.

…

The amendment was adopted by 25 votes ta 4, with 10 abstentions.

…

Mr. Chang (China) had voted against the amendment on account of its wording, although his delegation had no objection to the principle on which it was based. The right to leisure was an abstract idea, the limitation of working hours was an abstract idea relating to a concrete reality and holidays with pay were a concrete matter. For that reason, he considered that the wording of the New Zealand amendment, in giving equal importance to ideas of a very different nature and in expressing them without establishing any logical relation between them, was somewhat inadequate.

He appealed to the New Zealand delegation to consent to change the wording of its amendment.

...

在第三委员会第 151 次会议上的发言

1948 年 11 月 22 日星期一上午 10:50 巴黎夏乐宫

......

79.《国际人权宣言（草案）》（第 E/800 号文件）（续）

第 25 条（续）

......

张先生（中国）提请委员会成员注意第 25 条的最后部分，特别是"并分享科学进步"的措辞。正如各代表团特别是法国代表团已经指出的，不仅必须保障人人享有科学进步福利的权利，而且必须保障参与科学创造工作的权利。在艺术、文学和科学领域，审美享受具有双重性：欣赏美是纯粹被动的一面，创造美则是主动的一面。基于这种关系，张先生指出，"参与"或"分享"的表述并未足够准确地表达这种双重性。该案文更明确地指向创造而不是被动享受。因此，他提议在第一款末尾加上"及其利益"的措辞（A/C.3/361 号文件）。

他说中国代表团接受秘鲁修正案（第 150 次会议），即建议在第 1 款的"参与"一词之前插入"自由地"一词。随后，他建议对古巴、法国和墨西哥的联合修正案第 2 款的措辞作一些修改。第 2 款将改为：

"人人对其本人之任何科学、文学或美术作品所获得之精神与物质利益，有享受保护之权。"

佩雷斯西斯内罗斯先生（古巴）感谢中国代表团对联合修正案的原文进行的澄清和改进。古巴代表团乐于接受这些改动以及秘鲁代表提出的修正案。

......

——第三委员会第 151 次会议简要记录（A/C.3/SR.151）

李一萌译，常健校

A/C.3/SR.151

22 November 1948

GENERAL ASSEMBLY
THIRD SESSION
THIRD COMMITTEE
SUMMARY RECORD OF THE HUNDRED AND FIFTY-FIRST
MEETING

Held at the Palais de Chaillot, Paris, on Monday, 22 November 1948,

at 10:50 a.m.

...

79. Draft International Declaration of Human Rights (E/800)
(Continued)

Article 25 (Continued)

...

Mr. Chang (China) drew the attention of the members of the Committee to the last part of article 25, particularly the words "and to share in scientific advancement". As various delegations, in particular that of France, had already pointed out, not only must the right to share in the benefits of scientific advancement be guaranteed to everyone but also the right to participate in the work of scientific creation. In the arts, letters and sciences alike, aesthetic enjoyment had a dual aspect: a purely passive aspect when man appreciates beauty and an active aspect when he creates it. In this connexion Mr. Chang indicated that the expression "participate in" or "share in" did not express this dual aspect as precisely as it might. The text referred more clearly to creation than to passive enjoyment. He therefore proposed the addition, at the end of the first paragraph, of the words "and its benefits" (A/C.3/361).

After stating that his delegation accepted the Peruvian amendment (150th meeting) proposing insertion of the word "freely" before the word "participate" in the first paragraph, he suggested a few drafting changes in the second paragraph of the joint amendment of Cuba, France and Mexico. The second paragraph would then read:

"Everyone has the right to the protection of the moral and material interests resulting from any scientific, literary or artistic production of which he is the author."

Mr. Pérez Cisneros (Cuba) thanked the Chinese delegation for having clarified and improved the original text of the joint amendment. His delegation was glad to accept those changes, together with the amendment suggested by the Peruvian representative.

…

在第三委员会第 152 次会议上的发言

1948 年 11 月 22 日星期一下午 3:00 巴黎夏乐宫

80.《国际人权宣言（草案）》（第 E/800 号文件）（续）

第 25 条（续）

张先生（中国）说，A/C.3/361 号文件中的案文是由中国代表团提出的。它实际上是一个综合各方建议的文本：插入"自由地"一词是秘鲁的建议，增加"及其利益"一词是中国代表团的建议，第 2 款实际上是古巴、法国和墨西哥的联合建议。他要求对第 2 款进行单独表决。

……

伦德先生（挪威）说，他对经修正的第 1 款投了赞成票，因为由于中国代表的娴熟文笔，该案文措辞非常好。

……

第 26 条

主席在开放对第 26 条的一般性辩论时评论道，要求删除该条的埃及修正案（第 A/C.3/264 号文件）将不会直接付诸表决，但愿意支持该修正案的成员可以对整个条款投反对票。

……

张先生（中国）不太确定"社会"一词是否包括"国际"的概念。他也不认为第 26 条可以被称为是对一项权利的陈述。他认为，将对第 26 条的决定推迟至委员会审议第 27 条和第 28 条之后，会更为明智。

……

——第三委员会第 152 次会议简要记录（A/C.3/SR.152）

李一萌译，常健校

A/C.3/SR.152
22 November 1948

GENERAL ASSEMBLY
THIRD SESSION
THIRD COMMITTEE
SUMMARY RECORD OF THE HUNDRED AND FIFTY-SECOND MEETING

Held at the Palais de Chaillot, Paris, on Monday, 22 November 1948, at 3:00 p.m.

80. Draft International Declaration of Human Rights (E/800) (Continued)

Article 25 (Continued)

...

Mr. Chang (China) said that the text which appeared in document A/C.3/361 had been attributed to the Chinese delegation. It was really a combined text: the insertion of the word "freely" was a Peruvian suggestion, the addition of the words "and its benefits" had been suggested by the Chinese delegation, and the second paragraph was really a joint Cuban, French and Mexican proposal. He asked that the second paragraph should be voted upon separately.

...

Mr. Lunde (Norway) stated that he had voted in favour of the first paragraph as amended because that text, thanks to the skillful drafting of the Chinese representative, was very well phrased.

...

Article 26

The Chairman, in opening the general debate on article 26, remarked that the Egyptian amendment (A/C.3/264) which called for the deletion of the article would not be put to the vote as such; those who wished to support it could vote against the article as a whole.

...

Mr. Chang (China) was not at all sure that the word "social" did not include the idea of "international". Nor was he convinced that article 26 could be claimed to be a statement of a right. In his opinion, it would be wiser to postpone a decision on article 26 until the Committee had considered articles 27 and 28.

…

在第三委员会第 153 次会议上的发言

1948 年 11 月 23 日星期二下午 3:20 巴黎夏乐宫

81.《国际人权宣言（草案）》（第 E/800 号文件）（续）

第 27 条

......

张先生（中国）赞同法国修正第 1 款的目的，但并不认为该目的已经实现。在英文文本中，"人格的自由发展"可能比使用"自由地发展其人格"这一短语更可取。改进第 1 款的起草并非易事；如果不能作出改进，就应当允许该款继续有效。

以在适当的位置引入乌拉圭修正案的方式重新起草第 2 款，同样是困难的。按照乌拉圭代表的用法，对"为法律所规定"一词不仅适用于公共秩序和一般福利这些可以适用的内容，而且也适用于道德以及承认和尊重他人权利这样肯定不能也不应由法律规定的概念。

张先生评论道，他认为第 27 条的原初案文基本令人满意，但他可能会在以后的会议上提出有关起草性质的修正案。

......

——第三委员会第 153 次会议简要记录（A/C.3/SR.153）

李一萌译，常健校

A/C.3/SR.153
23 November 1948

GENERAL ASSEMBLY
THIRD SESSION
THIRD COMMITTEE
SUMMARY RECORD OF THE HUNDRED AND

FIFTY-THIRD MEETING

Held at the Palais de Chaillot, Paris, on Tuesday, 23 November 1948,
at 3:20 p.m.

81. Draft International Declaration of Human Rights (E/800) (Continued)

Article 27

...

Mr. Chang (China) sympathized with the purpose of the French amendment to paragraph 1, but did not think that it had been achieved. It might perhaps be preferable, in the English text, to speak of the "free development of personality" rather than use the phrase "freely to develop his personality". It was not simple to improve the drafting of paragraph 1; unless an improvement could be effected the paragraph should be permitted to stand.

It was equally difficult to re-draft paragraph 2 in such a manner as to introduce the Uruguayan amendment in its proper place. As used by the Uruguayan representative, the words "prescribed by law" applied not only to public order and general welfare, which they might properly qualify, but also to such concepts as morality and recognition and respect for the rights of others, which surely could not and should not be prescribed by law.

Mr. Chang remarked that he found the original text of article 27 satisfactory in the main, but that he might at a later meeting present amendment of a drafting nature.

...

在第三委员会第 154 次会议上的发言

1948 年 11 月 24 日星期三上午 11:00 巴黎夏乐宫

82.《国际人权宣言（草案）》（第 E/800 号文件）（续）

第 27 条（续）

......

瓦特先生（澳大利亚）建议在第 1 款中的"社会"一词之后插入"只有在其中其人格才可能得到自由和充分的发展"，而不是"它使其能够自由发展其人格"。

德乌斯先生（比利时）认为，澳大利亚代表建议的案文有一个不准确的说法，因为虽然社会无疑有助于个人人格的发展，但这种发展还会受到其他因素的制约，这也是不争的事实。

康德玛先生（希腊）完全同意比利时代表的意见。

罗斯福夫人（美国）建议删除"只有"一词。

本着折中主义精神，张先生（中国）提议将澳大利亚修正案第 1 款的结尾改为："它使其人格得以充分发展"。

阿兹库勒先生（黎巴嫩）赞成中国代表提出的案文。不过，他建议将"其人格"改为"人的人格"。新的措辞可规避一些代表团已指出的隐患，即该案文被解释为只有当社会确保了个人人格充分发展，个人才对社会负有义务。

张先生（中国）认为，第 27 条第一句中的"人人"一词已经包含了"人"的含义，因此无需重复。

......

主席将澳大利亚之前提交的修正案付诸表决，该修正案已被苏联代表团接受。

张先生（中国）要求对修正案分部分进行表决，以便对"只有"一词进行单独表决。

主席将关于把"只有"一词写入苏联修正案文本的提议付诸表决。

该提案以 23 票赞成、5 票反对、14 票弃权获得通过。

主席将苏联修正案整体付诸表决。

该修正案以 35 票对 0 票、6 票弃权获得通过。

......

——第三委员会第 154 次会议简要记录（A/C.3/SR.154）

李一萌译，常健校

A/C.3/SR.154

24 November 1948

GENERAL ASSEMBLY
THIRD SESSION
THIRD COMMITTEE
SUMMARY RECORD OF THE HUNDRED AND FIFTY-FOURTH MEETING

Held at the Palais de Chaillot, Paris, on Wednesday, 24 November 1948, at 11 a.m.

82. Draft International Declaration of Human Rights (E/800) (Continued)

Article 27 (Continued)

...

Mr. Watt (Australia) suggested inserting the phrase "in which alone the free and full development of his personality is possible", in paragraph 1 after the word "community", instead of the words "which enables him freely to develop his personality".

Mr. Dehousse (Belgium) considered that the text proposed by the representative of Australia contained an inaccurate statement, for while there was no doubt that society contributed to the development of the individual's personality, it was no less true that that development was conditioned by other factors.

Mr. Contoumas (Greece) fully agreed with the Belgian representative.

Mrs. Roosevelt (United States of America) proposed deletion of the word "alone".

In a spirit of compromise, Mr. Chang (China) proposed that the end of the first paragraph of the Australian amendment should read as follows: "which makes possible the full development of his personality".

Mr. Azkoul (Lebanon) preferred the text proposed by the Chinese representative. He suggested, however, that the words "his personality" should be replaced by the term "human personality". That new wording would avoid the danger, already pointed out by some delegations, that the text might be interpreted as implying that the individual had duties to society only in so far as the latter secured the full development of his own personality.

Mr. Chang (China) considered that the word "everyone" in the first sentence of article 27 already contained the meaning of the word "human", therefore need not be repeated.

...

The Chairman put to the vote the amendment formerly submitted by Australia, which had been taken up by the USSR delegation.

Mr. Chang (China) asked that the amendment should be voted upon in parts so that the word "alone" might be voted on separately.

The Chairman put to the vote the proposal to include the word "alone" in the text of the USSR amendment.

That proposal was adopted by 23 votes to 5, with 14 abstentions.

The Chairman put to the vote the USSR amendment as a whole.

The amendment was adopted by 35 votes to none, with 6 abstentions.

...

在第三委员会第 156 次会议上的发言

1948 年 11 月 25 日星期四上午 11:00 巴黎夏乐宫

84.《国际人权宣言（草案）》（第 E/800 号文件）（续）

第 28 条（续）

......

张先生（中国）指出，他同意乌拉圭代表的意见，即将乌拉圭代表提交的修正案（第 A/C.3/268 号文件）英文文本中的"从事任何行动"改为"参与任何行动"。

希梅内斯·德·阿雷查加先生（乌拉圭）说，他准备接受中国代表提出的修正案，并指出该修正案不会影响法文文本，该法文文本应保留现有的措辞。

主席回顾说，委员会在结束其工作之前，将要求联合国五种官方语言的代表任命专家，确保以官方语言拟定的五份文本之间绝对一致，所有这些文本将具有同等效力。

在谈到依照中国修正案来修改的乌拉圭修正案时，他强调第 28 条基本案文中的"活动"一词与乌拉圭建议的"行动"一词之间存在差异。他回顾道，人权委员会倾向于使用"活动"一词，因为它比"行动"一词有更广的含义。

格伦巴赫先生（法国）同意主席的解释。他认为，用"行动"来替代"活动"是危险的。人权委员会使用"活动"一词，希望赋予第 28 条以预防的意义，因为最好可以防止最后行动的出现，最后的行动一般来说是长期活动的结果。以纳粹主义和法西斯主义为例，其活动显然已经存在了许多年。如果想使人权宣言所规定的权利和自由得到真正的保护，应该从一开始就规定要防止任何旨在破坏这些权利和自由的活动。

法国代表询问乌拉圭代表，是否准备接受在"参与任何活动"之后增加"从事任何行动"这一短语。

阿基诺先生（菲律宾）指出，中国代表提议的修改并不仅仅是指措辞上的修改。他认为，"参与任何行动"的表述是不正确的；他建议采用"从事任何行动"或"参与任何活动"的措辞。像人权宣言这样的案文，其措辞应使用具有明确法律含义的表述。

柯伯特夫人（英国）支持菲律宾代表的意见。

她说，她支持法国代表提出的将这两个表述并列使用的建议，并正式要求将该提议付诸表决。

张先生（中国）说，鉴于他的提议引起的反对，他不会坚持这一提议。

……

张先生（中国）感谢第 3 小组委员会及其报告员起草了一份明显优于先前的案文。他希望第三委员会本着曾鼓舞小组委员会的成员们的和解和公正的精神开展工作。

在分析第 21 条拟议的新案文时，他对在第 1 款中巧妙地引入自由选择就业的理念表示满意。在该款中删除"和薪酬"一词，以便将与工人薪酬有关的所有内容归入第 2 款，这一点颇具争议，但中国代表团不会对其表示反对。关于非歧视条款，虽然他发现已获通过的折中方案并没有发挥作用，但他还是赞同不去列举产生歧视的各种可能的原因。

中国代表说，中国代表团不希望第 2 款第 2 项保持现有的形式，因为如果薪酬的概念属于第 21 条的范围，那么满足工人家庭需求所要求的社会保护则应属于第 22 条，似乎没有必要在第 21 条中对其重复表述。

中国代表团尽管接受第 1 款和第 3 款不作改动，但希望第 2 款措辞只保留以下两项原则：第 1 项应写入每个工作者都有权获得公正报酬的原则；第 2 项应写入同工同酬的原则。

……

瓦特先生（澳大利亚）感谢小组委员会成员及其杰出的报告员清晰客观的报告。

他支持中国代表关于小组委员会提议的案文第 2 款第 2 项的评论，因为他认为，已经通过的第 22 条不仅涵盖了对个人的保护，也涵盖了对其家庭的保护。

……

——第三委员会第 156 次会议简要记录（A/C.3/SR.156）

李一萌译，常健校

A/C.3/SR.156
25 November 1948

GENERAL ASSEMBLY
THIRD SESSION
THIRD COMMITTEE
SUMMARY RECORD OF THE HUNDRED AND FIFTY-
SIXTH MEETING

Held at the Palais de Chaillot, Paris, on Thursday, 25 November 1948,
at 11:00 a.m.

84. Draft International Declaration of Human Rights (E/800) (Continued)

Article 28 (Continued)

...

Mr. Chang (China) pointed out that he had agreed with the representative of Uruguay to replace the words "perform any acts" in the English text of the amendment submitted by the latter (A/C.3/268) by the words "engage in any acts".

Mr. Jiménez de Aréchaga (Uruguay) said he was prepared to accept the amendment proposed by the Chinese representative, and pointed out that the amendment would not affect the French text, which should retain its present wording.

The Chairman recalled that, before the end of its work, the Committee would ask the representatives of the five official languages to appoint experts in order to ensure absolute agreement between the five texts established in the official languages, which would all be equally authentic.

Referring to the Uruguayan amendment amended by the Chinese amendment he stressed the difference between the word "activity" in the basic text of article 28 and the word "acts" proposed by Uruguay. He recalled that the

Commission on Human Rights had preferred the word "activity", as having a wider meaning than the word "acts".

Mr. Grumbach (France) agreed to the explanation given by the Chairman. He thought that it would be dangerous to replace the word "activity" by the word "acts". In employing the former, the Human Rights Commission had wished to give a preventive sense to article 28, considering that it was preferable to prevent the final act which, in general, was the outcome of a long activity. In the case of Nazism and Fascism, for example, the activity had been evident for many years. If the rights and the freedoms laid down in the Declaration of Human Rights were really to be protected, provision should be made to prevent, at the very beginning, any activity aimed at their destruction.

The French representative asked the representative of Uruguay whether he would be prepared to accept the addition of the phrase "perform any acts" after the words "engage in any activity".

Mr. Aquino (Philippines) pointed out that the modification proposed by the Chinese representative was not simply a drafting change. In his opinion, the expression "engage in any acts" was incorrect; he suggested the wording "perform any acts" or "engage in any activity". In the wording of texts such as that of the Declaration of Human Rights, expressions with a clear legal meaning should be used.

Mrs. Corbet (United Kingdom) supported the Philippine representative's observation.

She stated that she supported the proposal made by the French representative to employ the two expressions side by side, and formally asked that that proposal should be put to the vote.

Mr. Chang (China) said that, in view of the objections which his proposal had raised, he would not insist on it.

......

Mr. Chang (China) thanked Sub-Committee 3 and its Rapporteur for having drawn up a decidedly better text than the previous one. He hoped that the Third Committee would work in the spirit of conciliation and impartiality, which had animated the members of the Sub-Committee.

Analysing the new text proposed for article 21, he expressed satisfaction at the skillful introduction of the idea of the free choice of employment in paragraph 1. The deletion of the words "and pay" in that paragraph, with a view to grouping everything connected with payment of the worker in paragraph 2, was a debatable point, but the Chinese delegation would not oppose it. With regard to the nondiscrimination clause, although he found the compromise formula adopted to be useless, he nevertheless approved the idea of not enumerating the possible causes of discrimination.

The representative of China said that his delegation would prefer not to keep the second sub-paragraph of paragraph 2 in its present form for, if the idea of payment came within the scope of article 21, that of the social protection required to meet the needs of the worker's family belonged, on the contrary, to article 22, and it did not seem necessary to repeat it in article 21.

The Chinese delegation, whilst accepting paragraphs 1 and 3 without alteration, would have preferred paragraph 2 to be worded so as to retain merely the two following principles: the first sub-paragraph should include the principle that every working person had the right to just remuneration; the second sub-paragraph should include the principle of equal pay for equal work.

...

Mr. Watt (Australia) thanked the members of the Sub-Committee and their distinguished Rapporteur for the clear and objective character of their report.

He supported the Chinese representative's remarks regarding the second sub-paragraph of paragraph 2 of the text proposed by the Sub-Committee, as he considered that protection, not only for the individual but also for his family, was covered by article 22, which had already been adopted.

...

在第三委员会第 157 次会议上的发言

1948 年 11 月 25 日星期四下午 3：00 巴黎夏乐宫

85.《国际人权宣言（草案）》（第 E/800 号文件）（续）

第 21 条：第三小组委员会的报告（第 A/C. 3/363 号文件）
（续）

......

卡雷拉·安德拉德先生（厄瓜多尔）对第 21 条第 2 款中的"歧视"一词表示不满。该词的确切意思是"识别"他建议用"区别"一词代替该词。

张先生（中国）指出，第 21 条如果宣布人人都享有工作的权利，不受任何歧视，或许能更准确地反映委员会的真实意图。如果人们因为各种歧视性理由而没有得到雇用，那么禁止同酬方面的歧视又有何用呢？

他认为，第 21 条第 2 款第 2 项从"辅以"开始的部分应该放在第 22 条，而不是第 21 条。

......

——第三委员会第 157 次会议简要记录（A/C.3/SR.157）

罗苇译，常健校

A/C.3/SR.157
25 November 1948

GENERAL ASSEMBLY
THIRD SESSION
THIRD COMMITTEE
SUMMARY RECORD OF THE HUNDRED AND FIFTY-
SEVENTH MEETING

Held at the Palais de Chaillot, Paris, on Thursday, 25 November 1948, at 3:00 p.m.

85. Draft International Declaration of Human Rights (E/800) (Continued)

Article 21: Report of Sub-Committee 3 (A/C.3/363) (Continued)

…

Mr. Carrera Andrade (Ecuador) expressed dissatisfaction with the word "discrimination" in paragraph 2 of article 21. The proper meaning of that word was "discernment"; he suggested that it might be replaced by the word "distinction".

Mr. Chang (China) indicated that article 21 might more accurately reflect the real feelings of the Committee if it stated that everyone, without discrimination, was entitled to work. Of what use was it to forbid discrimination with respect to equal pay if people were not hired for discriminatory reasons?

He thought that the phrase beginning "supplemented by" in the second sub-paragraph of paragraph 2 should be in article 22 rather than article 21.

…

在第三委员会第 158 次会议上的发言

1948 年 11 月 25 日星期四上午 8∶30 巴黎夏乐宫

86.　《国际人权宣言（草案）》（第 E/800 号文件）（续）

第 21 条：第三小组委员会的报告（第 A/C. 3/363 号文件）（续）

……

张先生（中国）表示，当对白俄罗斯修正案的讨论仍在进行时，他反对现在结束讨论，因为他希望能有更多时间来审查该修正案。引入该修正案，使得第 21 条与第 22 条的重合度比先前更高。中国代表团对第 2 款的第 2 句投了弃权票。新案文的第 3 款有了明显的改进。

在对第 21 条整体作最后表决时，中国代表团投了弃权票，尽管中国代表团感觉新的案文比其最初（在第 141 次会议上）投反对票的案文肯定有所改进。

……

——第三委员会第 158 次会议简要记录（A/C.3/SR.158）

罗苇译，常健校

A/C.3/SR.158
25 November 1948

GENERAL ASSEMBLY
THIRD SESSION
THIRD COMMITTEE

SUMMARY RECORD OF THE HUNDRED AND FIFTY-EIGHTH MEETING

Held at the Palais de Chaillot, Paris, on Thursday, 25 November 1948, at 8.30 p.m.

86. Draft International Declaration of Human Rights (E/800) (Continued)

Article 21: Report of the Sub-Committee 3 (A/C.3/363) (Continued)

…

Mr. Chang (China) stated that he had objected to the closure of the debate when the Byelorussian amendment had been under discussion as he had wanted more time in which to examine it. The introduction of that amendment had made article 21 more of a duplication of article 22 than before, and the Chinese delegation had abstained from voting on the second sentence of paragraph 2. Paragraph 3 of the new text was a definite improvement.

In the final vote on the article as a whole, the Chinese delegation had abstained, although it felt that the new text was certainly an improvement on the earlier text against which it had voted originally (141st meeting).

…

在第三委员会第 166 次会议上的发言

1948 年 11 月 30 日星期二下午 3：00 巴黎夏乐宫

94.《国际人权宣言（草案）》（第 E/800 号文件）（续）

序言（续）

……

张先生（中国）希望就序言第 1 段提出的修正案发表一些意见。他回顾道，自己有幸参加了人权委员会的工作，委员会成员那时已经认为第一段的叙述太长了。而荷兰修正案会使得该文本更加冗长、复杂。

此外，如果要在宣言中体现人起源于神的观念，就应该用单独一段来写，以强调其重要性。但是正如一些代表团已经指出的，不可能通过只反映政治因素的投票表决来决定如此重要的问题。为审议这样的问题，每个国家的可投票数应与其人口规模成比例。

基于所有这些理由，他希望荷兰代表团撤回其修正案。

……

张先生（中国）认为，人权委员会提交的案文中，前两段应予以保留。至于第 3 段，接受英国代表团提出的修改建议是一个明智的选择。同时，他不赞成在第 4 段增加对《联合国宪章》里的观点加以概述的建议。虽然宣言要涉及人的所有权利，但是没有必要在序言中谈及所有这些权利。

……

波戈莫洛夫先生（苏联）认为，须在小组委员会内设立一个语言小组。将用五种官方语言撰写的文本相互联系起来的责任，不应交给秘书处的技术部门。鉴于人权宣言的重要性，其文本必须由成员国代表在合格的翻译人员的协助下加以确定。

他认为：在小组委员会举行会议期间，第三委员会的工作不应继续。他认为，第三委员会会议暂停一两天是明智之举。

张先生（中国）同意苏联代表关于在小组委员会会议期间暂停第三委

员会工作的建议。

……

——第三委员会第 166 次会议简要记录（A/C.3/SR.166）

罗苇译，常健校

A/C.3/SR.166
30 November 1948

GENERAL ASSEMBLY
THIRD SESSION
THIRD COMMITTEE
SUMMARY RECORD OF THE HUNDRED AND SIXTY-SIXTH MEETING

Held at the Palais de Chaillot, Paris, on Tuesday, 30 November 1948, at 3:00 p.m.

94. Draft International Declaration of Human Rights (E/800) (Continued)

Preamble (Continued)

…

Mr. Chang (China) wished to make certain remarks concerning the amendments proposed to the first recital of the preamble. He recalled that he had had the honour of taking part in the work of the Commission on Human Rights and that the members of the Commission had then considered that first recital too long. The Netherlands amendment would make the text even more lengthy and more complex.

Moreover, if the idea of the divine origin of man were to be embodied in the declaration, it should be done in a separate paragraph so as to stress its importance; but as certain delegations had pointed out, it was impossible to decide so important a problem by a vote which would only reflect political factors; for the consideration of such a question the number of votes for each country should be proportional to the size of its population.

For all those reasons, he hoped that the Netherlands delegation would withdraw its amendment.

...

Mr. Chang (China) considered that the two first recitals in the text as submitted by the Commission on Human Rights should be retained. As for the third recital, it would be wise to accept the modification proposed by the United Kingdom delegation. On the other hand, he did not approve of the proposed additions to the fourth recital recapitulating ideas expressed in the Charter. Although the declaration dealt with all the rights of man, it was not necessary to refer to all of them in the preamble.

...

Mr. Bogomolov (Union of Soviet Socialist Republics) considered that it was indispensable to set up a language group within the Sub-Committee. The responsibility of correlating the texts in the five official languages could not be left to the technical services of the Secretariat.

In view of the importance of the Declaration of Human Rights the text must be established by representatives of the Member States with the assistance of qualified translators.

In his opinion the Committee should not continue to work while the subcommittee held its meetings and he thought it would be wise to suspend the Committee's meetings for a day or two.

Mr. Chang (China) shared the USSR representative's views on the adjournment of the Committee's work during the meetings of the sub-committee.

...

在第三委员会第 167 次会议上的发言

1948 年 11 月 30 日星期二下午 9:00 巴黎夏乐宫

95. 《国际人权宣言（草案）》（第 E/800 号文件）（续）

序言（续）

......

桑塔·克鲁兹先生（智利）对表决结果发表评论，他询问苏联代表是否同意将刚刚通过的苏联修正案中的第 2 段和第 3 段增加到序言里，而不是取代原来的内容。

波戈莫洛夫先生（苏联）同意在序言中增加上述两段内容。

戴维斯先生（英国）反对这一程序，他认为这是不可接受的。委员会已明确就用一个新案文取代另一个案文进行了表决，因此，在那时当然是可以对序言作出补充的，但现在为时已晚。

此外，苏联代表没有将他的意图表达得非常清楚，他应该对其再作解释。

张先生（中国）说，他对表决过程中代表们的主张出现的改变感到非常惊讶。主席应就是否应该用已通过的两个段落取代整个序言进行表决，因为将它们补充进序言的决定将会造成一种全新的局面。

......

张先生（中国）想知道，如果原则上接受将这两段内容补充进序言中，那么应该将该案文插在何处。进而言之，这两段是补充到实际的序言中，还是补充到厄瓜多尔代表团建议的案文中？

张先生建议，为了同时解决上述问题，应该首先进行表决。然后由苏联代表解释他希望以何种形式添加这两段内容。

主席同意了中国代表的建议。

......

主席提请委员会注意澳大利亚和法国对委员会起草的序言第 2 段提出

的联合修正案（第 A/C.3/383 号文件）。

张先生（中国）正式提议，用澳大利亚第一个修正案的最后一句话来取代修正案第 2 段，即："……并明确了承认和保障基本自由的极端重要性"。

他认为，每个人都熟悉罗斯福总统宣布的并在澳大利亚-法国联合修正案中提出的基本自由。因此，提及基本自由就足够清楚了，但重要的是规定对这些基本自由的承认和保障。

……

佩雷斯·西斯内罗斯先生（古巴）根据程序规则第 112 条正式提议，应当重新考虑所作出的表决结果，以便委员会能够通过法国代表提出的修正案。

桑迪弗先生（美国）反对该提议。委员会已经用了足够多的时间审查序言执行部分的案文。在几乎全票通过一项决定后，对其进行重新审议将是一个糟糕的流程。

张先生（中国）表示，古巴代表的提议不可取，因为委员会尚未完成对序言的表决。一旦结束对整个序言的表决，委员会才有可能就重新审议其投票结果的提议作出决定。

由于中国代表的意见，佩雷斯·西斯内罗斯先生（古巴）撤回了他的提议。

主席宣读了经修正的委员会序言草案全文。

经修正的序言以 36 票对 0 票、1 票弃权获得通过。

……

——第三委员会第 167 次会议简要记录（A/C.3/SR.167）

罗苇译，常健校

A/C.3/SR.167
30 November 1948

GENERAL ASSEMBLY
THIRD SESSION
THIRD COMMITTEE
SUMMARY RECORD OF THE HUNDRED AND

SIXTY-SEVENTH MEETING

Held at the Palais de Chaillot, Paris, on Tuesday, 30 November 1948, at 9:00 p.m.

95. Draft International Declaration of Human Rights (E/800) (Continued)

Preamble (Continued)

...

Mr. Santa Cruz (Chile) commenting on the result of the vote, asked the USSR representative if he would consent to the second and third paragraphs of his amendment, which had just been adopted, being added to the preamble instead of being substituted for it.

Mr. Bogomolov (Union of Soviet Socialist Republics) agreed to the two paragraphs in question being added to the preamble.

Mr. Davies (United Kingdom) objected to that procedure, which he declared was unacceptable; the Committee had plainly voted on a new text to substitute for the other; there could thus be no question, at that juncture, of an addition to the preamble.

The USSR representative, moreover, had not made his intentions very clear; he should explain them again.

Mr. Chang (China) said he was very surprised at the change of position which had occurred during the voting. The Chairman should take a vote on whether the two paragraphs which had been adopted should be submitted for the whole of the preamble or not, because a decision to add them to the preamble would create an entirely new situation.

...

Mr. Chang (China) wondered where the text should be inserted, if the principle were accepted that the two paragraphs should be added to the preamble. Furthermore, should the two paragraphs be added to the actual preamble, or to the text proposed by the Ecuador delegation?

Mr. Chang proposed that, in order to same time, they should first take a vote, and then the USSR representative should explain in what form he wished the two paragraphs to be added.

The Chairman agreed with the Chinese representative's proposal.

…

The Chairman drew the Committee's attention to the joint Australian and French amendment (A/C.3/383) to the second paragraph of the preamble prepared by the Commission.

Mr. Chang (China) proposed formally that the second paragraph of the amendment should be replaced by the last sentence of the first Australian amendment (A/C.3/257): "… and have made apparent the supreme importance of the recognition and guarantee of fundamental freedoms".

He thought that everyone was acquainted with the fundamental freedoms proclaimed by President Roosevelt and set forth in the joint Australian-French amendment. To mention them would therefore be sufficient, but it was essential to provide for the recognition and guarantee of those fundamental freedoms.

…

Mr. Pérez Cisneros (Cuba) formally proposed, in accordance with rule 112 of the rules of procedure, that the vote should be reconsidered so that the Committee could adopt the amendment proposed by the French representative.

Mr. Sandifer (United States of America) objected to that proposal. The Committee had had sufficient time to examine the text of the operative part of the preamble. It would be a bad procedure after an almost unanimous vote to reconsider a decision already taken.

Mr. Chang (China) said the Cuban representative's proposal could not be accepted as the Committee had not yet finished voting on the preamble. Once the whole of the preamble had been voted upon, it would be possible for the Committee to take a decision on a proposal to reconsider its vote.

Mr. Pérez Cisneros (Cuba) withdrew his proposal as a result of the observations made by the Chinese representative.

The Chairman read out the whole of the Commission's text of the draft preamble, as amended.

The preamble, as amended, was adopted by 36 votes to none, with 1 abstention.

...

在第三委员会第 175 次会议上的发言

1948 年 12 月 4 日星期六下午 4:15 巴黎夏乐宫

105.《世界人权宣言（草案）》（第 E/800 号文件）：第四小组委员会的报告
（第 A/C. 3/400 号文件和第 A/C. 3/400/rev. 1 号文件）

……

主席指出，小组委员会对第 1 条没有作出改动，现在开始讨论第 2 条。

第 2 条

……

张先生（中国）出于形式的原因，赞同小组委员会提交的文本。

……

张先生（中国）建议采用以下措辞："……语言、宗教、国籍或门第、政治或他种主张、出生、财产或他种身份"。

……

——第三委员会第 175 次会议简要记录（A/C.3/SR.175）

罗苇译，常健校

A/C.3/SR.175
4 December 1948

GENERAL ASSEMBLY
THIRD SESSION
THIRD COMMITTEE

SUMMARY RECORD OF THE HUNDRED AND SEVENTY-FIFTH MEETING

Held at the Palais de Chaillot, Paris, on Saturday, 4 December 1948,
at 4:15 p.m.

105. Draft Universal Declaration of Human Rights (E/800): Report of Sub-Committee 4 (A/C.3/400 and A/C.3/400/Rev.1)

…

The Chairman pointed out that article 1 had not been altered by the Sub-Committee, and opened discussion on article 2.

Article 2

…

Mr. Chang (China) favoured the text submitted by the Sub-Committee, for reasons of form.

…

Mr. Chang (China) suggested the following wording: "… language, religion, national or social origin, political or other opinion, birth, property or other status".

…

在第三委员会第 177 次会议上的发言

1948 年 12 月 6 日星期六下午 3：30 巴黎夏乐宫

107.《世界人权宣言（草案）》（第 E/800 号文件）：第四小组委员会的报告（第 A/C. 3/400 和 A/C. 3/400/Rev. 1 号文件）（续）

......

第 16 条

在回答张先生（中国）的问题时，主席说，法语中的 ou 替换为 et 必须涉及对英文文本的相应修改。然而，他指出，英文文本中的"either"（要么）一词清楚地表明，在公开场合表明宗教或信仰的自由绝不排除在私下这样做的自由。

......

第 19 条

......

张先生（中国）回顾道，第 3 款第 1 个短语目前采用的形式是一个折中的解决方案，这是法国代表团作出让步的结果。法国代表团一直表示倾向于使用现在时陈述语气。经过一番辩论，委员会决定支持现在的措辞。

虽然他表示没有个人偏好，但他建议，为了避免浪费时间，以及避免法文文本与英文文本之间可能出现的差异，这一句应保持原样。

......

第 23 条

张先生（中国）称：他对第 23 条第 1 款作出一项轻微改动的修正案（第 A/C.3/397 号文件），主要是为了统一风格。该款前两句保持不变；第 3 句如下：

"初级教育应属强迫性质；技术与职业教育应广为设立；高等教育应予人人平等机会，以成绩为准。"

波戈莫洛夫先生（苏联）要求对第 3 款付诸表决。按照该款的措辞，它可能被解释为：如果一个 23 或 24 岁的青年希望学习某一科目，他的父母有权阻止他这样做。

他要求在"儿童"一词之前插入"未成年人"一词。

……

主席指出，如果加上"未成年人"一词，委员会就必须决定儿童达到什么年龄就不再是未成年人；这个年龄在不同的国家是不一样的。

张先生（中国）建议将"对其子女"改为"对其幼年后代"。

……

——第三委员会第 177 次会议简要记录（A/C.3/SR.177）

罗苇译，常健校

A/C.3/SR.177
6 December 1948

GENERAL ASSEMBLY
THIRD SESSION
THIRD COMMITTEE
SUMMARY RECORD OF THE HUNDRED AND SEVENTY-SEVENTH MEETING

Held at the Palais de Chaillot, Paris, on Saturday, 6 December 1948,
at 3:30 p.m.

107. Draft Universal Declaration of Human Rights (E/800): Report of Sub-Committee 4 (A/C.3/400 and A/C.3/400/Rev.1) (Continued)

…

Article 16

…

In reply to a question by Mr. Chang (China), the Chairman stated that the replacement of *ou* by *et* in French must involve a corresponding change in the English text. He pointed out, however, that the word "either" in the English text made it clear that freedom to manifest religion or belief in public by no means excluded the freedom to do so in private.

...

Article 19

...

Mr. Chang (China) recalled that the current form of the first phrase of paragraph 3 had been established as a compromise solution, as the result of a concession by the French delegation, which had always expressed preference for the use of the present indicative. After some debate, the Committee had decided in favour of the current wording.

While expressing no personal preference, he suggested that, in order to avoid loss of time and a possible disparity between the French and English texts, the sentence should be retained as it stood.

...

Article 23

Mr. Chang (China) observed that he had submitted a slight amendment (A/C.3/397) to paragraph 1 of article 23, chiefly for the sake of uniformity of style. The first two sentences of the paragraph would remain unchanged; the third would read as follows:

"Elementary education shall be compulsory; technical and professional education shall be made generally available; and higher education shall be equally accessible to all on the basis of merit."

...

Mr. Bogomolov (Union of Soviet Socialist Republics) asked that paragraph 3 should be put to a vote. As the paragraph was worded, it might be interpreted to mean that if a young man of 23 or 24 wished to study a certain subject, his parents had the right to prevent him from so doing.

He asked that the word "minor" should be inserted before the word "children".

...

The Chairman pointed out that if the word "minor" were added, the

Committee would then have to decide at what age a child ceased to be a minor; that age differed in different countries.

Mr. Chang (China) suggested replacing the words "to their children" by the word's "to their offspring in their early childhood".

...

在第三委员会第 178 次会议上的发言

1948 年 12 月 6 日星期一下午 8:30 巴黎夏乐宫

108.《世界人权宣言（草案）》（第 E/800 号文件）：第四小组委员会的报告（第 A/C. 3/400 和 A/C. 3/400/Rev. 1 号文件）（续）

......

附加条款

......

坎波斯·奥尔蒂斯先生（墨西哥）、张先生（中国）和阿兹库勒先生（黎巴嫩）建议措辞变更，将法文文本中的"还"一词改为"完全平等"。其英文文案如下：

"本宣言所提出的权利，平等地适用于托管领土和非自治领土的所有居民。"

主席将经修正的附加条款付诸表决。

经修正的附加条款获得通过。

条款顺序

张先生（中国）提请注意这样一个事实，即：各机构已就宣言进行了为期两年的工作，各国政府都有机会对其进行审议并发表评论。各条款在宣言中的顺序经受住了时间的考验。该文件具有有机统一性，不应在委员会工作即将结束时轻率改动。

关于古巴的提议，因为第 7、8、9 条涉及纯粹法定权利的赋予，第 10 条仅顺带提及家庭，并要求对若干其他事项提供法律保护，所以如果将第 14 条插入第 7、8、9 条与第 10 条之间，就会破坏逻辑顺序。

黎巴嫩的建议同样是不可接受的，因为涉及行动自由、庇护和国籍的第 11、12 和 13 条在含义上与第 10 条的关系比第 14 条更密切。

他恳请委员会不要改变任何条款的顺序，除非有充分的理由。

……

张先生（中国）建议重新调整某些条款的顺序，以确保从有关生命权和自由权的条款到有关保护和享有这些权利的条款的有机进程不会中断。

他同意巴西代表的意见，即给予第 16 条优先地位，它应被放在第 3 条之后。但是他觉得第 17、18 和 19 条都涉及与社会相关的个人权利，应继续紧随第 16 条之后。

如果苏联关于附加条款的提案得到委员会的批准，他不会反对该提案。

……

主席将中国关于在第 16 条和第 17 条之后插入第 18 条和第 19 条的新提案付诸表决。

该提案以 21 票对 3 票、12 票弃权获得通过。

会议一致同意，第 4 条 a 款应成为第 5 条。

……

张先生（中国）撤回他先前的建议。他指出，第 16 条和第 17 条的新位置造成了混乱。

他支持海地代表关于重新审议委员会决定的提议。

……

桑塔·克鲁兹先生（智利）、张先生（中国）和柯伯特夫人（英国）敦促就重新审议委员会关于第 16、17、18 和 19 条的排序决定进行一次表决，他们认为这几条是一个统一的整体。

……

对《世界人权宣言（草案）》整体进行表决

主席说，由于委员会分别通过了《世界人权宣言（草案）》的实质内容和安排，他将对整个案文付诸表决。

智利代表要求进行唱名表决。

唱名表决如下：

经主席抽签，菲律宾被要求首先投票。

赞成：菲律宾、瑞典、叙利亚、土耳其、英国、美国、委内瑞拉、阿富汗、阿根廷、澳大利亚、比利时、玻利维亚、巴西、智利、中国、古巴、丹麦、多米尼加共和国、法国、希腊、海地、洪都拉斯、印度、伊朗、黎巴嫩、墨西哥、荷兰、新西兰、秘鲁。

弃权：波兰、乌克兰、苏联、南斯拉夫、白俄罗斯、加拿大、捷克斯洛伐克。

《世界人权宣言（草案）》以 29 票对 0 票、7 票弃权获得通过。

法国代表团提出的关于《世界人权宣言》的决议草案（第 A/C.3/381 号文件）

......

张先生（中国）建议将古巴修正案的（c）款改为：

"......不仅用官方语言，而且要用所掌握的一切手段，用所有可能的语言"。

该提议获得一致同意。

......

新西兰代表团提出的关于《世界人权宣言》的决议草案（第 A/C.3/405 号文件）

坎波斯·奥尔蒂斯先生（墨西哥）同意智利代表的意见，但是不认为通过新西兰的决议草案是明智之举。他认为，第 3 段不能令人满意，因为它强调说，如果没有公约和执行措施，宣言就无足轻重。

圣洛特先生（海地）认为，新西兰决议草案的执行部分是危险的，因为它会削弱宣言的效果。联合国大会不应承认宣言具有无法实施的性质，因为这可能被解释为宣布免除各国履行宣言规定的任何道德义务。

张先生（中国）支持海地和墨西哥代表的意见，并提议删除新西兰决议草案的第 3 段。

科贝特女士（英国）赞同那些认为公约和执行措施是人权法案重要组成部分的代表的意见。任务中较容易的部分已经完成，重点必须放在前面的困难工作上。

她可以接受中国代表的建议，即删除新西兰决议草案第 3 段，或将决议第 3 段中的"必要"改为"令人满意"。

......

——第三委员会第 178 次会议简要记录（A/C.3/SR.178）

罗苇译，常健校

A/C.3/SR.178
6 December 1948

GENERAL ASSEMBLY
THIRD SESSION
THIRD COMMITTEE
SUMMARY RECORD OF THE HUNDRED AND SEVENTY-EIGHTH MEETING

Held at the Palais de Chaillot, Paris, on Monday, 6 December 1948,
at 8:30 p.m.

108. Draft Universal Declaration of Human Rights (E/800): Report of Sub-Committee 4 (A/C.3/400 and A/C.3/400/Rev.1) (Continued)

...

Additional Article

...

Mr. Campos Ortiz (Mexico), Mr. Chang (China) and Mr. Azkoul (Lebanon) suggested drafting changes whereby the word également, in the French text, would be replaced by the words en pleine égalité, and the English text would read as follows:

"The rights set forth in this Declaration apply equally to all inhabitants of Trust and Non-Self-Governing Territories."

The Chairman put the additional article, as amended, to the vote.

The additional article, as amended, was adopted.

Arrangements of Articles

...

Mr. Chang (China) called attention to the fact that various bodies had worked on the declaration for two years, and that all the Governments had had an opportunity of considering it and making comments. The order in which the articles appeared in the declaration had stood the test of time. The document possessed an organic unity which should not be tampered with lightly, at the very end of the Committee's work.

With regard to the Cuban proposal, if article 14 were inserted between articles 7, 8 and 9, which granted purely legal rights, and article 10, which dealt only incidentally with the family and called for legal protection with respect to a number of other matters, a logical sequence would be destroyed.

The Lebanese suggestion was equally unacceptable since articles 11, 12 and 13, dealing with freedom of movement, asylum, and nationality, were much more closely associated in meaning with article 10 than was article 14.

He pleaded with the Committee not to alter the order of any of the articles save for good and sufficient reasons.

…

Mr. Chang (China) suggested a rearrangement of certain articles with a view to ensuring that there was no break in the organic progression from articles on the right to life and the right to liberty to articles on the protection and enjoyment of those rights.

He agreed with the Brazilian representative that priority should be given to article 16, which should follow article 3; he felt, however, that articles 17, 18 and 19, which all dealt with the rights of the individual in relation to society, should continue to follow immediately upon article 16.

He would not object to the USSR proposal concerning the additional article if it met with the Committee's approval.

…

The Chairman put to the vote the Chinese proposal for the insertion of articles 18 and 19 after articles 16 and 17 in their new position.

The proposal was adopted by 21 votes to 3, with 12 abstentions.

It was agreed that article 4a should become article 5.

…

Mr. Chang (China) withdrew his earlier suggestions. He pointed out that the new position of articles 16 and 17 had caused the confusion.

He supported the Haitian proposal for the reconsideration of the Committee's decisions.

...

Mr. Santa Cruz (Chile), Mr. Chang (China) and Mrs. Corbet (United Kingdom) urged that a single vote should be taken on the question of reconsidering the Committee's decisions on the arrangement of articles 16, 17, 18 and 19, which, they considered, represented a unified whole.

...

Vote On The Draft Universal Declaration of Human Rights As A Whole

The Chairman said that since the Committee had adopted separately the substance and the arrangement of the draft universal declaration of human rights, he would put to the vote the text as a whole.

A vote by roll-call had been requested by the representative of Chile.

A vote was taken by roll-call, as follows:

The Philippines, having been drawn by lot by the Chairman, was called upon to vote first:

In favour: Philippines, Sweden, Syria, Turkey, United Kingdom, United States of America, Venezuela, Afghanistan, Argentina, Australia, Belgium, Bolivia, Brazil, Chile, China, Cuba, Denmark, Dominican Republic, France, Greece, Haiti, Honduras, India, Iran, Lebanon, Mexico, Netherlands, New Zealand, Peru.

Abstaining: Poland, Ukrainian Soviet Socialist Republic, Union of Soviet Socialist Republics, Yugoslavia, Byelorussian Soviet Socialist Republic, Canada, Czechoslovakia.

The Draft Universal Declaration of Human Rights was adopted by 29 votes to none, with 7 abstentions.

Draft Resolution Submitted by the Delegation of France (A/C.3/381) concerning the Universal Declaration of Human Rights

...

Mr. Chang (China) suggested that paragraph (c) of the Cuban amendment should be changed to read as follows:

"... not only in the official languages, but also, using every means at his disposal, in all possible languages".

It was so agreed.

...

Draft Resolution Submitted by the Delegation of New Zealand (A/C.3/405) concerning the Universal Declaration of Human Rights

...

Mr. Campos Ortiz (Mexico) agreed with the Chilean representative, but wondered whether it would be advisable to adopt the New Zealand draft resolution. In his opinion, the third paragraph was unsatisfactory because it emphasized the fact that the declaration would have very little weight without the covenant and measures of implementation.

...

Mr. Saint-Lot (Haiti) considered that the operative part of the New Zealand draft resolution was dangerous because it would weaken the effect of the declaration. It would not be appropriate for the Assembly to recognize the inoperative character of the declaration, as that could be construed as exonerating States from any moral obligation to fulfil its provisions.

...

Mr. Chang (China) supported the views of the representatives of Haiti and Mexico and proposed that the third paragraph of the New Zealand draft resolution should be deleted.

Mrs. Corbet (United Kingdom) associated herself with those representatives who considered that the covenant and measures of implementation were the important parts of the Bill of Human Rights. The easier part of the task had been completed and the emphasis had to be placed on the difficult work ahead.

She could accept the Chinese representative's suggestion for the deletion of the third paragraph of the New Zealand draft resolution, or the substitution of the words "renders desirable" for "necessitates" in the third paragraph of the resolution.

...

第三届联合国大会

在联合国大会第 182 次会议上的发言

1948 年 12 月 10 日星期五下午 3:20 巴黎夏乐宫

118. 继续讨论《世界人权宣言（草案）》：第三委员会的报告（第 A/777 号文件）、英国提出的修正案（第 A/788/Rev. 1 号文件）、苏联对宣言（草案）提出的修正案（第 A/784 号文件）、苏联提出的决议草案（第 A/785/Rev. 2 号文件）

张先生（中国）指出，在关于《世界人权宣言》的长期辩论过程中，只要代表们将维护人权作为首要和最重要的关切，就会达成一致意见。分歧是由于纯粹政治性的考量。

张先生做了两年该宣言的起草工作了，他希望宣言能够在人类的期盼中滋养繁盛。

在 18 世纪，当西方对人的权利作出庄严宣告时，强调的是人权，与国王们所主张的神权形成鲜明对照。他强调，中国思想对西方世界这些思想的进化并非没有影响。维护人的权利的首要条件，是包容世界各地的不同观点和信仰。拒不妥协的教条主义加剧了纷争，并为这些纷争提供了意识形态基础，造成了巨大的危害。在当今时代，特别是在第一次世界大战之后的这些年里，出现了一种将某一标准化的思维方式和单一的生活方式强加于人的倾向。要想用这种方式达到平衡，只能以背离真相或使用武力为代价。然而，无论采用的方法如何暴力，以这种方式实现的均衡绝不会持久。如果要维持人类共同体的和谐，拯救人性本身，每个人都必须本着真诚包容的精神，接受其同胞们的不同观点和信仰。

此外，概念的定义必须非常准确，这一点非常重要；这不是一个纯粹的学术问题。在现代世界，使对手混淆被认为是一种精明的政治才能；但一个真正的政治家不能容忍混淆。只有当人们学会用准确的语言表达清楚的思想时，社会秩序与和平合作才能实现。使用不准确和模棱两可的措辞——不管是有意的还是无意的——所造成的混淆，经常是导致各种分歧的原因。

中国代表团通过呼吁包容所有的观点和信仰，并坚持用词的精确性，努力使《世界人权宣言》得到完善。

——联合国大会第 182 次全体会议逐字记录（A/PV.182）

罗苇译，常健校

A/PV.182
10 December 1948

GENERAL ASSEMBLY
THIRD SESSION
VERBATIM RECORD OF THE HUNDRED AND EIGHTY-SECOND PLENARY MEETING

Held at the Palais de Chaillot, Paris, on Friday, 10 December 1948, at 3:20 p.m.

118. Continuation of the Discussion e Draft Universal Declaration of Human Rights: Report of the Third Committee (A/777), Amendment proposed by the United Kingdom (A/788/Rev.1) and Amendments proposed by the Union of Soviet Socialist Republics (A/784) to the Draft Declaration
Draft resolution proposed by the Union of Soviet Socialist Republics (A/785/Rev.2)

…

Mr. Chang (China) pointed out that, in the course of the long debate on the Universal Declaration of Human Rights, representatives had reached agreement whenever they were concerned first and foremost with the defence of human rights. The disagreements had been due to preoccupation of a purely political nature.

Mr. Chang, who had worked for two years on drafting the declaration, hoped that it might prosper, nourished by the hope of mankind.

In the eighteenth century, when solemn declarations of the rights of man had been made in the west, the emphasis had been laid on human rights as contrasted with the divine right claimed by kings. The speaker stressed that Chinese thought had not been without influence on the evolution of those ideas in the western world. The first condition for defence of the rights of man was tolerance towards the various opinions and beliefs held throughout the world. Uncompromising dogmatism had caused much harm, by accentuating disputes, and lending them an ideological basis. In the present times, and more particularly during the years following the First World War, there had been a tendency to impose a standardized way of thinking and single way of life. With that approach, equilibrium could be reached only at the cost of moving away from the truth, or employing force. But, however violent the methods employed, equilibrium achieved in that way could never last. If harmony was to be maintained in the human community and humanity itself was to be saved, everyone had to accept, in a spirit of sincere tolerance, the different views and beliefs of his fellow men.

On the other hand, it was important that conceptions should be very accurately defined; that was no purely academic question. In the modern world, it was considered clever statesmanship to confuse one's adversary; but a real statesman could not tolerate confusion. Social order and peaceful co-operation could be achieved only if people learned to express clear ideas in precise terms. The disagreements all around were only too often the result of confusion spread by the use—whether wilful or not—of inaccurate and ambiguous terms.

By pleading for tolerance of all opinions and beliefs and by insisting on precision of terminology, the Chinese delegation had striven to introduce certain improvements into the Universal Declaration of Human Rights.

...

1949 年

联合国人权委员会第四届会议

人权委员会第 82 次会议简要记录

1949 年 4 月 11 日星期一上午 10:45 纽约成功湖

选举新闻和出版自由小组委员会成员（第 E/CN.4/159 号，第 E/CN.4/159/Add.1 to Add.7 号文件）

......

应主席邀请，张先生（中国）和马利克先生（黎巴嫩）进行唱票。

投票采取不记名方式，结果如下。

投票数：18 票

有效票：18 票

简单多数：10 票

候选人获得的票数：

甘地先生	17 票
宾德先生	16 票
张彭春先生	16 票
杰拉德先生	16 票
威廉姆斯先生	16 票
德迪耶尔先生	15 票
佐诺夫先生	15 票
洛佩兹先生	13 票
西尔瓦·卡瓦罗先生	13 票
阿祖尔先生	11 票
阿兹米先生	10 票
克利斯坦森先生	9 票
方泰纳先生	8 票
莱特先生	8 票
凡赫温·哥德哈特先生	6 票

鲍尼拉先生	4 票
帕拉维斯尼先生	4 票
肖维特先生	3 票
侯赛因先生	2 票
德・拉奥萨先生	2 票
瓦尔敦先生	2 票
加西亚・培纳先生	1 票

下列人士获得法定多数票，当选为和新闻和出版自由小组委员会成员：甘地先生、宾德先生、张彭春先生、杰拉德先生、威廉姆斯先生、德迪耶尔先生、佐诺夫先生、洛佩兹先生、西尔瓦・卡瓦罗先生、阿祖尔先生、阿兹米先生。

......

——人权委员会第 82 次会议简要记录（E/CN. 4/SR. 82）

常健译校

E/CN.4/SR.82

13 April 1949

COMMISSION ON HUMAN RIGHTS
FOURTH SESSION
SUMMARY RECORD OF THE EIGHTY-SECOND MEETING

Held at Lake Success, New York, on Monday, 11 April 1949, at 10:45 a.m.

Election of New Members of the Sub-Commission on Freedom of Information and of the Press (E/CN.4/159, E/CN.4/159/Add.1 to Add.7)

...

At the invitation of the Chairman, Mr. Chang (China) and Mr. Charles Malik (Lebanon) acted as tellers.

A vote was taken by secret ballot, as follows:

Number of votes cast: 18

Valid votes: 18

Simple majority:　　　　　　　10

Number of votes obtained:

Mr. Gandhi ························· 17

Mr. Binder ························· 16

Mr. Chang ························· 16

Mr. Geraud ························· 16

Mr. Williams ························· 16

Mr. Dedijer ························· 15

Mr. Zonov ························· 15

Mr. Lopez························· 13

Mr. Silva Carvallo ················· 13

Mr. Azkoul························· 11

Mr. Azmi························· 10

Mr. Christensen ·····················9

Mr. Fontaina·····················8

Mr. Leite ·····················8

Mr. Van Heuven Goedhart ··········6

Mr. Bonilla ·····················4

Mr. Palavicini ·····················4

Mr. Chauvet ·····················3

Mr. Husain·····················2

Mr. de la Ossa·····················2

Mr. Walton·····················2

Mr. Garcia Pena·····················1

　　　The required majority having been obtained, the following were elected members of the Sub-Commission on Freedom of Information and of the Press: Mr. Gandhi, Mr. Binder, Mr. Chang, Mr. Geraud, Mr. Williams, Mr. Dedijer, Mr. Zonov, Mr. Lopez, Mr. Silva Carvallo, Mr. Azkoul, Mr. Azmi.

　　　…

联合国人权委员会第五届会议

在人权委员会第 83 次会议上当选第一副主席

1949 年 5 月 9 日星期一上午 10:00 纽约成功湖

通过议程
选举主席团
邀请妇女地位委员会官员
关于人权委员会程序的建议（第 E/CN.4/167 号文件）

卡森先生（法国）提议罗斯福夫人应连任委员会主席。

马利克先生（黎巴嫩）、圣克鲁兹先生（智利）、胡德先生（澳大利亚）、梅塔夫人（印度）和卢特菲先生（埃及）附议了法国代表的提议。

罗斯福夫人被一致推选为委员会主席。

圣克鲁兹先生（智利）提议，其他主席团成员也应连任。

勒博先生（比利时）和恩特扎姆先生（伊朗）同意智利代表的提议。

张彭春先生（中国）和卡森先生（法国）分别当选为人权委员会第一副主席和第二副主席；马利克先生（黎巴嫩）当选为报告员。

主席表示，她本人和其他主席团成员感谢委员会再次选举他们，这是委员会对他们的信任和尊重。

——人权委员会第 83 次会议简要记录（E/CN.4/SR.83）

常健译校

E/CN.4/SR.83
9 May 1949

COMMISSION ON HUMAN RIGHTS
FIFTH SESSION

SUMMARY RECORD OF THE EIGHTY-THIRD MEETING

Held at Lake Success, New York, on Monday, 9 May 1949, at 10:00 a.m.

Adoption of the Agenda
Election of Officers
Invitation to the Officers of the Commission on the Status of Women
Suggestions Regarding the Procedure of the Commission (E/CN.4/167)

Election of officers

Mr. Cassin (France) proposed that Mrs. Roosevelt should be re-elected Chairman of the Commission.

Mr. Malik (Lebanon), Mr. Santa Cruz (Chile), Mr. Hood (Australia), Mrs. Mehta (India), and Mr. Loutfi (Egypt) seconded the French representative's proposal.

Mrs. Roosevelt was unanimously elected Chairman of the Commission.

Mr. Santa Cruz (Chile) proposed that the other officers should also be re-elected.

Mr. Lebeau (Belgium) and Mr. Entezam (Iran) seconded the Chilean representative's proposal.

Mr. Chang (China) and Mr. Cassin (France) were elected respectively first and second Vice-Chairmen of the Commission; Mr. Malik (Lebanon) was elected Rapporteur.

The Chairman expressed her own and the other officers' thanks to the Commission for the confidence and esteem it had shown them by re-electing them.

...

在人权委员会第 84 次会议上的发言

1949 年 5 月 12 日星期四上午 11:00 纽约成功湖

防止歧视和保护少数委员会的报告（第 E/CN.4/181 号文件）

会议主席：张彭春先生（中国）

……

主席建议人权委员会审查关于防止歧视和保护少数委员会的报告（第 E/CN.4/181 号文件）。

……

主席对秘书处延迟分发有关文件表示遗憾，这是由于秘书处为联合国大会承担了极其繁重的工作。他向苏联代表保证，他提出的建议将得到落实。

他还承认，法国代表的发言是完全有道理的。

关于防止歧视和保护少数小组委员会职权范围的决议草案

……

主席指出，该小组委员会的职权范围与许多其他委员会的职权相似。

……

主席在回答苏联代表关于程序的问题时说，每个代表团都有权提出休会动议。然而应当记住，小组委员会的职权范围问题已经列入人权委员会多次会议的议程上，要求休会似乎没有道理。

决议草案通过后，任何代表团都可以在遵守议事规则的前提下提出修正案。他提请委员会注意决议草案（b）款。根据该款，任何代表团都可以向人权委员会或经济及社会理事会提出建议，以便向小组委员会发出具体指示。通过这种方式，小组委员会可以承担苏联代表团所设想的职能，而不改变决议草案（a）款所界定的职权范围。

会议于下午 1:30 结束。

——人权委员会第 84 次会议简要记录（E/CN.4/SR.84）

常健译校

E/CN.4/SR.84
14 May 1949

COMMISSION ON HUMAN RIGHTS
FIFTH SESSION
SUMMARY RECORD OF THE EIGHTY-FOURTH MEETING

Held at Lake Success, New York, Thursday, 12 May 1949, at 11:00 a.m.

Report of the Committee on the Prevention of Discrimination and the Protection of Minorities (E/CN.4/181).

Chairman: Mr. P. C. Chang China

...

The Chairman proposed that the Commission examine the report of the Committee on the prevention of discrimination and the protection of minorities (E/CN.4/181).

...

The Chairman expressed the Secretariat's regret for the delay in distributing the document in question, which was due to the Secretariat's extremely heavy work load for the General Assembly. He assured the representative of the Union of Soviet Socialist Republics that his remarks would be acted on.

He also recognized that the remarks of the representative of France were fully justified.

Draft Resolution on the Terms of Reference of the Sub-Commission on the Prevention of Discrimination and the Protection of Minorities

...

The Chairman pointed out that the Sub-Commission's terms of reference were similar to those of many other Committees or Commissions.

...

The Chairman, replying to the questions of the representative of the Union of Soviet Socialist Republics concerning procedure, stated that every delegation had the right to submit a motion for adjournment. It should be remembered however that the question of the Sub-Commission's terms of reference had been on the Commission's agenda for several meetings and a request for adjournment did not seem to be justified.

When the draft resolution was adopted any delegation could submit amendments subject to observance of the rules of procedure. He called the attention of the Commission to paragraph (b) of the draft resolution. According to that paragraph any delegation could submit proposals to the Commission on Human Rights or to the Economic and Social Council with a view to giving specific instructions to the Sub-Commission. The Sub-Commission could in this way be entrusted with the functions the delegation of the Union of Soviet Socialist Republics had in mind without alteration of the terms of reference defined in paragraph (a) of the draft resolution.

The meeting rose at 1:30 p.m.

在人权委员会第 85 次会议上的发言

1949 年 5 月 12 日星期四下午 3:15 纽约成功湖

防止歧视和保护少数委员会的第一份报告
（第 E/CN.4/181 号文件）

会议主席：张彭春先生（中国）

……

主席宣读了发言者名单，他们是南斯拉夫、比利时、法国和乌克兰的代表。

……

主席说，将遵循该程序。

……

主席指出，苏联代表没有提交关于推迟对决议草案 A 进行表决的正式动议。虽然发言名单已经确定，但苏联代表将有机会在表决前澄清其对程序问题的立场。

……

主席问苏联代表，他是否希望提交一项正式动议，推迟对该决议草案的表决，或者他是否同意在此时进行表决，并保留随后提交修正案的权利。

……

主席将暂停辩论的动议付诸表决。该动议以 7 票反对、4 票赞成被否决。

……

主席打断了苏联代表的发言，由于发言者名单已经确定，对前几位发言者的任何答复都不符合程序。他要求对苏联代表的发言进行翻译，但当其开始回答法国代表时，他要求中止翻译。

主席裁定，苏联代表可以在表决后完成发言；然后他可以解释投票的理由。

……

主席裁定，由于只有 9 名有表决权的成员出席，而法定人数需要 10 名，会议将休会。

会议于下午 5:30 结束。

——人权委员会第 85 次会议简要记录（E/CN.4/SR.85）

常健译校

E/CN.4/SR.85

13 May 1949

COMMISSION ON HUMAN RIGHTS
FIFTH SESSION
SUMMARY RECORD OF THE EIGHTY-FIFTH MEETING
Held at Lake Success, New York, on Thursday, 12 May 1949, at 3:15 p.m.

First Report of the Committee on the Prevention of Discrimination and the Protection of Minorities (E/CN.4/181)

Chairman: Mr. P. C. Chang (China)

The Chairman read the list of speakers, who were the representatives of Yugoslavia, Belgium, France and the Ukrainian SSR.

…

The Chairman stated that that procedure would be followed.

…

The Chairman pointed out that the USSR representative had not submitted a formal motion for postponement of the vote on draft resolution A. Although the list of speakers was closed, the USSR representative would be given an opportunity to clarify his position on the procedural matter before a vote was taken.

…

The Chairman asked the USSR representative whether he wished to submit a formal motion for postponement of the vote on the draft, resolution or whether he would agree that a vote should be taken at that point and reserve his right subsequently to submit amendments.

…

The Chairman put the motion to adjourn the debate to the vote. The motion was rejected by 7 votes to 4.

…

The Chairman interrupted the USSR representative on the ground that any reply to previous speakers was not in order as the speakers' list had been closed. He called for an interpretation of the speech only to the point where the USSR representative had begun to reply to the representative of France.

The Chairman ruled that the USSR representative could complete his speech after the vote was taken; he would then be able to explain the reasons for his vote.

…

The Chairman ruled that since only nine voting members were present, and ten were required to form a quorum, the meeting would adjourn.

The meeting rose at 5:30 p.m.

在人权委员会第 87 次会议上的发言

1949 年 5 月 16 日星期一下午 3:00 纽约成功湖

防止歧视和保护少数委员会的第一份报告（第 E/CN.4/181、
E/CN.4/181/Corr.2、E/CN.4/183、E/CN.4/185、
E/CN.4/185/Corr.1 号文件）（继续讨论）：
决议草案：小组委员会的职权范围（续）；
决议草案：小组委员会成员的任期（第 E/CN.4/181 和
E/CN.4/181/Corr.1 号文件）；
决议草案 C：工作重点。
以两种工作语言对巴甫洛夫先生（苏联）在人权委员会
第八十五次会议上发言第二部分的翻译

......

汉弗莱先生（秘书处）宣读了委员会的职权范围（第 E/248 号文件）。

主席亦认为，确实很难决定人权委员会是否有能力处理与人民平等权利及其自决原则有关的问题。她认为这一点应由经济及社会理事会决定。因此，人权委员会应谨慎处理此事，因为国际法委员会正在讨论此事，而国际法委员会很可能是这方面真正有能力的机构。

张先生（中国）询问，迄今由经济及社会理事会设立的人权委员会是否纯粹是研究委员会，没有任何行政职能。

主席认为是这样的。

......

索伦森先生（丹麦）说，防止歧视和保护少数委员会决定在延长其任期后才增加小组委员会成员的人数，且增加成员是因为延长了任期。他要求对这两段按此顺序进行表决，这既符合时间顺序也符合逻辑顺序，而且这也是它们在案文草案中出现的顺序。

张先生（中国）赞同这一观点。

……

张彭春先生（中国）主持了委员会第八十五次会议的讨论，他希望作出解释。

在巴甫洛夫先生被要求发言时，关于决议草案 A 实质内容的讨论已经结束。他只能回答会议主席向他提出的问题，即他是否希望提出一项推迟对决议草案进行表决的正式动议，或者他是否同意在该时点进行表决，并保留随后提交修正案的权利。巴甫洛夫先生没有明确请求回答法国和智利的代表。因此，会议主席认为，苏联代表应该只限于回答向他提出的程序问题，其他任何评论都与此无关。由于会议主席不懂俄语，他无法听懂苏联代表的讲话，也无法在他偏离主题时打断他。一旦意识到发言者偏离了主题，他就有责任立即中止对该发言的翻译。张先生确信，如果巴甫洛夫先生担任委员会主席，他也会采取同样的行动。

——人权委员会第 87 次会议简要记录（E/CN.4/SR.87）

常健译校

E/CN.4/SR.87
26 May 1949

COMMISSION ON HUMAN RIGHTS
FIFTH SESSION
SUMMARY RECORD OF THE EIGHTY-SEVENTH
MEETING

Held at Lake Success, New York, on Monday, 16 May 1949, at 3:00 p.m.

First Report of the Committee on The Prevention of Discrimination and the Protection of Minorities (E/CN.4/181, E/CN.4/181/Corr.2, E/CN.4/183, E/CN.4/185, E/CN.4/185/Corr.1) (Discussion Continued): Draft Resolution: Terms of reference of the Sub-Commission (Continued); Draft Resolution: Term of Office of the Members of the Sub-Commission (E/CN.4/181, E/CN.4/181/Corr.1); Draft Resolution C: Prioriy of Work.

Interpretation, in the Two Working Languages, of the Second Part of a Speech by Mr. Pavlov (Union of Soviet Socialist Republics) at the Eighty-fifth Meeting of the Commission

...

Mr. Humphrey (Secretariat) read the Commission's term of reference (E/248).

The Chairman agreed that it was indeed rather difficult to decide whether the Commission was competent or not to deal with problems connected with the principle of equal rights of peoples and their self-determination. She thought it was for the Economic and Social Council to decide on that point. The Commission should therefore proceed with caution in the matter, the more so as it was being discussed by the International Law Commission, which might well be the organ which was really competent in that respect.

Mr. Chang (China) asked whether it was not true that the Commission so far set up by the Economic and Social Council were intended purely as study commissions without any executive functions.

The Chairman agreed that that was so.

...

Mr. Soerensen (Denmark) said the Committee had decided to increase the number of members of the Sub-Commission only after it had extended their term of office, and had done so owing to that extension. He asked that the vote be taken on the two paragraphs in that order, which was both chronological and logical and which was, moreover, the order in which they appeared in the draft text.

Mr. Chang (China) shared that view.

...

Mr. P. C. Chang (China), who had presided over the discussions of the eighty-fifth meeting of the Commission, wished to make an explanation.

At the time when Mr. Pavlov had been called upon to speak, the discussion of the substance of draft resolution A had been closed. He had bad to answer only the question which the Chairman had put him, namely whether he wished to submit a formal motion for postponement of the vote on the draft resolution, or whether he would agree that a vote should be taken at that point and reserve his right subsequently to submit amendments. Mr. Pavlov had not explicitly asked for permission to reply to the representatives of France and Chile. Therefore the Chairman had considered that the USSR representative should have confined himself to answering the question of procedure which had been addressed to him, any other remark being irrelevant. As the Chairman did not know Russian, he had been unable to follow the speech of the USSR representative and to interrupt him to the moment when he had digressed from the subject. It had been his duty to stop the interpretation of the speech as soon as he had become aware of that fact. Mr. Chang was convinced that Mr. Pavlov would have acted in the same way, had he been Chairman of the Commission.

...

在人权委员会第 88 次会议上的发言

1949 年 5 月 17 日星期二上午 10:30 纽约成功湖

（1）防止歧视和保护少数小组委员会的 职权范围（继续讨论） ## （2）犹太组织协调委员会代表的发言 ## （3）《国际人权公约（草案）》（第 E/800 号文件）

......

张先生（中国）指出，根据以往的经验，不应认为经济及社会理事会期望其任何附属机构去做研究以外的工作；此外，埃及提案中提到的"措施准备"工作，也确认了小组委员会成员参与访问托管领土的目的是收集数据资料，而不是试图作出行政性质的改变。如果埃及提案的意图是进行研究，那么该领域应尽可能广泛。因此，张先生建议在埃及原提案中的"充分享受人权和基本自由"之后加上"对自治人民"。这样，小组委员会就可以参与对托管领土的访问，以便在统计抽样的基础上获得科学数据，用以研究如何使充分享有人权和基本自由扩展到非自治人民这一普遍性问题。

谈到埃及提案中使用的"定期访问"一词，张先生建议删除"定期"一词。除了小组委员会认为有助于推进其正在进行的研究的访问之外，小组委员会不应参加其他任何访问。

卢特菲先生（埃及）要求对中国的修正案进行单独表决。

梅塔女士（印度）完全理解苏联代表希望小组委员会研究殖民地领土的情况，因为在这些领土上人权往往得不到遵守。然而，这项研究不需要托管理事会的授权。因此，埃及的建议只应提及托管领土。

她同意中国代表的意见，即应删除"定期"一词。这个词意味着小组委员会是一个常设机构，但事实并非如此。

英格尔斯先生（菲律宾）承认，托管理事会的权限仅限于托管领土，但小组委员会的权限不限于此。该机构的任务是研究将人权和基本自由的充分享受扩大到所有领土的措施，无论其是否自治。在访问托管领土时进行的研究，在将人权扩展到非自治领土方面无疑将被证明是非常宝贵的。

因此，英格尔斯先生支持苏联的修正案，如果该修改案未能通过，作为替代，他也支持中国的修正案。

科瓦连科先生（乌克兰）不同意中国代表的观点，即小组委员会工作的主要目的是进行科学研究。除非采取具体措施制止歧视，否则这些研究将毫无意义。

他支持苏联关于恢复埃及提案最后一部分的提议，并指出，对非自治领土和殖民地的提及，独立于提案第一部分，该部分提到定期访问托管领土，且无意冒犯托管理事会的权利或违反《联合国宪章》的规定。另一方面，任何将人权和基本自由的充分享受扩大到包括殖民地在内的非自治领土的努力，都是在努力落实《联合国宪章》的一些最基本条款。

……

主席将苏联的修正案付诸表决，其大意是埃及的提案应以"包括殖民地在内的非自治领土的人口"作为结尾。

苏联的提案以 4 票反对、5 票赞成、4 票弃权被否决。

主席将删除"定期"一词的中国修正案付诸表决。

该修正案以 6 票赞成、3 票反对、4 票弃权获得通过。

主席将中国的修正案付诸表决，其大意是埃及的提案应以"非自治人民"作为结尾。

该修正案以 9 票赞成、3 票反对、1 票弃权获得通过。

随后，主席将埃及的提案付诸表决，埃及代表接受了法国的修正案，以及刚刚通过的中国修正案。

埃及的提案以 9 票赞成、2 票反对、1 票弃权获得通过。

……

——人权委员会第 88 次会议简要记录（E/CN.4/SR.88）

常健译校

E/CN.4/SR.88
19 May 1949

COMMISSION ON HUMAN RIGHTS

FIFTH SESSION
SUMMARY RECORD OF THE EIGHTY-EIGHTH MEETING

Held at Lake Success, New York, on Tuesday, 17 May 1949, at 10:30 a.m.

(1) Terms of Reference of the Sub-Commission on the Prevention of Discrimination and Protection of Minorities (Discussion Continued)
(2) Statement by the Representative of the Co-Ordinating Board of Jewish Organizations
(3) Draft International Covenant on Human Rights (E/800).

...

Mr. Chang (China) observed that on the basis of previous experience, there was no reason to think that the Economic and Social Council expected any of its subsidiary organs to do more than make studies; moreover, the works "the preparation of measures" in the Egyptian proposal confirmed that the purpose of the participation of members of the Sub-Commission in the visits to Trust Territories was to collect data and not to attempt to make changes of an administrative nature. If, then, the intention of the Egyptian proposal was that a study should be made, the field should be as wide as possible. Mr. Chang therefore suggested that the words "to the self-governing populations" should be added after the words "the full enjoyment of human rights and fundamental freedoms" in the original Egyptian proposal. Thus, the Sub-Commission might participate in visits to Trust Territories in order to obtain scientific data, on the basis of statistical sampling, for a study of the general question of how the full enjoyment of human rights and fundamental freedoms could be extended to Non-Self-Governing peoples everywhere.

Speaking of the expression "periodical visits" used in the Egyptian proposal, Mr. Chang proposed the deletion of the word "periodical". The Sub-Commission should not be expected to take part in any visits other than those which it considered useful for the furtherance of the study it was making.

Mr. Loutfi (Egypt) asked that the Chinese amendments should be voted on separately.

Mrs. Mehta (India) fully appreciated the USSR representative's desire to have the conditions in the colonial territories studies by the Sub-Commission, since it was in those territories that human rights were often not observed. There was, however, no need for authorization from the Trusteeship Council for such a study. Consequently, the Egyptian proposal should refer only to the Trust Territories.

She agreed with the Chinese representative that the word "periodical" should be deleted. That word implied that the Sub-Commission was a permanent body, which it was not.

Mr. Ingles (Philippines) recognized that the competence of the Trusteeship Council was limited to Trust Territories, but the competence of the Sub-Commission was not limited in the same way. That body had the task of studying measures for the extension of the full enjoyment of human rights and fundamental freedoms to all territories, whether self-governing or not. Studies made in visits to the Trust Territories would undoubtedly prove invaluable in connexion with the extension of human rights to Non-Self-Governing Territories.

Mr. Ingles therefore supported the USSR amendment and, as an alternative, would support the Chinese amendment.

Mr. Kovalenko (Ukrainian Soviet Socialist Republic) could not agree with the Chinese representative that the chief purpose of the work of the Sub-Commission was to carry out scientific studies. Such studies could have no meaning unless they were followed by the adoption of specific measures to put an end to discrimination.

He supported the USSR proposal to reinstate the last part of the Egyptian proposal and pointed out that the reference made to the Non-Self-Governing Territories and colonies was independent of the first part of the proposal, which mentioned the periodical visits to the Trust Territories. There was no intention of infringing the rights of the Trusteeship Council or violating the provisions of the Charter. On the other hand, any attempt to extend to the Non-Self-Governing Territories, including the colonies, the full enjoyment of human rights and fundamental freedom would be an attempt to implement some of the most fundamental provisions of the Charter.

...

The Chairman put to the vote the USSR amendment to the effect that the Egyptian proposal should end with the words "populations of Non-Self-Governing territories, including colonies".

The USSR proposal was rejected by 4 votes to 5, with 4 abstentions.

The Chairman put to the vote the Chinese amendment to delete the word "periodical".

The amendment was adopted by 6 votes to 3, with 4 abstentions.

The Chairman put to the vote the Chinese amendment to the effect that the Egyptian proposal should end with the words "to the Non-Self-Governing populations".

The amendment was adopted by 9 votes to 3, with 1 abstention.

The Chairman then put to the vote the Egyptian proposal, with the French amendments which had beenaccepted by the Egyptian representative and with the Chinese amendments just adopted.

The Egyptian proposal as amended was adopted by 9 votes to 2, with 1 abstention.

...

在人权委员会第 90 次会议上的发言

1949 年 5 月 18 日星期三上午 11:00 纽约成功湖

黎巴嫩关于人权国际公约和执行措施草案的决议草案（第 E/CN.4/191 号文件）（继续讨论）
《国际人权公约（草案）》（第 E/800、E/CN.4/170、E/CN.4/188、E/CN.4/193 号文件）（继续讨论）

......

张先生（中国）表示，虽然他完全理解黎巴嫩代表希望就公约草案展开工作，但他觉得有义务提请人权委员会关注更大的目标，它是人权委员会存在的原因，而公约只是其中的一部分。这一目标就是确保每个人充分行使人权和基本自由；它可以通过联合国施加充分的道德力量对各国政府和公共舆论产生影响来加以实现。世界最需要的是最广义的教育。

公约草案终究只是另一项多边条约，应当现实地看待这些条约在当前文明状态下的效力。确保遵守关于如麻醉药品等特定主题的公约总是比较容易的。在像人权这样一个广阔的领域，应该注意在公约启动之前做好准备，以免公约成为律师可以利用的另一项国际文书。

因此，尽管张先生不反对该决议草案，但他认为不应明确该公约草案的确定完成日期。人权委员会最好冷静理智地致力于编写出一份令人满意的文件，并在道德上集中精力开展世界人权教育。

......

第 5 条

......

张先生（中国）提醒人权委员会，其真正目标是补充《世界人权宣言》第 3 条所述的目标，特别是"人人享有生命权……"的原则。他指出，公约实际上只是一项国际条约，第 5 条应该从这一角度来看待。应当记住，条约是可能被规避的，如果人权委员会希望保护生命，最好去研究各国当时保护其公民生命的方法。

关于美国的案文，他指出，如果一个国家希望剥夺一个人的生命，那么它在提供必要的法庭记录和判决以证明其程序正当性方面几乎没有困难。因此，第 5 条草案并不会对国家形成实际的约束，该公约也不会对个人提供任何实际保护。

关于英国的案文，他认为可能难以强制履行公约所规定的义务。

中国代表团认为，编写一份有关保护个人的国家法律汇编可能更明智。这样一份文件将有效地支持甚至执行《世界人权宣言》，中国代表团认为这对保护个人极为重要。编纂这一领域的国际立法汇编当然地属于国际机构的职权范围，这似乎是解决这一问题的最实际方法。中国代表团不相信按美国和英国的建议案来措辞的公约会取得任何实际效果。

......

——人权委员会第 90 次会议简要记录（E/CN.4/SR.90）

常健译校

E/CN.4/SR.90
20 May 1949

COMMISSION ON HUMAN RIGHTS
FIFTH SESSION
SUMMARY RECORD OF THE NINTIETH MEETING

Held at Lake Success, New York, on Wednesday, 18 May 1949, at 11:00 a.m.

Lebanese Draft Resolution on the Draft International Covenant on Human Rights and Measures of Implementation (E/CN.4/191) (Discussion Continued)

...

Mr. Chang (China) observed that, while he fully appreciated the desire of the Lebanese representative to expedite the work on the draft covenant, he felt obliged to remind the Commission of the larger objective which was its reason for being, and of which the covenant would be but a part. That objective was to assure to every individual the full exercise of human rights and fundamental freedoms; it could best be attained by bringing the full moral force of the United Nations to bear on Governments and public opinion. What the world needed most was education in the broadest sense of the word.

The draft covenant, would after all, be but another multilateral treaty, and a realistic view should be taken of the effectiveness of such treaties in the present state of civilization. It was always easier to ensure the observance of conventions on specific subjects, such as narcotic drugs. In a vast field like that of human rights, care should be taken to prepare the ground before a convention was launched, lest it should become merely another international instrument for lawyers to play with.

For that reason, while he did not oppose the Lebanese draft resolution, Mr. Chang did not think it wise to set definite dates for the completion of the draft covenant. The Commission would do better to devote cool intellectual attention to the production of a satisfactory document and a concentrated moral effort to the education of the world in the respect of human rights.

...

Draft international covenant on human rights (E/800, E/CN.4/170, E/CN.4/188, E/CN.4/193) (discussion continued)

Article 5

...

Mr. Chang (China) reminded the Commission that its real objective was to supplement the aims outlined in article 3 of the Universal Declaration of Human Rights and in particular the principle that "everyone has the rights to life…". He pointed out that a covenant was really nothing more that an international treaty and that article 5 should be viewed in that light. It should be remembered that a treaty could be circumvented and that if the Commission wished to protect life it might do better to study the methods by which States protected the lives of their citizens at that time.

With regard to the United States text, he pointed out that if a State wished to deprive a person of life, it would have very little trouble in producing the requisite court records and sentence to justify its procedure. Consequently that draft of article 5 would not hamper the State and the covenant would really offer no protection to the individual.

With regard to the United Kingdom text, he considered that it might be difficult to enforce the fulfillment of contractual commitments assumed under the covenant.

The Chinese delegation thought it might be wiser to prepare a compendium of States' laws concerning the protection of individuals. Such a document would effectively support and perhaps even enforce the Universal Declaration of Human Rights, which his delegation considered to be extremely valuable for the protection of individuals. The compilation of a compendium of international legislation in that field would certainly be within the purview of an international body and would seem to be the most practical way of attacking the problem. The Chinese delegation was not convinced that the covenant, as then worded, would achieve any affective practical results.

...

在人权委员会第 91 次会议上的发言

1949 年 5 月 18 日星期三下午 2:30 纽约成功湖

《国际人权公约（草案）》（第 E/800、E/CN.4/170、E/CN.4/170/Add.2、E/CN.4/188、E/CN.4/192、E/CN.4/193、E/CN.4/195、E/CN.4/197 号文件）（继续讨论）：第 5（继续讨论）、6、7 条

......

张先生（中国）建议，已就第 5 条提出了相似建议的英国、法国和黎巴嫩代表团应举行非正式会晤，以便起草一份包括卡森先生改进建议的联合案文，并提交人权委员会。

......

张先生（中国）支持黎巴嫩的修正案，即在公约草案第 7 条中复述《世界人权宣言》第 5 条的案文。他认为，一般来说，公约草案的条款应尽可能复述《世界人权宣言》的规定。

中国代表团不反对在第 6 条中列出该条所述的对权利的各种限制。在起草这样一份清单时，应考虑到各种现行的国家法律。可以要求秘书处汇编必要的资料。

因此，他建议暂时删除第 6 条，并以《世界人权宣言》第 5 条的形式保留第 7 条。

——人权委员会第 91 次会议简要记录（E/CN.4/SR.91）

常健译校

E/CN.4/SR 91

31 May 1949

COMMISSION ON HUNAN RIGHTS
FIFTH SESSION
SUMMRY RECORD OF THE NINETY-FIRST MEETING

Held at Lake Success, New York on Wednesday, 18 May 1949, at 2:30 p.m.

Draft International Covenant on Human Rights (E/800, E/CN.4/170, E/CN.4/170/Add.2, E/CN.4/188, E/CN.4/192, E/CN.4/193, E/CN.4/195, E/CN.4/197) (Discussion Continued): Articles 5 (Discussion Continued), 6 and 7

...

Mr. Chang (China) suggested that the delegations of the United Kingdom, France and Lebanon, which had presented similar proposals for article 5, should meet informally in order to prepare and submit to the Commission a joint text containing the improvements suggested by Mr. Cassin.

...

Mr. Chang (China) supported the Lebanese amendment to reproduce, in article 7 of the draft Covenant, the text of article 5 of the Declaration. He thought that, generally speaking, the articles of the draft Covenant should, whenever possible, repeat the provisions of the Declaration.

The Chinese delegation did not object to listing in article 6 the limitations of the right stated in that article. In drawing up such a list, account should be taken of various existing national laws. The Secretariat might be asked to compile the necessary material.

He therefore proposed that article 6 be deleted for the time being, and that article 7 might be retained in the form of article 5 of the Declaration.

在人权委员会第 93 次会议上的发言

1949 年 5 月 19 日星期四下午 2:30 纽约成功湖

《国际人权公约（草案）》（第 E/800、E/CN.4/170/Add.3、E/CN.4/202、E/CN.4/204、E/CN.4/205、E/CN.4/206、E/CN.4/207、E/CN.4/208 号文件）（继续讨论）：第 8 条和第 5 条（继续讨论）

······

张先生（中国）支持推迟审议第 8 条第二部分。丹麦代表提出的更仔细地审议所涉及的众多复杂问题这一要求的理由非常合理。人权委员会本应在 6 月 22 日前完成工作，现在应立即就第 8 条第一部分作出决定；如果人权委员会认为可以在本届会议结束之前重新审议第二部分，它仍然可以这样做。

······

张先生（中国）与危地马拉代表一样，本打算要求英国或黎巴嫩代表删除（b）分项。当然，曾经发生过许多战争，但如果这项公约规定了新战争的可能性，那将使战争几乎不可避免。因此，战争必须被明确宣布为非法。

······

——人权委员会第 93 次会议简要记录（E/CN.4/SR.93）

常健译校

E/CN.4/SR 93
27 May 1949

COMMISSION ON HUNAN RIGHTS
FIFTH SESSION
SUMMRY RECORD OF THE NINETY-THREE MEETING

Held at Lake Success, New York, on Thursday, 19 May 1949, at 2:30 p.m.

Draft International Covenant on Human Rights (E/800, E/CN.4/170/Add.3, E/CN.4/202, E/CN.4/204, E/CN.4/205, E/CN.4/206, E/CN.4/207, E/CN.4/208) (Discussion Continued): Articles 8 and 5 (Discussion Continued).

...

Mr. Chang (China) supported deferment of consideration of the second part of article 8. The very valid reasons advanced by the representative of Denmark called for more careful consideration of the numerous and complex problems involved. The Commission, which was to complete its work before 22 June should immediately take a decision on the first part of article 8; it could still return to the consideration of the second part if it felt it could do so before the end of the current session.

...

Mr. Chang (China), like the representative of Guatemala, had intended to ask the representatives of the United Kingdom or Lebanon to delete sub-paragraph (b). Of course there had been wars, but by providing for the possibility of new wars, the covenant would make them almost inevitable. On the contrary, war must be definitely outlawed.

...

在人权委员会第 95 次会议上的发言

1949 年 5 月 20 日星期五下午 2:30 纽约成功湖

《国际人权公约（草案）》（第 E/800、E/CN.4/170/Add.1、E/CN.4/188、E/CN.4/206 号文件）（继续讨论）：第 9 条

......

张先生（中国）指出，限制一项权利的行使所产生的困难不仅出现在当前审议的情况中，它也出现在第 5 条及其他条款中。

如果要提到某些例外情况，它们必须被限制在所有成员国立法中规定的那些基本和普遍的情况。

如果从一开始就试图起草这样一份公约，它可以预见所有可能的情况，并给出所有后续定义，那就过于雄心勃勃了。虽然人权委员会起草的公约并不完美，但它将作为一个法理基础而变得越来越重要和有意义。这一法理将使初始的公约有可能完成，并在随后的几年中修订其某些条款。

因此，张先生认为，就目前而言，人权委员会应将其活动限制在陈述一般原则，这些原则的法理可以通过议定书加以澄清和具体化，一旦可能和需要，这些议定书将形成初始的公约。通过这种渐进的行动，可以建立越来越完善的定义，对于某些条款，可以制定越来越完整的例外清单。

如果要立即寻求一个过于完美的公约，有可能取得相反的结果，并有损《世界人权宣言》的道德威信。

因此，他将投票反对保留一份例外清单，即反对拟议条款的第 2 款。

......

——人权委员会第 95 次会议简要记录（E/CN.4/SR.95）

常健译校

E/CN.4/SR 95
31 May 1949

COMMISSION ON HUHAN RIGHTS
FIRTH SESSION
SUMMARY RECORD OF TEE NINETY-FIFTH MEETING
Held at Lake Success, New York, on Friday, 20 May 1949, at 2:30 p.m.

Draft International Covenant on Human Rights
(E/800, E/CN.4/170/Add.1, E/CN.4/188, E/CN.4/206)
(Discussion Continued): Article 9

...

Mr. Chang (China) pointed out that the difficulty raised by restricting the exercise of a right occurred not only in the case under consideration. It also occurred in article 5 inter alia.

If certain exceptions were to be mentioned, they must be limited to the essential and general cases provided for in the legislation of all States.

It would be overambitious to try from the very beginning to draft a covenant anticipating all possible cases and giving all the consequent definitions. Even if the covenant which the Commission was drafting was not perfect, it would serve as a basis for a jurisprudence which would become increasingly important and significant. That jurisprudence would make it possible to complete the original covenant and to revise certain of its articles during the subsequent years.

Mr. Chang was therefore of the opinion that, for the time being, the Commission should limit its activities to the statement of general principles which jurisprudence could clarify and make concrete by protocols which would complete the original covenant whenever such action seemed possible and desirable. By such progressive action, increasingly perfect definitions could be established and, for certain articles, increasingly complete lists of exceptions could be drawn up.

If a too perfect covenant was sought immediately, there would be the risk that the opposite result would be achieved and the moral prestige of the Declaration encroached upon.

He would therefore vote against the retention of a list of exceptions, namely, against paragraph 2 of the proposed article.

　…

在人权委员会第 98 次会议上的发言

1949 年 5 月 24 日星期二下午 2:30 纽约成功湖

《国际人权公约（草案）》（第 E/800、E/CN.4/W.21、E/CN.4/W.22、E/CN.4/W.23、E/CN.4/W.212 号文件）（继续讨论）：第 5 条（继续讨论）和第 9 条

......

张先生（中国）提出，智利修正案的第一段应分两部分进行表决，"任意"一词应单独表决。

智利修正案第一段除"任意"一词外，以 14 票对 0 票、无弃权获得通过。

"任意"一词未获得通过，7 票赞成，7 票反对，1 票弃权。

......

——人权委员会第 98 次会议简要记录（E/CN.4/SR.98）

常健译校

E/CN.4/SR.98
2 June 1949
COMMISSION ON HUMAN RIGHTS
FIFTH SESSION
SUMMARY RECORD OF THE NINETY-EIGHTH MEETING
Held at Lake Success, New York, on Tuesday, 24 May 1949, at 2:30 p.m.

Draft International Covenant on Human Rights (E/800, E/CN.4/W.21, E/CN.4/W.22, E/CN.4/W.23, E/CN.4/W.212)(Discussion Continued)

Article 5 (Discussion Continued) and article 9

...

Mr. Chang (China) requested that the first paragraph of the Chilean amendment should be voted in two parts, the word "arbitrarily" to be voted on separately.

The first paragraph of the Chilean amendment, with the exception of the word "arbitrarily" was adopted by 14 votes to none with no abstention.

The word "arbitrarily" was not adopted, 7 votes being in favour and 7 against, with one abstention.

...

在人权委员会第 99 次会议上的发言

1949 年 5 月 25 日星期三上午 11:30 纽约成功湖

《国际人权公约（草案）》（第 E/800、E/CN.4/170/Add.1、E/CN.4/l88、E/CN.4/206、E/CN.4/212、E/CN.4/250 号文件）（继续讨论）：第 9 条

会议主席：张彭春先生（中国）

主席回顾说，委员会已经通过了第 9 条的前两款。

美国代表团提出了对第 3 款的修正案（第 E/CN.4/170 号文件），法国代表团随后也提出了修正案。美国的案文旨在取代起草委员会的案文。

最后，苏联代表团提交了对英国草案（第 E/CN.4/188 号文件）第 2 款的修正案（第 E/CN.4/250 号文件）。

……

主席解释说，苏联的建议是将"刑事指控中的被告"改为"任何因犯有罪行或为防止犯下正在准备实施的罪行而被捕的人"；案文的其余部分是美国提出的。他认为，"刑事指控中的被告"一词包括了苏联文本所规定的情况。

……

主席说，"在刑事指控中"这一表述既涵盖了犯罪，又涵盖了意图犯罪。

……

恩特扎姆先生（伊朗）接受法国代表建议的表述。然而，他注意到，该表述并没有涵盖任意和非法逮捕的情况。

主席回答说，该问题是草案下一段的主题。

……

恩特扎姆先生（伊朗）支持比利时代表的建议。他指出，如果第 4 款获得通过，他的提案将毫无意义。然而，只要人权委员会不确定是否会保留该款，他就很难放弃他的建议。

主席认为，为了加快工作，最好不要推迟对第 3 段的表决。他向伊朗代表保证，人权委员会完全意识到第 3 款和第 4 款之间的联系。如果第 4 款被否决，委员会可以返回来重新审议其关于第 3 款的决定，以便考虑到伊朗代表的意见。

恩特扎姆先生（伊朗）说，在这种情况下，伊朗代表团将同意暂时撤回口头修正案。

会议于下午 2:00 结束。

——人权委员会第 99 次会议简要记录（E/CN.4/SR.99）

常健译校

E/CN.4/SR.99

3 June 1949

COMMISSION ON HUMAN RIGHTS
FIFTH SESSION
SUMMARY RECORD OF THE NINETY-NINTH MEETING

Held at Lake Success, New York, on Wednesday, 25 May 1949, at 11:30 a.m.

Draft International Covenant on Human Rights (E/800, E/CN.4/170/Add.1, E/CN.4/188, E/CN.4/206, E/CN.4/212, E/CN.4/250) (Discussion Continued): Article 9

Chairman: Mr. Chang China

The Chairman recalled that the Commission had already adopted the first two paragraphs of article 9.

The United States delegation had presented an amendment (E/CN.4/170) to paragraph 3, to which the French delegation, in turn, had presented an amendment. The United States text was intended to replace the Drafting Committee's text.

Finally, the USSR delegation had submitted an amendment (E/CN.4/250) to paragraph 2 of the United Kingdom draft (E/CN.4/188).

...

The Chairman explained that the USSR proposal was to replace the words: "The accused in a criminal charge" by the words "Any person who is arrested on a charge of having committed a crime, or to prevent the commission of a crime for which he is making preparation, shall be"; then came the remainder of the text proposed by the United States of America. In his opinion, the words "the accused in a criminal charge" included the cases provided for by the USSR text.

...

The Chairman said that the expression "in a criminal charge" covered both the commission of the crime and the intent to commit the crime.

...

Mr. Entezam (Iran) accepted the formula suggested by the French representative. He noted, however, that cases of arbitrary and illegal arrests were not covered.

The Chairman answered that that question was the subject of the next paragraph of the draft.

...

Mr. Entezam (Iran) supported the Belgian representative's suggestion. He pointed out that there would be no purpose to his proposal if paragraph 4 were adopted. It would be difficult, however, for him to withdraw his proposal as long as there was no certainty that the Commission would retain the paragraph.

The Chairman thought that, in order to speed up the work, it would be better not to delay the vote on paragraph 3. He assured the representative of Iran that the Commission was fully conscious of the connexion which existed between paragraphs 3 and 4. If paragraph 4 was rejected, the Commission could go back on its decision with regard to paragraph 3 so as to take into consideration the observations by the representative of Iran.

Mr. Entezam (Iran) stated that in those circumstances his delegation would agree to withdraw provisionally its verbal amendment.

The meeting rose at 2:00 p.m.

在人权委员会第 100 次会议上的发言

1949 年 5 月 25 日星期三下午 2:30 纽约成功湖

《国际人权公约（草案）》（第 E/800、E/CN.4/170/Add.4、E/CN.4/200、E/CN.4/212、E/CN.4/250、E/CN.4/252、E/CN.4/259、E/CN.4/260 号文件）（继续）：第 9 条第 3 款和第 4 款（继续讨论）

会议主席：张彭春先生（中国）

主席回顾说，摆在人权委员会面前的有起草委员会编写的原文（第 E/CN.4/212 号文件）、美国提出的案文（第 E/CN.4/170/Add.4 号文件）、英国提出的案文以及苏联（第 E/CN.4/250 号文件）、法国（第 E/CN.4/259 号文件）和黎巴嫩（第 E/CN.4/260 号文件）提出的修正案。

……

主席将"任何被逮捕或拘留的人……"付诸表决。

这一表述以 11 票对 1 票、4 票弃权获得通过。

主席将修正案其余部分付诸表决。

修正案其余部分以 8 票对 6 票、2 票弃权获得通过。

苏联修正案整体以 10 票对 5 票，1 票弃权获得通过。

……

主席将经修正的美国提案的第一部分付诸表决。

经修正的美国文案以 13 票对 0 票、3 票弃权获得通过。

罗斯福夫人（美国）恢复主持会议。

……

——人权委员会第 100 次会议简要记录（E/CN.4/SR.100）

常健译校

E/CN.4/SR.100
3 June 1949

COMMISSION ON HUMAN RIGHTS
FIFTH SESSION
SUMMARY RECORD OF THE ONE HUMREDTH MEETING

Held at Lake Success, New York, on Wednesday, 25 May 1949, at 2:30 p.m.

Draft International Covenant on Human Rights (E/800, E/CN.4/170/Add.4, E/CN.4/200, E/CN.4/212, E/CN.4/250, E/CN.4/252, E/CN.4/259, E/CN.4/260) (Continued): Article 9, paragraphs 3 and 4 (Discussion Continued)

Chairman: Mr. P. C. Chang China

The Chairman recalled that the Commission had before it the original text prepared by the Drafting Committee (E/800, E/CN.4/212), the text proposed by the United States of America (E/CN.4/170/Add.4), the text proposed by the United Kingdom, and the amendments proposed by the USSR (E/CN.4/250), France (E/CN.4/259), and Lebanon (E/CN.4/260).

...

The Chairman put to the vote the words "Any person arrested or detained...".

Those words were adopted by 11 votes to 1, with 4 abstentions.

The Chairman put to the vote the rest of the amendment.

The rest of the amendment was adopted by 8 votes to 6, with 2 abstentions.

The USSR amendment as a whole was adopted by 10 votes to 5, with 1 abstention.

...

The Chairman put to the vote the first part of the United States proposal as amended.

The United States text, as amended, was adopted by 13 votes to none, with 3 abstentions.

Mrs. Roosevelt (United States of America) resumed the Chair.

…

在人权委员会第 102 次会议上的发言

1949 年 5 月 26 日星期四下午 2:30 纽约成功湖

《国际人权公约（草案）》（第 E/800、E/CN.4/212、E/CN.4/266、E/CN.4/219 号文件）第 6 条（继续讨论）、第 9 条（继续讨论）、第 10 条和第 11 条

第 9 条（继续讨论）

......

张先生（中国）认为，将原始措辞与法国代表团提议的措辞相结合，也许可以达成能得到一致同意的文本。该文本的英文版本如下。

"每一个被非法逮捕或剥夺自由的受害者都有获得赔偿的强制执行权。"

卡森先生（法国）接受对其案文的新的英文译本。他强调，在法语中，没有比"获得赔偿的权利"更有力的术语了，因为授予个人一项权利就是赋予他在法庭上捍卫这项权利的能力。因此，如果委员会接受了法国的建议，该款目前的法文文本就不必修改，也不必为"可强制执行"这一英文词语寻找适当的翻译。

......

主席将法国代表提出的案文付诸表决，但前提是其英文译文将是由张彭春先生起草的案文。

法国提出的第 5 款案文以 11 票对 1 票、4 票弃权获得通过。

......

——人权委员会第 102 次会议简要记录（E/CN.4/SR.102）

常健译校

E/CN.4/SR.102

7June 1949

COMMISSION ON HUMAN RIGHTS
FIFTH SESSION
SUMMARY RECORD OF THE ONE HUMRED AND SECOND MEETING

Held at Lake Success, New York, on Thursday, 26 May 1949, at 2:30 p.m.

Draft International Covenant on Human Rights (E/800, E/CN.4/212, E/CN.4/266, E/CN.4/219) Article 6 (Discussion Continued), 9 (Discussion Continued), 10 and 11

Article 9 (Discussion Continued)

...

Mr. Chang (China) believed that agreement might perhaps be reached on a text combining the original wording and that proposed by the French delegation. The English version of that text would read as follows:

"Every person who has been the victim of unlawful arrest or deprivation of liberty shall have an enforceable right to compensation."

Mr. Cassin (France) accepted the new English translation of his text. He stressed the fact that no stronger term existed in French than "droit a reparation" (right to compensation) because to grant an individual a right was to give him the faculty to defend that right before the courts. If therefore the Commission accepted the French proposal, the present French text of the paragraph would not have to be modified and there would he no need to find an adequate translation for the English term "enforceable".

...

The Chairman put to the vote the text proposed by the French representative, it being understood that the English translation would be the text drawn up by Mr. Chang.

The text of paragraph 5 proposed by France was adopted on that understanding by 11 votes to 1, with 4 abstentions.

在人权委员会第 103 次会议上的发言

1949 年 5 月 27 日星期五上午 11:30 纽约成功湖

1950 年人权委员会常会的会议地点（第 E/CN.4/268 号和第 E/CN.4/268/Add.1 号文件）
世界工会联合会代表在会议上发言的请求
《国际人权公约（草案）》（第 E/800 和 E/CN.4/W.25 号文件）：
第 8 条（继续讨论）

……

张先生（中国）感到惊讶的是，在秘书处提交的文件第 3 款中，规定了所有官方语言的同声传译，只是将中文除外。

主席回答说，鉴于中国代表对英语的精通，秘书处毫无疑问认为中国代表很擅长使用这种语言，并已作出了相应的安排。

张先生（中国）认为，在这样的原则事项上不应引入个人因素的考量。他补充说，他的代表团一直认为，如此重要的会议只应在本组织的常设总部举行。

……

张先生（中国）认为，法国代表提议的表述，即委员会 1950 年第一届会议应在欧洲举行，在一定程度上预设了经济及社会理事会的决定。事实上，经济及社会理事会可以决定人权委员会在 1950 年只举行一届会议。

卡森先生（法国）认识到中国代表意见的恰当性，并建议改用以下措辞："人权委员会 1950 年常会在日内瓦举行。"他希望委员会接受法国的提议，该提议已经得到一些非欧洲代表团的认可。

……

张先生（中国）指出，一般在日内瓦参加人权委员会会议的公众人数有限，仅由日内瓦人组成。因此，不能说该公众代表了欧洲舆论。

此外，日内瓦与世界其他地区之间的电话和无线通信，相比纽约与全世界的通信联系，完全不在一个规模层次。因此，如果从新闻传播和公众出席会议的角度来考虑宣传因素，就必须认识到，人权委员会会议在纽约举行会有相当多的好处，在那里会有众多的新闻记者定期对辩论进行跟踪报道。

张先生承认，欧洲是现代文明的摇篮，欧洲公共舆论对人权问题有浓厚的兴趣。但是，从声望和与公共舆论密切接触的角度来看，人权委员会并无必要在日内瓦举行会议。

……

张先生（中国）指出，中国代表团并不坚持人权委员会和联合国各机构应在美国举行会议；他本想传达的是，他的代表团认为联合国各机构应该在联合国总部举行会议，无论这些总部设于何处。

……

——人权委员会第 103 次会议简要记录（E/CN.4/SR.103）

常健译校

E/CN.4/SR.103

7June 1949

COMMISSION ON HUMAN RIGHTS
FIFTH SESSION
SUMMARY RECORD OF THE ONE HUMRED AND THIRD MEETING

Held at Lake Success, New York, on Friday, 27 May 1949, at 11:30 a.m.

Meeting Place of the Regular Session of the Commission on Human Rights in 1950 (E/CN.4/268 and E/CN.4/268/Add.1)
Request by the Representative of the World Federation of Trade Unions to Address the Meeting
Draft International Covenant on Human Rights (E/800, E/CN.4/W.25): Article 8 (Discussion Continued)

…

Mr. Chang (China) was surprised that in paragraph 3 of the document submitted by the Secretariat, provision was made for simultaneous interpretation in all the official languages except Chinese.

The Chairman replied that the Secretariat had no doubt supposed, in view of the Chinese representative's perfect knowledge of English, that he would be so good as to use that language, and had made its arrangements accordingly.

Mr. Chang (China) thought that personal considerations should not be introduced in a matter of principle. He added that his delegation had always been of the opinion that such an important session as that contemplated should be held only at the permanent Headquarters of the Organization.

...

Mr. Chang (China) thought that the formula proposed by the French representative, whereby the first session of the Commission in 1950 should be held in Europe, to a certain extent prejudged the decision of the Economic and Social Council. In point of fact, the Council could decide that the Commission on Human Rights should hold only one session in 1950.

Mr. Cassin (France) recognized the aptness of the Chinese representative's observation and proposed that the following wording should be used instead: "that the regular session of the Commission in 1950 be held in Geneva." He hoped that the Commission would accept the French proposal which had already been approved by a number of non-European delegations.

...

Mr. Chang (China) pointed out that the public which generally attended the meetings of the Commission in Geneva was limited, composed only of Genevese. It could not be said therefore that that public represented European public opinion.

Moreover, telephonic and wireless communications between Geneva and other parts of the world, were not at all on the same scale as those connecting New York with the whole world. Therefore, if the publicity factor were considered from the angle of press communications and public attendance of meetings, it had to be recognized that the Commission on Human Rights had everything to gain by meeting in New York, where a considerable number of press correspondents followed the debates regularly.

Mr. Chang recognized that Europe was the cradle of modern civilization and that European public opinion was deeply interested in the question of human rights. But it could not be said that from the point of view of prestige and of close contact with public opinion, it was necessary for the Commission on Human Rights to meet in Geneva.

...

Mr. Chang (China) pointed out that his delegation did not insist that the Commission on Human Rights and the organs of the United Nations in general should meet in the United States; what he had intended to convey was that his delegation felt the organs of the United Nations should meet at the Headquarters of the Organization wherever those Headquarters were situated.

...

在人权委员会第 104 次会议上的发言

1949 年 5 月 27 日星期五下午 2:45 纽约成功湖

《国际人权公约（草案）》（第 E/800、E/CN.4/158、 E/CN.4/170、E/CN.4/170/Add.3、E/CN.4/202/Rev.l、 E/CN.4/204、E/CN.4/207、E/CN.4/208、E/CN.4/270 号文件） （继续讨论）

……

张先生（中国）支持危地马拉代表的提议。他希望苏联代表现在对他的第二个选择感到满意，前提是在重新安排案文的最后阶段，可以决定是否在同一段落中提及奴隶制和奴役。

……

张先生（中国）认为，以良心为由反对杀人是一个非常高尚的想法，但他想知道有多少国家真正承认这一点。如果发现承认的人数很少，也许公约应该提到这一事实，除非它想鼓励承认依良心拒服兵役者的概念。

……

——人权委员会第 104 次会议简要记录（E/CN.4/SR.104）

常健译校

E/CN.4/SR.104
31 May 1949
COMMISSION ON HUMAN RIGHTS
FIFTH SESSION
SUMMARY RECORD OF THE HUNDRED AND FOURTH MEETING
Held at Lake Success, New York, on Friday, 27 May 1949, at 2:45 p.m.

Draft International Covenant on Human Rights (E/800, E/CN.4/158, E/CN.4/170, E/CN.4/170/Add.3, E/CN.4/202/Rev.l, E/CN.4/204, E/CN.4/207, E/CN.4/208, E/CN.4/270) (Discussion Continued)

…

Mr. Chang (China) supported the proposal of the representative of Guatemala. He hoped the USSR representative would be satisfied with his second choice for the time being, on the understanding that when the final stage of rearrangement of the text was reached it could be decided whether slavery and servitude should be mentioned in the same paragraph.

…

Mr. Chang (China) felt that the objection to killing on grounds of conscience was a very noble idea, but he wondered how many countries actually recognized it. If the number was found to be very small perhaps the Covenant should mention that fact, unless it wanted to encourage the recognition of the concept of the conscientious objector.

…

在人权委员会第 115 次会议上的发言

1949 年 6 月 6 日星期一下午 2:30 纽约成功湖

《国际人权公约（草案）》：执行措施（第 E/CN.4/82.Add.10、E/CN.4/276、E/CN.4/292、E/CN.4/293 号文件）

……

张先生（中国）表示，他对执行措施含义的理解与大多数代表所表达的观点有些不同。他所说的执行意味着为使公约生效而采取的积极措施。不应该仅仅从消极的角度来处理它；重点不应放在投诉和请愿上，而应放在实现人权方面的国际合作上。

张先生指出，在过去 150 年中，个人地位得到显著提高，特别是在工业化程度较高的国家，这些国家也受到了中国哲学思想的影响。尽管人权理想在一些国家比在其他国家得到了更充分的落实，但它们得到了所有国家的承认。高度工业化国家（如美国）与其他国家（如中国）在人权方面的立场自然存在差异，高度工业化国家有个人扩展的机会，而其他国家虽然继承了伟大的文化传统，但在工业上更为落后。因此，一个国家投诉另一个国家侵犯人权的行为很容易，但在政治层面上，这种投诉只会导致报复，没有建设性价值。

关于个人请愿权问题，他同意印度和黎巴嫩代表的意见。然而，他认为，积极执行的问题更为重要，并建议，与其规定如何处理申诉，不如采取积极措施，以促进国际合作，激发人们对落实人权的兴趣。

加布西亚·鲍尔先生（危地马拉）在提到中国代表的发言时指出，危地马拉代表团在其拟议的工作文件（第 E/CN.4/293 号文件）中审议了实施人权的积极方面。他保留稍后就其提案发言的权利。

……

鲍伊女士（英国）在提到中国代表的发言时说，人权委员会的讨论并不妨碍其审议保护人权的积极方面，许多联合国机关、专门机构和非政府组织也对此表示关注。

......

卡森先生（法国）在回答中国代表时指出，公约的第一部分处理了该问题的积极方面，他准备进一步强调这一方面。在这方面，他提请注意危地马拉的建议，即会员国应在国家和国际上采取适当步骤，确保其居民享有人权。

......

——人权委员会第 115 次会议简要记录（E/CN.4/SR.115）

常健译校

E/CN.4/SR.115

9 June 1949

COMMISSION ON HUMAN RIGHTS

FIFTH SESSION

SUMMARY RECORD OF THE HUNDRED AND FIFTEENTH MEETING

Held at Lake Success, New York, on Monday, 6 June 1949, at 2:30 p.m.

Draft International Covenant on Human Rights: Measures for Implementation (E/CN.4/82.Add.10, E/CN.4/276, E/CN.4/292, E/CN.4/293)

...

Mr. Chang (China) stated that he took la somewhat different view of the meaning of measures of implementation from that expressed by the majority of representatives. By implementation he meant positive measures for putting the Covenant into effect. It should not be dealt with merely from the negative angle; the emphasis should be less on complaints and petitions and more on international co-operation in the realization of human right.

Mr. Chang pointed put that great advances had been made in the status of the individual during the past 150 years, particularly in the more highly industrialization countries, which had, incidentally been influenced by Chinese philosophical thought. Although the ideals of human rights had been more fully put into effect in some countries than in others, they were recognized by all. Differences in the individual's position with regard to human rights natural existed between highly industrialized countries, with opportunities for individual expansion, such as the United States of America, and others such as China which, although heirs to a great tradition of culture, were more backward industrially. It would therefore be easy for one country to complain of violations of human rights in the other but, on the political plane, such a complaint would merely lead to retaliation and would be of no constructive value.

On the question of the individual right of petition he agreed with the representatives of India and Lebanon. He felt, however, that the question of positive implementation was of much greater importance and proposed that, instead of provisions dealing with complaints, positive measures to stimulate international co-operation and encourage interest in the implementation of human rights should be taken.

Mr. Gabcia Bauer (Guatemala) noted, with reference to the Chinese representative's remarks, that his delegation had considered the positive aspects of the implementation of human rights in its proposed working paper (E/CN.4/293) . He reserved the right to speak on his proposal at a later date.

...

Miss Bowie (United Kingdom), with reference to the statement by the representative of China, stated that the Commission's discussion did not preclude it from considering the positive aspects of the protection of human rights with which many United Nations organs, specialized agencies and non-governmental organizations were also concerned.

...

Mr. Cassin (France), in reply to the representative of China, pointed out that the first part of the Covenant dealt with the positive aspects of the question which he was prepared to stress even further. He drew attention, in that connexion, to the Guatemalan proposal that States Members should take suitable steps, nationally and internationally, to ensure the enjoyment of human rights by their inhabitants.

...

在人权委员会第 117 次会议上的发言

1949 年 6 月 7 日星期二下午 2:30 纽约成功湖

《国际人权公约（草案）》：第 16 条（第 E/CN.4/272、E/CN.4/300、E/CN.4/301 号文件）

......

张先生（中国）说，乌克兰代表引发了一个非常有意思的话题，但他将对乌克兰代表关于中国宗教自由的评论作出保留，因为在中国，人们完全可以自由改变信仰。

他认为最好采用《世界人权宣言》第 18 条，它是被 58 个国家在联合国大会第三届会议第一期会议上讨论过的。如果将这样的案文纳入公约，将比一个更详细、可能更具争议的草案更容易被联合国大会接受。

......

张先生（中国）建议人权委员会对第 1 款或第 16 条的法美联合案文进行表决。

......

第 16 条法美联合案文的第 1 款被付诸表决。

第 1 款以 11 票对 0 票、4 票弃权获得通过。

——人权委员会第 117 次会议简要记录（E/CN.4/SR.117）

常健译校

E/CN.4/SR.117

9 June 1949

COMMISSION ON HUMAN RIGHTS
FIFTH SESSION
SUMMARY RECORD OF THE HUNDRED AND SENVENTEENTH MEETING

Held at Lake Success, New York, on Tuesday, 7 June 1949, at 2:30 p.m.

Draft International Covenant on Human Rights: Article 16 (Discussion Continued) (E/CN.4/272, E/CN.4/300, E/CN.4/301)

...

Mr. Chang (China) stated that a very interesting field had been opened up by the representative of the Ukrainian SSR but he would reserve his remarks on freedom of religion in China, where persons had complete liberty to change their beliefs.

He thought that it would be best to adopt article 18 of the Universal Declaration which had been discussed by fifty-eight nations at the first part of the third session of the Assembly. Such a text, if incorporated in the Covenant, would be more acceptable to the General Assembly than a more detailed and possibly more controversial draft.

...

Mr. Chang (China) proposed that the Commission should vote on paragraph 1 or the joint France-United States text of article 16.

...

Paragraph 1 of the joint France-United States text of article 16 was put to the vote.

Paragraph 1 was adopted by 11 votes to none, with 4 abstentions.

...

在人权委员会第 118 次会议上的发言

1949 年 6 月 8 日星期三上午 10:30 纽约成功湖

人权公约草案
执行措施：确认个人和组织的申诉权（第 E/800、E/CN.4/292 号文件、第 1 部分第二章；第 E/CN.4/299 号文件）（继续讨论）

……

张先生（中国）认为，出现的唯一问题，就是与个人和组织请愿权有关的条款是否应该被写入公约。对秘书处起草的决议草案进行表决，可以表明人权委员会成员在这一问题上的立场。

然而，鉴于菲律宾代表所作的评论，有理由怀疑对决议草案进行表决是否会成为对采纳请愿原则同时推迟确定实施该原则的手段；或者相反，正如他自己所理解的那样，这将是就是否立即将保障个人和组织行使由此赋予他们的权利的条款纳入公约所进行的表决。

他请主席就秘书处起草的决议草案的含义作出裁决。

主席承认，这个问题非常微妙；她只能敦促人权委员会成员仔细考虑他们即将作出决定的含义。

……

张先生（中国）担心法国的提案有严重的缺点，因为它倾向于将原则与其在实践中的实现分开。如果法语文本的第一部分被接受，而第二部分被拒绝，那么这样一个决定的唯一结果将是唤醒全世界人民的巨大希望，但随后却立即让他们失望。人权委员会成员绝不能忘记，人权公约不能与《世界人权宣言》相提并论；公约是签字国承诺执行的条约。

……

张先生（中国）建议推迟对该问题的表决，以便对刚刚提交的提案和建议进行更彻底的讨论。

主席说，在推迟表决之前，委员会应该知道它正在处理哪些提案。

……

张先生（中国）认为，这个问题很重要，委员会应在对其进行表决之前，设法商定一个适当的案文。

他回顾说，危地马拉和伊朗代表提出了一些建议，其中包含一些新的想法。伊朗代表表示，案文很可能以否定形式起草。张先生想知道法国代表是否不能接受伊朗代表的建议。

卡森先生（法国）说，他不能修改他的提案，但建议中国代表自行提交丹麦代表提到的修正案，以便可以否定法国的提案。

张先生（中国）撤回了推迟投票的提议，并建议将法国的提案修改如下："决定目前不应将个人和团体请愿的规定列入执行措施"。

恩特扎姆先生（伊朗）接受了中国代表提出的案文。

主席将中国代表提出的修正案付诸表决。

加西亚·鲍尔先生（危地马拉）要求进行唱名表决。

唱名表决如下：

赞成：中国、埃及、伊朗、乌克兰、苏联、英国、美国、南斯拉夫。

反对：澳大利亚、丹麦、法国、危地马拉、印度、黎巴嫩、菲律宾、乌拉圭。

修正案未获得通过，投票结果是 8 票赞成，8 票反对。

梅塔女士（印度）想知道，如果在拒绝中国提交的修正案之后，人权委员会也拒绝了法国的原始提案，该委员会的立场会是什么。

加西亚·鲍尔先生（危地马拉）提请委员会注意印度代表提出的这一点的重要性。

主席解释说，如果法国提案也被否决，委员会可以审议其任何成员提出的任何新提案。

卡森先生（法国）认为，如果他的提案也被拒绝，人权委员会应向所有会员国提供备选方案，说明在每种情况下应采取的程序。

卡森先生要求进行唱名表决。

巴甫洛夫先生（苏联）回顾说，人权委员会面前还有一份菲律宾提案。该提案的大意是，关于个人或个人团体请愿权的规定应纳入人权公约，甚至比法国的提案更进一步。因此，如果法国的提案被否决，菲律宾的提案应被付诸表决。

英格尔斯先生（菲律宾）说，他将投票支持法国的提案，但如果该提案被否决，他自己的提案应该被付诸表决。

马利克先生（黎巴嫩）要求将法国提案分部分付诸表决，第一部分包括"在执行措施中"，第二部分包括"在此时"。

张先生（中国）指出，对法国提案第二部分投反对票的人也不得不对第一部分投反对票，因为在如此重要的问题上，原则问题不能与程序问题分开。不可能向世界宣布承认个人和个人团体的请愿权，同时宣布不能行使这一权利。使行使这一权利成为可能的程序尚未确定。因此，法国提案的第一部分应以与第二部分相同的理由被否决。

对法国提案的第一部分进行的唱名表决结果如下：

赞成：澳大利亚、丹麦、法国、危地马拉、印度、黎巴嫩、菲律宾、乌拉圭。

反对：中国、埃及、伊朗、乌克兰、苏联、英国、美国、南斯拉夫。

提案的第一部分没有获得通过，有 8 票赞成，8 票反对。

主席说，由于第一部分未获得通过，法国提案整体失去了意义。她将菲律宾的提案付诸表决。

加西亚·鲍尔先生（危地马拉）要求将该提案分部分付诸表决，第一部分只包括"此时"，第二部分是案文的其余部分。

主席将菲律宾提案的第一部分付诸表决。

第一部分以 8 票反对、6 票赞成、1 票弃权被否决。

加西亚·鲍尔先生（危地马拉）要求对第二部分进行唱名表决，内容如下："决议人权公约应包括个人和团体请愿的规定"。

投票结果如下：

赞成：澳大利亚、法国、危地马拉、印度、黎巴嫩、菲律宾、乌拉圭。

反对：中国、埃及、伊朗、乌克兰、苏联、英国、美国、南斯拉夫。

弃权：丹麦。

菲律宾提案的第二部分以 8 票反对、7 票赞成、1 票弃权被否决。

会议于下午 1:00 结束。

——人权委员会第 118 次会议简要记录（E/CN.4/SR.118）

常健译校

E/CN.4/SR.118

20 June 1949

COMMISSION ON HUMAN RIGHTS
FIFTH SESSION
SUMMARY RECORD OF THE HUNDRED AND
EIGHTEENTH MEETING

Held at Lake Success, New York, on Wednesday, 8 June 1949, at 10:30 a.m.

Draft Covenant on Human Rights: Measures of Implementation: Recognition of the Right of individuals and Organizations to Petition (E/800, E/CN.4/292, Part I, Chapter 2; E/CN.4/299) (Discussion Continued)

...

Mr. Chang (China) thought the only question which arose was whether or not provisions relating to the right of individuals and organizations to petition should already be included in the Covenant. A vote on the draft resolution prepared by the Secretariat would make clear the position of the members of the Commission on that point.

Nevertheless, in view of the comments made by the representative of the Philippines, there was some excuse for wondering whether a vote on the draft resolution would be a vote for the adoption of the principle of petitions, while at the same time postponing the establishment of the means whereby that principle would be put into practice to a later date, or whether, on the contrary, as he himself understood it, it would be a vote for the immediate inclusion in the Covenant of provisions guaranteeing individuals and organizations the exercise of the right thus conferred upon them.

He asked the Chairman to give a ruling on the meaning to be attached to the draft resolution drawn up by the Secretariat.

The Chairman admitted that the question was a very delicate one; she could only urge the members of the Commission to give careful consideration to the meaning of the decision they were about to take.

...

Mr. Chang (China) feared that the French proposal had serious disadvantages, in that it tended to separate the principle from its realization in practice. If the first part of the French text were accepted and the second rejected, the sole result of such a decision would be to awaken great hopes throughout the world, only to disappoint them immediately after. The members of the Commission must not forget that a Covenant on Human Rights was not to be compared with a Universal Declaration of Human Rights; a covenant was a treaty which the signatory States undertook to put into effect.

...

Mr. Chang (China) suggested that the vote on that question should be postponed, so that a more thorough discussion of the proposals and suggestions which had just been submitted could take place.

The Chairman said that before postponing the vote the Commission should know what proposals it was dealing with.

...

Mr. Chang (China) felt that the matter was important, and that the Commission should try to agree on an adequate text before voting on it.

He recalled that the representatives of Guatemala and of Iran had submitted suggestions which introduced new ideas. The representative of Iran had shown that a text might well be drafted in a negative form. Mr. Chang wondered whether the French representative could not accept the suggestion of the Iranian representative.

Mr. Cassin (France) said he could not modify his proposal, but suggested that the Chinese representative submit as his own the amendment referred to by the Danish representative in order to give the French proposal a negative sense.

Mr. Chang (China) withdrew his proposal to defer the vote and suggested that the French proposal should be amended to read as follows: "Resolves that provisions for individual and group petitions shall not be included in the measures of implementation at this time".

Mr. Entezam (Iran) accepted the text proposed by the Chinese representative.

The Chairman put to the vote the amendment submitted by the representative of China.

Mr. Garcia Bauer (Guatemala) asked that the vote be taken by roll-call.

A vote was taken by roll-call, as follows:

In favour: China, Egypt, Iran, Ukrainian Soviet Socialist Republic, Union of Soviet Socialist Republics, United Kingdom, United States of America, Yugoslavia.

Against: Australia, Denmark, France, Guatemala, India, Lebanon, Philippines, Uruguay.

The amendment was not adopted, the result of the vote being 8 votes in favour and 8 against.

Mrs. Mehta (India) wondered what would be the position of the Commission if, after rejecting the amendment submitted by China, it also rejected the original French proposal.

Mr. Gabcia Bauer (Guatemala) drew the Commission's attention to the importance of the point raised by the Indian representative.

The Chairman explained that, if the French proposal was also rejected, the Commission could then consider any new proposal submitted by any of its members.

Mr. Cassin (France) thought that, if his proposal was also rejected, the Commission should place before all Member States the alternative indicating, in each case, the procedure to be adopted.

Mr. Cassin requested that the vote be taken by roll-call.

Mr. Pavlov (Union of Soviet Socialist Republics) recalled that the Commission also had before it a Philippine proposal. That proposal, to the effect that the provisions concerning the right of individuals or groups of individuals to petition should be included in the Covenant on Human Rights, went much further even than the French proposal. Consequently, if the latter was rejected the Philippine proposal should be put to the vote.

Mr. Ingles (Philippines) said that he would vote for the French proposal but that if it was rejected his own proposal should then be put to the vote.

Mr. Malik (Lebanon) requested that the French proposal should be put to the vote in parts, the first part being up to and including the words: "in the measures of implementation" and the second part being the words "at this time".

Mr. Chang (China) pointed out that those who voted against the second part of the French proposal would likewise have to vote against the first part because, in a matter of such importance, the question of principle could not be separated from that of procedure. It was not possible to proclaim to the world that the right of petition by individuals and by groups of individuals was recognized, and at the same time declare that that right could not be exercised. The procedure making it possible to exercise that right had not yet been established. Consequently, the first part of the French proposal should be rejected for the same reason as the second part.

A vote was taken by roll-call on the first part of the French proposal as follows:

In favour: Australia, Denmark, France, Guatemala, India, Lebanon, Philippines, Uruguay.

Against: China, Egypt, Iran, Ukrainian Soviet Socialist Republic, Union of Soviet Socialist Republics, United Kingdom, United States of America, Yugoslavia.

The first part of the proposal was not adopted, there being 8 votes in favour and 8 against.

The Chairman stated that as the first part had not been adopted, the French proposal as a whole lost its meaning. She put to the vote the Philippine proposal.

Mr. Garcia Bauer (Guatemala) asked that that proposal should be put to the vote in parts, the first part comprising only the words: "at this time", and the seoond part the remainder of the text.

The Chairman put to the vote the first part of the Philippine proposal.

The first part was rejected by 8 vote to 6, with one abstention.

Mr. Garcia Bauer (Guatemala) asked that a roll-call vote be taken on the second part, reading as follows: "Resolves that the Covenant on human rights should include provisions for individuals and groups of individuals to petition".

A vote was taken by roll-call on the second part as follows:

In favour: Australia, France, Guatemala, India, Lebanon, Philippines, Uruguay.

Against: China, Egypt, Iran, Ukrainian Soviet Socialist Republic, Union of Soviet Socialist Republics, United Kingdom, United States of America, Yugoslavia.

Abstentions: Denmark.

The second part of the Philippine proposal was rejected by 8 votes to 7, with one abstention.

The meeting rose at 1:00 p.m.

在人权委员会第 119 次会议上的发言

1949 年 6 月 8 日星期三下午 2:30 纽约成功湖

人权公约草案
执行措施：第二章：关于个人权利的议案（第 E/CN.4/292 和 E/CN.4/299 号文件）

……

张先生（中国）认为，经济及社会理事会已商定，在同一届会议上不能重新审议关于实质性问题的表决，但关于程序性问题的表决没有这一规则；他同意人权委员会应在 6 月 20 日前完成工作，但指出，在其掌控的短时间内，人权委员会无望完成公约草案和关于执行建议的工作。

……

张先生（中国）说，他没有投票，因为他觉得第一次表决并不清楚。他询问黎巴嫩的提案是否意味着人权委员会将继续讨论公约草案，直至 6 月 16 日。

……

张先生（中国）无法理解，在宗教或信仰自由这样一个严肃的问题上，人权委员会为什么要施加在其他条款中被认为没有必要的限制。他认为，那些真正信奉宗教的人不会因为受到这些限制而感觉受到赞扬。张先生希望委员会最终能够决定删除该条第二款，并以一般限制取代。在他看来，一方面促进宗教信仰自由，另一方面不仅通过法律而且出于公共安全、公共秩序和健康的考虑来限制这种自由，似乎是前后矛盾的。

在这方面，他提到了在中国的传教活动。曾经有一段时间，宗教与“文明”没有联系，就像在 17 世纪和 18 世纪，耶稣会士前往中国不是为了开化，只是为了宣扬宗教。双方进行了愉快的合作，而耶稣会士也从他们的中国朋友那里学到了很多。在 19 世纪，人们形成了一种不同的态度，贸易、金融和其他利益与宗教活动联系在一起。张先生很高兴地注意到这种态度正在发生变化，他希望宗教和"文明"保持分离。

......

——人权委员会第 119 次会议简要记录（E/CN.4/SR.119）

常健译校

E/CN.4/SR.119

13 June 1949

COMMISSION ON HUMAN RIGHTS
FIFTH SESSION
SUMMARY RECORD OF THE HUNDRED AND NINETEENTH MEETING

Held at Lake Success, New York, on Wednesday, 8 June 1949, at 2:30 p.m.

Draft Covenant on Human Rights; measures of implementation: chapter 2: proposals relating to the question of the rights of individuals (E/CN.4/292, E/CN.4/299)

…

Mr. Chang (China) felt that it had been agreed in the Economic and Social Council that votes on matters of substance could not be reconsidered at the same session, but that there was no such rule regarding votes on procedural questions; He agreed that the Commission should finish its work by 20 June, but pointed out that in the short time at its disposal it could not hope to finish work on the draft covenant and the proposals regarding implementation.

…

Mr. Chang (China) stated that he had not voted because he felt that the first vote was not clear. He asked whether the Lebanese proposal signified that the Commission would continue its discussion on the draft Covenant up to and including 16 June.

…

Mr. Chang (China) could not understand why, in connexion with such a serious question as freedom of religion or beliefs, the Commission should have imposed limitations which had not been considered necessary in other articles. He felt that those who really practised their religion would not feel complimented by the restrictions which had imposed on them. Mr. Chang hoped that the Committee might eventually decide to delete the second paragraph of that article and replace it by a general limitation. It seemed to him inconsistent to promote, on the one hand, freedom of religious beliefs and, on the other, to limit such freedom not only by law but also by considerations of public safety, public order and health.

In that connexion, he mentioned the missionary effort in China. There had been a time when religion was not linked to "civilization", as in the seventeenth and eighteenth centuries when the Jesuits had gone to China not to civilize but simply to preach religion. A happy collaboration had existed and the Jesuits learned also a great deal from their Chinese friends. In the nineteenth century a different attitude had developed and trade and financial and other interests became linked to religious activities. Mr. Chang was glad to note that a change of attitude was developing and he hoped that religion and "civilization" would remain separate.

...

在人权委员会第 120 次会议上的发言

1949 年 6 月 9 日星期四上午 10:30 纽约成功湖

人权公约草案（第 E/800、E/CN.4/272、E/CN.4/272/Corr.1 号文件）（继续讨论）
第 17 和第 18 条

……

第 17 条

……

张先生（中国）指出，联合国新闻自由会议起草的第 17 条第 1 款涉及非常广泛的领域，也涉及思想和言论自由。

他建议，在就推迟审议第 17 条进行表决之前，人权委员会应决定征求各国政府对以下两个问题的意见：（1）公约是否应载有关于新闻自由的条款；（2）　如果是的话，该条款应该包括哪些具体款项？

……

第 18 条

……

张先生（中国）认为美国修正案的案文比起草委员会的案文更好，因为它比后者更清晰、更简洁。尽管如此，他认为应该对美国案文进行某些修改。特别是，他提议用《世界人权宣言》第 20 条第 1 款，即"每个人都有权享有和平集会和结社的自由"，来代替美国案文的第一句表述，该表述采用否定的形式，这是他不赞成的。

此外，他认为最好不要在第 18 条中引入限制性条款，而是提供一个适用于整个公约草案的一般性限制条款。然而，如果委员会不同意他的意见，他将建议对美国提出的限制性条款进行如下修改：（1）"合理的"一词过于模糊，无法纳入《国际人权公约（草案）》，不宜采用；（2）应使用逗号来代替（a）、（b）和（c）的分节；（3）"公益"这个表述不够具体，应该改为："防止社会动乱"。

主席以美国代表的身份发言，她解释说，美国代表团准备按照中国代表的建议，用《世界人权宣言》第 20 条第 1 款代替其修正案的第一句。

卡森先生（法国）又提议用《世界人权宣言》第 20 条第 1 款取代美国修正案的第一句，并删除"合理的"一词。他还建议将该修正案中的清单替换为："在一个民主社会中，为国家安全、公共秩序、保护健康或道德以及保护他人的权利和自由所必需的。"

......

——人权委员会第 120 次会议简要记录（E/CN.4/SR.120）

常健译校

E/CN.4/SR.120
21 June 1949

COMMISSION ON HUMAN RIGHTS
FIFTH SESSION
SUMMARY RECORD OF THE HUNDRED AND TWENTIETH MEETING

Held at Lake Success, New York, on Thursday, 9 June 1949, at 10:30 a.m.

Draft Covenant on Human Rights (E/800, E/CN.4/272, E/CN.4/272/Corr.1) (Discussion Continued) Articles 17 and 18

Article 17

...

Mr. Chang (China) observed that paragraph 1 of article 17 as drafted by the United Nations Conference on Freedom of Information covered a very wide field and also dealt with freedom of thought and expression.

He suggested that, before taking a vote on the postponement of the consideration of article 17, the Commission should decide to request the views of Governments on the following two questions: (1) whether the Covenant should contain an article concerning freedom of information; (2) if so, what should the terms of that article be?

...

Article 18

...

Mr. Chang (China) considered the text of the United States amendment preferable to that of the Drafting Committee since it was clearer and more concise than the latter. All the same, he thought certain changes should be made in the United States text. In particular, he proposed to substitute for the first sentence, the negative form of which he did not approve, article 20, paragraph 1 of the Universal Declaration of Human Rights, which stated that "Everyone has the right to freedom of peaceful assembly and association."

Furthermore, it would seem to him preferable not to introduce restrictive provisions in article 18, but to provide for a general limiting clause applicable to the draft Covenant as a whole. If, however, the Commission did not share his opinion, he would suggest that the restrictive clauses proposed by the United States should be amended aa follows: (1) the word "reasonable" which was too vague to be included in the Draft International Covenant on Human Rights should be suppressed; (2) instead of sub-divisions (a), (b) and (c) commas should be used; (3) the words "the general interest" which were not specific enough, should be replaced by: "the prevention of public disorder."

The Chairman, speaking as the representative of the United States of America, explained that her delegation was prepared to substitute article 20, paragraph 1 of the Universal Declaration of Human Rights for the first sentence of its amendment, as suggested by the representative of China.

Mr. Cassin (France) in turn proposed to replace the first sentence of the United States amendment by article 20, paragraph 1 of the Universal Declaration of Hunan Rights and to delete the word "reasonable". He also proposed to replace the list included in that amendment by the following: "necessary for national security, public order, the protection of health or morals and the protection of the rights and freedoms of others in a democratic society."

...

在人权委员会第 121 次会议上的发言

1949 年 6 月 9 日星期四下午 2:30 纽约成功湖

人权公约草案（第 E/800、E/CN.4/227、E/CN.4/230、E/CN.4/272、E/CN.4/272/Corr.1、E/CN.4/296、E/CN.4/296/Corr.1、E/CN.4/206、E/CN.4/207、E/CN.4/208、E/C.2/196 号文件）（继续讨论）：
第 17、18、19 条

……

第 18 条

……

关于对起草委员会第 18 条案文的中国修正案（第 E/CN.4/307 号文件），张先生（中国）同意接受法国代表团提出的某些修改（第 E/CN.4/306 号文件）。然而，他希望强调，在中国修正案的第二句中，在"安全"之前保留"国家"一词。他特别强调国家安全和社会安全之间不能混淆。

卡森先生（法国）无法同意在法国修正案中插入"国家"一词。

张先生（中国）撤回了他的修正案，并代之以提议在任何作为表决的基础案文中，都要在"安全"之前插入"国家"一词。

主席说，法国修正案（第 E/CN.4/306 号文件）的案文将作为表决的基础案文，美国、中国和智利代表团提出的备选建议将被视为对该案文的修正。

……

主席将提议对在法国修正案第三行"安全"之前插入"国家"一词的中国修正案付诸表决。

中国修正案以 7 票对 4 票、4 票弃权获得通过。

……

第 19 条

……

张先生（中国）说，根据第 20 条，对法律的保护不一定限于享有公约规定的权利和自由；出于某种原因可能没有纳入公约的其他自由，可能应该得到同等程度的保护。他强调，他的发言不是作为正式提案，而是作为供委员会审议的探索性建议。

……

——人权委员会第 121 次会议简要记录（E/CN.4/SR.121）

常健译校

E/CN.4/SR.121
14 June 1949

COMMISSION ON HUMAN RIGHTS
FIFTH SESSION
SUMMARY RECORD OF THE HUNDRED AND TWENTY-FIRST MEETING

Held at Lake Success, New York, on Thursday, 9 June 1949, at 2:30 p.m.

Draft Covenant on Human Rights (E/800, E/CN.4/227, E/CN.4/230, E/CN.4/272, E/CN.4/272/Corr.1, E/CN.4/296, E/CN.4/296/Corr.1, E/CN.4/206, E/CN.4/207, E/CN.4/208, E/C.2/196) (Discussion Continued): Articles 18, 19 and 20

Article 18

Mr. Chang (China) agreed to accept certain modifications proposed by the French delegation (E/CN.4/306) in the Chinese amendment to the Drafting Committee's text of article 18 (E/CN.4/307). However, he wished to press for the retention of the word "national" before "security" in the second sentence of the Chinese amendment. He was anxious that there should be no confusion between national and social security.

Mr. Cassin (France) was unable to agree to the insertion of the word "national" in the French amendment.

Mr. Chang (China) withdrew his amendment and proposed instead the insertion of the word "national" before "security" in whatever text was taken as a basis for voting.

The Chairman said that the text of the French amendment (E/CN.4/306) would be taken as a basis for the vote, and the alternative suggestions put forward by the delegations of the United States, China and Chile, would be regarded as amendments to that text.

....

The Chairman put to the vote the Chinese amendment proposing the insertion of the word "national"' before "security"' in the third line of the French amendment.

The Chinese amendment was adopted by 7 votes to 4, with 4 abstentions.

...

Article 19

...

Mr. Chang (China) remarked that protection of the law under article 20 should not necessarily be restricted to the enjoyment of rights and freedoms set forth in the Covenant; other freedoms which, for some reason, might not be incorporated in the Covenant might deserve an equal measure of protection. He stressed that his remark was not intended as a formal Proposal but only as a tentative suggestion for consideration by the Commission.

...

在人权委员会第 122 次会议上的发言

1949 年 6 月 10 日星期五上午 10:30 纽约成功湖

人权公约草案（第 E/800、E/CN.4/311、E/CN.4/312 号文件）
（继续讨论）

会议主席：张彭春先生（中国）

第 20 条

主席说，法国、菲律宾和美国代表团提交了第 20 条的联合案文（第 E/CN.4/131 号文件）。

然而，该提案第一句中的"和"应改为"享有"，这样该文本将改为："人人有权在享有所有权利和自由等方面受到法律的平等保护"。

......

主席指出，《世界人权宣言》第 7 条第一句说："法律面前人人平等，有权不受歧视地得到法律的平等保护"，这远远超出了法国、菲律宾和美国联合提案第一段所包含的观点，联合提案只提到"在享受本公约规定的所有权利和自由方面法律的保护"。

因此，他认为可能的解决办法是：在第 20 条中重申《世界人权宣言》第 7 条的第一句。这样，联合提案的规定就可以被写入第 20 条。

......

主席认为，通过以下方式起草第 20 条，就可能在不同代表团的意见之间达成折中解决办法：应使用《世界人权宣言》第 7 条的第一句；接着是"不受任何种类的歧视，如种族……"，不提"本公约规定的权利和自由"。

最后，应增加一段关于"防止违反本公约的任何歧视"的内容。

查尔斯·马利克先生（黎巴嫩）认为主席提出的两项建议是可以接受的，如果其中一项建议成为正式建议，他愿意支持。

胡德先生（澳大利亚）指出，主席的建议使我们能够非常清楚地区分正在审议的三个理念：第一，在享有该公约所规定的权利和自由方面的法律保护；第二，防止任何煽动歧视的行为；第三，正如主席所指出的，根据《世界人权宣言》第 7 条第一句的规定，法律保护的一般问题。

因此，胡德先生支持主席的提议。

……

主席指出，人权委员会因此审议了两份案文：一份是菲律宾、法国和美国的联合草案（第 E/CN.4/311 号文件），另一份是印度草案（第 E/CN.4/312 号文件）。

……

主席解释说，"或其他地位"这一表述涵盖了这一概念；为了避免在那个关键时刻重开一场历史悠久的辩论，就没有用更多的话语来阐述这一观点。

……

主席强调，拟议案文写的是"法律"而不是"诸项法律"，显然，受法律影响的所有人在法律面前都是平等的。

……

——人权委员会第 122 次会议简要记录（E/CN.4/SR.122）

常健译校

E/CN.4/SR.122
17 June 1949
COMMISSION ON HUMAN RIGHTS
FIFTH SESSION
SUMMARY RECORD OF THE HUNDRED AND TWENTIETH
MEETING
Held at Lake Success, New York, on FRIDAY, 10 June 1949, at 10:30 a.m.

Draft Covenant on Human Rights (E/800, E/CN.4/311,
E/CN.4/312) (Discussion Continued)

Chairman: Mr. Chang (China)

Article 20

The Chairman stated that the French, Philippine and United States delegations had submitted a joint text for article 20 (E/CN.4/131).

However, the words "and to" in the first sentence of that proposal should be replaced by the words "in the enjoyment of" so that the text would read: "Everyone is entitled to equal protection of the law in the enjoyment of all the rights and freedoms, etc.".

...

The Chairman pointed out that the first sentence of article 7 of the Declaration of Human Rights, which stated: "All are equal before the law and are entitled without discrimination to equal protection of the law", went far beyond the idea contained in the first paragraph of the joint proposal, which spoke only of the "protection of the law in the enjoyment of all the rights and freedoms defined in this Covenant."

He consequently thought that the solution might be to repeat, in article 20, the first sentence of article 7 of the Declaration; the provisions of the joint proposal would then be included in article 20.

...

The Chairman thought that it was possible to reach a compromise solution between the views of the different delegations by drafting article 20 in the following manner: the first sentence of article 7 of the Declaration should be used; followed by the words "without discrimination of any kind, such as race ... " and without mentioning "the rights and freedoms defined in this Covenant".

Finally, a paragraph should be added concerning "protection against any discrimination in violation of this Covenant".

Mr. Charles Malik (Lebanon) thought that the two suggestions submitted by the Chairman were quite acceptable, and, if one of those suggestions became a formal proposal, he was ready to support it.

Mr. Hood (Australia) noted that the Chairman's suggestion had made it possible to distinguish very clearly the three ideas under consideration: first, the protection of law in the enjoyment of the rights and freedoms defined in the Covenant; secondly, protection against any incitement to discrimination and, lastly, as the Chairman had pointed out, the general question of the protection of the law, according to the provisions of the first sentence of article 7 of the Declaration.

For that reason, Mr. Hood supported the Chairman's proposal.

…

The Chairman pointed out that the Commission was therefore seized of two texts: one being the joint draft of the Philippines, France and the United States (E/CN.4/311), and the other the Indian draft (E/CN.4/312).

…

The Chairman explained that that idea was covered by the words "or other status"; it had not been stated in so many words in order to avoid reopening a very old debate at that juncture.

…

The Chairman stressed that the proposed text read "the law" and not "the laws," and that it was evident that all those affected by the law were equal before that law.

…

在人权委员会第 123 次会议上的发言

1949 年 6 月 10 日星期五下午 2:45 纽约成功湖

人权公约草案（第 E/800、E/CN.4/296、E/CN.4/312 号文件）第 17 条（继续讨论）、第 21 条、第 22 条

会议主席：张彭春先生（中国）

第 20 条（继续讨论）

主席重新开放对第 20 条的讨论，并建议人权委员会将印度对该条的修正案（E/CN.4/312 号文件）作为其基本工作文件。

......

第 21 条

主席开放对上述问题的讨论，并请各位成员参阅 E/CN.4/296 号文件，其中载有起草委员会前一年删除的第 21 条的原文和苏联提出的案文。

......

主席将是否要将第 21 条的审议推迟到讨论第 17 条之后这一问题付诸表决。

该提案以 5 票对 3 票、4 票弃权获得通过。

主席说，当最终重新审议第 21 条时，法国和苏联代表提出的两份案文将提交人权委员会。

第 22 条

主席提请注意美国代表在 E/CN.4/296 号文件中发表的意见，大意是该条含糊不清，没有必要。在与卡森先生（法国）和胡德先生（澳大利亚）协商后，将法国代表团提出的草案修改如下：

"本公约的任何规定均不得解释为暗示任何国家、团体或个人有权从事任何旨在破坏或损害本公约规定的任何权利和自由的活动或实施任何这样的行动。"

应马利克先生（黎巴嫩）的建议，将"可能是"替换为"应该是"，因

为这是两个表达中比较强的一个。法语文本没有受到影响。

　　……

　　——人权委员会第 123 次会议简要记录（E/CN.4/SR.123）

常健译校

E/CN.4/SR.123

14 June 1949

COMMISSION ON HUMAN RIGHTS
FIFTH SESSION
SUMMARY RECORD OF THE HUNDRED AND TWENTY-THIRD MEETING

Held at Lake Success, New York, on Friday, 10 June 1949, at 2:45 a.m.

Draft Covenant on Human Rights (E/800, E/CN.4/296, E/CN.4/312)
Article20 (Discussion Continued), Articles 17 and Article 18

Chairman: Mr. P. C. Chang (China)

Article 20 (Discussion Continued)

The Chairman reopened the discussion on article 20 and suggested that the Commission should treat the Indian amendment to that article (E/CN.4/312) as its basic working document.

　　…

Article 21

The Chairman opened the discussion on the above and referred members to document E/CN.4/296, which contained the original text of article 21, deleted by the Drafting Committee the previous year, and the text proposed by the USSR.

　　…

The Chairman put to the vote the question whether consideration of article 21should be postponed until article 17 was discussed.

The proposal was adopted by 5 votes to 3, with 4 abstentions.

The Chairman stated that when article 21 was eventually reconsidered, the two texts proposed by the French and USSR representatives would be submitted to the Commission.

Article 22

The Chairman drew attention to the opinion expressed by the United States representative in document E/CN.4/296, to the effect that the article was vague and unnecessary. After consultation with Mr. Cassin (France) and Mr. Hood (Australia), be amended the draft proposed by the French delegation as follows:

"Nothing in this Covenant shall be interpreted as implying for any State, group or individual any right to engage in any activity or to perform any act aimed at the destruction or impairment of any of the rights and freedoms defined herein."

At the suggestion of Mr. Malik (Lebanon) the words "may be" were substituted for the words "shall be", as being the stronger of the two expressions. The French text was not affected.

...

在人权委员会第 124 次会议上的发言

1949 年 6 月 13 日星期一上午 10:30 纽约成功湖

人权公约草案：第 22 条（第 E/CN.4/315 号文件）
审议该公约草案第一部分（第 E/800 号文件）

......

张先生（中国）对该事项的具体内容没有发表任何意见，但他认为，法国的提案在含义上与澳大利亚的备选案文相似，但其措辞更为简单。

......

张先生（中国）支持英国的建议。他指出，起草委员会没有对该款进行充分讨论，也没有打算在一条中包括这两款。他建议，人权委员会可将对该款和英国修正案的审议推迟到稍后日期。

......

主席将推迟审议第 2 段的提议付诸表决。

推迟审议第 22 条第 2 款的提案以 22 票对 9 票、5 票弃权获得通过。

......

张先生（中国）指出，自起草公约案文以来，人权委员会制定了《世界人权宣言》，其中"文明国家"一词在任何地方都被删除，因为它难以界定。因此，他希望人权委员会也能从公约第 1 条中删除"文明国家"的表述。

......

——人权委员会第 124 次会议简要记录（E/CN.4/SR.124）

常健译校

E/CN.4/SR.124
14 June 1949
COMMISSION ON HUMAN RIGHTS
FIFTH SESSION

SUMMARY RECORD OF THE HUNDRED AND TWENTY-FOURTH MEETING

Held at Lake Success, New York, on Thursday, 13 June 1949, at 10:30 a.m.

Draft Covenant on Human Rights: Article 22 (E/CN.4/315)
Consideration of Part I of the draft Covenant (E/800)

...

Mr. Chang (China), without expressing any opinion on the substance of the matter, thought that the French proposal was similar in meaning to the Australian alternative version – the formulation of which was, however, simpler.

...

Mr. Chang (China) supported the United Kingdom suggestion. He pointed out that the paragraph had not been sufficiently discussed in the Drafting Committee, and that there had been no intention that both paragraphs should be included in one article. He suggested that the Commission might postpone consideration of both the paragraph and the United Kingdom amendment until a later date.

...

The Chairman put the proposal to postpone consideration of paragraph 2 to the vote.

The proposal to postpone consideration of paragraph 2 of article 22 was adopted by 22 votes to 9, with 5 abstentions.

...

Mr. Chang (China) pointed out that since the drafting of the text of the Covenant, the Commission had formulated the Declaration in which the term "civilized nations" had been deleted wherever it occurred, because of the difficulty of defining it. He therefore hoped that the Commission would see fit also to delete "civilized nations" from article 1 of the Covenant.

...

在人权委员会第 126 次会议上的发言

1949 年 6 月 14 日星期二上午 10:30 纽约成功湖

审议《国际人权公约（草案）》：第 4 条（第 E/800、E/CN.4/319、E/CN.4/324、E/CN.4/325 号文件）

会议主席：张彭春先生（中国）

主席宣布开始讨论国际公约草案第 4 条以及美国、英国、法国和苏联提交的修正案（第 E/CN.4/319 号、第 E/CN.4/324 号、第 E/CN.4/325 号文件）。

……

主席注意到提案中的三个观点：（1）在某些情况下，某些权利可以被克减；（2）虽然在公共紧急情况下允许克减这些权利，但某些必须始终不受损害的权利应作为例外；（3）任何权利受到克减时，都必须通知联合国秘书长。

第一个和第三个观点似乎具有更一般的性质，而第二个观点涉及列举不应克减的条款。鉴于公约条款的数目顺序尚未确定，而且根据各国政府的评论意见，以后可能会列入更多条款，他建议，人权委员会应推迟就英国提案第 2 款作出任何决定，直到明确公约草案第二部分将包含哪些条款。

……

主席以中国代表的身份发言，他认为，如果有一条款包括拟议的第 4 条中所陈述的观点，该条款就不应出现在第一部分。拟议的条款在处理限制方面的基本特点与第 22 条的内容有明显的相似之处；因此，它应该被置于该条款之前或之后。

人权委员会应该记得在通过《世界人权宣言》之前进行的讨论。人权委员会现在看到的起草委员会案文在日期早于《世界人权宣言》。在起草后者时，人权委员会处理了限制问题，并同意将其置于列举各项权利之后。如果将公约中的限制条款列入第一部分，他将被迫投票反对该条款。

他反对将战争作为允许克减公约的条件。他并不是不考虑未来战争可能发生的实际情况，但如果把战争作为允许克减某些人权的条件，那就意味着承认战争规则的概念，他认为这至少是有问题的。

关于在某些条件下可能允许限制的条款细目，张先生认为，这应该在以后审议，因为在这方面需要审议的条款可能会有所增减。

......

主席将对公约第 4 条的审议推迟到公约第二部分完成后进行的建议付诸表决。

该提案以 7 票反对、2 票赞成、6 票弃权被否决。

会议于下午 1:00 结束。

——人权委员会第 126 次会议简要记录（E/CN.4/SR.126）

常健译校

E/CN.4/SR.126

17 June 1949

COMMISSION ON HUMAN RIGHTS

FIFTH SESSION

SUMMARY RECORD OF THE HUNDRED AND TWENTY-SIXTH MEETING

Held at Lake Success, New York, on Tuesday, 14 June 1949, at 10:30 a.m.

Consideration of the Draft International Covenant on Human Rights: Article 4 (E/800, E/CN.4/272, E/CN.4/319, E/CN.4/324, E/CN.4/325)

Chairman: Mr. Chang (China)

The Chairman opened the discussion on article 4 of the draft international covenant and the amendments submitted to it by the United States of America, the United Kingdom, France, and the Union of Soviet Socialist Republics (E/CN.4/3l9, E/CN.4/324, E/CN.4/325).

...

The Chairman noted three ideas in the proposal: (1) certain rights could be derogated from in certain circumstances; (2) while derogation from those rights was permissible in public emergencies, an exception should be made in respect of certain rights which must always remain unimpaired; (3) whenever there was a derogation from any rights, the Secretary-General must be informed thereof.

The first and third ideas seemed of a more general nature, whereas the second idea involved enumeration of the articles from which there should be no derogation. In view of the fact that the numerical order of the articles of the Covenant had not yet been determined and that more articles might later be included in the light of comments which would be received from Governments, he suggested that the Commission should postpone any decision in respect of paragraph 2 of the United Kingdom proposal until it had become clear what provisions Part II of the draft Covenant would contain.

　　…

The Chairman, speaking as the representative of China, expressed the view that if there were to be an article containing the ideas stated in the proposed article 4, it should not appear in part I. Those ideas were linked by their nature to the terms of article 22, as adopted. The essential character of the proposed article, dealing as it did with limitations, bore a marked resemblance to the subject matter of article 22; it should therefore be placed before or after that article.

The Commission would remember the discussions that had preceded the adoption of the Universal Declaration of Human Rights. The text of the Drafting Committee which was before the Commission was of an earlier date than the Universal Declaration of Human Rights. When, in drafting the latter, the Commission had dealt with the matter of limitations, it had agreed to place them after the enumeration of' rights. If the limitation clause in the Covenant were placed in part I, he would be compelled to vote against the article.

He was opposed to mentioning war as a condition permitting derogation from the Covenant. It was not that he was unrealistic so far as the possibility of future wars was concerned, but to mention war as a condition permitting derogation of certain human rights would involve recognition of the concept of rules of war, which he deemed questionable, at the very least.

With regard to the enumeration of articles the limitation of which might be permitted under certain conditions, Mr. Chang believed that that should be considered later since the articles subject to consideration in that respect might yet be added to or subtracted from.

…

The Chairman put the proposal to postpone consideration of article 4 until part II of the Covenant was completed to the vote.

The proposal was rejected by 7 votes to 2, with 6 abstentions.

The meeting rose at 1:00 p.m.

在人权委员会第 127 次会议上的发言

1949 年 6 月 14 日星期二下午 2:50 纽约成功湖

人权公约草案（第 E/800、E/CN.4/319、E/CN.4/324 号文件）（继续讨论）
第 23 条（第 E/CN.4/296 号文件）

会议主席：张彭春（中国）

《国际人权公约（草案）》
第 4 条（第 E/800 号、第 E/CN.4/3L9 号、第 4/324 号文件）（继续讨论）

……

主席在回答英国和菲律宾代表的发言时同意，除非原则是用文字表述的，否则很难对其进行表决。他指出，如果委员会通过一项临时案文，就可以在下届会议续会期间随时改进案文。因此，委员会成员可立即就以下事项进行表决（1）"战时"克减公约规定的原则；（2）"其他公共紧急情况"的克减原则；（3）苏联修正案；以及如果有机会；（4）英国修正案第 2 款和第 3 款。

……

主席说，他将对印度的第二项提案付诸表决，该提案要求人权委员会就英国的案文作出临时决定，并在处理公约第二部分的工作结束后重新审议这个问题。

……

主席说，他将对苏联对英国案文提出的修正案（E/CN.4/319）付诸表决，然后对英国案文本身进行表决。

……

罗斯福夫人（美国）继续主持会议。

......

张先生（中国）说，他一贯反对在公约草案中列入这一条，并希望人权委员会在仔细考虑后最终决定将该条全文删除。人权委员会应决定保留第 4 条，但应改变其位置；它可能应该被放在第 22 条之后，该条是以一项限制性规定结束的。

......

——人权委员会第 127 次会议简要记录（E/CN.4/SR.127）

常健译校

E/CN.4/SR.127

17 June 1949

COMMISSION ON HUMAN RIGHTS
FIFTH SESSION
SUMMARY RECORD OF THE HUNDRED AND TWENTY-SEVENTH MEETING

Held at Lake Success, New York, on Tuesday, 14 June 1949, at 2:50 p.m.

Draft Covenant on Human Rights (E/800, E/CN.4/319, E/CN.4/324)
Articles 23 (E/CN.4/296)

Chairman: Mr. Chang (China)

Draft International Covenant on Human Rights
Article 4 (E/800, E/CN.4/3l9, E/CN.4/324) (Discussion Continued)

...

The Chairman, replying to the remarks of the United Kingdom and Philippine representatives, agreed that principles could hardly be voted upon unless they were formulated in words. He pointed out that, if the Commission adopted a provisional text, it would remain free to improve it during its next succeeding session. The members of the Commission could, therefore, proceed to vote immediately on (1) the principle of derogations from provisions of the Covenant "in time of war"; (2) the principle of derogations in the event of "other public emergency"; (3) the USSR amendment; and (4) paragraphs 2 and 3 of the United Kingdom amendment, should occasion arise.

...

The Chairman said he would take a vote on the second Indian proposal that the Commission should take a provisional decision on the United Kingdom text and reconsider the question when it had finished dealing with the second part of the Covenant.

...

The Chairman said that he would take a vote on the USSR amendment to the United Kingdom text (E/CN.4/319) and then on the United Kingdom text itself.

...

Mrs. Roosevelt (United States of America) resumed the Chair.

...

Mr. Chang (China) said that he had always opposed the inclusion of such an article in the draft Covenant, and expressed the hope that the Commission would ultimately decide, after careful consideration, to omit the article in its entirety. Should the Commission decide to maintain article 4, however, its position should be changed; it might perhaps be inserted after article 22, which concluded with a limitative provision.

...

在人权委员会第 129 次会议上的发言

1949 年 6 月 9 日星期四上午 10:30 纽约成功湖

人权公约草案（第 E/800、E/CN.4/296、E/CN.4/328、E/CN.4/337 号文件）（继续讨论）
第 23 条（继续讨论）

......

第 17 条

......

张先生（中国）指出，在联合国主持下制定的所有公约中都出现了有关殖民地的条款，但对必须承认所有人民享有相同权利和自由的普遍认识来说，它并没有产生多少变革性影响。

然而，就人权公约而言，人权委员会似乎不能仅限于复述先前通过的条款。人权公约的目标与在新闻国际传播和纠正权方面通过的公约完全不同，那些公约主要涉及行政当局行使的权力，在那些公约中托管领土或非自治领土的人民所扮演的角色是被动的。然而，在人权方面，他们的角色应该是非常积极的。因此，公约应如《世界人权宣言》已经明确宣布人权普遍性原则那样，以更直接的方式适用于这些民族。

因此，最好考虑一个新的表述，在第一部分中复述美国修正案的第二项，该项要求签约国尽快采取必要措施，以便在其负有国际关系责任的领土上执行公约。考虑到许多领土已经享有自行决定这些事项的权利，还应列入关于领土同意的限制条款。该条的其余部分可能会对某些例外作出规定，签约国为这些例外的正当性进行辩护，其理由必须是它们符合宪法文本所产生的真正需要。

起草这一条款会产生一些棘手的宪法问题。应当首先由有关问题的专家对这些问题进行研究。因此，中国代表建议，应将第 25 条的案文连同所有相关的修正和评论转交各国政府，在各代表团能够对其采取明确态度之前，不应就此作出任何决定。

……

主席请委员会就中国的提案进行表决，该提案要求推迟就第 25 条作出决定，并向各国政府转交该条草案、与该条有关的所有提案和修正案，以及人权委员会第五届会议讨论有关问题的会议记录。

该提案以 7 票对 4 票、2 票弃权获得通过。

会议于下午 6:30 结束。

——人权委员会第 129 次会议简要记录（E/CN.4/SR.129）

常健译校

E/CN.4/SR.129
27 June 1949

COMMISSION ON HUMAN RIGHTS
FIFTH SESSION
SUMMARY RECORD OF THE HUNDRED AND TWENTY-NINTH MEETING

Held at Lake Success, New York, on Wednesday, 15 June 1949, at 2:30 p.m.

Draft Covenant on Human Rights (E/800, E/CN.4/296, E/CN.4/328, E/CN.4/337) (Discussion Continued)
Articles 23(Discussion Continued)

…

Mr. Chang (China) noted that the colonial clause had appeared in all the conventions prepared under the auspices of the United Nations, but that it had not effected much change in general appreciation of the necessity for recognizing the same rights and liberties for all peoples.

In the case of the Covenant on Human Rights, however, the Commission could not, it seemed, confine itself to reproducing one of the previously adopted clauses. The object of the Covenant was completely different from that of a convention such as had been adopted in connexion with the international transmission of news and the right of correction, which dealt primarily with the rights exercised by the Administering Authority and where the role played by the peoples of the Trust Territories or Non-Self-Governing territories was passive. In respect of human rights, however, their role should be eminently an active one. For that reason the Covenant should apply in a more direct manner to such peoples, the more so as the Declaration had already expressly proclaimed the principle of the universality of human rights.

It would, therefore, be well to consider a new formula which would reproduce, in the first part, the second sub-paragraph of the United States amendment which would require the signatory State to take the necessary measures as soon as possible with a view to the implementation of the Covenant in territories for whose international relations it was responsible. The limitation clause regarding the consent of the territories could also be included in view of the fact that a number of them already enjoyed the right to decide such matters themselves. The rest of the article might make provision for certain exceptions which the signatory State would have to justify on the grounds that they met a real necessity arising out of a constitutional text.

The drafting of such an article raised a number of knotty questions of constitutional law which should first be studied by experts on the matter. The representative of China therefore suggested that the text of article 25 should be transmitted to Governments with all pertinent amendments and comments and that no decision should be taken on it until the various delegations were able to adopt a definite attitude towards it.

...

The Chairman asked the Commission to vote on the Chinese proposal to postpone decision on article 25, and to transmit to the Governments the draft of the article, all proposals and amendments to it, pertaining to it as well as the records of the meetings of the fifth session of the Commission at which the article in question had been discussed.

The proposal was adopted by 7 votes to 4, with 2 abstentions.

The meeting rose at 6:30 p.m.

在人权委员会第 131 次会议上的发言

1949 年 6 月 16 日星期四下午 2:40 纽约成功湖

人权公约草案：关于经济和社会权利的补充条款（第 E/CN.4/313 和 E/CN.4/333 号文件）（继续讨论）

......

张先生（中国）担心丹麦的决议草案可能不如初看上去那么令人满意，它可能会回避真正的问题，即将经济和社会权利纳入公约。在他看来，提案中规定的调查将只涉及与执行《世界人权宣言》第 22 至 27 条有关的国际行动；但是，在就将经济和社会权利纳入公约作出任何决定之前，人权委员会应设法获得关于政府层面为执行《世界人权宣言》第 22 至 27 条而采取的措施的信息。因此，为了改进丹麦的决议草案，他建议将"或在该领域的其他机构"改为"与实现……有关的"。

他还建议，在"专门机构"之前的"他们的"一词应改为定冠词"the"。

......

——人权委员会第 131 次会议简要记录（E/CN.4/SR.131）

常健译校

E/CN.4/SR.131

27 June 1949

COMMISSION ON HUMAN RIGHTS

FIFTH SESSION

SUMMARY RECORD OF THE HUNDRED AND THIRTY-FIRST MEETING

Held at Lake Success, New York, on Thursday, 16 June 1949, at 2:40 a.m.

Draft Covenant on Human Rights: Additional Articles Concerning Economic and Social Rights (E/CN.4/313, E/CN.4/333) (Discussion Continued)

...

Mr. Chang (China) was afraid the Danish draft resolution might be less satisfactory than it appeared at first sight and might by-pass the real question, which was the inclusion of the economic and social rights in the Covenant. It seemed to him that the survey provided for in the proposal would be concerned exclusively with international action in connexion with the implementation of articles 22 to 27 of the Declaration; but, before taking any decision regarding the inclusion of the economic and social rights in the Covenant, the Commission should try to obtain Information on measures taken at the governmental level for the implementation of articles 22 to 27 of the Declaration. In order to improve the Danish draft resolution, therefore, he proposed that the words "or other bodies... within the scope" should be replaced by the words "in connexion with the realization of".

He also proposed that the word "their" before "specialized agencies" should be replaced by the word "the".

...

在人权委员会第 133 次会议上的发言

1949 年 6 月 9 日星期五下午 2:30 纽约成功湖

申诉权（第 E/CN.4/316 和 E/CN.4/347 号文件）

......

张先生（中国）投了弃权票，因为如果要适用《世界人权宣言》和后来的公约，首先应该尽一切努力找到一些切实可行的措施来促进国家间的合作。因此，应减少相互指责和摩擦的可能性。该决议过分强调消极行动。

......

——人权委员会第 133 次会议简要记录（E/CN.4/SR.133）

常健译校

E/CN.4/SR.133
28 June 1949

COMMISSION ON HUMAN RIGHTS
FIFTH SESSION
SUMMARY RECORD OF THE HUNDRED AND THIRTY-THIRD MEETING

Held at Lake Success, New York, on Friday, 17 June 1949, at 2:30 p.m.

Right of Petition (E/CN.4/316, E/CN.4/347)

…

Mr. Chang (China) had abstained because, if the Declaration on Human Rights and later the Covenant were to be applied, every effort should first be made to find some practical measures to promote cooperation between nations. Any possibility of mutual recrimination and friction should therefore be reduced. The resolution gave too much weight to negative action.

…

在人权委员会第 134 次会议上的发言

1949 年 6 月 20 日星期一上午 10:30 纽约成功湖

第五届人权委员会报告草案（第 E/CN.4/332 号、第 E/CN.4/332/Corr.1 号、第 E/CN. 4/332/Add.1 号、第 E/CN.4/332/Add.2 号、第 E/CN.4/332/Add.3 号、第 E/CN.4/332/Add.4 号文件）

……

张先生（中国）希望秘书处也能尽快将报告翻译成中文。

……

张先生（中国）说，他的候补者查先生名字的首字母缩写是"H"。

……

《人权年鉴》第十一章

张先生（中国）希望决议执行部分第 1 段提到的语言按照《联合国宪章》中出现的顺序排列，即"中文、俄文、西班牙文"。

……

张先生（中国）说，起草委员会已将乌克兰的提案（第 E/CN. 4/AC. 8/1 号文件）和危地马拉的提案（第 E/CN. 4/AC. 8/2 号文件）连同其报告一并转交人权委员会。因此，第十一章第一段可以提到这三个文件。

如此作出决定。

经修正的十一章获得通过。

……

附件IV
决议草案 C 所涉经费问题

......

张先生（中国）重申，在口译和笔译方面，五种官方语言不应被区别对待。

......

——人权委员会第 134 次会议简要记录（E/CN.4/SR.134）

常健译校

E/CN.4/SR.134
28 June 1949

COMMISSION ON HUMAN RIGHTS
FIFTH SESSION
SUMMARY RECORD OF THE HUNDRED AND THIRTY
FOURTH MEETING

Held at Lake Success, New York, on Monday, 20 June 1949, at 10:30 a.m.

Draft Report of the Fifth Session of the Commission on Human Rights
(E/CN.4/332, E/CN.4/332/Corr.1, E/CN. 4/332/Add.1, E/CN.4/332/Add.2, E/CN.4/332/Add.3, E/CN.4/332/Add.4)

…

Mr. Chang (China) hoped that the Secretariat would also see that the report was translated with as little delay into Chinese.

…

Mr. Chang (China) said that the initial of his alternate, Mr. Cha, was "H".

…

Chapter XI: Yearbook on Human Rights

Mr. Chang (China) would have preferred the languages mentioned in paragraph 1 of the operative part of the resolution, to have been listed in the order in which they appeared in the Charter, namely: "Chinese, Russian, Spanish".

...

Mr. Chang (China) said that the Committee had transmitted the proposals submitted by Ukraine (E/CN.4/AC.8/1) and by Guatemala (E/CN.4/AC.8/2) to the Commission together with its report. The first paragraph of Chapter XI could therefore mention all three documents.

It was so decided.

Chapter XI, as amended, was adopted.

...

Annex IV
Financial implications of draft resolution C

...

Mr. Chang (China) requested that no distinction should be made between the five official languages, as regards both interpretation and translation.

...

人权委员会第 135 次会议简要记录

1949 年 6 月 20 日星期一下午 2:30 纽约成功湖

第五届人权委员会报告草案（第 E/CN.4/332、E/CN.4/332/Corr.1、E/CN. 4/332/Add.1、E/CN.4/332/Add.2、E/CN.4/332/Add.3、E/CN.4/332/Add.4 号文件）（继续讨论）

......

主席对人权委员会成员在本届会议期间的合作表示感谢，特别要感谢在她缺席期间经常主持会议的副主席张彭春先生和卡森先生、工作尚未完成的报告员以及协助委员会工作的秘书处成员。

会议于下午 6:45 结束。

——人权委员会第 135 次会议简要记录（E/CN.4/SR.135）

常健译校

E/CN.4/SR.135

29 June 1949

COMMISSION ON HUMAN RIGHTS
FIFTH SESSION
SUMMARY RECORD OF THE HUNDRED AND THIRTY-FIFTH MEETING

Held at Lake Success, New York, on Monday, 20 June 1949, at 2:30 p.m.

Draft Report of the Fifth Session of the Commission on Human Rights
(E/CN.4/332, E/CN.4/332/Corr.1, E/CN. 4/332/Add.1, E/CN.4/332/Add.2, E/CN.4/332/Add.3, E/CN.4/332/Add.4) (Discussion Continued)

...

The Chairman expressed her gratitude to the members of the Commission for their co-operation during the session and, in particular, wished to thank the Vice-Presidents, Mr. Chang and Mr. Cassin, who had so often presided in her absence, the Rapporteur, whose work was yet to be completed, and the members of the Secretariat who had assisted the Commission in its work.

The meeting rose at 6:45 p.m.

1950 年

联合国人权委员会第六届会议

人权委员会第 136 次会议简要记录

1950 年 3 月 27 日星期一上午 11:00 纽约成功湖

苏联提交的关于中国在委员会中的代表权的决议草案（第 E/CN.4/369 号文件）

1. 察拉普金先生（苏联）回顾了最近在中国发生的事件。国民党反动集团腐化堕落，在政治、经济和军事上都遭受了失败，被逐出中国大陆。

2. 中华人民共和国中央政府目前对中国领土及其 4.5 亿居民行使一切政府管理职能，并正式通知联合国由国民党代表来代表中国人民是非法的，要求将他们驱逐出联合国。与此同时，中央人民政府行使其作为联合国会员国的合法权利，任命了自己的安全理事会和经济及社会理事会代表。

3. 苏联代表团一再申明，支持中国中央人民政府的合法要求，不承认国民党代表是中国的代表。也认为国民党代表的存在是非法的，并要求将他们驱逐出去。

4. 然而，中国人民在联合国的代表权和参加联合国工作的权利，却被国民党集团的少数代表篡夺了，而国民党的代表只能以他们自己的名义发言。这种情况是前所未有，并且已经持续了四个多月，必须毫不拖延地结束这种局面。为此，国民党的代表应被驱逐出所有联合国机构，而中国的真正代表应被允许占据他们有权占据的位置。有鉴于此，苏联代表团提交了一项决议草案（第 E/CN.4/369 号文件），根据该决议草案，人权委员会将决定取消国民党集团代表的委员会成员资格。

5. 最后，他说，只要国民党的代表继续担任人权委员会的成员，苏联代表团就不会参加委员会的工作。

6. 主席宣读了议事规则第44条,并裁定苏联的决议草案不符合程序。

7. 经济及社会理事会第二届会议决定,在当选人权委员会成员的政府提名其代表后,这些代表应由理事会加以确认。中国政府提名了张先生,经济及社会理事会确认他为人权委员会成员。

8. 因此,如果苏联代表希望对张先生参加人权委员会的权利质疑,他应该向经济及社会理事会而不是人权委员会提出这个问题。

9. 察拉普金先生(苏联)说,他提出的问题不能用程序性理由来加以回避。这是一个具有重大政治意义的问题,影响到联合国的所有活动。

10. 为了联合国组织本身的利益,察拉普金先生敦促对他的决议草案进行讨论和表决。的确,某些国家——特别是美国——在中国问题上采取了与苏联不同的政策,但只是声称苏联的决议草案不符合程序,这就是一种武断和不公正的程序。

11. 主席指出,她的裁决受到质疑,因此要求根据议事规则进行表决。**主席的裁决以 13 票对 2 票获得支持。**

12.张先生(中国)说,这项提交给委员会的提案是在意料之中的。他认为无法容忍这些发表的言论,这种千篇一律的重复已经成为一种陈词滥调。

13. 承认或不承认政府的问题超出了人权委员会的职权范围。中国驻联合国代表团代表中国国民政府。尽管冲突在中国肆虐,但它是唯一合法的政府。

14. 中国代表团一贯维护中国人民的利益,表达中国人民的愿望。在联合国内广泛存在的紧张局势是由苏联代表撤出联合国各机构造成的,而不是由中国的冲突造成的。这种对中国代表的拒绝为报纸头条提供了素材,但并没有促进联合国的进步。

15. 他呼吁人权委员会不要偏离其宗旨,而是继续其工作。

16. 察拉普金先生（苏联）坚持认为，苏联的提议是公正和必要的。主席的裁决造成了这样一种局面，使人权委员会的工作无法正常进行。

17. 主席也是美国代表；她对苏联提议的反对只是美国政府企图利用联合国来达到其自身目的的延续，这不仅违背了联合国自身的利益，也与维护和平背道而驰。其目的是路人皆知的：令人痛恨的国民党集团被赶出中国领土，它正在寻求对中国人民进行报复。美国飞机被用来实施这些轰炸。美国政府向台湾输送了包括坦克在内的武器，以使国民党集团能够在这个最后的避难地站稳脚跟。

18. 主席提醒苏联代表，人权委员会不是发表宣传演说的适当场所。她请他结束讲话。

19. 察拉普金先生（苏联）回顾说，1950 年 3 月 23 日，加拿大阿戈诺特船运公司的一艘 10000 吨级运输船载着一批坦克从温哥华前往台湾。

20. 除此之外，美国推行的对中华人民共和国的仇恨政策，正在联合国反映出来，它有损联合国的工作。

21. 所有维持腐败政权的企图都注定要失败。历史的进程不可逆转；绝不能再让穷兵黩武的反动集团在中国人民头上作威作福了。

22. 只要不把国民党代表驱逐出人权委员会，苏联代表团就不会参加人权委员会的工作。此外，苏联代表团也不承认人权委员会在国民党代表的参与下所作出决定的有效性。

苏联代表离开了会议室。

……

34. 张先生（中国）回顾说，中国人民已经明确表示，他们永远不会放弃独立和主权。他们决不会屈服于来自任何一方的外国统治。完全支持主席的决定。这个问题已经非常清楚地说明了：苏联代表并不关心由谁在联合国代表中国的问题，而只是要把自己的方针强加给人权委员会。

......

选举主席

应主席邀请，劳吉尔先生（助理秘书长）主持会议。

41. 劳吉尔先生（助理秘书长）请人权委员会就美国代表罗斯福夫人当选委员会主席的提议进行表决。

罗斯福夫人（美国）以鼓掌方式当选为主席。

罗斯福夫人（美国）恢复主持会议。

选举副主席

42. 主席请人权委员会就中国代表张彭春先生当选第一副主席的提议进行表决。

43. 杰夫列莫维奇先生（南斯拉夫）重申，南斯拉夫代表团反对选举中国代表为副主席。

44. 主席说，在这种情况下，将根据议事规则第 62 条以无记名投票方式进行表决。

投票以无记名投票方式进行。

应主席要求，马利克先生（黎巴嫩）和圣克鲁兹先生（智利）担任计票员。

张彭春先生（中国）以 12 票对 0 票、2 票弃权当选第一副主席。

45. 主席随后请人权委员会就法国代表卡森先生当选第二副主席的提议进行表决。

一致选举卡森先生（法国）为第二副主席。

选举报告员

46. 主席请人权委员会就选举黎巴嫩代表马利克先生担任报告员的提议进行表决。

一致选举马利克先生（黎巴嫩）担任报告员。

......

会议时间表

......

在开始详细审查公约草案之前，主席请想作一般性发言的人权委员会成员马上告知主席。

张彭春先生（中国）指出，各代表团已有三年多的时间表明立场。人权委员会无疑希望在下次会议就开始起草公约草案的最后案文。

如此作出决定。

会议于下午 12:45 结束。

——人权委员会第 136 次会议简要记录（E/CN.4/SR.136）

常健译校

E/CN.4/SR.136

3 April 1950

COMMISSION ON HUMAN RIGHTS
SIXTH SESSION
SUMMARY RECORD OF THE HUNDRED AND THIRTY-SIXTH MEETING

Held at Lake Success, New York, on Monday, 27 March 1950, at 11:00 a.m.

Draft Resolution Submitted by the USSR Concerning the Representation of China on the Commission (E/CN.4/369)

1. Mr. Tsarapkin (Union of Soviet Socialist Republics) recalled the events which had recently taken place In China and which had culminated in the establishment of the People's Republic of China. Corrupt and demoralized, the reactionary clique of the Kuomintang had suffered political, economic and military defeat and been driven from the mainland of China.

2. The Central Grvernmant of the People's Republic of China was currently exercising all the functions of government over the territory of China and its 450 million inhabitants. That Government had officially informed the United Nations that it did not recognize the representatives of the Kuomintang as representing the Chinese people. It had stated that their presence was illegal and asked that they should be excluded. At the same time, exercising its legitimate rights as a State Member of the organization, the Central People's Government had appointed its own representatives to the Security Council and the Economic and Social Council.

3. The USSR delegation had repeatedly affirmed that it supported the legitimate request of the Central People's Government of China and that it did not recognize the agents of the Kuomintang as representative of China. It too thought that their presence was illegal and asked that they should be excluded.

4. Yet the right of the Chinese people to be represented in the United Nations and to take part in its work had been usurped by a small number of representatives of the Kuomintang group, who could speak only in their own name. That was an unprecedented situation which had already lasted for over four months and which must be brought to an end without delay. For that purpose the representatives of the Kuomintang should be excluded from all United Nations organs and the true representatives of China permitted to occupy the places to which they were entitled. That being so, the USSR delegation was submitting a draft resolution (E/CN.4/369) according to which the Commission on Human Rights would decide to exclude the representative of the Kuomintang group from membership of the Commission.

5. In conclusion, he said that his delegation would not take part in the work of the Commission so long as the representative of the Kuomintang continued to sit on that body.

6. The Chairman read rule 44 of the rules of procedure, and ruled that the USSR draft resolution was out of order.

7. At its second session, the Economic and Social Council had decided that after the Governments elected to the Commission on Human Rights had nominated their representatives, those representatives should be confirmed by the Council itself. The Government of China had nominated Mr. Chang and the Economic and Social Council had confirmed him as a member of the Commission on Human Rights.

8. Accordingly, if the representative of the USSR wished to challenge the right of Mr. Chang to sit on the Commission on Human Rights, he should raise the matter in the Economic and Social Council and not in the Commission.

9. Mr. Tsarapkin (Union of Soviet Socialist Republics) stated that the question which he had raised could not be evaded by procedural arguments. It was a question of considerable political importance which affected all the

activities of the United Nations.

10. In the interests of the organizations itself, Mr. Tsarapkin urged that his draft resolution should be discussed and voted upon. It was true that certain States – particularly the United States of America – followed a different policy from the USSR on the Chinese question, but merely to state that the USSR draft resolution was out of order was an arbitrary and unjust procedure.

11. The Chairman noted that her ruling had been challenged and called for a vote, in accordance with the rules of procedure.

The ruling of the Chairman was upheld by 13 votes to 2.

12. Mr. Chang (China) remarked that the proposal which had been laid before the Commission had not been unexpected. He considered it impossible to tolerate statements such as those which had been made, and which, moreover, had become hackneyed through stereotyped repetition.

13. The question of the recognition or non-recognition of Governments was outside the scope and competence of the Commission. The Chinese delegation to the United Nations represented the National Government of China. Notwithstanding the conflict which was raging in China, it was the only legal Government.

14. The Chinese delegation had always defended the interests of the Chinese people and voiced their aspirations. The tension which prevailed in the United Nations was caused by the withdrawal of the representatives of the USSR from its various organs rather than by the Chinese conflict. That refusal provided material for newspaper headlines; it did not contribute to the progress of the United Nations.

15. He appealed to the Commission not to allow itself to be diverted from its purposes but to continue its work.

16. Mr. Tsarapkin (Union of Soviet Socialist Republics) maintained that the USSR proposal had been just and necessary. The Chairman's ruling had created a situation which made it impossible for the work of the Commission to follow its normal course.

17. The Chairman was also the representative of the United States of America; her objections to the USSR proposal were merely a continuation of the

attempts of the United States Government to use the United Nations to further its own ends, which were contrary to the interests of the Organization and to the maintenance of peace. Those ends were well known: the detested Kuomintang clique, which had been driven from Chinese territory, was seeking to wreak vengeance on the Chinese people. American aeroplanes were used to carry out those bombings. The United States Government was sending arms, including tanks, in order to enable the Kuomintang clique to entrench itself in that last refuge.

18. The Chairman reminded the USSR representative that the Commission on Human Rights was not the appropriate place for propaganda speeches. She asked him to conclude his remarks.

19. Mr. Tsarapkin (Union of Soviet Socialist Republics) recalled that on 23 March 1950, a 10,000-ton ship belonging to the Canada Argonaut Shipping Company had left Vancouver for Formosa with a cargo of tanks.

20. More than that, the policy of the United States, a policy of hatred for the People's Republic of China, was being reflected in the United Nations, to the detriment of the work of the Organization.

21. All those attempts to sustain a corrupt regime were doomed to failure. The course of history could not be turned back; a militarist clique could not once again be forced upon the Chinese people.

22. The delegation of the USSR would not take part in the work of the Commission so long as the Kuomintang representative bad not been excluded from it. Moreover, it would not recognize the validity of decisions taken by the Commission with the participation of the Kuomintang representative.

The USSR representative left the conference room.

…

34. Mr. Chang (China) recalled that the Chinese people had made it clear that they would never renounce their independence and sovereign rights. They would never submit to foreign domination from any quarter. Wholeheartedly supported the Chairman's decision. The problem had been stated in perfectly clear terms: the representative of the USSR had not been concerned with the question of who was to represent China in the United Nations, but with imposing

a specific policy on the Commission.

…

Election of the Chairman

At the invitation of the Chairman, Mr. Laugier (Assistant Secretary-General) took the Chair.

41. Mr. Laugier (Assistant Secretary-General) asked the Commission to vote on the proposal that Mrs. Roosevelt, representative of the United States of America, should be elected Chairman of the Commission.

Mrs. Roosevelt (United States of America) was elected Chairman by acclamation.

Mrs. Roosevelt (United States of America) resumed the Chair.

Election of Vice-Chairmen

42. The Chairman asked the Commission to vote on the proposal that Mr. Chang, representative of China, should be elected first Vice-Chairman.

43. Mr. Jevremovic (Yugoslavia) reiterated that his delegation opposed the election of the representative of China as Vice-Chairman.

44. The Chairman said that in the circumstances a vote would be taken by secret ballot in accordance with rule 62 of the rules of procedure.

A vote was taken by secret ballot.

At the request of the Chairman, Mr. Malik (Lebanon) and Mr. Santa Cruz (Chile) acted as tellers.

Mr. Chang (China) was elected first Vice-Chairman by 12 votes to none, with 2 abstentions.

45. The Chairman then requested the Commission to vote on the proposal that Mr. Cassin, representative of France, should be elected second Vice-Chairman.

Mr. Cassin (France) was unanimously elected second Vice-Chairman.

Election of the Rapporteur

46. The Chairman requested the Commission to vote on the proposal that

Mr. Malik, representative of Lebanon, should be elected Rapporteur.

Mr. Malik (Lebanon) was unanimously elected Rapporteur.

...

Time-Table of Meetings

...

The Chairman asked members of the Commission who intended to make statements of a general character before beginning the detailed examination of the Draft Covenant to inform the Chair immediately of the fact.

Mr. Chang (China) pointed out that the various delegations had had more than three years in which to state their positions. The Commission would no doubt desire to start drafting the final text of the draft covenant at its next meeting.

It was so decided.

The meeting rose at 12:45 p.m.

在人权委员会第 137 次会议上的发言

1950 年 3 月 29 日星期三上午 11:00 纽约成功湖

委员会会议简要记录

......

27. 张先生（中国）指出，在目前阶段，就构成公约草案第一部分的一般性条款交换意见，无疑是非常有用的，前提是人权委员会在后期给予改变其意见的机会，因为由于印度和黎巴嫩代表提出的理由，很难在人权委员会确定公约草案第二部分的一般要旨之前对这些条款作出最后决定。

28. 在这种情况下，张先生建议首先就序言和前四条进行一般性辩论。然后，委员会将研究公约草案第二部分的规定，并根据一般性辩论过程中出现的原则进行讨论。然后，再回到序言和一般性条款，并在充分考虑的基础上对其作出决定。

......

对序言的一般性讨论

......

54. 张先生（中国）认为，人权委员会从讨论序言开始做得很好，因为这样的讨论将使它能够理解它正在准备的公约的范围和真正性质。事实上，这是人权委员会应该努力解决的基本问题。在过去，该公约被认为是《国际人权宪章》最重要的部分，《世界人权宣言》将成为其序言。然而，《世界人权宣言》自通过以来，其重要性和意义越来越大，超出了起草者的期望。它现在已经成为一份历史性文件，它将超越政治动荡，任何事情，甚至公约，都不能减损或削弱它的重要性。在这种情况下，正在制定的公约的具体目的是什么？它是为了确保落实《世界人权宣言》中宣布的权利和基本自由。显然，与《世界人权宣言》被正确地描述为具有"普遍性"不同，公约只能具有国际性，因为它应该约束签约国。但是，立即出现的问题是，鉴于国际法发展的当前阶段，如何确保有效执行公约？在没有一部保障其实施的普遍宪法的情况下，可以预见的是，各国将试图通过依据其主权来逃避其责任，并因未能适用公约的规定而相互指责。

55. 尽管如此，至少应该做的是提请各国政府注意《联合国宪章》规定的它们在人权和基本自由方面的义务。考虑到这一目的，张先生认为，公约的序言部分可能会重申《世界人权宣言》中导言条款结尾部分所宣布的内容。

56. 此外，澳大利亚代表在其草案中删除了涉及《联合国宪章》一般原则的内容，张先生认为这是正确的，《世界人权宣言》从未提及原则；它只提到了具体的权利和自由。必须尽一切努力避免关于原则的声明，因为各国总是可以提出这样的论点，即不能在所有情况下都使实践符合原则。因此，澳大利亚草案非常正确地强调了一个事实，即通过签署《联合国宪章》，各国承诺促进普遍尊重人权。

57. 张先生认为，澳大利亚代表团提案中序言的执行部分的措辞，应使其不被解释为缔约方不保证公约中未明确规定的权利。此外，张先生并不特别喜欢澳大利亚文本中的"同意以下条款"这一短语：他更愿意用"同意遵行……"或类似于法语文本中出现的短语来代替。

......

——人权委员会第 137 次会议简要记录（E/CN.4/SR.137）

常健译校

E/CN.4/SR.137

5 April 1950

COMMISSION ON HUMAN RIGHTS
SIXTH SESSION
SUMMARY RECORD OF THE HUNDRED AND THIRTY-SEVENTH MEETING

Held at Lake Success, New York, on Wednesday, 29 March 1950, at 11:00 a.m.

Summary Records of the Meetings of the Commission

...

27. Mr. Chang (China) pointed out that an exchange of views on the general articles which would constitute part I of the draft covenant would undoubtedly exceedingly useful at the current stage, provided that the Commission were given

the possibility of changing its opinion at a later date, for it would be difficult, on account of the reasons given by the representatives of India and Lebanon, to take a final decision on those articles before the Commission had established the general purport of part II of the draft covenant.

28. In the circumstances, Mr. Chang suggested that a general debate should first take place on the preamble and the first four articles. The Commission would then study the provisions of part II of the draft covenant, basing its discussion on the principles which would have emerged in the course of the general debate. It would then return to the preamble and the general articles and take its decision upon them on the basis of ripe consideration.

...

General Discussion of the preamble

...

54. Mr. Chang (China) thought that the Commission had done well to begin by discussing the preamble because that discussion would enable it to understand the scope and the true nature of the covenant which it was preparing. That was in fact the essential point which the Commission should try to settle. In the past, the covenant had been considered the most important part of the Charter of Human Rights and the Declaration was to constitute a kind of preamble to it. However, ever since its adopticon, the Declaration had assumed more and more importance and meaning, exceeding the hopes of those who had drafted it. It had now become an historic document which would outlive political disturbances and nothing, not even the covenant, could diminish or weaken its significance. In the circumstances, what was the specific purpose of the covenant which was being prepared? It was to ensure the implementation of the rights and fundamental freedoms proclaimed in the Declaration. It was clear that the covenant, unlike the Declaration which had rightly been described as "universal", could only have an international character inasmuch as it was supposed to bind the signatory States. But the question which immediately, arose was how to ensure the effective implementation of the covenant, given the present stage of development of international law? In the absence of an universal constitution which would guarantee its implementation, it could be anticipated

that States would seek to evade their responsibilities by invoking their sovereignty, and would reproach one another for failure to apply the provisions of the covenant.

55. That being so, the least that should be done was to draw the attention of Governments to their duties under the Charter in respect of human rights and fundamental freedoms. With that purpose in mind, Mr. Chang thought that the preamble of the covenant might reiterate the end of the introductory clause of the proclamation as it appeared in the Declaration.

56. Moreover, Mr. Chang thought that the representative of Australia had been right in deleting any reference in his draft to the general principles of the Charter, The Universal Declaration never mentioned principles; it spoke only of specific rights and freedoms. Every effort must be made to avoid statements concerning principles because States could always use the argument that practice could not in all cases be made to conform to principles. The Australian draft therefore quite rightly emphasized the fact that, by signing the Charter, States had undertaken to promote universal respect for human rights.

57. Mr. Chang thought that the operative part of the preamble proposed by the Australian delegation should be drafted so that it could not be construed to mean that the rights which were not specifically stated in the covenant were not guaranteed by the contracting parties. Furthermore, Mr. Chang did not especially like the phrase "agree on the following articles" in the Australian text: he would prefer to replace it with "agree to give effect…" or a similar phrase such as that which appeared in the French text.

...

在人权委员会第 138 次会议上的发言

1950 年 3 月 29 日星期三上下 2:30 纽约成功湖

《国际人权公约（草案）》（第 E/CN.4/1371、E/CN.4/365、E/CN.4/353/Add.10、E/CN.4/370、E/CN.4/374、E/CN.4/375、E/CN.4/379、E/CN.4/380 号文件）（续）

第 1 条：一般性辩论

......

12. 张先生（中国）支持普遍认为的观点，即第 1 条应予删除，其中可能包含的任何有价值的想法应在进一步审议后放在序言部分。

13. 他认为，鉴于人权问题的争议性，公约草案与《世界人权宣言》一样，不应具体提及人权的起源。

......

第 2 条：一般性辩论

......

51. 张先生（中国）保留对迄今为止在讨论中作出的许多重要和有启发性的贡献进行更全面讨论的权利，他表示，他准备接受澳大利亚的建议，即用"公认"一词代替"定义"一词。他也可以接受添加"尊重和"这两个词，正如法国所建议的那样。

52. 英国对第 2 条第 1 款的修正提出了一个最重要的问题。尽管正在审议的文件被称为盟约，但实际上它是一项条约或公约，与以往所有此类文书的不同之处在于，它将涵盖各种各样的主题。而公约通常只涉及一个主题。如果只是为了避免未来的失望和幻灭，那么应该记住，本公约草案旨在涵盖的主题比任何其他主题都多。

53. 各国立法机构如何批准这样一项复杂的公约草案，这是公认的最困难的问题，但绝非毫无希望。

54. 英国的修正案是切实可行的，因为它提出了对特定条款进行具体保留的可能性。然而，他想知道，哪个国家会坦诚地承认自己的立法可能达不到公约草案中规定的标准。他认为这个问题非常困难，建议认真研究这一点。作为一个原则问题，他赞成对特定问题作出某种具体保留的规定，但目前不会就执行该原则的方法作出承诺。

55. 另一个需要铭记的事实是，各国在立法和宪法实践方面存在差异。第 2 条第一款第二句可能可以接受。他可以理解那些对"合理的时间"这个短语表示怀疑的人，但他认为，确定时间限制也会带来困难。他建议，这一问题应暂时搁置，人权委员会应研究公约草案第二部分中的每一条，同时铭记所提到的要点。然后，人权委员会可以回到第一部分，很可能会发现，它对第二部分的审议使其更容易找到一个合适的案文。

......

——人权委员会第 138 次会议简要记录（E/CN.4/SR.138）

常健译校

E/CN.4/SR.138

6 April 1950

COMMISSION ON HUMAN RIGHTS
SIXTH SESSION
SUMMARY RECORD OF THE HUNDRED AND THIRTY-EIGHTH MEETING

Held at Lake Success, New York, on Wednesday, 29 March 1950, at 2:30 p.m.

Draft International Covenant on Human Rights (E/CN.4/1371, E/CN.4/365, E/CN.4/353/Add.10, E/CN.4/370, E/CN.4/374, E/CN.4/375, E/CN.4/379, E/CN.4/380) (Continues)

Article 1: General Debate

…

12. Mr. Chang (China) supported the widely held view that article 1 should be deleted and that any valuable idea it might contain should, after further consideration, be placed in the preamble.

13. He felt that the draft covenant - like the Declaration - should contain no specific mention of the origin of human rights, in view of the controversial nature of the subject.

…

Article 2: General Debate

…

51. Mr. Chang (china), reserving the right to enter into a fuller discussion of the many important and suggestive contributions made in the discussion so far, stated that he was prepared to accept the Australian suggestion that the word "recognized" should be substituted for the word "defined". He could also accept the addition of the words "respect and", as suggested by France.

52. The United Kingdom amendment to article 2, paragraph 1, raised a most important problem. Although the document under consideration was called a covenant, it was in effect a treaty or convention, differing from all other previous instruments of that kind in that it would cover a great variety of subjects. A convention normally covered one subject only. The fact that the present draft Convention was intended to cover more subjects than any other should be borne in mind, if only to avoid future disappointments and disillusions.

53. The problem of how such a complex draft convention was to be ratified by the various national legislatures was admittedly most difficult but by no means hopeless.

54. The United Kingdom amendment was practical in that it introduced the possibility of specific reservations on particular provisions. He wondered, however, what nation would be frank enough to admit that its own legislation might not be up to the standards specified in the draft Covenant. He saw in that question a very real difficulty and suggested that serious study should be made of that point. He favoured some sort of provision for specific reservations on particular points, as a matter of principle, but would not at the moment commit himself concerning the methods to be used in the implementation of that principle.

55. Another fact to be borne in mind was that States differed in their legislative and constitutional practices. The second sentence of the first

paragraph of article 2 might be acceptable. He sympathised with those who had doubts concerning the phrase "reasonable time" but considered that the fixing of a time-limit would also involve difficulties. He suggested that the matter should be left open for the time being and that the Commission should study each article in part II of the draft Convention, bearing in mind the points to which allusion had been made. The Commission could then return to part I and might well find that its consideration of part II had made it easier to free upon a suitable text.

……

在人权委员会第 139 次会议上的发言

1950 年 3 月 30 日星期四上午 11:00 纽约成功湖

《国际人权公约（草案）》和执行措施（第 E/CN.4/365、E/CN.4/353/Add.10、E/CN.4/371、E/CN.4/378、E/1371 号文件）（续）

第 5 条

······

43. 张先生（中国）认为，并不是在人权委员会中各国利益之间存在冲突，而是在两个或三个法律制度之间存在对立。人权委员会代表联合国开展工作，代表了世界上所有的法律制度和哲学思想，因此它必须努力协调这些不同的制度。因此，最好的解决办法是将与第 5 条有关的各种建议结合起来，以便尽可能达成一致意见，并调和关于这一问题的不同观点。

44. 因此，他建议保留第 5 条草案初稿第一款的原本形式，省略任何意向性或武断性的观点，这样的观点会严重削弱其重要性。然而，为了满足那些其法律规定有死刑的国家的要求，可以在案文后面加上第二款，起草如下：

"在实行死刑的国家，死刑只能作为对最严重罪行的惩罚，并由主管法院依法作出判决。任何被判处死刑的人都可以获得大赦、特赦或减刑。"

45. 张先生认为，在国际法发展的现阶段，只有这样草拟的条款才能获得普遍支持。在这时不宜在第 5 条中列入太多的详细规定，例如英国提案第三款中的规定，无论这些规定多么重要。任何这类规定肯定会造成混乱，人权委员会在起草第一项人权公约时必须不惜一切代价避免这样做。随着时间的推移，一定会根据各国政府的意见，建立一种关于这一问题的法理，并随后有可能根据这一法理对公约进行补充。就第 5 条而言，英国的贡献极为重要，并将成为任何此类法理的基本要素之一，他对此表示敬意。

会议于下午 1:00 结束。

——人权委员会第 139 次会议简要记录（E/CN.4/SR.139）

常健译校

E/CN.4/SR.139

6 April 1950

COMMISSION ON HUMAN RIGHTS
SIXTH SESSION
SUMMARY RECORD OF THE HUNDRED AND THIRTY-SEVENTH MEETING

Held at Lake Success, New York, on Thursday, 30 March 1950, at 11:00 a.m.

Draft International Covenant on Human Rights, and Measures of Implementation (E/CN.4/365, E/CN.4/353/Add.10, E/CN.4/371, E/CN.4/378, E/1371) (Continued)

Article 5

...

43. Mr. Chang (China) thought that there was no conflict between national interests in the Commission, but rather an opposition between two or three legal systems. As the Commission was working on behalf of the United Nations, in which all the legal systems and philosophical ideas of the world were represented, it must try to reconcile those different systems. The best solution would therefore be to combine the various proposals relating to article 5 in such a way as to achieve as large a measure of agreement as possible and to reconcile the different viewpoints on the subject.

44. He therefore proposed that the first paragraph of the original draft article 5 should be retained in its absolute form, omitting any idea of intention or arbitrariness, which would considerably diminish its significance. In order, however, to satisfy States whose legislation provided for the death penalty, the text might be followed by a second paragraph drafted as follows:

"In countries where capital punishment exists, a sentence of death may be imposed only as a penalty for the most serious crimes pursuant to sentence by a competent court and in accordance with the law. Anyone sentenced to death may be granted amnesty or pardon or commutation of the sentence."

45. Mr. Chang thought that only an article so drafted could obtain general support at the present stage in the evolution of international law. It would not be advisable at that time to include in article 5 too many detailed provisions, such as those which appeared in the third paragraph of the United Kingdom proposal, however important they might be. Any provisions of that sort would certainly create confusion and the Commission must at all costs avoid doing that when it was drafting the first covenant on human rights. In time a sort of jurisprudence on the subject would certainly be established, based on the comments of governments, and it would subsequently be possible to supplement the covenant in the light of that jurisprudence. So far as article 5 was concerned, the United Kingdom contribution, to which he paid tribute, was extremely important and would form one of the basic elements in any jurisprudence of that sort.

The meeting rose at 1:00 p.m.

在人权委员会第 140 次会议上的发言

1950 年 3 月 30 日星期四下午 2:30 纽约成功湖

《国际人权公约（草案）》（第 E/CN.4/1371、E/CN.4/365、E/CN.4/353/Add.10、E/CN.4/371、E/CN.4/378、E/CN.4/383、E/CN.4/384、E/CN.4/385、E/CN.4/386 号文件）（续）

第 5 条（续）

......

59. 张先生（中国）指出，就公约草案而言，案文和实质内容密切相关，几乎不可能区分它们，也不可能单独对它们进行表决。同时，该公约是一份最重要的文件，需要仔细考虑和反思。因此，他建议人权委员会同意进行两次宣读；投票将在一读时进行，并知晓任何严重的错误都可以在第二次更快速的重读时纠正。

60. 关于第 5 条，完全省略第 1 款将是不幸的，这样会使公约中包括人权条款的部分将首先说明的不是一项权利，而是一项例外。如果秘书处准备一份文件，列出所有修正案，并建议按照什么顺序进行表决，人权委员会就会更容易就该条款作出决定。

61. 豪尔先生（英国）说，不应删除第 1 款。如果删除它的话，第 5 条将只适用于死刑，而不适用于任何其他剥夺人命的情况，如由警察或军事行动造成的剥夺生命。

......

64. 主席支持中国代表的建议，即公约草案应进行两读。

65. 在回答圣克鲁兹先生（智利）时，张彭春先生（中国）说，在他看来，在二读期间，应允许对内容的修改和措辞的变化，只要它们能够提出新的论点。

......

68. 主席认为，可以相信人权委员会的所有成员在一读时都会仔细考虑每一条，只有在他们认为已经基于所面对的各种考量作出了最后决定时才进行投票；在二读期间，只提出他们认为至关重要的建议。二读不应被视为改变主意的机会；同时，辩论不会受到限制，所有错误都可以纠正。

69. 基于这一理解，她将中国代表的建议付诸表决，即应进行两读。

人权委员会以 10 票对 9 票、3 票弃权同意对公约草案进行两读。

会议于下午 5:25 结束。

——人权委员会第 140 次会议简要记录（E/CN.4/SR.140）

常健译校

E/CN.4/SR.140

7 April 1950

COMMISSION ON HUMAN RIGHTS
SIXTH SESSION
SUMMARY RECORD OF THE HUNDRED AND THIRTY-
SEVENTH MEETING

Held at Lake Success, New York, on Thursday, 30 March 1950, at 2:30 p.m.

Draft International Covenant on Human Rights (E/CN.4/1371, E/CN.4/365, E/CN.4/353/Add.10, E/CN.4/371, E/CN.4/378, E/CN.4/383, E/CN.4/384, E/CN.4/385, E/CN.4/386)
Article 5 （Continued）

...

59. Mr. Chang (China) observed that in the case of the draft covenant text and substance were so closely related that it was next to impossible to distinguish between them and to vote on them separately. At the same time, the covenant was a most important document, which required careful consideration and reflection. He therefore proposed that the Commission should agree to have two readings; votes would be taken at the first reading in the knowledge that any serious errors could still be corrected at the second and more rapid reading.

60. With respect to article 5, it would be unfortunate to omit paragraph 1 altogether, as the part of the covenant containing provisions on human rights

would then begin by stating not a right but an exception to it. The Commission would find it much easier to reach a decision on that article if the Secretariat were to prepare a paper listing all the amendments and proposing in what order they should be put to the vote.

...

61. Mr. Hoare (United Kingdom) said that paragraph 1 should not be delete. If it were, article 5 would apply exclusively to the death penalty and would no cover any other cases of taking human life, as by police or military action.

...

64. The Chairman supported the suggestion of the Chinese representative that there should be two readings of the draft covenant.

65. In reply to Mr. Santa Cruz (Chile), and Mr. Chang (China) said that in his view amendments of substance as well as drafting changes should be permitted during the second reading, provided that new arguments were adduced.

...

68. The Chairman felt that all members of the Commission could be trusted to give careful thought to every article during the first reading and to vote only when they felt they had arrived at a final decision on the basis of the considerations before them; and, during the second reading, to suggest only such changes as they deemed vital. The second reading should not be regarded as an opportunity for a change of mind; at the same time, there would be no limitation of debate, and all errors could be rectified.

69. On that understanding, she put to the vote the Chinese representative's suggestion that two readings should be held.

The Commission agreed, by 10 votes to 9, with 3 abstentions, that there should be two readings of the draft covenant.

The meeting rose at 5:25 p.m.

在人权委员会第 142 次会议上的发言

1950 年 3 月 31 日星期五下午 2:30 纽约成功湖

《国际人权公约（草案）》（第 E/CN.4/1371、E/CN.4/365、E/CN.4/353/Add.10、E/CN.4/388、E/CN.4/390、E/CN.4/391 号文件）（续）

......

第 8 条

......

73. 张先生（中国）支持黎巴嫩代表关于第 2 款和第 3 款的发言。他提到《世界人权宣言》第 4 条中关于"奴役"一词的使用，并得出结论认为，在目前的后期阶段，没有必要对"奴役"一词加以限定。

......

——人权委员会第 142 次会议简要记录（E/CN.4/SR.142）

常健译校

E/CN.4/SR.142
10 April 1950

COMMISSION ON HUMAN RIGHTS
SIXTH SESSION
SUMMARY RECORD OF THE HUNDRED AND FORTY-SECOND MEETING

Held at Lake Success, New York, on Friday, 31 March 1950, at 2:30 p.m.

Draft International Covenant on Human Rights (E/CN.4/1371, E/CN.4/365, E/CN.4/353/Add.10, E/CN.4/388, E/CN.4/390, E/CN.4/391)(continued)

...

Article 8

...

73. Mr. Chang (China) supported the remarks of the Lebanese representative concerning paragraphs 2 and 3. He referred to article 4 of the Universal Declaration of Human Rights in connexion with the use of the word "servitude" and concluded that there was no need to qualify the word "servitude" at the present late stage.

...

在人权委员会第 143 次会议上的发言

1950 年 4 月 3 日星期一上午 11:00 纽约成功湖

任命来文委员会成员
任命年鉴委员会成员
任命防止歧视和保护少数群体委员会成员
《国际人权公约（草案）》（第 E/CN.4/1371、E/CN.4/365、E/CN.4/353/Add.10、E/CN.4/370、E/CN.4/374、E/CN.4/375、E/CN.4/379、E/CN.4/380 号文件）（续）
第 8 条（续）

......

57. 张先生（中国）认为，问题并不在于规定各代表团之间的定期协商，而在于确保在成员们清楚地意识到问题所在时进行这样协商。虽然人权委员会可以在二读之前暂停讨论第 4 款，但他认为大多数成员都赞成立即作出决定。他认为，短时间的磋商就足够了，因此他建议人权委员会立即休会，以便在下一次会议上审议商定的案文。

58. 主席说，虽然她原则上赞同张先生所建议的程序的有用性，但她认为，在这种情况下，很难在下次会议之前的有限时间内达成商定的解决办法。

......

72. 张先生（中国）建议人权委员会在起草委员会完成工作之前暂停对第 8 条的讨论。起草委员会的工作应以将进行二读为前提。

如此作出决定。

会议于下午 1:00 结束。

——人权委员会第 143 次会议简要记录（E/CN.4/SR.143）

常健译校

E/CN.4/SR.143

10 April 1950

COMMISSION ON HUMAN RIGHTS
SIXTH SESSION
SUMMARY RECORD OF THE HUNDRED AND FORTY-THIRD MEETING

Held at Lake Success, New York, on Monday, 3 April 1950, at 11:00 a.m.

Appointment of members to the Committee on Communications
Appointment of members to the Committee on the Yearbook
Appointment of members to the Committee on Prevention of Discrimination and Protection of Minorities
Draft International Covenant on Human Rights (E/CN.4/1371, E/CN.4/365, E/CN.4/353/Add.10, E/CN.4/370, E/CN.4/374, E/CN.4/375, E/CN.4/379, E/CN.4/380) (Continued)
Article 8 （Continued）

...

57. Mr. Chang (China) felt that it was not so much a question of making regular provision for consultation among delegations as of ensuring that such consultations took place while the points at issue were clearly in members' minds. While it was open to the Commission to suspend discussion of paragraph 4 until the second reading, he felt that most members were in favour of reaching an immediate decision. He felt that a short period of consultation would be sufficient and he therefore suggested that the Commission should adjourn forthwith with a view to considering an agreed text at the following meeting.

58. The Chairman said that, while she agreed with Mr. Chang in principle on the usefulness of the procedure he suggested, she thought that, in the given instance, it would be difficult to reach an agreed solution in the limited time available before the following meeting.

...

72. Mr. Chang (China) proposed that the Committee should suspend its discussion of article 8 until the drafting committee had completed its work. The

drafting committee should work on the assumption that a second reading would take place.

It was so decided.

The meeting rose at 1 p.m.

在人权委员会第 145 次会议上的发言

1950 年 4 月 4 日星期二下午 3:00 纽约成功湖

**《国际人权公约（草案）》（人权委员会第五届会议的报告的附件
一和附件二，第 E/1371 号文件）
第 8 条（第 E/CN.4/353/Add.10、E/CN.4/365、E/CN.4/388、
E/CN.4/391、E/CN.4/404 号文件）（续）
第 9 条（第 E/C.4/353/Add.10、E/CN.4/3b5、E/CN.4/396、
E/CN.4/397、E/CN.4/399、E/CN.4/400、E/CN.4/401、
E/CN.4/402、E/CN.4/405、E/CN.4/406 号文件）（续）**

……

47. 张先生（中国）指出，人权委员会已经详细讨论了第 9 条。该条
已提交给各国政府，那些认为其适于实施的国家已经提出了意见和建议。
在这一阶段，修改一个被如此仔细研究过的案文似乎是不可取的。不能忘
记，人权委员会已经到了为公约草案提供最后形式的阶段。它应该全力以
赴，并且只应该试图修改那些受到严重批评的条款——而第 9 条不在其中。
否则，它将无法在本届会议期间完成面前的工作。

……

50. 张先生（中国）认为很难在一句话中作出如此细微的时间区分。他
更喜欢原来的案文。

……

——人权委员会第 145 次会议简要记录（E/CN.4/SR.145）

常健译校

E/CN.4/SR.145

13 April 1950

COMMISSION ON HUMAN RIGHTS
SIXTH SESSION
SUMMARY RECORD OF THE HUNDRED AND FORTY-FIFTH MEETING

Held at Lake Success, New York, on Tuesday, 4 April 1950, at 3:00 p.m.

Draft International Covenant on Human Rights (Annexes I and II of the Report of the Commission on Human Rights on Its fifth session, Document E/1371)
Article 8 (E/CN.4/353/Add.l0, E/CN.4/365, E/CN.4/388, E/CN.4/391, E/CN.4/404) (Continued)
Article 9 (E/C.4/353/Add.10, E/CN.4/365, E/CN.4/396, E/CN.4/397, E/CN.4/399, E/CN.4/400, E / CN.4/401, E/CN.4/402, E/CN.4.405, E/CN.4/406) (Continued)

...

47. Mr. Chang (China) observed that the Commission had already discussed article 9 at length. The article had been submitted to Governments and those which had thought fit to do so had sent their comments and suggestions. It did not seem advisable at that stage to modify a text which had been so closely studied. It must not be forgotten that the Commission had reached the stage of giving final form to the draft covenant. It should devote its entire attention to and should only attempt to modify those articles which had been the subject of serious criticism – and article 9 was not among them. Otherwise it would not complete the work before it during the current session.

...

50. Mr. Chang (China) thought that it was very difficult to make such subtle time distinctions in a single sentence. He preferred the original text.

...

在人权委员会第 146 次会议上的发言

1950 年 4 月 5 日星期三上午 11:00 纽约成功湖

《国际人权公约（草案）》（第 E/1371、E/CN.4/365、E/CN.4/353/Add.10、E/CN.4/394、E/CN.4/397、E/CN.4/399、E/CN.4/400、E/CN.4/401、E/CN.4/402、E/CN.4/405、E/CN.4/406、E/CN.4/408、E/CN.4/409 号文件）（续）

第 9 条（续）

……

张先生（中国）赞成现在的第 1 款和第 2 款。

……

> ——人权委员会第 146 次会议简要记录（E/CN.4/SR.146）
>
> 常健译校

E/CN.4/SR.146

12 April 1950

COMMISSION ON HUMAN RIGHTS

SIXTH SESSION

SUMMARY RECORD OF THE HUNDRED AND FORTY-SIXTH MEETING

Held at Lake Success, New York, on Wednesday, 5 April 1950, at 11:00 a.m.

Draft International Covenant on Human Rights (E/1371, E/CN.4/365, E/CN.4/353/Add.10, E/CN.4/394, E/CN.4/397, E/CN.4/399, E/CN.4/400, E/CN.4/401, E/CN.4/402, E/CN.4/405, E/CN.4/406, E/CN.4/408, E/CN.4/409) (Continued)

Article 9 (Continued)

…

Mr. Chang (China) was in favour of paragraphs 1 and 2 as they stood.

…

在人权委员会第 147 次会议上的发言

1950 年 4 月 5 日星期三下午 2:45 纽约成功湖

《国际人权公约（草案）》（人权委员会第五届会议的报告的附件一和附件二，第 E/1371 号文件）
第 9 条（第 E/C.4/353/Add.10、E/CN.4/365、E/CN.4/394、E/CN.4/397、E/CN.4/399、E/CN.4/400、E/CN.4/401、E/CN.4/402、E/CN.4.405 号文件）

......

26. 张先生（中国）说，马利克先生的发言有两个非常有趣的观点。

27. 他高兴地注意到，马利克先生承认现代国家的行为是可怕的，并试图保护个人不受国家滥用权力的侵害。因此，马利克先生对自己的修正案投反对票似乎是合乎逻辑的，因为在该修正案中，每句话都提到了"法律"一词。法律直接来自国家，投票支持黎巴嫩修正案将是为了加强国家已经过大的权力，正是国家制定了适合自己的法律。此外，马利克先生宣称，该公约不会一成不变，可能会被修改。如果是这样的话，所有提到的例外情况都可以纳入立法中，随着公约条款的适用而发展。他希望人权委员会每年收到秘书处关于该领域立法进展情况的报告。同时，他认为，人权委员会成员不应忽视这样一个事实，即法律基本上是武断的，看上去像是对人权的威胁。因此，他认为人权委员会第五届会议通过的案文并不像某些人所说的那样不堪，他将对其投赞成票。

......

46. 张先生（中国）认为现在不是对"任意"一词作出最后解释的适当时机。希望明确定义该词的代表团应就此提出具体建议，以便委员会在草案二读期间对其进行审查。

47. 主席意识到这个问题很复杂，值得进一步审议。

......

50. 主席说，鉴于中国代表的反对，几乎没有任何理由将"任意"一词定义为"非法和不合法"的提议付诸表决。

51. 她指出，在这方面，这个词是特意选择的，是为了涵盖所有可能发生的不应逮捕或拘留的情况。

52. 马利克先生（黎巴嫩）对其对投票的解释导致人权委员会改变意见表示遗憾。一些代表团，特别是智利、中国、丹麦、法国和希腊以及他的代表团，已经对"任意"一词作出了解释。因此，令人遗憾的是，人权委员会重新考虑其立场，因为他对投票的解释而排除了任何界定该术语的可能性。

53. 张先生（中国）向黎巴嫩代表保证，他提出在研究是否可能或适宜对"任意"一词进行定义之前，不应对其加以定义，这一建议并没有受到该代表的解释的启发。

54. 奥多诺先生（法国）说，他不反对推迟就这个问题作出决定，前提是各代表团有机会在适当时候重新讨论这个问题。

如此作出决定。

……

——人权委员会第 147 次会议简要记录（E/CN.4/SR.147）

常健译校

E/CN.4/SR.147
17 April 1950

COMMISSION ON HUMAN RIGHTS
SIXTH SESSION
SUMMARY RECORD OF THE HUNDRED AND FORTY-SEVENTH MEETING

Held at Lake Success, New York, on Wednesday, 5 April 1950, at 2:45 p.m.

Draft international covenant on human rights (annexes I and II of the report of the Commission on Human Rights on Its fifth session, document E/1371) Article 9 (E/CN.4/353/Add.10, E/CN.4/365, E/CN.4/394, E/CN.4/397, E/CH.4/399, E/CN.4/400, E/CN.4/401, E/CN.4/402 and E/CN.4/405)

...

26. Mr. Chang (China) said that there were two very interesting points in Mr. Malik's statement.

27. He was happy to note that Mr. Malik had acknowledged that the actions of the modern State were monstrous and was trying to protect individuals against State abuse of power. It would therefore seem logical for Mr. Malik to vote against his own amendment, in which the word "law" was mentioned in each sentence. Law emanated directly from the State and to vote for the Lebanese amendment would be to strengthen the already excessive power of the State, which itself enacted the laws which suited it. Mr. Malik had declared, moreover, that the covenant would not be immutable and might be revised. If that was so, all the exceptions that had been mentioned could be incorporated in the legislation which would develop as the provisions of the covenant were applied. He hoped that the Commission would have before it each year a report by the Secretariat on the progress of legislation in that fields. Meanwhile, he considered that the members of the Commission should not lose sight of the fact that laws were essentially arbitrary and hung like a threat over human rights. For that reason he thought that the text adopted by the Commission at its fifth session was not as imperfect as some made out, and he would vote for it.

...

46. Mr. Chang (China) thought that was not the proper time to try to give a final interpretation of the word "arbitrary". Delegations which wished to define the word clearly should present concrete proposals to that effect so that the Commission could examine them during the second reading of the draft.

47. The Chairman realized that the question was complicated and deserved further consideration.

...

50. The Chairman said that in view of the Chinese representative's objection, there was hardly any reason to put the proposal to define the word "arbitrary" as "illegal and unjust" to the vote.

51. She pointed out, in that connexion, that the word had been purposely chosen in order to cover all possible cases in which an arrest or detention should not take place.

52. Mr. Malik (Lebanon) regretted that the explanation of his vote had led the Commission to change its opinion. Several delegations, particularly those of Chile, China, Denmark, France and Greece as well as his own, had already stated their interpretation of the word "arbitrary". It would therefore be regrettable for the Commission to reconsider its position by removing any possibility of defining the term because of his explanation of his vote.

53. Mr. Chang (China) assured the Lebanese representative that his suggestion that the word "arbitrary" should not be defined until a study had been made of whether it was possible or desirable to define it had not been inspired by that representative's interpretation.

54. Mr. Ordonneau (France) said that he had no objection to postponing a decision on the question, provided it was understood that delegations would have an opportunity of reopening the matter in due course.

It was so decided.

...

在人权委员会第 148 次会议上的发言

1950 年 4 月 6 日星期四上午 11:00 纽约成功湖

《国际人权公约（草案）》（第 E/1371、E/CN.4/365、E/C.4/353/Add.10、E/CN.4/394、E/CN.4/404、E/CN.4/408 号文件）（续）

第 9 条（续）

......

25. 张先生（中国）建议，美国的修正案（第 E/CN.4/394 号文件）应分两部分进行表决，第一次表决包括"赔偿"一词，第二次表决其余部分。他之所以提出这一建议，是因为他认为美国修正案的第一部分确实是必要的，而第二部分则处理了根本不需要考虑的问题。他将美国修正案的第一部分与公约草案第 6 款的案文进行比较后得出结论，两个版本几乎完全相同，但美国草案的优点是更加明确。

26. 他同意那些认为这个问题不能在起草委员会中解决的人们的意见。

......

第 8 条（续）

......

60. 张先生（中国）对过于详细地起草该条款是否明智感到有些疑虑，因为从逻辑上讲，这种方法可能必须适用于其他条款。起草小组成功地解决了由于最初将第 3 款和第 4 款分开而产生的问题，但他不相信详细规定是一种完全可取的方法。

......

69. 张先生（中国）解释说，他投了弃权票，因为他怀疑把该条款写得如此详细是否明智。他希望不要为在其他条款中写入过多细节开创先例。

会议于下午 1:00 结束。

——人权委员会第 148 次会议简要记录（E/CN.4/SR.148）

常健译校

E/CN.4/SR.148
14 April 1950
COMMISSION ON HUMAN RIGHTS
SIXTH SESSION
SUMMARY RECORD OF THE HUNDRED AND THIRTY-SEVENTH MEETING

Held at Lake Success, New York, on Thursday, 6 April 1950, at 11:00 a.m.

Draft International Covenant on Human Rights (E/1371, E/CN.4/365, E/C.4/353/Add.10, E/CN.4/394, E/CN.4/404, E/CN.4/408) (Continued)

Article 9 (Continued)

…

25. Mr. Chang (China) suggested that the United States amendment (E/CN.4/394) should be voted on in two parts, a first vote to be taken up to and including the word "compensation", and a second vote on the remainder. He was making that suggestion because he felt that the first part of the United States amendment was really all that was necessary, and that the second half dealt with matters that need not enter into the picture at all. He concluded from a comparison of the first part of the United States amendment with the text of paragraph 6, as worded in the draft covenant, that both versions were almost identical, but that the United States draft had the merit of greater clarity.

26. He agreed with those who had held that the question was not one which could be resolved in a drafting committee.

…

Article 8 (Continued)

...

60. Mr. Chang (China) felt some misgivings about the wisdom of drafting the article in too great detail, because that method might logically have to be extended to other articles. The Drafting Group had successfully solved the problems which had arisen as a result of the original separation of paragraphs 3 and 4, but he was not convinced that stipulation in detail was a wholly desirable method.

...

69. Mr. Chang (China) explained that he had abstained from voting because he doubted the wisdom of making the article so detailed. He hoped that a precedent would not be set for the inclusion of excessive detail in other articles.

The meeting rose at 1:00 p.m.

在人权委员会第 149 次会议上的发言

1950 年 4 月 6 日星期四下午 2:30 纽约成功湖

**《国际人权公约（草案）》（人权委员会第五届会议的报告的附件
一和附件二，第 E/1371 号文件）
第 8 条（第 E/CN.4/365、E/CN.4/353/Add.10、E/CN.4/388、
E/CN.4/391、E/CN.4/404、E/CN.4/408 号文件）（续）
第 5 条（第 E/CN.4/387、E/CN.4/393、E/CN.4/398 号文件）
（续）**

第 17 条

......

4. 张先生（中国）指出，菲律宾的提案主张删除第一款的原文。然而，人权委员会面前还有影响该款案文的其他几项修正案，在知道要删除什么之前，很难对删除该款进行表决。

......

18. 张先生（中国）指出，黎巴嫩案文的第 2 款完全可以被添加到原文第 1 款中，而不是将其替换。

......

44. 张先生（中国）认为，"主管"一词足以说明主管法庭是指独立的法庭。此外，"故意"是该款的关键词。这与黎巴嫩修正案第 4 款所列例外情况的解释密切相关。因此，张先生要求对该词进行单独表决。

......

48. 张先生（中国）询问美国的修正案是否适用于第 5 条第 2 款或第 3 款。

......

82. 张先生（中国）提醒人权委员会，它正在起草一份能够被所有国家接受的公约草案，而不是关于每一条所涵盖的各种事项的详细公约。

83. 他承认埃及代表的论点有一定的根据，并认为从人道的角度来看他是正确的。尽管如此，在公约草案的条款中加入过多的细节还是不可取的，这可能会使整个文件变得相当不平衡。

84. 公约应构成一个合乎逻辑的整体，只有在得到各国政府批准后，人权委员会才有能力起草若干详细的公约，并请秘书处向它提供关于各种法律制度的报告。

85. 张先生回顾说，这就是他投票反对第 8 条中提出的详细规定的原因，并表示他将对第 5 条采取同样的做法。

86. 主席同意中国代表的意见。

——人权委员会第 149 次会议简要记录（E/CN.4/SR.149）

常健译校

E/CN.4/SR.149

17 April 1950

COMMISSION ON HUMAN RIGHTS
SIXTH SESSION
SUMMARY RECORD OF THE HUNDRED AND FORTY-NINTH MEETING

Held at Lake Success, New York, on Thursday, 6 April 1950, at 2:30 p.m.

Draft International Covenant on Human Rights (Annexes I and II of the Report of the Commission on Human Rights on Its Fifth Session, Document E/137I)
Article 8 (E/CN.4/365, E/CN.4/353/Add.l0,E/CN.4/388, E/CN.4/391, E/CN.4/404、E/CN.4/408) (Continued)
Article 5 (E/CN.4/387, E/CN.4/393, E/CN.4/398) (Continued)

...

4. Mr. Chang (China) observed that the Philippine proposal advocated the deletion of the original text of the first paragraph. There were, however, several other amendments affecting the text of that paragraph before the Commission, and it would hardly be possible to vote on its deletion before knowing just what

was to be deleted.

...

18. Mr. Chang (China) pointed out that paragraph 2 of the Lebanese text could very well be added to the original text of paragraph 1 instead of replacing it.

...

44. Mr. Chang (China) thought that the word "competent" would suffice for competent tribunal meant independent tribunal. Moreover, "intentional" was the key word of the paragraph. It was closely related to the interpretation of the exceptions listed in paragraph 4 of the Lebanese amendment. Therefore, Mr. Chang asked that a separate vote should be taken on that word.

...

48. Mr. Chang (China) asked whether the United States amendment applied to paragraph 2 or paragraph 3 of article 5.

...

82. Mr. Chang (China) reminded the Committee that it was working on a draft covenant capable of being accepted by all States and not on detailed conventions bearing on the various matters covered by each article.

83. He admitted that there was some foundation for the Egyptian representative's arguments and thought that he was quite right from the humane point of view. Nevertheless it would be somewhat inadvisable to overload the articles of the draft covenant with details which might make the document as a whole rather unbalanced.

84. The covenant should constitute a logical whole and only when it had been approved by Governments would the Commission be in a position to draw up a certain number of detailed conventions and to request the Secretariat to provide it with reports on the various legal systems.

85. Mr. Chang recalled that that was the reason why he had voted against the detailed provisions which it had been sought to introduce into article 8 and stated that he would do the same for article 5.

86. The Chairman agreed with the representative of China.

...

在人权委员会第 150 次会议上的发言

1950 年 4 月 10 日星期一上午 11:00 纽约成功湖

防止歧视和保护少数小组委员会的组成；
人权委员会和起草委员会会议；
《国际人权公约（草案）》（人权委员会第五届会议的报告的附件一和附件二，第 E/1371 号文件）（续）
第 5、10、11 条（第 E/CN.4/353/Add.10、E/CN.4/365、E/CN.4/367、E/CN.4/392、E/CN.4/393、E/CN.4/395、E/CN.4/398、E/CN.4/407 号文件）

......

2. 凯罗先生（希腊）建议委员会不应在 4 月 12 日星期三开会，以便主席能够参加纪念罗斯福总统的纪念仪式。这也将使委员会有机会向最热心的人权捍卫者之一致敬。

3. 主席感谢希腊代表的周到考虑，并说她实际上必须在 4 月 12 日星期三缺席，才能参加在海德公园举行的仪式。然而，人权委员会可以在张先生的主持下举行会议。

4. 张先生（中国）虽然很愿意在委员会希望的情况下担任会议主席，但由于希腊代表提出的理由，他赞成在 4 月 12 日星期三不举行会议。

......

——人权委员会第 150 次会议简要记录（E/CN.4/SR.150）

常健译校

E/CN.4/SR.150
17 April 1950
COMMISSION ON HUMAN RIGHTS
SIXTH SESSION
SUMMARY RECORD OF THE HUNDRED AND FIFTIETH

MEETING

Held at Lake Success, New York, on Monday, 10 April 1950, at 11:00 a.m.

Composition of the Sub-Commission on Prevention of Discrimination and
Protection of Minorities;
Meetings of the Commission and the Committees;
Draft International Covenant on Human Rights (Annexes I and II of the Report of the Fifth Session of the Commission on Human Rights, Document E/1371) (Continued);
Article 5, 10 and 11(E/CN.4/353/Add.10, E/CN.4/365, E/CN.4/367, E/CN.4/392, E/CN.4/393, E/CN.4/395, E/CN.4/398 and E/CN.4/407)

...

2. Mr. Kyrou (Greece) suggested that the Commission should not meet on Wednesday 12 April, so that the Chairman could attend the commemoration service in honour of President Roosevelt. That would also give the Commission an opportunity to pay tribute to one of the most ardent defenders of human rights.

3. The Chairman thanked the Greek representative for his consideration and said that she would in fact have to be absent on Wednesday 12 April in order to attend the ceremonies to be held at Hyde Park. The Commission could, however, meet under the chairmanship of Mr. Chang.

4. Mr. Chang (China), although quite prepared to act as chairman if the Commission so desired, was nevertheless in favour of holding no meeting on Wednesday 12 April, for the reasons given by the Greek representative.

在人权委员会第 151 次会议上的发言

1950 年 4 月 10 日星期一下午 2:30 纽约成功湖

《国际人权公约（草案）》（第 E/1371、E/CN.4/365、E/CN.4/353/Add.10、E/CN.4/412 号文件）（续）

第 11 条（续）

······

14. 张先生（中国）认为，第 11 条的实质内容应该体现在正在讨论的公约中，尽管起草一个令人满意的文案存在着困难。该原则可以在该阶段通过，但可能有必要将关于措辞的决定推迟到二读之前。迁徙自由权是一项重要的权利，尤其是对以前没有享受过该权利的人而言。

15. 他同意黎巴嫩代表的意见，认为该条款的形式需要进一步审议。他认为，在考虑这些限制的所有条款中，限制的措辞应该是相似的，一般原则应该在限制之前说明。然而，这必须根据对后续条款所作的决定来最终决定。

16. 他无法接受美国修正案（第 E/CN.4/365 号文件，第 34 页）中的"不受政府干预"一词。所有法律都是政府干预的一种形式，尽管它们是为了大多数人民的利益而制定的。如果干预发生在不受法律管辖的环境中，它一定会被认为是任意的；而如果它是依法作出的，人权委员会似乎会对相关法律提出挑战，但这是不可取的。

······

51. 张先生（中国）认为，澳大利亚和美国的修正案不是相互排斥的，因此可以合并，可以在美国修正案中加入"并返回自己的国家"的措辞。

······

——人权委员会第 151 次会议简要记录（E/CN.4/SR.151）

常健译校

E/CN.4/SR.151
19 April 1950

COMMISSION ON HUMAN RIGHTS
SIXTH SESSION
SUMMARY RECORD OF THE HUNDRED AND FIFTY-FIRST MEETING

Held at Lake Success, New York, on Monday, 10 April 1950, at 2:30 p.m.

Draft International Covenant on Human Rights (E/1371, E/CN.4/365, E/CN.4/353/Add.10, E/CN.4/412) (Continued); Article 11 (Continued)

...

14. Mr. Chang (China) thought that the substance of article 11 ought to be embodied in the covenant under discussion, despite the difficulty of drafting it satisfactorily. The principle could be adopted at that stage, but it might be necessary to postpone the decision on the wording until the second reading. The right of liberty of movement was a very important one, particularly for peoples who had not previously enjoyed it.

15. He agreed with the Lebanese representative that the form of the article required further consideration. He felt that the wording of the limitations should be similar in all articles regarding them and that the general principle should be stated before the limitations. That would, however, have to be decided finally in the light of the decisions taken upon subsequent articles.

16. He could not accept the words "free from governmental interference in", which were in the United States amendment (E/CN.4/365, page 34). All laws were a form of governmental interference, even though they were enacted in the interests of the majority of the people. If the interference occurred in circumstances not governed by a law, it must be assumed to be arbitrary, while if it was under the law, the Commission would be seeming to challenge the law, and that would be undesirable.

...

51. Mr. Chang (China) thought that the Australian and the United States

amendments were not mutually exclusive, and could therefore be combined, possibly by adding the phrase "and to return to his own country" to the United States amendment.

 …

在人权委员会第 152 次会议上的发言

1950 年 4 月 11 日星期二上午 11:00 纽约成功湖

《国际人权公约（草案）》（人权委员会第五届会议的报告的附件
一和附件二，第 E/1371 号文件）
第 5 条（续）（第 E/CN.4/365、E/CN.4/378、E/CN.4/383、
E/CN.4/384、E/CN.4/385、E/CN.4/387、E/CN.4/393、
E/CN.4/398、E/CN.4/413 号文件）

......

42. 张先生（中国）认为，如此迅速地合并案文，不可能不出现重复或不幸遗漏的危险。

43. 他担心，投票赞成从修正后的黎巴嫩对第 2 款的修正案（E/CN.4/413）中删除"故意的"一词，可能会引起一些混乱，因为许多代表会认为，这一删除也意味着删除黎巴嫩为第 5 条提出的案文（E/CN.4/398）中的第 4 款。

44. 英国代表这时表示，第 4 段中有一些理念应该保留。张先生表示同意，但提议推迟对该问题的表决，直到委员会收到书面的具体提案。

45. 马利克先生（黎巴嫩）回答说，如果人权委员会没有决定赞成法国的修正案，中国代表对删除"故意的"一词的解释是正确的，该修正案还载有一系列例外情况。在这种情况下，人权委员会在投票中明确表示，它认为有必要限制第 5 条所述的权利。因此，英国代表提出的完成例外清单的建议是完全合理的，不能说这会引起混淆。

......

49. 奥多诺先生（法国）敦促投票应适用于原文的所有部分。例如，第 2 款表达了法国代表团希望在第 5 条中看到的想法。

50. 张先生（中国）支持这一观点。没有什么可以阻止人权委员会首先对美国提出的修正案进行表决，该修正案要取代原文第 2 款和第 3 款。如果该修正案被否决，人权委员会就可以就这两款作出决定。重要的一点是，不应遗漏任何可能对整个条款具有重要意义的因素。

......

——人权委员会第 152 次会议简要记录（E/CN.4/SR.152）

常健译校

E/CN.4/SR.152

18 April 1950

COMMISSION ON HUMAN RIGHTS
SIXTH SESSION
SUMMARY RECORD OF THE HUNDRED AND FIFTY-SECOND MEETING

Held at Lake Success, New York, on Tuesday, 11 April 1950, at 11:00 a.m.

Draft international Covenant on Human Rights (Annexes I and II of the Report of the Fifth Session of the Commission on Human Rights, Document E/1371)
Article 5 (Continued) (E/CN.4/365, E/CN.4/378, E/CN.4/383, E/CN.4/384, E/CN.4/385, E/CN.4/387, E/CN.4/393, E/CN.4/398, E/CN.4/413)

...

42. Mr. Chang (China) did not think it possible to combine the texts so rapidly without the danger of either repetitions or unfortunate omissions.

43. He feared that some confusion might have arisen from the fact that in voting for the deletion of the word "intentional" from the revised Lebanese amendment to paragraph 2 (E/CN.4/413), many representatives had considered that that deletion also implied the deletion of paragraph 4 of the text proposed by Lebanon for article 5 (E/CN.4/398).

44. The United Kingdom representative now expressed the opinion that there were ideas in paragraph 4 which should be kept. Mr. Chang agreed, but proposed that the vote on the question should be postponed until the commission

had a concreted proposal in writing before it.

45. Mr. Malik (Lebanon) replied that the Chinese representative's interpretation of the deletion of the word "intentional" would have been correct if the Commission had not decided in favour of the French amendment, which also contained a list of exceptions. In the circumstances, the Commission had clearly indicated by its vote that it considered it necessary to limit the right sated in article 5. The United Kingdom representative's proposal to complete the list of exceptions was therefore fully justified and it could not be said that it would give rise to confusion.

...

49. Mr. Ordonneau (France) urged that the vote should bear on all parts of the original text. Paragraph 2, for example, expressed an idea which the French delegation would like to see in article 5.

50. Mr. Chang (China) supported that point of view. There was nothing to prevent the Commission from voting first on the amendment proposed by the United States as a substitute for paragraphs 2 and 3 of the original text. If the amendment was rejected, the Commission could very well decide on those two paragraphs. The essential point was that no factor which might be of importance to the article as a whole should be omitted.

...

在人权委员会第 153 次会议上的发言

1950 年 4 月 11 日星期二下午 2:45 纽约成功湖

《国际人权公约（草案）》（第 E/1371、E/CH.4/365、E/CN./353/Add.10、E/CN.4/387、E/CN.4/393、E/CN.4/398、E/CN.4/413、E/CH.4/414、E/CN./417、E/CN.4/420 号文件）

（续）
妇女地位委员会代表的陈述
第 5 条（续）
第 12 条
第 13 条

......

12. 应张先生（中国）的请求，他希望能够就"根据主管法院的判决"等词语分别进行表决，因为这些词语已包含在法语文本中，美国对第 2 款和第 3 款的修正案分四部分付诸表决。

"在存在死刑的国家，死刑只能作为对最严重罪行的惩罚"以 13 票对 0 票、1 票弃权获得通过。

"根据主管法院的判决"等措辞以 9 票对 0 票、5 票弃权获得通过。

"依法"一词以 12 票对 0 票、2 票弃权获得通过。

"不违反《世界人权宣言》"的表述以 9 票对 2 票、3 票弃权获得通过。

美国的修正案以 12 票对 0 票、3 票弃权获得通过，成为第 5 条第 3 款。

......

——人权委员会第 153 次会议简要记录（E/CN.4/SR.153）

常健译校

E/CN.4/SR.153
19 April 1950

COMMISSION ON HUMAN RIGHTS
SIXTH SESSION
SUMMARY RECORD OF THE HUNDRED AND FIFTY-
THIRD MEETING

Held at Lake Success, New York, on Tuesday, 11 April 1950, at 2:45 p.m.

Draft International Covenant on Human Rights (E/1371,
E/CH.4/365, E/CN./353/Add.10, E/CN.4/387, E/CN.4/393,
E/CN.4/398, E/CN.4/413, E/CH.4/414, E/CN./417, E/CN.4/420)
(Continued);
Statement by the Representative of the Commission on the Status
of Women;
Article 5 (Continued)
Article 12
Article 13

...

12. At the request of Mr. Chang (China), who wished to be able to vote separately on the words, "pursuant to the sentence of a competent court and", inasmuch as they were covered in the French text, the United States amendment to paragraphs 2 and 3 was put to the vote in four parts.

The words "In countries where capital punishment exists, sentence of death may be imposed only as a penalty for the most serious crimes" were adopted by 13 votes to none, with one abstention.

The words "pursuant to the sentence of a competent court and" were adopted by 9 votes to none, with 5 abstentions.

The words "in accordance with law" were adopted by 12 votes to none, with 2 abstentions.

The words "not contrary to the Universal Declaration of Human Rights" were adopted by 9 votes to 2, with 3 abstentions.

The United States amendment as a whole was adopted by 12 votes to none, with 3 abstations, becoming paragraph 3 of article 5.

...

在人权委员会第 155 次会议上的发言

1950 年 4 月 14 日星期五下午 4:00 纽约成功湖

《国际人权公约（草案）》（续）
第 12 条和第 13 条（第 E/1371、E/CH.4/365、E/CN.4/423、
E/CH.4/426、E/CN./414 号文件）

......

51. 张先生（中国）解释说，他对美国的修正案投了弃权票，因为他认为"有资格享有"一词不能用"应当"一词来限定，因为它指的是一种固有的权利，不能使之成为强制性的。他不反对使用条约中常用的"应当"一词，但希望二读时能找到"有资格享有"一词的替代词。

......

——人权委员会第 155 次会议简要记录
（E/CN.4/SR.155，第二部分）

常健译校

E/CN.4/SR.155, Part II
24 April 1950
COMMISSION ON HUMAN RIGHTS
SIXTH SESSION
SUMMARY RECORD OF THE HUNDRED AND FIFTY-
FIFTH MEETING

Held at Lake Success, New York, on Friday, 14 April 1950, at 4:00 p.m.

Draft International Covenant on Human Rights (Continued) Article 12 and 13 (E/1371, E/CH.4/365, E/CN.4/423, E/CH.4/426, E/CN./414)

...

51. Mr. Chang (China) explained that he had abstained from voting on the United States amendment because he thought that the word "entitled" could not be qualified by the words "shall be", since it referred to an inherent right, which could not be made mandatory. He did not object to the use of the words "shall be" –the form usual in treaties – but hoped that a substitute for the word "entitled" would be found on second reading.

...

在人权委员会第 157 次会议上的发言

1950 年 4 月 17 日星期一下午 3:00 纽约成功湖

《国际人权公约（草案）》（人权委员会第五届会议的报告的附件一和附件二，第 E/1371 号文件）（续）

第 13 条（第 E/CH.4/365、E/CN.4/353/Add.10、E/CH.4/358、E/CN./422/Rev.1、E/CN./426、E/CN./428 号文件）（续）

······

41. 张先生（中国）接受英国代表提出的最后案文。他建议人权委员会进行表决，并请秘书处在二读之前就案文发表意见。

42. 主席以美国代表的身份发言，撤回了美国的修正案，赞成英国代表提出的最后案文。

······

44. 主席将英国对第 2 款（b）项的修正案付诸表决（第 E/CN.4/428 号文件）。

该修正案获得一致通过。

······

——人权委员会第 157 次会议简要记录（E/CN.4/SR.157）

常健译校

E/CN.4/SR.157

26 April 1950

COMMISSION ON HUMAN RIGHTS
SIXTH SESSION
SUMMARY RECORD OF THE HUNDRED AND FIFTY-
SEVENTH MEETING

Held at Lake Success, New York, on Monday, 17 April 1950, at 3:00 p.m.

Draft International Covenant on Human Rights (Annexes I and II of the Report of the Fifth Session of the Commission on Human Rights, Document E/1371) (Continued)
Article 13 (E/CH.4/365, E/CN.4/353/Add.10, E/CH.4/358, E/CN./422/Rev.1, E/CN./426, E/CN./428) (Continued)

...

41. Mr. Chang (China) accepted the last text proposed by the United Kingdom representative. He suggested the Commission should proceed to a vote and should request the Secretariat to give its opinion on the text before the second reading.

42. Speaking as representative of the United States of America, the Chairman withdrew the United States amendment in favour of the last text proposed by the United Kingdom representative.

...

44. The Chairman put to the vote the United Kingdom amendment to paragraph 2, sub-paragraph (b) (E/CN.4/428).

That amendment was unanimously adopted.

...

在人权委员会第 158 次会议上的发言

1950 年 4 月 18 日星期二上午 11:00 纽约成功湖

《国际人权公约（草案）》（第 E/1371 和 E/CN.4/365 号文件）
第 13 条（续）

......

30. 张先生（中国）指出，"赔偿"一词没有明确定义。该条应规定，在错误定罪的情况下，不仅要给予物质赔偿，还要给予精神赔偿。

31. 关于将要通过的案文，他倾向于法国对第 3 款的原始草案进行的修正。

32. 他同意黎巴嫩代表提出的应遵循的程序。他希望在决定是否删除该款之前先研究最后案文。

......

——人权委员会第 158 次会议简要记录（E/CN.4/SR.158）

常健译校

E/CN.4/SR.158
26 April 1950
COMMISSION ON HUMAN RIGHTS
SIXTH SESSION
SUMMARY RECORD OF THE HUNDRED AND FIFTY-EIGHTH MEETING

Held at Lake Success, New York, on Tuesday, 18 April 1950, at 11:00 a.m.

Draft International Covenant on Human Rights (E/1371, E/CN.4/365)
Article 13 (Continued)

...

30. Mr. Chang (China) pointed out that the word "compensation" had not been clearly defined. The article should provide for moral as well as material compensation in cases of erroneous convictions.

31. As to the text to be adopted, he preferred the French amendment to the original draft of paragraph 3.

32. He agreed with the representative of Lebanon with regard to the procedure to be followed. He would like to study a final text before deciding whether the paragraph should be deleted.

...

在人权委员会第 159 次会议上的发言

1950 年 4 月 18 日星期二下午 3:00 纽约成功湖

《国际人权公约（草案）》（人权委员会第五届会议的报告的附件一和附件二，第 E/1371 号文件）（续）

第 13 条（第 E/CH.4/365、E/CN.4/353/Add.10、E/CH.4/358、E/CN4./422、E/CN4./426、E/CN4./429、E/CN4./430、E/CN4./431 号文件）（续）

第 14 条（第 E/CN.4/365、E/CN.4/353/Add.10、E/CN.4./425 号文件）；

第 15 条（第 E/CN.4/365 和 E/CN.4/353/Add.10 号文件）
……

51. 张先生（中国）赞同美国代表的评论。他确认，人权委员会决定不保留英国提出的案文，这不仅因为它认为该案文没有价值，而且因为担心它可能导致混乱，并被用于与作者意图无关的目的。纽伦堡审判是国际判例中的一个例外案例；因此，它不应成为关于基本人权和自由的一般性公约中一项特别条款的主题。
……

——人权委员会第 159 次会议简要记录（E/CN.4/SR.159）

常健译校

E/CN.4/SR.159
27 April 1950

COMMISSION ON HUMAN RIGHTS
SIXTH SESSION
SUMMARY RECORD OF THE HUNDRED AND FIFTY-NINTH MEETING

Held at Lake Success, New York, on Tuseday, 18 April 1950, at 3:00 p.m.

Draft International Covenant on Human Rights (Annexes I and II of the Report of the fifth Session of the Commission on Human Rights, Document E/1371) (Continued);
Article 13 (E/CH.4/365, E/CN.4/353/Add.10, E/CH.4/358, E/CN.4/422, E/CN.4/426, E/CN.4/429, E/CN.4/430, E/CN.4/431) (Continued);
Article 14 (E/CN.4/365, E/CN.4/353/Add.10, E/CN.4./425);
Article 15 (E/CN.4/365, E/CN.4/353/Add.10)

...

51. Mr. Chang (China) associated himself with the comments of the United States representative. He confirmed the fact that the Commission had decided against retaining the text proposed by the United Kingdom, not only because it thought that it was without value but also because it was afraid that it might lead to confusion and be exploited for purposes foreign to the intention of its authors. The Nuremberg Trial was an exceptional case in international jurisprudence; it outer not therefore to be the subject of a special provision in a general convention on fundamental human rights and freedoms.

...

在人权委员会第 161 次会议上的发言

1950 年 4 月 19 日星期三下午 3:00 纽约成功湖

《国际人权公约（草案）》（人权委员会第五届会议的报告的附件一和附件二，第 E/1371 号文件）（续）
第 16 条（第 E/CH.4/365、E/CN.4/353/Add.10、E/CH.4/358、E/CN.4/382、E/CN4./429 号文件）
第 17 条（第 E/CN.4/365、E/CN.4/353/Add.10、E/CN.4/360、E/CN.4/360/Corr.1、E/CN.4/415 号、第 E/CN.4/424 号文件）
任命体裁委员会

......

41. 张先生（中国）指出，如果出于欺诈意图改变宗教，显然不会得到民事当局的承认。一般来说，任何出于欺诈意图的行为都不被承认；这是民法的一般原则。无论如何，涉及一般限制的条款涵盖了欺诈行为。因此，埃及的修正案似乎没有必要。

42. 主席以美国代表的身份发言，同意中国代表的意见；她认为，在第 16 条中增加埃及代表提议的条款是没有任何用处的。

埃及修正案以 8 票反对、3 票赞成、2 票弃权被否决。

......

——人权委员会第 161 次会议简要记录（E/CN.4/SR.161）

常健译校

E/CN.4/SR.161

28 April 1950

COMMISSION ON HUMAN RIGHTS
SIXTH SESSION
SUMMARY RECORD OF THE HUNDRED AND SIXTY-FIRST
MEETING

Held at Lake Success, New York, on Wednesday, 19 April 1950, at 3:00 p.m.

**Draft International Covenant on Human Rights (Annexes I and
II of the Report of the Fifth Session of the Commission on
Human Rights, Document E/1371) (Continued);
Article 16 (E/CH.4/365, E/CN.4/353/Add.10, E/CH.4/358,
E/CN.4/382, E/CN.4/429);
Article 17 (E/CN.4/365, E/CN.4/353/Add.10, E/CN.4/360,
E/CN.4/360/Corr.1, E/CN.4/415, E/CN.4/424) (Continued)
Appointment of a style Committee**

...

41. Mr. Chang (China) pointed out that if a change of religion was made, with fraudulent intent, it would obviously not be recognized by the civil authorities. In general, any act committed with fraudulous intent was not recognized; that was a general principle of civil codes. In any case fraud was covered by the paragraph which dealt with general limitations. The Egyptian amendment therefore seemed unnecessary.

42. The Chairman, speaking as the representative of the United States of America, agreed with the Chinese representative; she felt that no useful purpose would be served by adding the provision proposed by the Egyptian representative to article 16.

The Egyptian amendment was rejected by 8 votes to 3, with 2 abstentions.

...

在人权委员会第 163 次会议上的发言

1950 年 4 月 20 日星期四下午 3:00 纽约成功湖

《国际人权公约（草案）》（人权委员会第五届会议的报告的附件一和附件二，第 E/1371 号文件）（续）

第 17 条（第 E/CN.4/365、E/CN.4/353/Add.10、E/CN.4/360、E/CN.4/360/Corr.1、E/CN.4/415、E/CN.4/424、E/CN.4/432、E/CN.4/433/Rev.1、E/CN.4/433/Rev.2、E/CN.4/434 号文件）

（续）

......

22. 张先生（中国）建议，鉴于人权委员会面前的提案和修正案数量众多，委员会应采取这样的程序：对一项基本提案进行单独研究，决定它是否需要修正，然后对修正案进行表决。

23. 根据他自己的建议，他将把他的评论局限于美国修正案的案文（第 E/CN.4/433/Rev.1 号文件）。该案文的第一款令人满意，但应在第一行的"言论"和"自由"之间插入"新闻和"。由于委员会三年来一直关注新闻自由，因此提及新闻自由似乎必不可少。他还建议，"不受政府干预"一词应单独表决，出于形式原因，最好将"任何其他媒体"之前的"由"替换为"通过"一词。

24. 他反对第 2 款开头的"这项权利"的措辞。参考第 1 款可见，该项权利包括"保持主张的自由、寻求、接受和传播信息和思想的自由"。表达主张的权利以及寻求和接受信息的自由并不属于"法律规定的限制"这一表述的约束范围，这些限制只能适用于传播信息的权利。因此，他建议将第 2 款第一行改为："传播信息和思想的权利只受……"。他还建议将"国家安全"之前的"为了保护"改为"根据……利益"，并在"他人的权利、名誉或自由"之前插入"为了保护"。

25 他解释说，他要求就"不受政府干预"的措辞进行单独表决，因为他认为这些措辞是危险的，因为它们可能会为许多滥用行为敞开大门。无论如何都会有政府干预，因为只有政府才能施加第 2 款所述的限制。但是，应防止任意干预，如果人权委员会对此作出决定，它可以在第 1 款中规定，新闻和发表自由权属于个人，政府不得任意干涉。

26. 人权委员会正在研究一个极其广泛的问题；在起草未来的公约和协议时，它可以返回到相同的问题，并以更详细的方式来研究它们。

......

27. 主席以美国代表的身份发言，接受了中国代表对美国案文第 1 款提出的修正案。然而，她希望保留第二款的开头，并删除第 1 款中的"保持主张"的措辞。

28. 关于"不受政府干预"的措辞，干涉的主要来源是国家实行的审查制度。因此，第 17 条中必须保留"不受政府干预"的措辞；它们为新闻自由提供了必要的保护。

......

52. 张先生（中国）正式提请人权委员会同意将 E/CN.4/433/Rev.2 号文件作为基础案文。

该提案以 12 票对 0 票、1 票弃权获得通过。

......

——人权委员会第 163 次会议简要记录（E/CN.4/SR.163）

常健译校

E/CN.4/SR.163
2 May 1950
COMMISSION ON HUMAN RIGHTS
SIXTH SESSION
SUMMARY RECORD OF THE HUNDRED AND SIXTY-THIRD MEETING

Held at Lake Success, New York, on Thursday, 20 April 1950, at 3:00 p.m.

Draft International Covenant on Human Rights (Annexes I and II of the Report of the Fifth Session of the Commission on Human Rights, Document E/1371) (Continued); Article 17 (E/CN.4/365, E/CN.4/353/Add.10, E/CN.4/360,

E/CN.4/360/Corr.1, E/CN.4/415, E/CN.4/424, E/CN.4/432, E/CN.4/433/Rev.1, E/CN.4/433/Rev.2, E/CN.4/434) (Continued)

...

22. Mr. Chang (China) suggested that, in view of the number of proposals and amendments before it, the Commission should adopt the procedure of making a separate study of a basic proposal, deciding whether it required amendments and then voting on the amendments.

23. Following his own suggestion, he would confine his comments to the text of the United States amendment (E/CN.4/433/Rev. l). The first paragraph of that text was satisfactory, but the words "of information and" should be inserted between the words "freedom" and "of expression" in the first line. Inasmuch as the Commission had been concerned for three years with the freedom of infonmation, mention of it appeared indispensable. He also suggested that the words "without governmental interference" should be voted on separately, and that, for reasons of form, it would be better to replace the word "by" before "any other media" by the word "through".

24. He was opposed to the words "This right" at the beginning of paragraph 2. Reference to paragraph 1 showed that the right in question included "freedom to hold opinions, to seek, receive and impart information and ideas". The right to express opinions and the freedom to seek and receive information could not be subject to "such limitations as are provided by law", which could apply only to the right to impart information. He therefore suggested that the first line of paragraph 2 might be re-drafted to read: "The right to impart information and ideas shall be subject only...". He also suggested that the words "for the protection of" before "national security" should be replaced by "in the interest of", and that the words "for the protection of" should be inserted before the phrase, "the rights, reputation or freedom of other persons".

25. He explained that he had asked for a separate vote on the words "without governmental interference" because he considered them dangerous in that they might open the door to many abuses. There would, in any case, be governmental interference as only Governments could impose the limitations mentioned in

paragraph 2. Arbitrary interference, however, should be prevented and if the Commission so decided, it could stipulate in paragraph 1 that the right to freedom of information and expression belonged to the individual and that there could be no arbitrary interference on the part of the Government.

26. The Commission wasengaged in the study of an extremely broad subject; when future conventions and protocols were being dramn up it could return to the same questions and study them in a more detailed manner.

27. The Chairman, speaking as the United States representative, accepted the amendments proposed by the Chinese representative to paragraph 1 of the United States text. She would however prefer to keep the beginning of the second paragraph in its present form, and to delete the words "to hold opinions" in paragraph 1. She was willing to accept the substitution of the words "in the interests of" for the term "for the protection of".

28. With regard to the words "to be free from governmental interference", the principal source of interference was censorship enforced by the State. The words "to be free from governmental interference" must therefore be retained in article 17; they provided the necessary protection for freedom of information.

...

52. Mr. Chang (China) formally asked the Commission to adopt document E/CN.4/433/Rev.2 as the basic text.

That proposal was adopted by 12 votes to none, with 1 abstention.

...

在人权委员会第 164 次会议上的发言

1950 年 4 月 21 日星期五上午 11:00 纽约成功湖

《国际人权公约（草案）》（第 E/1371、E/CN.4/365、E/CN.4/415、E/CN.4/424、E/CN.4/432、E/CN.4/433/Rev.2、E/CN.4/434、E/CN.4/435、E/CN.4/438/Rev.1、E/CN.4/440 号文件）（续）
第 17 条（续）

……

2. 奥多诺先生（法国）解释说，他对第 1 款第一行的第二次修正案（第 E/CN.4/438/Rev.1 号文件）可以被视为主要是措辞上的修改。他已经为其更广泛的含义进行了辩护。应该区分表达自由的两个方面，即接受信息和传递信息。前者意味着主张自由，后者是新闻自由。本条其他部分对这些方面作了说明，因此在第 1 款第一行中提及这一点是多余的。

……

4. 张先生（中国）强调，第 17 条的整个历史表明，它一直被视为一条涉及新闻自由而不是表达自由的条款。在基本案文中重复"新闻"一词是完全有理由的，因为首先要说明一般权利，然后再进行具体定义。

5. 梅塔女士（印度）不同意中国代表的意见。基本概念是表达自由；新闻自由是一个从表达自由衍生而来的狭义概念。因此，她将支持法国的修正案。

6. 主席以美国代表的身份发言，她解释说，她接受插入"新闻和"的措辞，因为她认为这使该条更加准确；接受信息和思想是表达信息和思想能力的先决条件。没有获得信息的自由，表达自由将是不完整的。

7. 梅塔女士（印度）指出，新闻自由这一更为有限的概念出现在本款后面，因此不应限制第一行中更广泛的表达自由。

8. 张先生（中国）指出，《世界人权宣言》第 19 条同时涵盖了主张自由和新闻自由——它们是形成意见和表达意见的必要条件。印度代表团本来希望将该条的案文纳入公约草案。该公约不应比《世界人权宣言》更加局限。他不反对复述《世界人权宣言》的案文，因为他同意美国代表的意见，即如果从中删除新闻自由的概念，该款将是不充分的。

……

12. 如果法国修正案获得通过，张先生（中国）保留提议将第三行中的"新闻"一词应改为"主张"一词的权利。这样，《世界人权宣言》第19条的内容可以纳入公约草案第17条，或许可以作为单独一款。

……

18. 主席将法国对第一行的第二项修正案付诸表决，建议删除"新闻和"字样。

法国修正案以9票对4票、1票弃权获得通过。

19. 张先生（中国）敦促增加"主张和"等字，以取代委员会刚刚投票决定删除的"新闻和"。他指出，《世界人权宣言》第19条提到"主张和发表自由"，并指出公约第17条旨在补充第16条，该条并未完全涵盖主张自由。

20. 在回答惠特拉姆（澳大利亚）关于如果中国提案获得通过，案文其余部分将出现重复的问题时，张先生（中国）指出，《世界人权宣言》第19条也出现了类似的重复，因此，人权委员会只会强化《世界人权宣言》的规定。如果人权委员会认为合适，可以在第1款第2行和第3行的"持有主张"之后加上"不受干涉"。

……

37. 张先生（中国）同意英国、印度和黎巴嫩代表的意见，并就第17条提出了一项提案，他希望法国代表团也能接受该提案。他建议以下三款取代两条单独的条款："1.每个人都有不受干涉的主张自由的权利。"第二款将采用第E/CN.4/433/Rev.2号文件的案文，并删除人权委员会已同意删除的内容，还要删除了第2行和第3行中的"保持主张"的字样。最后，第三款将说明第2款中提到的权利将受到所列举的各种限制。

38. 门德斯先生（菲律宾）指出，以上的讨论表明，大家都普遍同意，在关于表达自由的草案中提及主张自由是偏离主题的。将这两个概念分离将使语言更流畅、更清晰。

39. 奥多诺先生（法国）表示，他的观点与中国和黎巴嫩代表的观点没有真正的区别。如果拟议的解决方案明确规定限制只涉及表达自由，而不涉及主张自由，他不会要求分成两条。

40. 梅塔女士（印度）不赞成分成两条或分成两款。在她看来，事情很简单，将两个理念分开似乎没有必要。

41. 主席以美国代表的身份发言，表示美国将支持中国代表关于分出第1款的建议。

42. 鲍伊女士（英国）认为不宜在公约中插入这类已经在《世界人权宣言》中写入的一般性条款。在接受中国提案之前，她必须对该提案进行研究 并考虑到这一因素。

43. 张先生（中国）在回答尼索特先生（比利时）时说，他理解"不受干涉"指的是那种不受欢迎的干涉。应当保留这一点，以避免在应当是一项切实可行的法律文书中包含一般性原则的陈述，正如英国代表所指出的。

……

51. 张先生（中国）担心乌拉圭修正案只会导致重新辩论。他认为，法国代表希望将表达自由的概念与主张自由的概念分开，而印度代表则认为这两项原则不应分开，如果在同一条中分成两款来表达这两个理念，他们都会感到满意。

52. 他认为可以由体裁委员会来编写一份符合黎巴嫩代表愿望的案文。

如此作出决定。

……

57. 张先生（中国）可以接受澳大利亚的案文。然而，他想知道，在做出决定之前，对该问题进行更通彻的考量是否会更好。

……

64. 主席在与秘书处协商后说，根据议事规则第 60 条，她将首先将中国关于将第 17 条第一款改写如下的建议付诸表决："人人享有主张自由的权利，不受干涉。"

该提案以 9 票对 2 票、4 票弃权获得通过。

65. 主席在回答阿兹库尔先生（黎巴嫩）时说，由于中国的提案已经通过，美国提案第一款中的"保持主张"的字样必须删除。然而，如果人权委员会愿意，她会将该修正案付诸表决。

会议于下午 1:50 结束。

——人权委员会第 164 次会议简要记录（E/CN.4/SR.164）

常健译校

E/CN.4/SR.164

1 May 1950

COMMISSION ON HUMAN RIGHTS
SIXTH SESSION
SUMMARY RECORD OF THE HUNDRED AND SIXTY-FOURTH MEETING

Held at Lake Success, New York, on Friday, 21 April 1950, at 11:00 a.m.

Draft International Covenant on Human Rights (E/1371, E/CN.4/365, E/CN.4/415, E/CN.4/424, E/CN.4/432, E/CN.4/433/Rev.2, E/CN.4/434, E/CN.4/435, E/CN.4/438/Rev.1, E/CN.4/440) (Continued)
Article 17 (Continued)

…

2. Mr. Ordonneau (France) explained that his second amendment (E/CN.4/438/Rev.1) to the first line of paragraph 1 might be regarded principally as a drafting change. He had already defended its wider implications. A distinction should be drawn between the two aspects of freedom of expression, namely, receiving information and imparting it. The former implied freedom of opinion, the latter freedom of information. These aspects were stated in other parts of the article, so that the reference to it in the first line of paragraph 1 was redundant.

…

4. Mr. Chang (China) stressed the fact that the entire history of article 17 went to show that it had always been regarded as an article dealing with freedom of information rather than with freedom of expression. The repetition of the word

"information" in the basic text was fully justified, because the general right was stated first and the specific definitions then followed.

5. Mrs. Mehta (India) could not agree with the Chinese representative. The fundamental concept was freedom of expression; freedom of information was a narrower concept deriving from that of freedom of expression. She would therefore support the French amendament.

6. The Chairman, speaking as the representative of the United States of America, explained that she had accepted the insertion of the words "information and" because she had believed that it made the article more precise; the reception of information and ideas was the prerequisite to the ability to express them. Freedom of expression would be incomplete without the freedom to obtain information.

7. Mrs. Mehta (India) pointed out that the more limited concept, freedom of information, appeared later in the paragraph and should therefore not limit freedom of expression the broader term, in the first line.

8. Mr. Chang (China) observed that article 19 of the Universal Declaration of Human Rights covered both the freedom of opinion and the freedom of information – the prerequiste for forming opinion and expressing it. The Indian delegation itself had originally wished to incorporate the text of that article in the draft covenant. The covenant should not more restrictive than the Declaration. He would not object to a reproduction of the text of the Declaration, because he agreed with the representative of the United States that the paragraph would be inadequate if the concept of freedom of information was deleted from it.

…

12. Mr. Chang (China) reserved the right to propose that the word "opinion" should be substituted for the word "information" in the third line, should the French amendment be adopted. The substance of article 19 of the Declaration could thus be incorporated in article 17 of the draft covenant, perhaps in a separate paragraph.

…

18. The Chairman put to the vote the second French amendment to the first line, proposing the deletion of the words "information and".

That French amendment was adopted by 9 votes to 4, with 1 abstention.

19. Mr. Chang (China) urged the addition of the words "opinion and" to replace the words "information and" which the Commission had just voted to delete. He pointed out that article 19 of the Universal Declaration of Human Rights referred to "freedom of opinion and expression" and indicated that article 17 of the covenant was intended to supplement article 16 which did not fully cover freedom of opinion.

20. In reply to a question by Whitlam (Australia) regarding the repetition which would occur in the rest of the text if the Chinese proposal were adopted, Mr. Chang (China) noted that similar repetition occurred in article 19 of the Declaration and that therefore the Commission would merely be reinforcing the provisions of the Declaration. If the Commission was fit, it could add the words "without interference" after the expression "to hold opinions" in lines 2 and 3 of paragraph 1.

…

37. Mr. Chang (China) agreed with the views of the representatives of the United Kindom, India and Lebanon and presented a proposal for article 17 which he hoped would also be acceptable to the French delegation. Instead of two separate articles, he suggested three paragraphs as follows: "1. Everyone has the right to freedom of opinion without interference." The second paragraph would reproduce the text of E/CN.4/433/Rev.2 with the deletion which the Commission had agreed to as well as the deletion of the words "to hold opinions" in lines 2 and 3. Finally a third paragraph would state that the rights referred to in paragraph 2 would be subject to the limitations enumerated.

38. Mr. Mendez (Philippines) noted that the discussion indicated general agreement that reference to freedom of opinion was out of context in a draft on freedom of expression. Separation of the two concepts made for smoother language and greater clarity.

39. Mr. Ordonneau (France) indicated that there was no real difference between his view and those of the representatives of China and Lebanon. He would not press for two separate articles if the proposed solution made it clear that the limitations referred only to freedom of expression and not to freedom of

opinion.

40. Mrs. Mehta (India) was not in favour or two separate articles of two separate paragraphs. In her opinion the matter was quite simple and separation of the two ideas seemed unnecessary.

41. The Chairman, speaking as the representative of the United States of America, indicated that the United States would support a separate paragraph 1 as suggested by the representative of China.

42. Miss Bowie (Unite Kingdom) thought it inappropriate to insert in the covenant general provisions of the type which had been included in the Universal Declaration of Human Rights. Before accepting the Chinese proposal, she would have to study the proposed text with that consideration in mind.

43. In reply to Mr. Nisot (Belgium), Mr. Chang (China) said he understood the phrase "without interference" to mean the undesirable type of interference. It should be retained to avoid including a general statement of principle in what should rightly be, as the representative of the United Kingdom had pointed out, a practical legal instrument.

…

51. Mr. Chang (China) feared that the Uruguayan amendment would only lead to renewed debate. He thought that both the representative of France, who wished to separate the concept of freedom of expression from that of freedom of opinion, and the representative of India, who did not think the two principles should be severed, would be satisfied if those ideas were presented in two separate paragraphs within the same article.

52. He thought it could be left to the Style Committee to prepare a text which would meet the wishes of the Lebanese representative.

It was so decided.

…

57. Mr. Chang (China) could accept the Australian text. He wondered, however, whether it would not be better to consider the matter more thoroughly before taking a decision.

…

64. The Chairman, after consultation with the Secretariat, said that, in

accordance with rule 60 of the rules of procedure, she would first put to the vote the Chinese proposal to redraft the first paragraph of article 17 as follows: "Everyone shall have the right to freedom of opinion without interference."

That proposal was adopted by 9 vote to 2, with 4 abstentions.

65. In reply to Mr. Azkoul (Lebanon), the Chairman said that, as the Chinese proposal had been adopted, the words "to hold opinions" would have to be deleted from the first paragraph of the United States proposal. If the Commission wished, however, she would put that amendment to the vote.

The meeting rose at 1:50 p.m.

在人权委员会第 165 次会议上的发言

1950 年 4 月 21 日星期五下午 3:00 纽约成功湖

**《国际人权公约（草案）》（人权委员会第五届会议的报告的附件
一和附件二，第 E/1371 号文件）（续）
第 17 条（第 E/CN.4/365、E/CN.4/433/Rev.2、
E/CN.4/438/Rev.1、E/CN.4/440 号文件）**

......

20. 张先生（中国）说，美国的案文应该有更明确的定义。该案文提到
了信息和思想，但这些概念并非排他性的。法国的修正案使案文更加具体，
他想知道该修正案是否意味着批评意见应该被否决。他认为最好只提事实
和思想。

......

31. 张先生（中国）说，如果人权委员会开始进行词源学讨论，辩论可
能会过度延长。他建议对法国修正案的几个部分进行单独表决；首先，对
写入"所有种类"的措辞进行表决；如果法国代表坚持，对"包括事实"
的措辞进行表决；最后，对"批判性评论"的措辞进行表决。此外，如果
需要，人权委员会可以对原文中出现的"和思想"进行表决。

......

41. 尼索特先生（比利时）要求接下来就美国为第 17 条提出的新案文
中的"和思想"的措辞进行表决。

42. 张先生（中国）想知道这些词将放在句子的哪个部分。

43. 主席说，由于人权委员会已经通过了"各种信息"的措辞，"和思
想"只能跟在其后。

44. 鲍伊女士（英国）不同意，认为如果将"和思想"放在"信息"和
"各种"之间，表达会更为有力。

45. 由于没有人反对该提案，主席将在"信息"和"各种"之间插入

"和思想"等字的提案付诸表决，这样，该短语将改为"各种信息和思想"。

该提案以 10 票对 1 票、4 票弃权获得通过。

……

53. 张先生（中国）认为，美国建议的第 1 款的措辞令人满意，采用英国建议的限制性表述是危险的。

54. 奥多诺先生（法国）在尼索特先生（比利时）的支持下，同意中国代表的意见。人权委员会成员必须考虑到这一事实：他们的工作涉及未来而不是过去；没有人能预见一百年后会使用什么样的新闻媒体。

……

74. 张先生（中国）认为，美国的案文对法律规定的限制的定义较窄。法国修正案的案文更加简洁，但将这些限制扩大到新闻自由，这似乎并不可取。

……

103. 张先生（中国）说，联合国新闻自由会议认为，宣布有关权利附带义务和责任是明智的，他对此感到满意。另一方面，他认为没有必要在国际人权公约草案中再次提醒新闻界这一事实。最好保留美国代表团提交的第 2 款案文。

104. 引入"特别"一词将使英国的修正案更不可接受；人们很可能想知道，要提到的特殊职责和责任是什么。

……

110. 张先生（中国）认为英文单词"保护"不合适。国家安全、公共秩序等抽象概念不应受到"保护"。

……

114. 在交换意见的过程中，中国、比利时、澳大利亚和英国的代表提议翻译短语"pour la sauvegarde"而不是"for the protection"，主席建议法国和英国代表商定一个法语和英语都令人满意的措辞。这样提交的新修正案可在人权委员会下次会议上审议。

如此作出决定。

会议于下午 5:35 结束。

——人权委员会第 165 次会议简要记录（E/CN.4/SR.165）

常健译校

E/CN.4/SR.165

2 May 1950

COMMISSION ON HUMAN RIGHTS
SIXTH SESSION
SUMMARY RECORD OF THE HUNDRED AND SIXTY-FIFTH MEETING

Held at Lake Success, New York, On Friday, 21 April 1950, at 3:00 p.m.

Draft International Covenant on Human Rights (Annexes I and II of the Report of the Fifth Session of the Commission on Human Rights, Document E/1371) (Continued); Article 17 (E/CN.4/365, E/CN.4/433/Rev.2, E/CN.4/438/Rev.1, E/CN.4/440)

...

20. Mr. Chang (China) said that the United States text should be more clearly defined. The text mentioned information and ideas, but those notions were not exclusive. He wished to know whether the French amendment, which made the text more specific, implied that critical comment should be deprecated. He thought it would be better to mention only facts and ideas.

...

31. Mr. Chang (China) remarked that if the Commission embarked upon an etymological discussion, the debate might be prolonged unduly. He proposed that separate votes should be taken upon the several parts of the French amendment; first, upon the inclusion of the words "of all kinds" ("de toute espèce"); then, if the French representative insisted, upon the words "including facts" ("notamment des felts") ; and lastly , upon the words "critical comment" ("des appréciations critiques"). Further, If it was so desired, the Commission might vote upon the words "and ideas", appearing in the original text.

...

41. Mr. Nisot (Belgium) asked for the vote to be taken next on the words

"and ideas" in the new text proposed for article 17 by the United States of America.

42. Mr. Chang (China) wanted to know in what part of the sentence those words would be placed.

43. The Chairman said that since the Commission had already adopted the words "information of all kinds", the words "and ideas" could only follow after them.

44. Miss Bowie (United Kingdom) did not agree and thought that expression would be more forceful if the words "and ideas" were placed between "information" and "of all kinds".

45. In the absence of any objection to that proposal, the Chairman put to the vote the proposal to insert the words "and ideas" between "information" and "of all kinds", so that the phrase would read "information and ideas of all kinds".

The proposal was adopted by 10 votes to 1, with 4 abstentions.

...

53. Mr. Chang (China) thought that the wording of paragraph 1 as proposed by the United States was satisfactory and that it would be dangerous to adopt the restrictive formula suggested by the United Kingdom.

54. Mr. Ordonneau (France) supported by Mr. Nisot (Belgium) agreed with the representative of China. The members of the Commission must take into account the fact that their work concerned the future and not the past; no one could foresses what information media would be employed in a hundred years' time.

...

74. Mr. Chang (China) considered that the United States text gave a narrower definition of the limitations provided by the law. The text of the French amendment was more concise but extended those limitations to freedom of information, which did not appear to be desirable.

...

103. Mr. Chang (China) was gratified that the United Nations Conference on Freedom of information had thought it wise to declare that the right in question carried with it duties and responsibilities. On the other hand, he did not

think it necessary to remind the press of that fact once again in the draft international covenant on human, rights. It would be well to retain the text of paragraph **2** submitted by the United States delegation.

104. The introduction of the word "special" would make the United Kingdom's amendment even less acceptable; it might well be wondered what were the special duties and responsibilities to which allusion was to be made.

…

110. Mr. Chang (China) did not think the English word "protection" suitable. Abstractions such as national security, public order etc. could not be "protected".

…

114. Following an exchange of views, in the course of which the representatives of China, Belgium, Australia and the United Kingdom proposed translation for the phrase "pour la sauvegarde" other than "for the protection", the Chairman suggested that the French and United Kingdom representatives should agree on a wording which would be satisfactory both in French and in English. The new amendment thus submitted could be examine during the Commission's next meeting.

It was so decided.

The meeting rose at 5:35 p.m.

在人权委员会第 166 次会议上的发言

1950 年 4 月 24 日星期一上午 11:15 纽约成功湖

《国际人权公约（草案）》（人权委员会第五届会议的报告的附件一和附件二，第 E/1371 号文件）（续）

会议主席：张彭春先生（中国）

第 13 条第 5 款（第 E/CN.4/365、E/CN.4/441、E/CN.4/445、E/CN.4/448、E.CN.4/L.4 号文件）（续）

1. 主席欢迎法国代表卡森先生，他此前一直未能参加委员会第六届会议的工作。

……

24. 主席以中国代表的身份发言，指出法语文本第 1 款中使用了"未成年人"一词，最好再使用一次。他建议委员会应采纳美国代表的建议，因此下次会议应在下午 3:00 而不是下午 2:30 举行。

如此作出决定。

……

第 17 条（第 E/CN.4/365、E/CN.4/424、E/CN.4/433/Rev.2、E/CN.4/434 号文件）

25. 主席回顾说，人权委员会尚未通过第 17 条第 3 款（原第 2 款）的最后案文。

……

36. 主席说，由于人权委员会所有成员似乎都同意法国修正案，因此没有必要将其付诸表决。

如此作出决定。

……

40. 主席随后请人权委员会成员审查英国的修正案，它将 "公共秩序" 改为 "防止混乱或犯罪"（第 E/CN.4./365 号文件，第 50 页）。

······

47. 梅塔女士（印度）在回答主席时确认，印度代表团没有撤回其修正案（第 E/CN.4/424 号文件）。她会在适当的时候介绍它。

······

——人权委员会第 166 次会议简要记录（E/CN.4/SR.166）

常健译校

E/CN.4/SR.166

1 May 1950

COMMISSION ON HUMAN RIGHTS
SIXTH SESSION
SUMMARY RECORD OF THE HUNDRED AND SIXTY-SIXTH MEETING

Held at Lake Success, New York, on Monday, 21 April 1950, at 11:15 p.m.

Draft International Covenant on Human Rights (Annexes I and II of the Report of the Fifth Session of the Commission on Human Rights, Document E/1371) (Continued)

Chairman: Mr. Chang (China)

Article 13, paragraph 5 (E/CN.4/365, E/CN.4/441, E/CN.4/445, E/CN.4/448, E.CN.4/L.4)

1. The Chairman welcomed Mr. Cassin, French representative, who had so far not taken part in the Commission's work during the sixth session.

…

24. The Chairman, speaking as representative of China, pointed out that the word "mineurs" had been used in paragraph 1 of the French text and that it might be advisable to use it again. He proposed that the Commission should adopt the

United States representative's suggestion and that its next meeting should accordingly be held at 3:00 p.m. and not at 2:30 p.m.

It was so decided.

Article 17 (E/CN.4/365, E/CN.4/424, E/CN.4/433/Rev.2, E/CN.4/434)

25. The Chairman recalled that the Commission he not yet adopted a final text for paragraph 3 (original paragraph 2) of article 17.

...

36. The Chairman said that, as all the members of the Commision appeared to be in agreement on the French amendment, it was unnecessary to put it to the vote.

It was so decided.

...

40. The Chairman then invited the members of the Commission to examine the United Kingdom amendment to replace the words "of public order" by the words "for prevention of disorder or crime" (E/CN.4./365, page 50).

...

47. Replying to the Chairman, Mrs. Mehta (India) confirmed that her delegation had not withdrawn its amendment (E/CN.4/424). She would introduce it in due course.

...

在人权委员会第 167 次会议上的发言

1950 年 4 月 24 日星期一下午 3:00 纽约成功湖

欢迎妇女地位委员会的成员
《国际人权公约（草案）》（续）
第 17 条（第 E/1371、E/CN.4/353、E/CN.4/365/Add.10、E/CN.4/365、E/CN.4/433/Rev.2、E/CN.4/434、E/CN.4/438/Rev.1、E/CN.4/439、E/CN.4/440、E/CN.4/441、E/CN.4/442、E/CN.4/445、E/CN.4/446、E/CN.4/424 号文件）
（续）
第 13 条（第 E/CN.4/449 和 E/CN.4/L.4 号文件）（续）

主席：张彭春先生（中国）

……

1. 主席向妇女地位委员会成员科尔德曼夫人表示热烈欢迎。

2. 主席请人权委员会继续讨论美国第 17 条草案（第 E/CN.4/433/Rev.2 号文件）以及英国（第 E/CN.4/440 号文件）、法国（第 E/CN.4/438/Rev.1 号文件）、埃及（第 E/CN.4/434 号文件）和印度（第 E/CN.4/424 号文件）对该提案第 2 款的修正案。

……

10. 主席以中国代表的身份发言，他指出，《世界人权宣言》第 29 条中使用了"民主社会"一词来限定整个条款，而不是仅仅限定"公共秩序"一词。然而，最好在第 17 条中不提及"民主社会"，并为整个公约起草一项总括条款。

……

19. 主席将英国对第 17 条第 2 款的修正案（第 E/CN.4/440 号文件）付诸表决。由于有人要求分两部分对修正案进行表决，他首先将"防止混乱"等字样付诸表决。

这些措辞以 7 票反对、6 票赞成、2 票弃权被否决。

20. 主席说，由于英国修正案的第一部分已经被否决，他不会再将"或犯罪"一词付诸表决。

大家都对此表示同意。

21. 主席将法国的修正案付诸表决，该修正案要求在第 17 条第 2 款"公共秩序"之后加上"在民主社会中"（第 E/CN.4/438/Rev.1 号文件）。

该修正案以 8 票反对、5 票赞成、2 票弃权被否决。

22. 主席随后将关于第 17 条的美国草案（第 E/CN.4/433/Rev.2 号文件）中第 2 款的"国家安全、公共秩序、安全、健康或道德"一语付诸表决。

该短语获得一致通过。

……

24.主席将经修正的关于第 17 条的美国草案第 2 款最后一句付诸表决（第 E/CN.4/433/Rev.2 号文件）。

该短语获得一致通过。

……

34. 主席以中国代表的身份发言，同意印度修正案对表达自由施加的额外限制。他想知道是否可以重新措辞以应对这一反对意见。

……

51. 主席将印度修正案（第 E/CN.4/424 号文件）付诸表决。

该提案以 6 票反对、5 票赞成、4 票弃权被否决。

……

54. 在没有人反对的情况下，主席注意到大家普遍认为，英国的修正案被第 2 段所涵盖，因此不需要单独表决。

55. 他要求对经修正的第 17 条案文进行表决。

经修正的第 17 条以 13 票赞成、0 票反对、2 票弃权获得通过。

……

67. 主席回顾说，人权委员会已同意首先审议第 17 条的美国案文及其各种修正案作为其基本案文，然后研究菲律宾提交的备选案文（第 E/CN.4/365 号文件）和南斯拉夫提交的备选案文（第 E/CN.4/415 号文件）。

……

71. 主席将关于第 17 条备选案文的南斯拉夫提案付诸表决。

南斯拉夫的提案（第 E/CN. 4/415 号文件）以 5 票反对、1 票赞成、8 票弃权被否决。

73. 主席注意到起草小组已提交了第 13 条第 2 款（e）项的商定案文（第 E/CN.4/449 号文件）。

......

85. 主席将起草小组提交的案文（第 E/CN.4/449 号文件）付诸表决。起草小组提交的案文被一致接受。

......

87. 主席将经修正的第 13 条付诸表决。

经修正的第 13 条获得一致通过。

会议于下午 5:35 结束。

——人权委员会第 167 次会议简要记录（E/CN.4/SR.167）

常健译校

E/CN.4/SR.167

5 May 1950

COMMISSION ON HUMAN RIGHTS
SIXTH SESSION
SUMMARY RECORD OF THE HUNDRED AND SIXTY-THIRD MEETING

Held at Lake Success, New York, on Monday, 24 April 1950, at 3:00 p.m.

Welcome to the member of the Commission on the Status of Women
Draft International Covenant on Human Rights (Continued)
Article 17 (E/1371, E/CN.4/353, E/CN.4/365/Add.10, E/CN.4/365, E/CN.4/433/Rev.2, E/CN.4/434, E/CN.4/438/Rev.1, E/CN.4/439, E/CN.4/440, E/CN.4/441, E/CN.4/442, E/CN.4/445, E/CN.4/446, E/CN.4/424) (Continued)
Article 13 (E/CN.4/449, E/CN.4/L.4) (Continued)

Chairman: Mr. Chang (China)

1. The Chairman extended a cordial welcome to Mrs. Coldman, the member of the Commission on the Status of Women.

2. The Chairman invited the Commission to continue its discussion of the United States draft article 17 (E/CN.4/433/Rev.2) and the amendments to paragraph 2 of that proposal by the United Kingdom (E/CN.4/440), France (E/CN.4/438/Rev.1) Egypt (E/CN.4/434) and India (E/CN.4/424).

…

10. The Chairman, speaking as representative of China, observed that the phrase "democratic society" had been used in article 29 of the Universal Declaration of Human Rights to qualify the article as a whole, and not merely the phrase "public order". It might be better, however, to omit the reference from article 17 and draft an omnibus clause for the covenant as a whole.

…

19. The Chairman put the United Kingdom amendment to paragraph 2 of article 17 (E/CN.4/440) to the vote. As a request had been made that the amendment should be voted upon in two parts, he first put to the vote the words "the prevention of disorder".

Those words were rejected by 7 votes to 6, with 2 abstentions.

20. The Chairman said that, as the first part of the United Kingdom amendment had been lost, he would not put the words "or crime" to the vote.

It was so agreed.

21. The chairman put to the vote the French amendment to add the words "in a democratic society" after the words "public order" in paragraph 2 of article 17 (E/CN.4/438/Rev.1).

That amendment was rejected by 8 votes to 5, with 2 abstentions.

22. The Chairman then put to the vote the phrase "of national security, public order, safety, health or morals" in paragraph 2 of the United States draft article 17 (E/CN.4/433/Rev.2).

That phrase was adopted unanimously.

…

24. The Chairman put to the vote the last phrase of the second paragraph of the United States draft article 17 as amended (E/CN.4/433/Rev.2).

That phrase was adopted unanimously.

…

34. The Chairman, speaking as representative of China, agreed that the Indian amendment as it stood imposed an additional limitation on freedom of expression. He wondered whether it could be rephrased to meet that objection.

…

51. The Chairman put the Indian amendment (E/CN.4/424) to the vote.

It was rejected by 6 votes to 5, with 4 abstentions.

…

54. In the absence of objection, the Chairman noted the general consensus that the United Kingdom amendments were covered by paragraph 2 and that a separate vote was therefore unnecessary.

55. He called for a vote on the text of article 17 as amended.

Article 17 as amended was adopted by 13 votes to none, with 2 abstentions.

…

67. The Chairman recalled that the Commission had agreed first to consider the United States text of article 17 and the various amendments thereto as its basic text and then to study the alternative texts submitted by the Philippines (E/CN.4/365) and Yugoslavia (E/CN.4/415).

…

71. The Chairman put the Yugoslav proposal for an alternative text of article 17 to the vote.

The Yugoslav proposal (E/CN.4/415) was rejected by 5 votes to 1, with 8 abstentions.

73. The Chairman noted that the drafting group had submitted an agreed text for paragraph 2 (e) of article 13 (E/CN.4/449).

…

85. The Chairman put the text submitted by the drafting group (E/CN.4/449) to the vote.

The text submitted by the drafting group was unanimously accepted.

87. The Chairman put article 13 as amended to the vote.

Article 13 as amended was unanimously adopted.

The meeting rose at 5:35 p.m.

在人权委员会第 170 次会议上的发言

1950 年 4 月 26 日星期三上午 11:00 纽约成功湖

《国际人权公约（草案）》（人权委员会第五届会议的报告的附件一和附件二，第 E/1371 号文件）（续）
新闻自由：埃及、法国、印度和黎巴嫩提交的联合决议草案（第 E/CN.4/439 和 E/CN.4/439/Corr.1 号文件）
美国对联合决议草案的修正案（第 E/CN.4/442 号文件）
……

43. 张先生（中国）回顾了新闻自由公约草案的历史，并指出世界局势不可避免地对联合国的工作进程产生了影响。根据两年前的一项决定，1948 年在日内瓦举行了新闻自由会议。会议起草了三项公约草案，经经济及社会理事会和大会轮流审议。事实证明，经济及社会理事会第九届会议不可能通过第三份草案，因为某些国家在后期提交了大量修正案；值得注意的是，当时的立场已经变得固化了。因此，等一段时间似乎更为明智。联合国大会已经放弃了对该事项的表决；它倾向于将其提交人权委员会，并确定将写入人权公约的有关新闻自由条款的总体思路。这就是实际情况；人权委员会起草了第 17 条，并将提交联合国大会，联合国大会当然将对此事项作出最后决定。

44. 根据所有这些情况，张先生觉得到了该投票表决的时候了。他概述了他对人权委员会面前的两份案文的看法，并在提到联合决议草案时指出，拟订一项公约是确保新闻自由的一种手段，但不是唯一手段，并建议对案文进行相应修订。就美国的修正案而言，四年前，联合国大会就已经认识到需要制定一项关于新闻自由的公约。仍然需要作出的唯一决定与该公约的案文有关。因此，最好使用"关于特别公约"这一短语。

45. 卡森先生（法国）、拉马丹先生（埃及）、梅塔夫人（印度）和马利克先生（黎巴嫩）同意按照中国代表的建议修改其联合决议草案。

46. 主席以美国代表的身份发言，她说，她倾向于美国代表团的原始修正案。但是，如果中国代表希望她这样做，她准备将中国代表的提案付诸表决。

47. 主席将美国的修正案付诸表决，该修正案要求以第 E/CN.4/442 号文件中的案文取代联合决议草案第 3 款。

该修正案以 7 票反对、3 票赞成、3 票弃权被否决。

……

——人权委员会第 170 次会议简要记录（E/CN.4/SR.170）

常健译校

E/CN.4/SR.170
5 May 1950

COMMISSION ON HUMAN RIGHTS
SIXTH SESSION
SUMMARY RECORD OF THE HUNDRED AND SEVENTIETH MEETING

Held at Lake Success, New York, on Wednesday, 26 April 1950, at 11:00 a.m.

Draft International Covenant on Human Rights (Annexes I and II of the Report of the Fifth Session of the Commission on Human Rights, Document E/1371) (Continued)
Freedom of Information: Joint Draft Resolution Submitted by Egypt, France, India and Lebanon (E/CN.4/439, E/CN.4/439/Corr.1)
United States Amendment to the Joint Draft Resolution (E/CN.4/442)

…

43. Mr. Chang (China) traced the history of the draft convention on freedom of information and pointed out that the world situation had inevitably had its effect on the course of the United Nations' work. The Conference on Freedom of Information had been convened in Geneva in 1948 in accordance with a decision taken two years earlier. The Conference had drawn up three draft conventions,

which had been examined in turn by the Economic and Social Council and by the General Assembly. It had not proved possible to adopt the third draft at the Council's ninth session on account of the large number of amendments submitted at a late stage by certain delegations; it should be borne in mind that at that time positions had hardened. It therefore seemed wiser to allow a certain period to elapse. The general Assembly had abstained from taking a final decision in the matter; it had preferred to refer it to the Commission on Human Rights and to ascertain the general lines of the article on freedom of information to be included in the covenant on human rights. Such was the actual situation; the Commission had drafted article 17 and would submit it to the General Assembly, which would of course take the final decision in the matter.

44. In all the circumstances, Mr. Chang felt that the time had come to take a vote. Outlining his views on the two texts before the Commission, he pointed out with reference to the joint draft resolution that the preparation of a convention was one means but not the only means of ensuring freedom of information and proposed that the text should be amended accordingly. Where the United States amendment was concerned, the desirability of preparing a convention on freedom of information had already been recognized by the General Assembly four years earlier. The only decision it was still required to take was related to the text of that convention. It would therefore be preferable to use the phrase "with respect to a special convention".

45. Mr. Cassin (France), Mr. Ramadan (Egypt), Mrs. Mehta (India) and Mr. Malik (Lebanon) agreed to amend their joint draft resolution on the lines suggested by the representative of China.

46. The Chairman, speaking as the representative of the United States of America, said that she preferred her delegation's amendment in its original form. She was, however, prepared to put the Chinese representative's proposal to vote, if he wished her to do so.

47. The Chairman put to the vote the United States amendment to replace the third paragraph of the joint draft resolution by the text in document E/CN.4/442.

That amendment was rejected by 7 votes to 3, with 3 abstentions.

...

在人权委员会第 171 次会议上的发言

1950 年 4 月 26 日星期三下午 2:30 纽约成功湖

《国际人权公约（草案）》
第 17 条（第 E/1371、E/CN.4/353/Add.10、E/CN.4/365、E/CN.4/439、E/CN.4/439/Corr.1、E/CN.4/442 号文件）（续）
第 19 条（第 E/1371、E/CN.4/353/Add.10、E/CN.4/365、E/CN.4/164、E/CN.4/164/Add.1 号文件）

......

4. 张先生（中国）认为，今后最好在进行表决之前提交所有修正案。

......

34. 张先生（中国）支持法国对第 1 款的修正案，该修正案的形式与第 18 条相似。但是，如果保留原文，第 2 款应修改为"这项权利仅受这种限制如……"。

35. 相对于第 19 条，他更喜欢第 18 条中限制条款的形式。他建议体裁委员会考虑将第 2 款修改为："确保国家安全、公共秩序、维护健康或道德，或保护他人的基本权利和自由。"

36. 为了确保整个公约的风格更加统一，如果要删除具体限制性条款，他可以接受英国的修正案。

......

84. 张先生（中国）认为这两项公约不可能发生冲突。本公约旨在成为一项法律文书，以强化《世界人权宣言》所宣布的权利，那些更具体地处理本公约所规定的各项保障的现有的或未来的公约，将进一步增强本公约的效力。只有联合国大会通过的一项新的结社自由公约，才有损于国际劳工组织公约。没有理由保留第 19 条第 3 款，特别是因为可以在第 22 条中引入进一步的保障措施，以防止与其他公约发生冲突。

......

88. 张先生（中国）建议，应推迟审议乌拉圭对第 3 款的修正案，直到该修正案以书面形式分发，他建议休会。然而，他接受英国代表的建议，即应立即对第 19 条第 1 款和第 2 款进行表决。

89. 奥瑞比先生（乌拉圭）接受了这一妥协方案。

......

——人权委员会第 171 次会议简要记录（E/CN.4/SR.171）
常健译校

E/CN.4/SR.171
8 May 1950

COMMISSION ON HUMAN RIGHTS
SIXTH SESSION
SUMMARY RECORD OF THE HUNDRED AND SEVENTY-FIRST MEETING

Held at Lake Success, New York, on Wednesday, 26 April 1950, at 2:30 p.m.

Draft International Covenant on Human Rights
Article 17 (E/1371, E/CN.4/353/Add.10, E/CN.4/365, E/CN.4/439, E/CN.4/439/Corr.1, E/CN.4/442) (Continued)
Article 19 (E/1371, E/CN.4/353/Add.10, E/CN.4/365, E/CN.4/164, E/CN.4/164/Add.1)

…

4. Mr. Chang (China) thought that in future it would be better to table all amendments before proceeding to the vote.

…

34. Mr. Chang (China) supported the French amendment to paragraph 1, which was similar in form to article 18. If the original text were retained, however, paragraph 2 should be amended to read "This right shall be subject only to such limitations…"

35. He also preferred the form of the limitation clause in article 18 to that in article 19. He proposed that the Style Committee should consider amending

paragraph 2 to read: "to ensure national security, public order, the preservation of health or morals, or the protection of the fundamental rights and freedom of others."

36. in the interests of securing a more uniform style throughout the covenant he could accept the United Kingdom amendment if the specific limitations clause were deleted.

...

84. Mr. Chang (China) saw no possibility of conflict between the two conventions. The covenant was intended to be a legal instrument to reinforce the rights proclaimed in the Declaration and to be further strengthened by existing conventions or future conventions dealing more specifically with the guarantees it provided. Only a new convention on freedom of association, adopted by the General Assembly, could prejudice the ILO Convention. There was no reason to retain paragraph 3 of article 19, especially since further safeguards against conflict with other conventions could be introduced in article 22.

...

88. Mr. Chang (China) suggested that consideration of the Uruguayan amendment to paragraph 3 should be deferred until it had been distributed in writing and moved the adjournment of the meeting. He accepted the United Kingdom representative's suggestion, however, that a vote should be taken forthwith on paragraphs 1 and 2 of article 19.

89. Mr. Oribe (Uruguay) accepted that compromise.

...

在人权委员会第 173 次会议上的发言

1950 年 4 月 27 日星期四下午 2:30 纽约成功湖

《国际人权公约（草案）》（续）
第 20 条（第 E/1371、E/CN.4/353/Add.10、
E/CN.4/353/Add.111、E/CN.4/358、E/CN.4/365、E/CN.4/418、
E/CN.4/447/Rev.1、E/CN.4/451、E/CN.4/455、E/CN.4/456 号文
件）（续）

会议主席：张彭春先生（中国）

1. 主席请人权委员会继续审议第 20 条。

……

23. 主席以中国代表的身份发言，强调第 20 条不是关于法律的条款，而在本质上是涉及平等的条款。人权几乎总是涉及比较和平等对待问题。尽管很难将《世界人权宣言》第 1 条写入法律条款，但公约至少可以规定法律面前人人平等的基本原则。

24. 中国代表说，长时间的讨论并没有影响他对人权委员会第 20 条案文的支持。

……

82. 主席以中国代表的身份发言，认为智利的修正案可能会引起误解。为了避免人们认为人权委员会对这一问题的看法不如过去那么严厉，"种族、肤色"的措辞应该保留，尽管可能缺乏清晰的定义。

……

88. 主席认为人权委员会可以对第 20 条的案文进行表决，并在二读时审议乌拉圭代表提出的问题。

……

94. 主席将休会动议付诸表决。

该动议以 7 票反对、6 票赞成、2 票弃权被否决。

95. 主席在回答奥瑞比先生（乌拉圭）时解释说，辩论尚未结束，黎巴嫩修正案可以接受。

......

97. 主席还提醒人权委员会，"歧视"一词已被选为法语文本中"区别"一词的最佳翻译。

......

——人权委员会第 173 次会议简要记录（E/CN.4/SR.173）

常健译校

E/CN.4/SR.173

9 May 1950

COMMISSION ON HUMAN RIGHTS
SIXTH SESSION
SUMMARY RECORD OF THE HUNDRED AND SEVENTY-THIRD MEETING

Held at Lake Success, New York, on Thursday, 27 April 1950, at 2:30 p.m.

**Draft International Covenant on Human Rights (Continued)
Article 20 (E/1371, E/CN.4/353/Add.10, E/CN.4/353/Add.11,
E/CN.4/358, E/CN.4/365, E/CN.4/418, E/CN.4/447/Rev.1,
E/CN.4/451, E/CN.4/455, E/CN.4/456) (Continued)**

Chairman: Mr. Chang (China)

1. The Chairman invited the Commission to proceed with its consideration of article 20.

...

23. The Chairman, speaking as the representative of China, stressed the fact that article 20 was not an article on law but rather an article dealing essentially with equality. Human rights almost always involved comparison and questions

of equal treatment. Although it was difficult to put article 1 of the Universal Declaration into legal terms, the covenant could at least provide for the essential of equality before the law.

24. The representative of China stated that the long discussion had not affected his support of the Commission's text of article 20.

...

82. The Chairman, speaking as the representative of China, suggested that the Chilean amendment might give rise to misunderstandings. To avoid any idea that the Commission took a less severe view of the matter than it had in the past, the words "race, colour" should be retained, ill-defined though they might be.

...

88. The Chairman thought that the Commission could vote on the text of article 20 and consider the point raised by the Uruguayan representative at the second reading.

...

94. The Chairman put to the vote the motion to adjourn.

That motion was rejected by 7 votes to 6, with 2 abstentions.

95. In reply to Mr. Oribe (Uruguay), the Chairman explained that the debate was not closed and that the Lebanese amendment could be admitted.

...

97. The Chairman too reminded the Commission that the word "discrimination" had been chosen as the best translation for the word "distinction" in the French text.

...

在人权委员会第 174 次会议上的发言

1950 年 4 月 28 日星期五上午 11:00 纽约成功湖

**《国际人权公约（草案）》（人权委员会第五届会议的报告的附件
一和附件二，第 E/1371 号文件）（续）
第 20 条（第 E/CN.4/365、E/CN.4/447、E/CN.4/455、
E/CN.4/455/Rev.1、E/CN.4/456 号文件）（续）
第 21 条（E/CN.4/365、E/CN.4/353/Add.10、
E/CN.4/353/Add.11、E/CN.4/358 号文件，第 52 段）**

……

11. 张先生（中国）指出，在黎巴嫩代表团以书面形式提交正式提案之前，最难作出决定。这一观点得到凯罗先生（希腊）的支持。

……

17. 张先生（中国）要求将关于第 20 条的讨论推迟到下一次会议，以便代表们能够研究黎巴嫩提案的书面文本，并对这一非常重要的条款进行应有的彻底审议。这一提议得到卡森先生（法国）的支持。

18. 主席将中国代表的提案付诸表决。

该提案以 10 票对 0 票、4 票弃权获得通过。

……

49. 张先生（中国）认为，为第 21 条提出的案文并不完全清楚。当然，法国草案具有建设性。它源于第二次世界大战的惨痛经历和对犹太人屡遭迫害的记忆。然而，苏联文本中出现的"法西斯-纳粹"一词不能被一些国家接受。事实上，这些词指的是意识形态，根据所涉及的不同国家可以被赋予各种其他名称，因此这一概念不应出现在像公约这样的文件中。

50. 法国草案表达了一项不容忽视的原则。应用这一原则无疑会遇到一些困难，正如美国代表所指出的，它可能会导致滥用。此外，使用"民族"和"宗教"等词来限定"敌意"一词是有争议的。很难给出什么构成国家或宗教领域的定义。因此，应谨慎使用此类词语。

51. 他希望法国代表复查其案文，作出必要的修改。无论如何，人权委员会都应该考虑到这一案文，因为它表达了一项原则，数百万人在中国和法国都为此献出了生命。

……

69. 张先生（中国）认为，澳大利亚代表的提议值得认真考虑，因此他提议暂停辩论。

作出暂停辩论的决定。

会议于下午 1:50 结束。

——人权委员会第 174 次会议简要记录（E/CN.4/SR.174）

常健译校

E/CN.4/SR.174
8 May 1950

COMMISSION ON HUMAN RIGHTS
SIXTH SESSION
SUMMARY RECORD OF THE HUNDRED AND SEVENTY-FOURTH MEETING

Held at Lake Success, New York, on Friday, 28 April 1950, at 11:00 a.m.

Draft International Covenant on Human Rights (Annexes I and II of the Report of the Fifth Session of the Commission on Human Rights, Document E/1371) (Continued); Article 20 (E/CN.4/365, E/CN.4/447, E/CN.4/455, E/CN.4/455/Rev.1, E/CN.4/456) (Continued) Article 21 (E/CN.4/365, E/CN.4/353/Add.10, E/CN.4/353/Add.11, E/CN.4/358, Paragraph 52)

…

11. Mr. Chang (China), supported by Mr. Kyrou (Greece), pointed out that it was most difficult to take a decision before the Lebanese delegation had submitted a formal proposal in writing.

...

17. Mr. Chang (China) supported by Mr. Cassin (France) asked that the discussion on article 20 should be postponed until the following meeting to enable representatives to study the written text of the Lebanese proposal and to give that very important article the thorough consideration it deserved.

18. The Chairman put the Chinese representative's proposal to the vote.

That proposal was adopted by 10 votes to none, with 4 abstentions.

...

49. Mr. Chang (China) felt that the texts proposed for article 21 were not entirely clear. The French draft was, of course, constructive. It resulted from the harrowing experiences of the Second World War and the memory of racial persecutions against the Jews. The words "fascist-Nazi" which appeared in the USSR text, could not, however, be accepted by some countries. Those words, in fact, designated ideologies which could be given other names, depending on the countries involved, and therefore had no place in a document such as the covenant.

50. The French draft expressed a principles which should not be overlooked. Application of that principle would no doubt meet with some difficulty and, as pointed out by the United States representative, might lead to abuse. Moreover, the use of such words as "national" and "religious" to qualify the word "hostility" was debatable. It would be difficult to give a definition of what constituted the national or religious domain. Caution should therefore be exercised to the use of such words.

51. He hoped that the French representative would review his text, making the necessary changes. The Commission should, in any event, take that text into account since it expressed a principle for which millions of men had given their lives in China as well as in France.

...

69. Mr. Chang (China) considered that the Australian representative's proposal deserved careful consideration and he accordingly moved the adjournment of the debate.

It was decided to adjourn the debate.

The meeting rose at 1:50 p.m.

在人权委员会第 175 次会议上的发言

1950 年 4 月 28 日星期五下午 2:30 纽约成功湖

分发保密的来文清单
《国际人权公约（草案）》（第 E/1371、E/CN.4/365、
E/CN.4/447/Rev.1、E/CN.4/455/Rev.1、E/CN.4/458 号
文件）（续）
第 21 条
第 20 条（续）

......

32. 张先生（中国）指出，虽然第 1 款与宣言密切相关，但必须从法律角度加以解释；尽管委员会可能相信更大的平等概念，但它仍然可以接受第 20 条的严格规定，从而在条约保护领域迈出重要一步。黎巴嫩文本强调平等的概念，而公约只能处理法律面前的平等。因此，他希望保留对第 1 款的立场。

33. 他还认为应该将第 2 款中插入第 2 条，这样它就可以适用于所有权利。

34. 他反对提出的两项措辞修正案。他认为，如果人权委员会决定保留黎巴嫩修正案，可以将这些问题留给体裁委员会处理。

......

43. 张先生（中国）认为智利的修正案是学术性的，因为"种族血统"一词对普通人的意义不大。

44. 由于欧洲的扩张助长了基于种族和肤色的歧视观念，多年来饱受折磨的人们不会对这个词感到满意。因此，为避免误解，人权委员会应遵循《联合国宪章》和《世界人权宣言》的措辞。

45. 这是一个实质问题，而不是选词问题，应该仔细权衡。在签署《联合国宪章》和宣布《世界人权宣言》时，许多国家郑重地批准了"种族"和"肤色"这两个词，尽管它们不是科学术语，但全世界都清楚地理解。

另一方面，"种族起源"包括语言和宗教的概念，过于宽泛和混乱。此外，许多国家仍然在官方文件中使用旧术语。因此，人权委员会在防止歧视方面也应使用同样的词语。如果人权委员会愿意，它可以在公约中同时使用加上引号的"种族"和"肤色"，但无论如何都应该保留。

46. 他向委员会保证，智利的修正案可能会产生误导性和深远的后果，并敦促将其撤回，直到将来某个时候公众舆论可以更好地理解其全部含义。

47. 他保留再次介入辩论的权利。

……

55. 张先生（中国）说，他毫不怀疑智利代表消除种族歧视的真诚愿望。在提到智利的修正案是学术性的时，他表达了他对该提案的意见，他认为该提案在现阶段是不合适的，因为它偏离了《联合国宪章》和《世界人权宣言》的措辞。

56. 在回答乌拉圭代表时，他明确表示，他提到了过去两百年来西方扩张造成的歧视。在谈到西方发展的不利方面时，他无意贬低西方对人类进步的宝贵贡献。

57. 主席表示，人权委员会正在寻找对普通人最有意义的措辞。不希望对任何文明进行反思。

58. 杰夫列莫维奇先生（南斯拉夫）说，由于基于种族和肤色的歧视仍然很普遍，人权委员会应该现实一些，并在案文中保留这些词语。

59. 卡森先生（法国）要求将智利修正案分两部分进行表决。

60. 主席将以"种族血统"取代"种族"的智利修正案付诸表决。

该修正案以 9 票反对、4 票赞成、2 票弃权被否决。

61. 主席将以"种族血统"取代"肤色"的智利修正案付诸表决。

该修正案以 9 票反对、3 票赞成、3 票弃权被否决。

……

——人权委员会第 175 次会议简要记录（E/CN.4/SR.175）

常健译校

E/CN.4/SR.175
10 May 1950

COMMISSION ON HUMAN RIGHTS
SIXTH SESSION
SUMMARY RECORD OF THE HUNDRED AND SEVENTY-FIFTH MEETING

Held at Lake Success, New York, on Friday, 28 April 1950, at 2:30 p.m.

Distribution of confidential List of Communications
Draft International Covenant on Human Rights (E/1371, E/CN.4/365, E/CN.4/447/Rev.1, E/CN.4/455/Rev.1, E/CN.4/458)
(Continued)
Article 21
Article 20 (Continued)

...

32. Mr. Chang (China) pointed out that while paragraph 1 was closely linked to the Declaration, it had to be interpreted in terms of the law; although the Commission might believe in the larger concept of equality, it could nevertheless accept the restrictive provisions of article 20 and thus take a significant step forward in the field of treaty protection. The Lebanese text stressed the notion of equality, whereas the covenant could only deal with equality before the law. He therefore wished to reserve his position on paragraph 1.

33. He also thought that paragraph 2 should be inserted in article 2, where it would apply to all rights.

34. He was opposed to the two drafting amendments which had been presented. He thought that if the Commission decided to retain the Lebanese amendment, it could leave such matters to the Style Committee.

...

43. Mr. Chang (China) thought the Chilean amendment was academic because the term "ethnic origin" would convey but little to the common man.

44. The people who had suffered for many years, as European expansion

fostered the concepts of discrimination based on race and colour, would not be satisfied with that term. To avoid misunderstanding, therefore, the Commission should adhere to the language of the Charter and the Universal Declaration of Human Rights.

45. It was a matter of substance and not of drafting, and should be weighed carefully. In signing the Charter and in proclaiming the Declaration many nations had solemnly given sanction to the words "race" and "colour", which although not scientific terms, were clearly understood throughout the world. On the other hand, "ethnic origin", which included the notion of language and religion, was too broad and confusing. Moreover, many nations still used the old terms in official documents. The Commission should therefore use those same words in preventing discrimination. If the Commission wished, it could use both "race" and "colour" in quotation marks in the covenant, but at all costs they should be retained.

46. He assured the Commission that the Chilean amendment could have misleading and far-reaching consequences and urged that it should be withdrawn until some future date, when public opinion was better prepared to understand its full implications.

47. He reserved the right to intervene again in the debate.

...

55. Mr. Chang (China) stated that he had no doubt of the sincere desire of the representative of Chile to wipe out racial discrimination. In referring to the Chilean amendment as academic, he had voiced his opinion of the proposal, which he felt was inappropriate at that stage since it departed from the wording of the United Nations Charter and the Universal Declaration of Human Rights.

56. In reply to the representative of Uruguay, he made it clear that he had referred to Western expansion during the last two hundred years which had spread discrimination. It had not been his intention in speaking of that unfavourable aspect of Western development to minimize the valuable contributions of the West to the progress of mankind.

57. The Chairman indicated that the Commission was seeking to find the wording which would be most meaningful for the common man. There was no

desire to cast refection on any civilization.

58. Mr. Jevremovic (Yugoslavia) stated that since discrimination on grounds of race and colour was still prevalent, the Commission should be realistic and maintain those words in the text.

59. Mr. Cassin (France) requested that the Chilean amendment should be voted on in two parts.

60. The Chairman put to the vote the Chilean amendment to replace "race" by "ethnic origin".

That amendment was rejected by 9 votes to 4, with 2 abstentions.

61. The Chairman put to the vote the Chilean amendment to replace "colur" by "ethnic origin".

That amendment was rejected by 9 votes to 3, with 3 abstentions.

...

在人权委员会第 182 次会议上的发言

1950 年 5 月 8 日星期一下午 3:00 纽约成功湖

《国际人权公约（草案）》
第 7 条（第 E/1371、E/CN.4.353/Add.10、E/CN.4/353/Add.11、
E/CN.4/359、E/CN.4/305、E/CN.4/372、E/CN.4/339、
E/CN.4/468、E/CN.4/471、E/CN.4/472 号文件）（续）

会议主席：张彭春先生（中国）

1. 主席请委员会继续讨论第 7 条草案。他特别提请注意世界卫生组织提交的关于该条的声明（第 E/CN.4/359 号、第 E/CN.4/389 号文件）。

......

24. 主席询问人权委员会是否希望说明，它认为第 7 条所思考的战争暴行确定无误地包含在第 6 条中。

......

41. 主席希望澄清，他只是根据法国代表的建议，提议以人权委员会名义作出一项声明，表示认为第 7 条的内容已经被第 6 条所涵盖。因此，他不能为这一建议本身负责。

......

61. 主席向黎巴嫩代表保证，将有充足的时间审议新案文。

......

——人权委员会第 182 次会议简要记录（E/CN.4/SR.182）

常健译校

E/CN.4/SR.182

17 May 1950

COMMISSION ON HUMAN RIGHTS
SIXTH SESSION
SUMMARY RECORD OF THE HUNDRED AND EIGHTY-SECOND MEETING

Held at Lake Success, New York, on Monday, 8 May 1950, at 3:00 p.m.

Draft International Covenant on Human Rights
Article 7 (E/1371, E/CN.4.353/Add.10, E/CN.4/353/Add.11, E/CN.4/359, E/CN.4/305, E/CN.4/372, E/CN.4/339, E/CN.4/468, E/CN.4/471, E/CN.4/472) (Continued)

Chairman: Mr. Chang (China)

1. The Chairman asked the Commission to continue its discussion of draft article 7. He drew attention in particular to statements concerning that article which had been submitted by the World Health Organization (E/CN.4/359, E/CN.4/389).

…

24. The Chairman asked the Commission whether it wished to state that it thought the atrocities contemplated under article 7 were definitely and categorically covered by article 6.

…

41. The Chairman wished to make it clear that in proposing a statement placing the Commission on record as believing that the substance of article 7 was covered by article 6, he had merely acted on the French representative's suggestion. He could therefore not claim credit for the suggestion itself.

…

61. The Chairman assured the Lebanese representative that ample time would be given for consideration of the new texts.

…

在人权委员会第 183 次会议上的发言

1950 年 5 月 9 日星期二上午 11:20 纽约成功湖

《国际人权公约（草案）》（人权委员会第五届会议的报告的附件一和附件二，第 E/1371 号文件）（续）
第 7 条（第 E/CN.4/365、E/CN.4/353/Add.10、E/CN.4/353/Add.11、E/CN.4/359、E/CN.4/372、E/CN.4/389 号文件）（续）
第 6 条（第 E/CN.4/365、E/CN.4/471、E/CN.4/472、E/CN.4/473 号文件）（续）

主席：张先生（中国）

......

2. 主席注意到英国代表的要求。

3. 主席请人权委员会继续研究第 7 条。他回顾道，已经向人权委员会提交了几项提案——法国代表团建议删除第 7 条，并将该条的内容纳入第 6 条（第 E/CN.4/471 号文件）；南斯拉夫代表团建议修订第 7 条（第 E/CN.4/372 号文件）；以及菲律宾代表团提交的对第 6 条的修正案（第 E/CN.4/472 号文件）。

......

7. 主席将希腊代表团的结束动议付诸表决。

该动议以 9 票对 2 票获得通过。

8. 主席说，他将按下列顺序将各项提案付诸表决：他将首先将删除第 7 条的提案付诸表决，如果该提案被否决，他将把南斯拉夫的修正案付诸表决。如果删除建议获得通过，他将对第 6 条的法国修正案（第 E/CN.4/471 号文件）进行表决，然后对关于第 6 条的菲律宾修正案（第 E/CN.4/472 号文件）进行表决。

......

11. 主席将法国关于从公约草案中删除第 7 条的建议付诸表决。

该提案以 11 票对 0 票、2 票弃权获得通过。

12. 主席说，鉴于人权委员会已作出的决定，没有必要再将南斯拉夫对第 7 条的修正案付诸表决。然后，他请人权委员会成员研究法国和菲律宾提交的修正案（第 E/CN.4/471 和 E/CN.4/472 号文件），将他们的意见限于这些修正案的案文，而不是实质内容。

……

44. 主席请天主教国际社会服务联盟和国际天主教妇女组织联盟的代表发表意见。

……

52. 主席宣布结束发言报名，发言名单中仍包括英国、菲律宾、澳大利亚和南斯拉夫的代表。

……

61. 主席宣读了法国提案（第 E/CN.4/471 号文件）第 2 款，并将其付诸表决。

法国提案第 2 款以 8 票赞成、4 票反对、3 票弃权获得通过。

62. 主席要求对菲律宾的提案（第 E/CN.4/472 号文件）进行表决。

菲律宾的提案以 5 票反对、4 票赞成、3 票弃权被否决。

63. 主席说，人权委员会必须在二读期间对第 6 条整体进行表决。

……

66. 主席请世界卫生组织代表发言。

……

——人权委员会第 183 次会议简要记录（E/CN.4/SR.183）

常健译校

E/CN.4/SR.183
17 May 1950

COMMISSION ON HUMAN RIGHTS
SIXTH SESSION
SUMMARY RECORD OF THE HUNDRED AND EIGHTY-THIRD MEETING

Held at Lake Success, New York, on Tuesday, 9 May 1950, at 11:20 a.m.

Draft International Covenant on Human Rights (Annexes I and II of the Report of the Fifth Session of the Commission on Human Rights, Document E/1371) (Continued); Article 7 (E/CN.4/365, E/CN.4/353/Add.10, E/CN.4/353/Add.11, E/CN.4/359, E/CN.4/372, E/CN.4/389) (Continued) Article 6 (E/CN.4/365, E/CN.4/471, E/CN.4/472, E/CN.4/473) (Continued)

Chairman: Mr. Chang (China)

…

2. The Chairman noted the request of the United Kingdom representative.

3. The Chairman invited the Commission to continue the study of article 7. He recalled that several proposals had been submitted to the Commission – the French delegation's proposal that article 7 should be deleted and the substance of that article incorporated in article 6 (E/CN.4/471), the Yugoslav delegation's proposal that article 7 should be amended (E/CN.4/372), and the amendment to article 6 submitted by the Philippine delegation (E/CN.4/472).

…

7. The Chairman put the Greek delegation's motion for closure to the vote.
The motion was adopted by 9 votes to 2.

8. The Chairman said he would put the various proposals to the vote in the following order: he would first put to the vote the proposal that article 7 should be deleted, and if that were rejected, he would put the Yugoslav amendment to

the vote. If the proposal for deletion were adopted, he would put the French amendment to article 6 (E/CN.4/471) to the vote, and then the Philippine amendment to the same article (E/CN.4/472).

...

11. The Chairman put to the vote the French proposal that article 7 should be deleted from the draft covenant.

The proposal was adopted by 11 votes to none, with 2 abstentions.

12. The Chairman said that in view of the Commission's decision it was unnecessary to put the Yugoslav amendment to article 7 to the vote. He then invited the members of the Commission to study the amendments submitted by France and the Philippines (E/CN.4/471, E/CN.4/472), confining their remarks to the text of those amendments and not to the substance.

...

44. The Chairman invited the representatives of the Catholic International Union for Social Service and the International Union of Catholic Women's Leagues to state their views.

...

52. The Chairman closed the list of speakers which still included the representatives of the United Kingdom, the Philippines, Australia and Yugoslavia.

...

61. The Chairman read out and put to the vote paragraph 2 of the French proposal (E/CN.4/471).

Paragraph 2 of the French proposal was adopted by 8 votes to 4, with 3 abstentions.

62. The Chairman called for a vote on the proposal of the Philippines (E/CN.4/472).

The proposal of the Philippines was rejected by 5 votes to 4, with 3 abstentions.

63. The Chairman said that the Commission would have to vote on the whole of article 6 during the second reading.

...

66. The Chairman called upon the representative of the World Health Organisation to make a statement.

...

在人权委员会第 184 次会议上的发言

1950 年 5 月 9 日星期二一下午 2:30 纽约成功湖

关于在公约草案第二部分中增加条款的建议
（第 E/1371、E/CN.4/351、E/CN.4/353/Add.10、
E/CN.4/353/Add.11、E/CN.4/358、E/CN.4/364、
E/CN.4/364/Corr.1、E/CN.4/364/Corr.2、E/CN.4/364/Corr.3、
E/CN.4/365、E/CN.4/395、E/CN.4/396、E/CN.4/403、
E/CN.4/435、E/CN.4/436、E/CN.4/470 号文件）

会议主席：张先生（中国）

1. 主席开放讨论关于在公约草案第二部分中增加条款的建议。

……

81. 主席在答复西姆萨里安先生（美国）时说，人权委员会在处理完手中的问题后，将继续审议第一部分。

82. 他询问人权委员会是否希望批准黎巴嫩关于将国际人权联盟代表的发言全文分发的建议。

如此作出决定。

会议于下午 5:40 结束。

——人权委员会第 184 次会议简要记录（E/CN.4/SR.184）

常健译校

E/CN.4/SR.184
19 May 1950
COMMISSION ON HUMAN RIGHTS
SIXTH SESSION

SUMMARY RECORD OF THE HUNDRED AND EIGHTY-ROURTH MEETING

Held at Lake Success, New York, on Tuesday, 9 May 1950, at 2:30 p.m.

Proposals for additional articles to be inserted in Part II of the draft covenant (E/1371, E/CN.4/351, E/CN.4/353/Add.10, E/CN.4/353/Add.11, E/CN.4/358, E/CN.4/364, E/CN.4/364/Corr.1, E/CN.4/364/Corr.2, E/CN.4/364/Corr.3, E/CN.4/365, E/CN.4/395, E/CN.4/396, E/CN.4/403, E/CN.4/435, E/CN.4/436, E/CN.4/470)

Chairman: Mr. Chang (China)

1. The Chairman opened the discussion on proposals for additional articles to be inserted in part II of the draft covenant.

...

81. In reply to Mr. Simsarian (United States of America), the Chairman said that when it had disposed of the question in hand, the Commission would resume its consideration of Part I.

82. He asked whether the Commission wished to approve the Lebanese suggestion to have the statement of the representative of the International League for the Rights of Man circulated in extenso.

It was so decided.

The meeting rose at 5:40 p.m.

在人权委员会第 186 次会议上的发言

1950 年 5 月 10 日星期三下午 3:00 纽约成功湖

《国际人权公约（草案）》：关于在公约草案第二部分中增加条款的建议（续）（第 E/1371、E/CN.4/365、E/CN.4/395、E/CN.4435、E/CN.4/436、E/CN.4/353/Add.10、E/CN.4/470、E/CN.4/351、E/CN.4/358、E/CN.4/364、E/CN.4/403、E/CN.4/478、E/CN.4/376、E/CN.4/377、E/CN.4/370、E/CN.4/379、E/CN.4/374、E/CN.4/380、E/CN.4/483、E/CN.4/484、E/CN.4/485 号文件）

......

30. 张先生（中国）支持美国、希腊和乌拉圭代表对决议草案（E/CN.4/484）的评论。反过来，他又对该案文提出了几项具体的修正案。在第 1 段中，他建议在 "人权公约" 之前的第一行插入 "草案" 一词。然后，应删除以下短语 "它参与了几年的起草工作" 和短语 "确实"。应在第二行 "基本权利" 之前插入 "一些"。第三行中的 "以及某些基本的公民自由" 一语也应删除，因为难以界定这类自由。第四行的 "标准" 一词和第五行的 "并确保尽早适用其主要原则" 也应删除。基于已经给出的理由，他反对使用 "标准" 一词；最后一句应该删除，因为《世界人权宣言》的条款恰当地说不是原则。"主要" 一词不够充分，"确保适用" 一词含糊不清。

31. 他还建议将第 2 款修改为 "审议关于经济、社会、文化、政治和其他人权的其他公约和措施，并为此目的"。基于乌拉圭代表提出的理由，他反对原初的表述。

......

70. 张先生（中国）就程序问题说，由于主席要求对修正案进行第二次表决，因此对其进行进一步讨论是不符合程序的。

......

74. 张先生（中国）说，他不会强调他的修正案的这一部分，特别是考虑到有关短语含有限定词"某些"。

……

84. 张先生（中国）同意法国代表的意见。他还提请大家注意"补充公约和措施"这一短语，它是被审议条款的争议焦点。

……

——人权委员会第 186 次会议简要记录（E/CN.4/SR.186）

常健译校

E/CN.4/SR.186

19 May 1950

COMMISSION ON HUMAN RIGHTS
SIXTH SESSION
SUMMARY RECORD OF THE HUNDRED AND EIGHTY-SIXTH MEETING

Held at Lake Success, New York, on Wednesday, 10 May 1950, at 3:00 p.m.

Draft International Covenant on Human Rights: Proposals for Additional Articles to be Inserted in Part II of the Draft Covenant (Continued) (E/1371, E/CN.4/365, E/CN.4/395, E/CN.4435, E/CN.4/436, E/CN.4/353/Add.10, E/CN.4/470, E/CN.4/351, E/CN.4/358, E/CN.4/364, E/CN.4/403, E/CN.4/478, E/CN.4/376, E/CN.4/377, E/CN.4/370, E/CN.4/379, E/CN.4/374, E/CN.4/380, E/CN.4/483, E/CN.4/484, E/CN.4/485)

…

30. Mr. Chang (China) supported the United States, Greek and Uruguayan representatives in their comments on the concolidated draft resolution (E/CN.4/484). He in turn had several specific amendments to propose to that text. In paragraph 1 he suggested that the word "draft" should be inserted in the first line before the words "Covenant on human rights". Then the following phrase

"on the drafting of which it has been engaged for several years" and the phrase "as it does" should be deleted. The words "some of" should be inserted in the second line before the words "the fundamental rights". In the third line the phrase "and to certain essential civil freedoms" should also be deleted because of the difficulty of defining that category of freedoms. In the fourth line the word "Standard" and in the fifth line the words "and secure the application of its primary principles as early as possible" should also be deleted. He objected to the word "Standard" for the reasons which had already been given; the last phrase should be deleted because the articles of the Universal Declaration were not, properly speaking, principles. The word "primary" was inadequate and the phrase "secure the application" was vague.

31. He also suggested that paragraph 2 should be amended to read "consideration of additional Covenants and measures dealing with economic, social, cultural, political and other human rights, and to this end". He objected to the original formulation for the reasons given by the representative of Uruguay.

...

70. Mr. Chang (China) on a point of order, stated that inasmuch as the Chairman had called for the second vote on the amendment, further discussion thereon was out of order.

...

74. Mr. Chang (China) stated that he would not press that part of his amendment, particularly in view of the fact that the phrase concerned contained the qualifying word "certain".

...

84. Mr. Chang (China) agreed with the French representative. He would also invite attention to the words "additional covenants and measures" which formed the crux of the paragraph under consideration.

...

在人权委员会第 189 次会议上的发言

1950 年 5 月 12 日星期五上午 11:15 纽约成功湖

《国际人权公约（草案）》和执行措施：（第 E/1371 号文件、附件三、第 E/CN.4/366、E/CN.4/366/Corr.1、E/CN.4/353/Add.10、E/CN.4/352/Add.11 号文件）（续）

法国、印度、英国和美国提交的关于执行措施的提案（第 E/CN.4/474 和 E/CN.4/488 号文件）（续）

第 4 条和第 6 条至第 11 条

……

17. 张先生（中国）希望人权委员会就"和投票"一词进行表决。人权事务委员会成员应当受到高度尊重，因此应当由大多数公约缔约方选出。

18. 梅塔女士（印度）同意中国代表的意见。她指出，除非人权委员会颁布适当的规定，否则人权事务委员会成员很可能由极少数公约缔约方选出。

19. 主席指出，丹麦代表提出的对乌拉圭修正案的修正符合中国代表提出的观点。

……

——人权委员会第 189 次会议简要记录（E/CN.4/SR.189）

常健译校

E/CN.4/SR.189

22 May 1950

COMMISSION ON HUMAN RIGHTS
SIXTH SESSION
SUMMARY RECORD OF THE HUNDRED AND EIGHTY-NINTH MEETING

Held at Lake Success, New York, on Friday 12 May 1950, at 11:15 a.m.

Draft International Covenant on Human Rights and Measures of Implementation: (E/1371, Annex III, E/CN.4/366, E/CN.4/366/Corr.1, E/CN.4/353/Add.10, E/CN.4/353/Add.11) (Continued)

Proposal Concerning Measures of Implementation Submitted by France, India, United Kingdom of Great Britain and Northern Ireland, and the United States of America (E/CN.4/474 and E/CN.4/488) (Continued)

Articles 4 and 6 to 11

...

17. Mr. Chang (China) wanted the Commission to vote on the words "and voting". The members of the committee ought to be highly respected and ought therefore to be elected by the majority of States parties to the covenant.

18. Mrs. Mehta (India) agreed with the Chinese representative. She observed that unless the Commission enacted an appropriate provision, the members of the committee might well be elected by a very small number of States parties to the covenant.

19. The Chairman pointed out that the amendment to the amendment of Uruguay proposed by the Danish representative, met the point raised by the Chinese representative.

...

在人权委员会第 192 次会议上的发言

1950 年 5 月 15 日星期一上午 11:00 纽约成功湖

人权国际公约草案

执行措施：（第 E/1371、Annex III、E/CN.4/164/Add.1、E/CN.4/353/Add.10、E/CN.4/353/Add.11、E/CN.4/358、E/CN.4/358、9 章第 E/CN.4/366、E/CN.4/419、E/CN.4/444、E/CN.4/452、E/CN.4/457、E/CN.4/474、E/CN.4/474/Corr.1、E/CN.4/487、E/CN.4/489、E/CN.4/L.9、E/CN.4/L.9/Add.1 号文件）（续）

……

46. 张先生（中国）认为，在这个阶段插入英国案文是多余的。国际法院发布咨询意见通常需要几天到一年的时间；如此冗长的程序很难解决人权事务委员会工作过程中可能出现的法律问题。如果出现需要国际仲裁的根本意见分歧，有关国家完全可以自由地将其提交法院。

……

57. 张先生（中国）说，英国的第二项提案比第一项提案更不可接受，因为它更容易混淆人权事务委员会职能的性质。在创建该委员会时，人权委员会并不打算设立一个司法机构，而是一个由政治家组成的机构，该机构的上诉法院将是全世界的舆论。英国的两项提案都使这一初衷变得模糊。

……

——人权委员会第 192 次会议简要记录（E/CN.4/SR.192）

常健译校

E/CN.4/SR.192

24 May 1950

COMMISSION ON HUMAN RIGHTS
SIXTH SESSION
SUMMARY RECORD OF THE HUNDRED AND NINETY-SECOND MEETING

Held at Lake Success, New York, on Monday 15 May 1950, at 11:00 a.m.

Draft International Covenant on Human Rights
Measures of Implementation: (E/1371, Annex III, E/CN.4/164/Add.1, E/CN.4/353/Add.10, E/CN.4/353/Add.11, E/CN.4/358, E/CN.4/358, Chapter IX, E/CN.4/366, E/CN.4/419, E/CN.4/444, E/CN.4/452, E/CN.4/457, E/CN.4/474, E/CN.4/474/Corr.1, E/CN.4/487, E/CN.4/489, E/CN.4/L.9, E/CN.4/L.9/Add.1) (Continued)

...

46. Mr. Chang (China) thought that insertion of the United Kingdom text would be superfluous at that stage. The International Court usually took from several months to a year to issue an advisory opinion: such a lengthy procedure was hardly appropriate for resolving the points of law likely to come up in the course of the committee's work. If fundamental differences of opinion requiring international arbitration should arise, the States concerned would in any event be free to put them before the Court.

...

57. Mr. Chang (China) remarked that the second United Kingdom proposal was still less acceptable that the first, since it tended even more to confuse the character of the committee's functions. In creating the committee, the Commission had not intended to set up a juridical organ but a body of statesmen whose court of appeal would be the public opinion of the world. Both the United Kingdom proposals allowed that original intention to become obscured.

...

在人权委员会第 193 次会议上的发言

1950 年 5 月 15 日星期一下午 2:30 纽约成功湖

执行措施：（第 E/1371、Annex III、E/CN.4/366、
E/CN.4/366/Corr.1、E/CN.4/353/Add.10、E/CN.4/353/Add.11 号
文件）（续）
澳大利亚代表团提交的决议草案（第 E/CN.4/489 和 E/CN.4/492
号文件）
《国际人权公约（草案）》（人权委员会第五届会议的报告的附件
一和附件二，第 E/1371 号文件）（续）
序言和第 1 条、第 2 条的文案（第 E/CN.4/491、E/CN.4/365、
E/CN.4/375、E/CN.4/380、E/CN.4/475、E/CN.4/486 号文件）

......

17. 张先生（中国）认为法国修正案措辞过于笼统。特别是，它不应提及非官方性质的提案。

......

——人权委员会第 193 次会议简要记录（E/CN.4/SR.193）

常健译校

E/CN.4/SR.193
26 May 1950

COMMISSION ON HUMAN RIGHTS
SIXTH SESSION
SUMMARY RECORD OF THE HUNDRED AND NINETY-
THIRD MEETING

Held at Lake Success, New York, on Monday 15 May 1950, at 2:30 p.m.

Measures of Implementation: (E/1371, Annex III, E/CN.4/366,

E/CN.4/366/Corr.1, E/CN.4/353/Add.10, E/CN.4/353/Add.11)
(Continued)
Draft Resolution Submitted by the Australian Delegation
(E/CN.4/489, E/CN.4/492)
Draft International Covenant on Human Rights (Annexes I and
II of the Report of the Fifth Session of the Commission on
Human Rights, Document E/1371) (Continued)
Text of the Preamble and Article 1; Article 2 (E/CN.4/491,
E/CN.4/365, E/CN.4/375, E/CN.4/380, E/CN.4/475, E/CN.4/486)

...

17. Mr. Chang (China) felt that the French amendment was couched in too general terms. In particular, it should not refer to proposals of an unofficial nature.

...

在人权委员会第 195 次会议上的发言

1950 年 5 月 16 日星期二下午 2:30 纽约成功湖

《国际人权公约（草案）》（人权委员会第五届会议的报告的附件一和附件二，第 E/1371 号文件）（续）

第 2 条（续），第 3 条和第 4 条（第 E/CN.4/365、E/CN.4/353/Add.10、E/CN.4/374、E/CN.4/380、E/CN.4/495、E/CN.4/497、E/CN.4/498 号文件）

......

16. 张先生（中国）认为插入"国内"一词没有意义。因此，他建议删除该词。

17. 马利克先生（黎巴嫩）建议将中国修正案的案文修改如下："由主管当局或一个有资格和独立的法庭……"。"独立法庭"的表述已在第 13 条中被使用。

......

19. 主席将中国修正案付诸表决。

中国修正案未获得通过，4 票赞成，4 票反对，6 票弃权。

......

22. 张先生（中国）建议删除第（c）项。

23. 主席将中国关于删除英国修正案第（c）项的提议付诸表决。

该提案未获得通过，6 票赞成，6 票反对，2 票弃权。

......

——人权委员会第 195 次会议简要记录（E/CN.4/SR.195）

常健译校

E/CN.4/SR.195

29 May 1950

COMMISSION ON HUMAN RIGHTS
SIXTH SESSION
SUMMARY RECORD OF THE HUNDRED AND NINETYFIFTH MEETING

Held at Lake Success, New York, on Tuesday 16 May 1950, at 2:30 p.m.

Draft International Covenant on Human Rights (Annexes I and II of the Report of the Fifth Session of the Commission on Human Rights, Document E/1371) (Continued)
Article 2 (Continued), 3 and 4 (E/CN.4/365, E/CN.4/353/Add.10, E/CN.4/374, E/CN.4/380, E/CN.4/495, E/CN.4/497, E/CN.4/498)

...

16. Mr. Chang (China) thought there was no point in inserting the word "domestic". He therefore suggested that the word should to be deleted.

17. Mr. Malik (Lebanon) proposed that the text of the Chinese amendment should be altered as follows: "by the competent authorities or a competent and independent tribunal...". The expression "independent tribunal" had already been used in article 13.

...

19. The Chairman put the Chinese amendment to the vote.

The Chinese amendment was not adopted, there being 4 votes in favour and 4 against, with 6 abstentions.

...

22. Mr. Chang (China) proposed that sub-paragraph © should be deleted.

23. The Chairman put to the vote the Chinese proposal to delete sub-paragraph (c) of the United Kingdom amendment.

That proposal was not adopted, there being 6 votes in favour and 6 against, with 2 abstentions.

...

在人权委员会第 196 次会议上的发言

1950 年 5 月 17 日星期直上午 10:00 纽约成功湖

《国际人权公约（草案）》
第 4 条和第 23 条（第 E/1371、E/CN.4/365、E/CN.4/353/Add.10 号文件）（续）

......

83. 张先生（中国）认为法国的修正案是不明智的。安全理事会常任理事国是对联合国运作产生重大影响的一个重要因素。然而，法国修正案引入了一个新概念，即要求得到安理会常任理事国中的大多数国家支持，这会产生非常严重的问题，不应被采纳。

......

——人权委员会第 196 次会议简要记录（E/CN.4/SR.196）

常健译校

E/CN.4/SR.196

26 May 1950

COMMISSION ON HUMAN RIGHTS
SIXTH SESSION
SUMMARY RECORD OF THE HUNDRED AND NINETY-SIXTH MEETING

Held at Lake Success, New York, on Wednesday 17 May 1950, at 10:00 a.m.

Draft International Covenant on Human Rights
Article 4 and 233 (E/1371, E/CN.4/365, E/CN.4/353/Add.10)

(Continued)

...

83. Mr. Chang (China) thought the French amendment was ill-advised. The permanent members of the Security Council were an important factor which vitally affected the functioning of the United Nations. The French amendment however introduced a new concept, namely the requirement of the support of a majority of these States, which raised very serious questions and should not be adopted.

...

在人权委员会第 197 次会议上的发言

1950 年 5 月 17 日星期三下午 2:15 纽约成功湖

《国际人权公约（草案）》（人权委员会第五届会议的报告的附件一和附件二，第 E/1371 号文件）（续）
英国（第 E/CN.4/375 号文件）和比利时（第 E/CN.4/486 号文件）提交的关于对公约作出保留的新条款
第 24、25 和 26 条（第 E/CN.4/365、E/CN.4/353/Add.10、E/CN.4/437、E/CN.4/494 号文件）
法国提交的决议草案（第 E/CN.4/501 号文件）

......

13. 张先生（中国）说，在听取了比利时代表的解释后，他无法支持比利时的案文。事实上，至关重要的是不要赋予该公约双边条约的性质，相反，要强调其更广的适用范围。

......

109. 张先生（中国）准备支持英国的修正案，但认为联合国大会对一项公约修正案的批准，意味着要对该修正案进行讨论。如果英国代表接受这一解释，他准备投票赞成英国的提议。

......

118. 张先生（中国）询问，非成员国的参与是否包括享有投票权。

119. 沙赫特先生（秘书处）回答说，在他提到的先例中，非成员国的参与不包括享有投票权。只有《国际法院规约》载有一项规定，允许非联合国会员国但是《国际法院规约》缔约方的国家享有投票权。在其他情况下，是否享有投票权是根据《联合国宪章》第十八条所作出的明确规定。

......

——人权委员会第 197 次会议简要记录（E/CN.4/SR.197）

常健译校

E/CN.4/SR.197

29 May 1950

COMMISSION ON HUMAN RIGHTS
SIXTH SESSION
SUMMARY RECORD OF THE HUNDRED AND NINETY-SEVENTH MEETING

Held at Lake Success, New York, on Wednesday 17 May 1950, at 2:15 p.m.

Draft International Covenant on Human Rights (Annexes I and II of the Report of the Fifth Session of the Commission on Human Rights, Document E/1371) (Continued)
New Articles Concerning Reservations to the Covenant, Submitted by the United Kingdom (E/CN.4/375) and Belgium (E/CN.4/486)
Articles 24, 25 and 26 (E/CN.4/365, E/CN.4/353/Add.10, E/CN.4/437, E/CN.4/494)
Draft Resolution Submitted by France (E/CN.4/501)

...

13. Mr. Chang (China) said that, having heard the explanation given by the representative of Belgium, he could not support the Belgian text. Indeed, it was essential not to give the covenant a bilateral character and, on the contrary, to lay stress on its wider scope.

...

109. Mr. Chang (China) was prepared to support the United Kingdom amendment but thought that approval of an amendment to the covenant made by the General Assembly implied discussion of that amendment. If the United Kingdom representative would accept that interpretation, he was prepared to vote in favour of the United Kingdom proposal.

...

118. Mr. Chang (China) asked whether the participation of non-member

States would include the right to vote.

119. Mr. Schachter (Secretariat) replied that, in the precedent he had mentioned, the participation of non-member States had not included the right to vote. Only the Statute of the International Court of Justice included a provision which made it possible to grant the right to vote to States which were not Members of the United Nations but were parties to the Statute of the Court. In other cases the right to vote was governed explicitly by Article 18 of the Charter.

...

在人权委员会第 198 次会议上的发言

1950 年 5 月 18 日星期二上午 10:15 纽约成功湖

《国际人权公约（草案）》
法国提出的决议草案（第 E/CN.4/501 号文件）（续）
黎巴嫩提出的决议草案（第 E/CN.4/493 和 E/CN.4/503 号文件）
丹麦提出的决议草案（第 E/CN.4/496 号文件）
英国提出的决议草案（第 E/CN.4/505 号文件）
......

14. 张先生（中国）认为，法国的决议草案，试图在比公约所设想的更大范围内实施《世界人权宣言》，这是一项值得称赞的尝试。他对拟议的案文没有重大的修改意见，但建议删除第三款中的"根据本国法律"一语。除通过立法促进对人权的尊重这一纯粹消极的做法外，该决议还可以被解释为包括促进尊重人权的其他积极措施。他经常表示，人权委员会在其工作中过分强调了实施人权的消极措施，他指出，这种做法可能会鼓励各国仅仅进行相互指责。为了确保有效遵守人权，他强调，最广泛意义上的教育措施和其他建设性方案不应被忽视。

15. 他建议对法国的提案进行几处措辞上的修改。最好将第六款插在第二款或第三款之后，因为在规定向有关机构提交年度报告的机制程序之前，先制定有关年度报告内容的规制更符合逻辑。他还认为第四和第五款是多余的，应该删除。

16. 他敦促人权委员会以最仔细的方式审议法国决议草案的含义，并设法采取建设性措施，执行《世界人权宣言》所宣布的原则。如果能够取得一些积极的成果，整个人权事业将得到推进，但如果必须完全依靠立法措施来实现这些目标，他认为人权委员会的努力取得巨大成功的希望就渺茫了。

17. 主席以美国代表的身份发言说，她同意中国的修正案，删除第三款中的"根据本国法律"一语。

......

——人权委员会第 198 次会议简要记录（E/CN.4/SR.198）

常健译校

E/CN.4/SR.198
31 May 1950

COMMISSION ON HUMAN RIGHTS
SIXTH SESSION
SUMMARY RECORD OF THE HUNDRED AND NINETY-EIGHTH MEETING

Held at Lake Success, New York, on Tuesday 18 May 1950, at 10:15 a.m.

Draft international covenant on human rights
Draft resolution proposed by France (E/CN.4/501) (Continued)
Draft resolution proposed by Lebanon (E/CN.4/493, E/CN.4/503)
Draft resolution proposed by Denmark (E/CN.4/496)
Draft resolution proposed by the United Kingdom (E/CN.4/505)

...

14. Mr. Chang (China) thought the French draft resolution was a praise worthy attempt the implementation of the Universal Declaration on a wider scale than that envisaged in the covenant. He held no strong views on the proposed text, but would suggest that in the third paragraph the phrase "by their national law" should be deleted. The resolution could then be interpreted to include other, positive measures for promoting the observance of human rights, in addition to the purely negative approach of fostering respect for those rights through legislation. He had often expressed the view that in its work the Commission unduly emphasized the negative aspect of the implementation of human rights, and he had pointed out that such an approach might encourage states merely to engage in recriminations. In the interests of ensuring the effective observance of human rights, he would stress that educational measures in their widest sense,

and other constructive programmes, should not be overlocked.

15. He had several drafting changes to suggest to the French proposal. It might be better to insert the sixth paragraph after either the second or the third paragraph, as it would be more logical to establish the regulations governing the contents of the annual report before laying down the mechanical procedure for transmitting them to the proper bodies. He also thought that the fourth and fifth paragraphs were superfluous and should be deleted.

16. He urged the Commission to consider the implications of the French draft resolution most carefully and to attempt to provide for constructive measures to implement the principles proclaimed by the Declaration. If some positive results could be achieved, the entire cause of human rights would be advanced, but if it became necessary to rely entirely on legislative measures to achieve those ends, he thought there was little hope that the Commission's efforts would be highly successful.

17. The Chairman, speaking as representative of the United States of America, said she agreed with the Chinese amendment to delete the phrase "by their national law", in the third paragraph.

...

在人权委员会第 199 次会议上的发言

1950 年 5 月 18 日星期四下午 2:30 纽约成功湖

《国际人权公约（草案）》（续）：
（1）法国提出的决议草案（第 E/CN.4/501 号文件）（续）
（2）黎巴嫩提出的决议草案（第 E/CN.4/493 和 E/CN.4/503 号文件）
（3）丹麦提出的决议草案（第 E/CN.4/496 号文件）
（4）英国提出的决议草案（第 E/CN.4/505 号文件）
二读《国际人权公约（草案）》：
（1）一读通过的公约草案第一部分条款案文（第 E/CN.4/L.11 和 E/CN.4/L.14 号文件）
（2）体裁委员会通过的公约草案第二部分第 3 至 12 条案文（第 E/CN.4/L.10 号文件）

……

8. 张先生（中国）认为黎巴嫩的提案应该获得一致通过。他认为，没有必要通知经济及社会理事会，说人权委员会在某些重大问题上出现了意见分歧，因为经济及社会理事会将收到人权委员会的报告和会议简要记录。他还认为，英国决议草案的最后一款毫无意义。将人权委员会的报告转交经济及社会理事会就足够了，经济及社会理事会将自行决定要采取的行动。

9. 他同意黎巴嫩决议草案的第一款，并提议在该款中增加以下文字："……和执行措施"。他还建议删除"本决议附件 A 中继续"等字。

10. 马利克先生（黎巴嫩）接受了中国代表的建议。

……

22. 张先生（中国）认为，人权委员会应向经济及社会理事会提交一份用最简单的措辞表述的决议草案；黎巴嫩文本非常适合这一目的。他还赞同希腊关于将英国决议草案第三款作为报告最后一句的建议。最后，他认为，人权委员会应提请经济及社会理事会注意人权委员会会议的简要记录。

......

——人权委员会第 199 次会议简要记录（E/CN.4/SR.199）

常健译校

E/CN.4/SR.199

31 May 1950

COMMISSION ON HUMAN RIGHTS

SIXTH SESSION

SUMMARY RECORD OF THE HUNDRED AND NINETY-NINTH MEETING

Held at Lake Success, New York, on Thursday 18 May 1950, at 2:30 p.m.

Draft International Covenant on Human Rights (Continued):

(a) Draft Resolution Proposed by France (E/CN.4/501) (Continued)

(b) Draft Resolution Proposed by Lebanon (E/CN.4/493, E/CN.4/503)

(c) Draft Resolution Proposed by Denmark (E/CN.4/496)

(d) Draft Resolution Proposed by the United Kingdom (E/CN.4/505)

Second Reading of the Draft International Covenant on Human Rights:

(a) Texts of Articles in Part I of the Draft Covenant as Adopted at the First Reading (E/CN.4/L.11, E/CN.4/L.14)

(b) Texts of Articles 3 to 12 of Part II of the Draft Covenant as Adopted by the Style Committee (E/CN.4/L.10)

...

8. Mr. Chang (China) thought that the Lebanese proposal should be carried

unanimously. In his opinion, there was no point in informing the Economic and Social Council that differences of opinion had arisen in the Commission on certain problems of major importance, because the Council would have before it the Commission's report and the summary records of it meetings. He also thought that the last paragraph of the United Kingdom draft resolution was pointless. It would be sufficient to transmit the Commission's report to the Council, which would decide for itself the stops to be taken.

9. He approved the first paragraph of the Lebanese draft resolution, and proposed that the following words would be added to that paragraph: "...and measures of implementation". He also suggested that the words "continued in annex A of this resolution" should be deleted.

10. Mr. Malik (Lebanon) accepted the alterations suggested by the Chinese representative.

...

22. Mr. Chang (China) thought that the Commission should submit to the Economic and Social Council a draft resolution couched in the simplest terms; the Lebanese text would answer that purpose admirably. He also endorsed the Greek proposal for the inclusion of the third paragraph of the United Kingdom draft resolution as the last sentence of the report. Finally, in his opinion the /commission should draw the attention of the Council to the summary records of its meetings.

...

在人权委员会第 201 次会议上的发言

1950 年 5 月 19 日星期五下午 2:30 纽约成功湖

《国际人权公约（草案）》（续）
法国代表团提交的决议草案（第 E/CN.4/501/Rev.1 号文件）
（续）
通过人权委员会第六届会议报告（第 E/CN.4/L.12、
E/CN.4/L.12/Add.1、E/CN.4/L.13/Add.2、E/CN.4/L.12/Add.3、
E/CN.4/L.14/Add.4 号文件）

······

77. 主席将人权委员会第六届会议报告草案整体付诸表决。

人权委员会第六届会议报告草稿获得一致通过。

······

80. 主席感谢秘书处成员，特别是新闻稿撰稿人和口译员的出色工作和对人权委员会的宝贵帮助。她还感谢专门机构和非政府组织的代表对人权委员会的辩论表现出的兴趣；这种兴趣极大地鼓舞了委员会。最后，她感谢人权委员会成员在经常遇到困难的情况下表现出的合作精神；正是这种合作精神使人权委员会得以完成第一项国际人权公约这一历史性文件的起草工作。

81. 张先生（中国）说，人权委员会成员很高兴在主席鼓舞人心的领导下进行工作，主席的智慧和人道主义精神对大家完成这一工作任务起到了极大的促进作用。

会议于下午 6:05 结束。

——人权委员会第 201 次会议简要记录（E/CN.4/SR.201）

常健译校

E/CN.4/SR.201

5 June 1950

COMMISSION ON HUMAN RIGHTS
SIXTH SESSION
SUMMARY RECORD OF THE TWO HUNDRED AND FIRST MEETING

Held at Lake Success, New York, on Friday 19 May 1950, at 2:30 p.m.

Draft International Covenant on Human Rights (Continued)
Draft Resolution Submitted by French Delegation
(E/CN.4/501/Rev.1) (Continued)
Adoption of the Report of the Sixth Session of the Commission on Human Rights (E/CN.4/L.12, E/CN.4/L.12/Add.1, E/CN.4/L.12/Add.2, E/CN.4/L.12/Add.3, E/CN.4/L.12/Add.4)

...

77. The Chairman put to the vote the draft report of the sixth session of the Commission on Human Rights, as a whole.

The draft report of the sixth session of the Commission on Human Rights as a whole was adopted unanimously.

...

80. The Chairman expressed her thanks to the members of the Secretariat, in particular the precise writers and interpreters, for their excellent work and valuable assistance to the Commission. She also thanked the representatives of specialized agencies and non-governmental organizations for the interest they had shown in the Commission's debates; that interest had greatly encouraged the Commission. Finally, she thanked the members of the Commission for the spirit of co-operation they had manifested in frequently trying circumstances; it was that spirit of co-operation which had made it possible for the Commission to complete the preparation of the historic document that the first international covenant on human right was.

81. Mr. Chang (China) said that it had been a pleasure for the members of

the Commission to work under the inspiring leadership of the Chairman, whose wisdom and humanitarian spirit had greatly facilitated the accomplishment of their task.

The meeting rose at 6:05 p.m.

附录

《世界人权宣言》通过时的中英文原文

一、中文文件繁体字原文

二一七（三）國際人權法案

甲

世界人權宣言

弁言

茲鑒於人類一家，對於人人固有尊嚴及其平等不移權利之承認確系世界自由、正義與和平之基礎；

複鑒於人權之忽視及侮蔑恒釀成野蠻暴行，致使人心震憤，而自由言論、自由信仰、得免憂懼、得免貧困之世界業經宣示為一般人民之最高企望；

複鑒於為使人類不致迫不得已鋌而走險以抗專橫與壓迫，人權須受法律規定之保障；

複鑒於國際友好關係之促進，實屬切要；

複鑒於聯合國人民已在憲章中重申對於基本人權、人格尊嚴與價值以及男女平等權利之信念，并決心促成大自由中之社會進步及較善之民生；

複鑒於各會員國業經誓願與聯合國同心協力促進人權及基本自由之普遍尊重與遵行；

複鑒於此種權利自由之公共認識對於是項誓願之徹底實現至關重大；

大會爰於此

頒佈世界人權宣言，作為所有人民所有國家共同努力之標的，務望個人及社會團體永以本宣言銘諸座右，力求藉訓導與教育激勵人權與自由之尊重，并借國家與國際之漸進措施獲得其普遍有效之承認與遵行；會員國本身人民及所轄領土人民均各永享咸遵。

第一條

人皆生而自由；在尊嚴及權利上均各平等。人各賦有理性良知，誠應和睦相處，情同手足。

第二條

人人皆得享受本宣言所載之一切權利與自由，不分種族、膚色、性別、語言、宗教、政見或他種主張、國籍或門第、財產、出生或他種身分。

且不得因一人所隸國家或地區之政治、行政或國際地位之不同而有所區別，無論該地區系獨立、托管、非自治或受其他主權上之限制。

第三條

人人有權享有生命、自由與人身安全。

第四條

任何人不容使為奴役；奴隸制度及奴隸販賣，不論出於何種方式，悉應予以禁止。

第五條

任何人不能加以酷刑，或施以殘忍不人道或侮慢之待遇或處罰。

第六條

人人於任何所在有被承認為法律上主體之權利。

第七條

人人在法律上悉屬平等，且應一體享受法律之平等保護。人人有權享受平等保護，以防止違反本宣言之任何歧視及煽動此種歧視之任何行為。

第八條

人人於其憲法或法律所賦予之基本權利被侵害時，有權享受國家管轄法庭之有效救濟。

第九條

任何人不容加以無理逮捕、拘禁或放逐。

第十條

人人於其權利與義務受判定時及被刑事控告時，有權享受獨立無私法庭之絕對平等不偏且公開之聽審。

第十一條

一、凡受刑事控告者，在未經依法公開審判證實有罪前，應視為無罪，審判時并須予以答辯上所需之一切保障。

二、任何人在刑事上之行為或不行為，於其發生時依國家或國際法律均不構成罪行者，應不為罪。刑罰不得重于犯罪時法律之規定。

第十二條

任何個人之私生活、家庭、住所或通訊不容無理侵犯，其榮譽及信用亦不容侵害。人人為防止此種侵犯或侵害有權受法律保護。

第十三條

一、人人在一國境內有自由遷徙及擇居之權。

二、人人有權離去任何國家，連其本國在內，並有權歸返其本國。

第十四條

一、人人為避迫害有權在他國尋并享受庇身之所。

二、控訴之確源於非政治性之犯罪或源於違反聯合國宗旨與原則之行為者，不得享受此種權利。

第十五條

人人有權享有國籍。

任何人之國籍不容無理褫奪，其更改國籍之權利不容否認。[①]

---

① 文件原文如此，疑遺漏兩款的序号。

第十六條

一、成年男女，不受種族、國籍或宗教之任何限制，有權婚嫁及成立家庭。男女在婚姻方面，在結合期間及在解除婚約時，俱有平等權利。

二、婚約之締訂僅能以男女雙方之自由完全承認為之。

三、家庭為社會之當然基本團體單位，并應受社會及國家之保護。

第十七條

一、人人有權單獨占有或與他人合有財產。

二、任何人之財產不容無理剝奪。

第十八條

人人有思想、良心與宗教自由之權；此項權利包括其改變宗教或信仰之自由，及其單獨或集體、公開或私自以教義、躬行、禮拜及戒律表示其宗教或信仰之自由。

第十九條

人人有主張及發表自由之權；此項權利包括保持主張而不受干涉之自由，及經由任何方法不分國界以尋求、接收并傳播消息意見之自由。

第二十條

一、人人有平和①集會結社自由之權。

二、任何人不容強使隸屬於某一團體。

第二十一條

一、人人有權直接或以自由選舉之代表參加其本國政府。

二、人人有以平等機會參加其本國公務之權。

三、人民意志應為政府權力之基礎；人民意志應以定期且真實之選舉表現之，其選舉權必須普及而平等，并當以不記名投票或相等之自由投票程序為之。

---

① 文件原文如此，疑為筆誤，似應為"和平"。

第二十二條

人既為社會之一員，自有權享受社會保障，并有權享受個人尊嚴及人格自由發展所必需之經濟、社會及文化各種權利之實現：此種實現之促成，端賴國家措施與國際合作并當依各國之機構與資源量力為之。

第二十三條

一、人人有權工作、自由選擇職業、享受公平優裕之工作條件及失業之保障。

二、人人不容任何區別，有同工同酬之權利。

三、人人工作時，有權享受公平優裕之報酬，務使其本人及其家屬之生活足以維持人類尊嚴，必要時且應有他種社會保護辦法，以資補益。

四、人人為維持其權益，有組織及參加工會之權。

第二十四條

人人有休息及閑暇之權，包括工作時間受合理限制及定期有給[①]休假之權。

第二十五條

一、人人有權享受其本人及其家屬康樂所需之生活程度，舉凡衣、食、住、醫藥及必要之社會服務均包括在內；且於失業、患病、殘廢、寡居、衰老或因不可抗力之事故致有他種喪失生活能力之情形時，有權享受保障。

二、母親及兒童應受特別照顧及協助。所有兒童，無論婚生與非婚生，均應享受同等社會保護。

第二十六條

一、人人皆有受教育之權。教育應屬免費，至少初級及基本教育應然。初級教育應屬強迫性質。技術與職業教育應廣為設立。高等教育應予人人平[②]機會，以成績為准。

二、教育之目標在於充分發展人格，加強對人權及基本自由之尊重。

---

① 文件原文如此，疑為遺漏，似應為"給薪"。
② 文件原文如此，疑為遺漏，似應為"平等"。

教育應謀促進各國、各種族或宗教團體間之諒解、容恕及友好關係，并應促進聯合國維繫和平之各種工作。

三、父母對其子女所應受之教育，有優先抉擇之權。

第二十七條

一、人人有權自由參加社會之文化生活，欣賞藝術，并共同襄享科學進步及其利益。

二、人人對其本人之任何科學、文學或美術作品所獲得之精神與物質利益，有享受保護之權。

第二十八條

人人有權享受本宣言所載權利與自由可得全部實現之社會及國際秩序。

第二十九條

一、人人對於社會負有義務；個人人格之自由充分發展厥為社會是賴。

二、人人於行使其權利及自由時僅應受法律所定之限制且此種限制之唯一目的應在確認及尊重他人之權利與自由並謀符合民主社會中道德、公共秩序及一般福利所需之公允條件。

三、此等權利與自由之行使，無論在任何情形下，均不得違反聯合國之宗旨及原則。

第三十條

本宣言所載，不得解釋為任何國家、團體或個人有權以任何活動或任何行為破壞本宣言之任何權利與自由。

一九四八年十二月十日
第一百八十三次全體會議

二、转换后的简体字版

二一七（三）国际人权法案

甲

世界人权宣言

弁言

兹鉴于人类一家，对于人人固有尊严及其平等不移权利之承认确系世界自由、正义与和平之基础；

复鉴于人权之忽视及侮蔑恒酿成野蛮暴行，致使人心震愤，而自由言论、自由信仰、得免忧惧、得免贫困之世界业经宣示为一般人民之最高企望；

复鉴于为使人类不致迫不得已铤而走险以抗专横与压迫，人权须受法律规定之保障；

复鉴于国际友好关系之促进，实属切要；

复鉴于联合国人民已在宪章中重申对于基本人权、人格尊严与价值以及男女平等权利之信念，并决心促成大自由中之社会进步及较善之民生；

复鉴于各会员国业经誓愿与联合国同心协力促进人权及基本自由之普遍尊重与遵行；

复鉴于此种权利自由之公共认识对于是项誓愿之彻底实现至关重大；

大会爰于此

颁布世界人权宣言，作为所有人民所有国家共同努力之标的，务望个人及社会团体永以本宣言铭诸座右，力求借训导与教育激励人权与自由之尊重，并借国家与国际之渐进措施获得其普遍有效之承认与遵行；会员国本身人民及所辖领土人民均各永享咸遵。

第一条

人皆生而自由；在尊严及权利上均各平等。人各赋有理性良知，诚应和睦相处，情同手足。

第二条

人人皆得享受本宣言所载之一切权利与自由，不分种族、肤色、性别、语言、宗教、政见或他种主张、国籍或门第、财产、出生或他种身份。

且不得因一人所隶国家或地区之政治、行政或国际地位之不同而有所区别，无论该地区系独立、托管、非自治或受其他主权上之限制。

第三条

人人有权享有生命、自由与人身安全。

第四条

任何人不容使为奴役；奴隶制度及奴隶贩卖，不论出于何种方式，悉应予以禁止。

第五条

任何人不能加以酷刑，或施以残忍不人道或侮慢之待遇或处罚。

第六条

人人于任何所在有被承认为法律上主体之权利。

第七条

人人在法律上悉属平等，且应一体享受法律之平等保护。人人有权享受平等保护，以防止违反本宣言之任何歧视及煽动此种歧视之任何行为。

第八条

人人于其宪法或法律所赋予之基本权利被侵害时，有权享受国家管辖法庭之有效救济。

第九条

任何人不容加以无理逮捕、拘禁或放逐。

第十条

人人于其权利与义务受判定时及被刑事控告时，有权享受独立无私法庭之绝对平等不偏且公开之听审。

第十一条

一、凡受刑事控告者，在未经依法公开审判证实有罪前，应视为无罪，审判时并须予以答辩上所需之一切保障。

二、任何人在刑事上之行为或不行为，于其发生时依国家或国际法律均不构成罪行者，应不为罪。刑罚不得重于犯罪时法律之规定。

第十二条

任何个人之私生活、家庭、住所或通讯不容无理侵犯，其荣誉及信用亦不容侵害。人人为防止此种侵犯或侵害有权受法律保护。

第十三条

一、人人在一国境内有自由迁徙及择居之权。

二、人人有权离去任何国家，连其本国在内，并有权归返其本国。

第十四条

一、人人为避迫害有权在他国寻求并享受庇身之所。

二、控诉之确源于非政治性之犯罪或源于违反联合国宗旨与原则之行为者，不得享受此种权利。

第十五条

人人有权享有国籍。

任何人之国籍不容无理褫夺，其更改国籍之权利不容否认。①

第十六条

一、成年男女，不受种族、国籍或宗教之任何限制，有权婚嫁及成立家庭。男女在婚姻方面，在结合期间及在解除婚约时，俱有平等权利。

二、婚约之缔订仅能以男女双方之自由完全承认为之。

三、家庭为社会之当然基本团体单位，并应受社会及国家之保护。

第十七条

一、人人有权单独占有或与他人合有财产。

二、任何人之财产不容无理剥夺。

---

① 文件原文如此，疑遗漏两款的序号。

第十八条

人人有思想、良心与宗教自由之权；此项权利包括其改变宗教或信仰之自由，及其单独或集体、公开或私自以教义、躬行、礼拜及戒律表示其宗教或信仰之自由。

第十九条

人人有主张及发表自由之权；此项权利包括保持主张而不受干涉之自由，及经由任何方法不分国界以寻求、接收并传播消息意见之自由。

第二十条

一、人人有平和①集会结社自由之权。

二、任何人不容强使隶属于某一团体。

第二十一条

一、人人有权直接或以自由选举之代表参加其本国政府。

二、人人有以平等机会参加其本国公务之权。

三、人民意志应为政府权力之基础；人民意志应以定期且真实之选举表现之，其选举权必须普及而平等，并当以不记名投票或相等之自由投票程序为之。

第二十二条

人既为社会之一员，自有权享受社会保障，并有权享受个人尊严及人格自由发展所必需之经济、社会及文化各种权利之实现：此种实现之促成，端赖国家措施与国际合作并当依各国之机构与资源量力为之。

第二十三条

一、人人有权工作、自由选择职业、享受公平优裕之工作条件及失业之保障。

二、人人不容任何区别，有同工同酬之权利。

三、人人工作时，有权享受公平优裕之报酬，务使其本人及其家属之

---

① 文件原文如此，疑为笔误，似应为"和平"。

生活足以维持人类尊严，必要时且应有他种社会保护办法，以资补益。

四、人人为维持其权益，有组织及参加工会之权。

第二十四条

人人有休息及闲暇之权，包括工作时间受合理限制及定期有给①休假之权。

第二十五条

一、人人有权享受其本人及其家属康乐所需之生活程度，举凡衣、食、住、医药及必要之社会服务均包括在内；且于失业、患病、残废、寡居、衰老或因不可抗力之事故致有他种丧失生活能力之情形时，有权享受保障。

二、母亲及儿童应受特别照顾及协助。所有儿童，无论婚生与非婚生，均应享受同等社会保护。

第二十六条

一、人人皆有受教育之权。教育应属免费，至少初级及基本教育应然。初级教育应属强迫性质。技术与职业教育应广为设立。高等教育应予人人平②机会，以成绩为准。

二、教育之目标在于充分发展人格，加强对人权及基本自由之尊重。教育应谋促进各国、各种族或宗教团体间之谅解、容恕及友好关系，并应促进联合国维系和平之各种工作。

三、父母对其子女所应受之教育，有优先抉择之权。

第二十七条

一、人人有权自由参加社会之文化生活，欣赏艺术，并共同襄享科学进步及其利益。

二、人人对其本人之任何科学、文学或美术作品所获得之精神与物质利益，有享受保护之权。

---

① 文件原文如此，疑为遗漏，似应为"给薪"。
② 文件原文如此，疑为笔误，似应为"平等"。

第二十八条

人人有权享受本宣言所载权利与自由可得全部实现之社会及国际秩序。

第二十九条

一、人人对于社会负有义务；个人人格之自由充分发展厥为社会是赖。

二、人人于行使其权利及自由时仅应受法律所定之限制且此种限制之唯一目的应在确认及尊重他人之权利与自由并谋符合民主社会中道德、公共秩序及一般福利所需之公允条件。

三、此等权利与自由之行使，无论在任何情形下，均不得违反联合国之宗旨及原则。

第三十条

本宣言所载，不得解释为任何国家、团体或个人有权以任何活动或任何行为破坏本宣言之任何权利与自由。

一九四八年十二月十日
第一百八十三次全体会议

三、英文文件原文

217 (III). International Bill of Human Rights
A
UNIVERSAL DECLARATION OF HUMAN RIGHTS
Preamble

Whereas recognition of the inherent dignity and of the equal and inalienable rights of all members of the human family is the foundation of freedom, justice and peace in the world,

Whereas disregard and contempt for human rights have resulted in barbarous acts which have outraged the conscience of mankind, and the advent of a world in which human beings shall enjoy freedom of speech and belief and freedom from fear and want has been proclaimed as the highest aspiration of the common people,

Whereas it is essential, if man is not to be compelled to have recourse, as a last resort, to rebellion against tyranny and oppression, that human rights should be protected by the rule of law,

Whereas it is essential to promote the development of friendly relations between nations,

Whereas the peoples of the United Nations have in the Charter reaffirmed their faith in fundamental human rights, in the dignity and worth of the human person and in the equal rights of men and women and have determined to promote social progress and better standards of life in larger freedom,

Whereas Member States have pledged themselves to achieve, in cooperation with the United Nations, the promotion of universal respect for and observance of human rights and fundamental freedoms,

Whereas a common understanding of these rights and freedoms is of the greatest importance for the full realization of this pledge,

Now, therefore,

The General Assembly

Proclaims this Universal Declaration of Human Rights as a common standard of achievement for all peoples and all nations, to the end that every individual and every organ of society, keeping this Declaration constantly in mind, shall strive by teaching and education to promote respect for these rights and freedoms and by progressive measures, national and international, to secure their universal and effective recognition and observance, both among the peoples of Member States themselves and among the peoples of territories under their jurisdiction.

Article 1

All human beings are born free and equal in dignity and rights. They are endowed with reason and conscience and should act towards one another in a spirit of brotherhood.

Article 2

Everyone is entitled to all the rights and freedoms set forth in this Declaration, without distinction of any kind, such as race, colour, sex, language, religion, political or other opinion, national or social origin, property, birth or other status. Furthermore, no distinction shall be made on the basis of the political, jurisdictional or international status of the country or territory to which a person belongs, whether it be independent, trust, non-self-governing or under any other limitation of sovereignty.

Article 3

Everyone has the right to life, liberty and the security of person.

Article 4

No one shall be held in slavery or servitude; slavery and the slave trade shall be prohibited in all their forms.

Article 5

No one shall be subjected to torture or to cruel, inhuman or degrading treatment or punishment.

Article 6

Everyone has the right to recognition everywhere as a person before the law.

Article 7

All are equal before the law and are entitled without any discrimination to equal protection of the law. All are entitled to equal protection against any discrimination in violation of this Declaration and against any incitement to such discrimination.

Article 8

Everyone has the right to an effective remedy by the competent national tribunals for acts violating the fundamental rights granted him by the constitution or by law.

Article 9

No one shall be subjected to arbitrary arrest, detention or exile.

Article 10

Everyone is entitled in full equality to a fair and public hearing by an independent and impartial tribunal, in the determination of his rights and obligations and of any criminal charge against him.

Article 11

1. Everyone charged with a penal offence has the right to be presumed innocent until proved guilty according to law in a public trial at which he has had all the guarantees necessary for his defence.

2. No one shall be held guilty of any penal offence on account of any act or omission which did not constitute a penal offence, under national or international law, at the time when it was committed. Nor shall a heavier penalty be imposed than the one that was applicable at the time the penal offence was committed.

Article 12

No one shall be subjected to arbitrary interference with his privacy, family, home or correspondence, nor to attacks upon his honour and reputation. Everyone has the right to the protection of the law against such interference or attacks.

Article 13

1. Everyone has the right to freedom of movement and residence within the borders of each State.

2. Everyone has the right to leave any country, including his own, and to return to his country.

Article 14

1. Everyone has the right to seek and to enjoy in other countries asylum from persecution.

2. This right may not be invoked in the case of prosecutions genuinely arising from non-political crimes or from acts contrary to the purposes and principles of the United Nations.

Article 15

1. Everyone has the right to a nationality.

2. No one shall be arbitrarily deprived of his nationality nor denied the right to change his nationality.

Article 16

1. Men and women of full age, without any limitation due to race, nationality or religion, have the right to marry and to found a family. They are entitled to equal rights as to marriage, during marriage and at its dissolution.

2. Marriage shall be entered into only with the free and full consent of the intending spouses.

3. The family is the natural and fundamental group unit of society and is entitled to protection by society and the State.

Article 17

1. Everyone has the right to own property alone as well as in association with others.

2. No one shall be arbitrarily deprived of his property.

Article 18

Everyone has the right to freedom of thought, conscience and religion; this right includes freedom to change his religion or belief, and freedom, either alone or in community with others and in public or private, to manifest his religion or belief in teaching, practice, worship and observance.

Article 19

Everyone has the right to freedom of opinion and expression; this right includes freedom to hold opinions without interference and to seek, receive and impart information and ideas through any media and regardless of frontiers.

Article 20

1. Everyone has the right to freedom of peaceful assembly and association.

2. No one may be compelled to belong to an association.

Article 21

1. Everyone has the right to take part in the government of his country, directly or through freely chosen representatives.

2. Everyone has the right to equal access to public service in his country.

3. The will of the people shall be the basis of the authority of government; this will shall be expressed in periodic and genuine elections which shall be by universal and equal suffrage and shall be held by secret vote or by equivalent free voting procedures.

Article 22

Everyone, as a member of society, has the right to social security and is entitled to realization, through national effort and international co-operation and in accordance with the organization and resources of each State, of the economic, social and cultural rights indispensable for his dignity and the free development of his personality.

Article 23

1. Everyone has the right to work, to free choice of employment, to just and favourable conditions of work and to protection against unemployment.

2. Everyone, without any discrimination, has the right to equal pay for equal work.

3. Everyone who works has the right to just and favourable remuneration ensuring for himself and his family an existence worthy of human dignity, and supplemented, if necessary, by other means of social protection.

4. Everyone has the right to form and to join trade unions for the protection of his interests.

Article 24

Everyone has the right to rest and leisure, including reasonable limitation of working hours and periodic holidays with pay.

Article 25

1. Everyone has the right to a standard of living adequate for the health and well-being of himself and of his family, including food, clothing, housing and medical care and necessary social services, and the right to security in the event of unemployment, sickness, disability, widowhood, old age or other lack of livelihood in circumstances beyond his control.

2. Motherhood and childhood are entitled to special care and assistance. All children, whether born in or out of wedlock, shall enjoy the same social protection.

Article 26

1. Everyone has the right to education. Education shall be free, at least in the elementary and fundamental stages. Elementary education shall be compulsory. Technical and professional education shall be made generally

available and higher education shall be equally accessible to all on the basis of merit.

2. Education shall be directed to the full development of the human personality and to the strengthening of respect for human rights and fundamental freedoms. It shall promote understanding, tolerance and friendship among all nations, racial or religious groups, and shall further the activities of the United Nations for the maintenance of peace.

3. Parents have a prior right to choose the kind of education that shall be given to their children.

Article 27

1. Everyone has the right freely to participate in the cultural life of the community, to enjoy the arts and to share in scientific advancement and its benefits.

2. Everyone has the right to the protection of the moral and material interests resulting from any scientific, literary or artistic production of which he is the author.

Article 28

Everyone is entitled to a social and international order in which the rights and freedoms set forth in this Declaration can be fully realized.

Article 29

1. Everyone has duties to the community in which alone the free and full development of his personality is possible.

2. In the exercise of his rights and freedoms, everyone shall be subject only to such limitations as are determined by law solely for the purpose of securing due recognition and respect for the rights and freedoms of others and of meeting the just requirements of morality, public order and the general welfare in a democratic society.

3. These rights and freedoms may in no case be exercised contrary to the purposes and principles of the United Nations.

Article 30

Nothing in this Declaration may be interpreted as implying for any State, group or person any right to engage in any activity or to perform any act aimed at the destruction of any of the rights and freedoms set forth herein.

Hundred and eighty-third plenary meeting.
10 December 1948